Just Deceivers

Just Deceivers

An Exploration of the Motif of Deception in the Books of Samuel

Matthew Newkirk

FOREWORD BY
Daniel I. Block

☙PICKWICK *Publications* • Eugene, Oregon

JUST DECEIVERS
An Exploration of the Motif of Deception in the Books of Samuel

Copyright © 2015 Matthew Newkirk. All rights reserved. Except for brief quotations in critical publications or reviews, no part of this book may be reproduced in any manner without prior written permission from the publisher. Write: Permissions. Wipf and Stock Publishers, 199 W. 8th Ave., Suite 3, Eugene, OR 97401.

Pickwick Publications
An Imprint of Wipf and Stock Publishers
199 W. 8th Ave., Suite 3
Eugene, OR 97401

www.wipfandstock.com

ISBN 13: 978-1-4982-0117-9

Cataloguing-in-Publication Data

Newkirk, Matthew

Just deceivers : an exploration of the motif of deception in the books of Samuel / Matthew Newkirk, with a foreword by Daniel I. Block

xviii + 244 p. ; 23 cm. Includes bibliographical references.

ISBN 13: 978-1-4982-0117-9

1. Bible. Samuel 1&2—Criticism and interpretation, etc. 2. First and Second Samuel. 3. Ethics in the Bible. I. Block, Daniel Isaac, 1943–. II. Title.

BS1325.53 N294 2015

Manufactured in the U.S.A.   04/16/2015

Scripture quotations marked "ESV" are taken from The Holy Bible, English Standard Version® (ESV®), copyright © 2001 by Crossway, a publishing ministry of Good News Publishers. Used by permission. All rights reserved.

Scripture quotations marked "KJV" are taken from The King James Version.

Scripture quotations marked "NASB" are taken from the New American Standard Bible®, Copyright © 1960, 1962, 1963, 1968, 1971, 1972, 1973, 1975, 1977, 1995 by The Lockman Foundation. Used by permission.

Scripture quotations marked "NETS" are taken from *A New English Translation of the Septuagint*, © 2007 by the International Organization for Septuagint and Cognate Studies, Inc. Used by permission of Oxford University Press. All rights reserved.

Scripture quotations marked "NIV" are taken from the HOLY BIBLE, NEW INTERNATIONAL VERSION®. NIV®. Copyright © 1973, 1978, 1984 by International Bible Society. Used by permission of Zondervan. All rights reserved worldwide.

Scripture quotations marked "NKJV" are taken from the New King James Version. Copyright © 1982 by Thomas Nelson, Inc. Used by permission. All rights reserved.

Scripture quotations marked "NLT" are taken from the *Holy Bible*, New Living Translation, copyright ©1996, 2004, 2007, 2013 by Tyndale House Foundation. Used by permission of Tyndale House Publishers, Inc., Carol Stream, Illinois 60188. All rights reserved.

Scripture quotations marked "NRSV" are taken from the New Revised Standard Version Bible, copyright 1989, Division of Christian Education of the National Council of the Churches of Christ in the United States of America. Used by permission. All rights reserved.

Scripture quotations marked "TNIV" are taken from the HOLY BIBLE, TODAY'S NEW INTERNATIONAL VERSION®. TNIV®. Copyright © 2001, 2005 by International Bible Society. Used by permission of Zondervan. All rights reserved worldwide.

To Caroline, who has taught me more about
faith in YHWH than any other.

"Charm is deceptive, and beauty is fleeting;
but a woman who fears YHWH is to be praised."

שקר החן והבל היפי
אשה יראת־יהוה היא תתהלל

Prov 31:30

Table of Contents

List of Tables | viii
Foreword by Daniel I. Block | ix
Acknowledgements | xiii
Abbreviations | xv

1 Introduction | 1

2 Deception in the Explicit Statements of the Old Testament | 15

3 Deception Intended to Prevent Death or Harm in the Books of Samuel | 53

4 Deception Intended to Cause Death or Harm in the Books of Samuel | 85

5 Deception Intended to Benefit Someone Else in the Books of Samuel | 120

6 Deception Intended to Benefit the Deceiver in the Books of Samuel | 140

7 Conclusion | 176

Bibliography | 207

Scripture Index | 227

List of Tables

1. David's Suggested Lie vs. Jonathan's Actual Lie | 69
2. YHWH's Command to Saul vs. David's Attacks | 78
3. Structural Comparison of 2 Samuel 3:27 and 2 Samuel 4:6 | 100
4. Abigail and the Tekoite's Audiences with David | 129
5. Tactic and Evaluation | 178
6. Motive and Evaluation | 180
7. Achievement of Goals and Evaluation | 183
8. Negative Consequences and Evaluation | 185

Foreword

IN THE LATE 1980S, when I was on the faculty of a small college in Canada, the students put on a children's musical, *Sir Oliver's Song*, an entertaining presentation of the "Ten Commandments" (more appropriately called the Ten Words).[1] I remember the musical well, because I witnessed it being performed every night for two weeks while on tour to churches on the prairies of Canada. The line interpreting the command against bearing false witness is particularly memorable: "God don't dig lyin'" (Exod 20:16; Deut 5:20). Cast into colloquial American English, at this stage the performance was quite humorous.

Although this rendering reflects a common interpretation of the command in the Decalogue, over the past forty years of study and teaching, my doubts whether or not the command speaks at all to the issue of lying in everyday speech have increased. On the one hand the vocabulary of the command in both the Exodus and Deuteronomy versions suggests a legal context, like that reflected in Deuteronomy 19:15–21. On the other hand, I have noticed for a long time that the biblical narratives report many instances involving deception, with no hint of punishment or even accusation. On the contrary, in many instances the deceitful speeches or actions actually succeed and the deceivers achieve their goals. How can this be, if "God don't dig lyin'"?

Ethicists have often commented on the midwives' half-truth—grounded in the fear of God—regarding the superior strength of pregnant Hebrew women vis-à-vis their Egyptian counterparts (Exod 1:15–21), or on Rahab's deceitful concealing of the Israelite scouts in Jericho (Josh 2:1–7). These cases contrast starkly with the New Testament case involving Ananias and Sapphira, whose efforts to deceive the apostles were punished with death (Acts 5:1–11). Recent work has also been done on the role of deceit and deceitfulness in the stories of Israel's ancestors in Genesis.

---

1. For discussion of this issue, see Block, "Reading the Decalogue Right to Left," 21–25.

In this volume Matt Newkirk surveys these and other responses to biblical narratives of deceit, and then sets out to explore the role and consequences of deceit in the books of Samuel, to determine the narrator's disposition toward the issue. After identifying twenty-eight episodes that involve deception, he classifies them on the basis of the narrator's apparent assessment of the deception. He discovered that of the twenty-eight cases, in twelve the deception was evaluated positively, and in fifteen it was assessed negatively. One case is unclear (2 Sam 18:19–30). Although the assessment is rarely declared explicitly, the narrator's disposition—negative or positive—is indicated by subtle features in the text, through descriptions of people's response to the deception, or through events that transpire after the deception.

Having carefully analyzed each of these twenty-eight texts, the author observes that deception was evaluated negatively when the goal of the deceit was to cause unjust harm or death to someone else, or when deceivers were only looking out for their own interests. By contrast, when the intent of the deception was to prevent unjust harm or death, and when the deception was intended to benefit someone else, it was assessed positively.

This study is significant for several reasons. First, the author has examined twenty-eight episodes from the events leading up to the establishment of Israel's monarchy and the early years under Saul and under David. With his particular interest in a specific feature of these narratives he has presented a nuanced interpretation of these texts that scholars writing commentaries on the books of Samuel will need to consider. Second, his work exposes the superficiality of previous evangelical ethicists' treatment of the motif of deception in Scripture. It will not do any more simply to say that persons involved in deceitful events were functioning with a lower ethic, and that God overlooked the evil of deceit itself. Rather, we must always inquire regarding the intent of the deceit. Newkirk is not the first to discover this, but in this study of the books of Samuel he has provided the most thorough study of the issue available. But this is true not only of Samuel, but coheres with the picture painted by the rest of the Scriptures, both Old and New Testaments.

As suggested by the title, a biblical ethic demands Christians have room for the category of "just deceivers," that is deceivers who are just in their deception. If the deception serves unjust ends—either the death or harm of another person or merely the deceiver's self-interest—it is to be condemned. However, a Christian who deceives to secure the well-being of another person or who does so self-sacrificially is to be honored. After reading this volume, we should no longer struggle over the decision of Corrie ten Boom and her family for helping many Jews escape the Nazi Holocaust, often through clever and deceitful means. The Jewish world has rightly recognized her with the epithet "righteous gentile," and with a tree planted in her honor on the grounds of the *Yad Vashem* memorial to Holocaust victims.

It has been a delight to work with Matt Newkirk on this project, and it is an honor to commend his work to the world. May the name of the living God be praised as his people take up the mantle of "righteousness, only righteousness" (Deut 16:2).

Daniel I. Block
Gunther H. Knoedler Professor of Old Testament
Wheaton College, IL

Acknowledgements

THIS STUDY IS A lightly revised version of my Wheaton College doctoral dissertation, defended and submitted in 2013. Although writing a dissertation involves much isolated time in the library and home study, ultimately such a project is not completed in isolation. As I look back over the time during which this work was written, I am struck with gratitude for the many people who have helped me along the way and enabled its completion. First and foremost I am thankful to God, who has saved me by his grace through the Lord Jesus Christ and has sustained my family and me throughout the course of my study. I am grateful also for my supervisor, mentor, and friend, Dr. Daniel Block. His wise guidance, careful scrutiny, and positive encouragement have been of inestimable value as I have sought to grow and mature as a scholar. My two examiners at my defense, Dr. Michael Graves and Dr. V. Philips Long, both offered generous encouragement as well as sound counsel for improvement. I would also like to express thanks to Mr. Don King and Dr. Elizabeth King for providing the doctoral fellowship that enabled me to devote myself to academic work full-time during my season at Wheaton, and to the staff at Wipf & Stock for accepting the manuscript for publication.

My parents, Mike and Marcia Newkirk, deserve special mention. They have nurtured my faith throughout my life and have always been supportive of my studies, both personally and financially. My late mother-in-law, Robin Candeto, was also a tireless encourager and assisted us financially during our time in Wheaton. The Dodd and Macrina families were also gracious and continued their support beyond my church ministry and into my seminary and doctoral work. The two churches I served during the writing of this dissertation—New Covenant Church in Naperville, IL and St. Paul's Presbyterian Church in Orlando, FL—are also to be commended for their grace and patience with me as I sought to balance life as both a pastor and a scholar.

Lastly, I owe the greatest debt of gratitude to my family. My children—Lydia, Silas, and Ethan—were all born during my time working on this project. They have brought me much joy and many needed breaks throughout its writing. However, it is my wife, Caroline, who deserves the most recognition. She has walked with me through every step of this study and has endured the many trials that accompany being married to a doctoral student. She believed that this work would come to completion even when I didn't, and she encouraged me to persevere in it when I was ready to give up. This project is as much hers as it is mine, and so it is to her that I gratefully dedicate it.

Abbreviations

AB	Anchor Bible
AKM	Abhandlungen für die Kunde des Morgenlandes
AnBib	Analecta biblica
Ant.	*The Jewish Antiquities, Books 1–19*. Flavius Josephus. Translated by H. St. J. Thackeray, et al. LCL. Cambridge: Harvard University Press, 1930–65.
AOTC	Apollos Old Testament Commentary
BCOTWP	Baker Commentary on the Old Testament Wisdom and Psalms
BDB	Francis Brown, S. R. Driver, and Charles A. Briggs. *A Hebrew and English Lexicon of the Old Testament*. Oxford: Clarendon, 1907.
BECNT	Baker Exegetical Commentary on the New Testament
BETL	Bibliotheca ephemeridum theologicarum lovaniensium
BHS	*Biblia Hebraica Stuttgartensia*. Edited by K. Elliger and W. Rudolph. Stuttgart, 1983.
Bib	*Biblica*
BibInt	*Biblical Interpretation*
BIS	Biblical Interpretation Series
BLS	Bible and Literature Series
BR	*Biblical Research*
BRev	*Bible Review*
BSac	*Bibliotheca sacra*
BSC	Bible Student's Commentary
BTB	*Biblical Theology Bulletin*
BWANT	Beiträge zur Wissenschaft vom Alten und Neuen Testament
BZ	*Biblische Zeitschrift*
BZABR	Beihefte zur Zeitschrift für Altorientalische und Biblische Rechtsgeschichte
BZAW	Beihefte zur Zeitschrift für die alttestamentliche Wissenschaft
CAT	Commentaire de l'Ancien Testament

CBC	Cambridge Bible Commentary
CBET	Contributions to Biblical Exegesis and Theology
CBQ	*Catholic Biblical Quarterly*
ConBOT	Coniectanea biblica: Old Testament Series
CTJ	*Calvin Theological Journal*
CV	*Communio viatorum*
DDD	*Dictionary of Deities and Demons in the Bible*. Edited by K. van der Toorn et al. Leiden, 1995.
ETL	*Ephemerides theologicae lovansienses*
EvQ	*Evangelical Quarterly*
ExAud	*Ex Auditu*
FCI	Foundations of Contemporary Interpretation
FOTL	Forms of the Old Testament Literature
HALOT	Koehler, L., W. Baumgartner, and J. J. Stamm, *The Hebrew and Aramaic Lexicon of the Old Testament*. Translated and edited under the supervision of M. E. J. Richardson. 4 vols. Leiden, 1994–99.
HAR	*Hebrew Annual Review*
HBM	Hebrew Bible Monographs
HS	*Hebrew Studies*
HTR	*Harvard Theological Review*
HUCA	*Hebrew Union College Annual*
IBC	Interpretation: A Bible Commentary for Teaching and Preaching
IBHS	*An Introduction to Biblical Hebrew Syntax*. B. K. Waltke and M. O'Connor. Winona Lake, IN: Eisenbrauns, 1990.
ICC	International Critical Commentary
IJAP	*International Journal of Applied Philosophy*
Int	*Interpretation*
ITC	International Theological Commentary
JANES	*Journal of the Ancient Near Eastern Society*
JBL	*Journal of Biblical Literature*
JBQ	*Jewish Bible Quarterly*
JETS	*Journal of the Evangelical Theological Society*
JHebS	*The Journal of Hebrew Scriptures*
JPhil	*Journal of Philosophy*
JPS	Jewish Publication Society
JR	*Journal of Religion*
JSem	*Journal for Semitics*
JSNTSup	Journal for the Study of the New Testament: Supplement Series

JSOT	*Journal for the Study of the Old Testament*
JSOTSup	Journal for the Study of the Old Testament: Supplement Series
JTS	*Journal of Theological Studies*
KAT	Kommentar zum Alten Testament
LAI	Library of Ancient Israel
LBI	Library of Biblical Interpretation
LCBI	Literary Currents in Biblical Interpretation
LCL	Loeb Classical Library
LHBOTS	Library of Hebrew Bible / Old Testament Studies
LXX	Septuagint
MSJ	*The Master's Seminary Journal*
MT	Masoretic Text
NAC	New American Commentary
NCB	New Century Bible
NETS	New English Translation of the Septuagint
NIBC	New International Biblical Commentary
NICNT	New International Commentary on the New Testament
NICOT	New International Commentary on the Old Testament
NIDOTTE	*New International Dictionary of Old Testament Theology and Exegesis.* 5 vols. Edited by Willem A. VanGemeren. Grand Rapids: Zondervan, 1997.
NIGTC	New International Greek Testament Commentary
NIV	New International Version
NIVAC	New International Version Application Commentary
NovT	*Novum Testamentum*
OBO	Orbis biblicus et orientalis
OBT	Overtures to Biblical Theology
OTE	*Old Testament Essays*
OTL	Old Testament Library
OTM	Old Testament Message
PNTC	The Pillar New Testament Commentary
PRSt	*Perspectives in Religious Studies*
RB	*Revue biblique*
RelLit	*Religion and Literature*
ResQ	*Restoration Quarterly*
RevExp	*Review and Expositor*
SABJT	*The South African Baptist Journal of Theology*
SAIS	Studies in the Aramaic Interpretation of Scripture
SBJT	*The Southern Baptist Journal of Theology*
SBLDS	Society of Biblical Literature Dissertation Series
SBLMS	Society of Biblical Literature Monograph Series

SBLWAW	Society of Biblical Literature Writings from the Ancient World
SBT	Studies in Biblical Theology
ScrHier	Scripta hierosolymitana
SHBC	Smyth & Helwys Bible Commentary
SJLA	Studies in Judaism in Late Antiquity
SJOT	*Scandinavian Journal of the Old Testament*
SSN	Studia semitica neerlandica
ST	*Studia theologica*
StBL	Studies in Biblical Literature
TDOT	*Theological Dictionary of the Old Testament*. 15 vols. Edited by G. Johannes Botterweck and Helmer Ringgren. Translated by Geoffrey W. Bromiley et al. Grand Rapids: Eerdmans, 1974–2006.
TLOT	*Theological Lexicon of the Old Testament*. 3 vols. Edited by Ernst Jenni and Claus Westermann. Translated by Mark Biddle. Peabody, MA: Hendrickson, 1997.
TLZ	*Theologische Literaturzeitung*
TOTC	Tyndale Old Testament Commentaries
TQ	*Theologische Quartalschrift*
TynBul	Tyndale Bulletin
TZ	*Theologische Zeitschrift*
VE	*Vox evangelica*
VT	*Vetus Testamentum*
VTSup	Vetus Testamentum Supplements
WBC	Word Biblical Commentary
WD	*Wort und Dienst*
WTJ	*Westminster Theological Journal*
ZAH	*Zeitschrift für Althebräistik*
ZAW	*Zeitschrift für die alttestamentliche Wissenschaft*

1

Introduction

IN MOST CONTEXTS DECEPTION is considered an immoral activity, and many view the Bible as supporting this conclusion. Passages such as the ninth command[1] of the Decalogue (Exod 20:16)[2] and the injunctions against false speech in the Book of the Covenant (Exod 23:1–8) are often said to prohibit all forms of lying and deception.[3] However, others read the same texts and conclude very differently. For example, Richard A. Freund writes: "a standard of absolute truthfulness does not seem to be a major issue in the Hebrew Bible."[4] Furthermore, in many biblical narratives, some acts of deception seem to be depicted positively. In Gen 38:13–18 Tamar disguised herself as a prostitute and deceived Judah to get him to impregnate her. At the end of the episode Judah himself evaluated her actions positively: "She is more righteous than I" (Gen 38:26, NIV).[5] In Exod 1:19 the midwives lied to Pharaoh to cover up their disobedience to his death sentence against the Hebrew

---

1. Although a plausible case exists for the Lutheran/Roman Catholic enumeration of the Decalogue, by which the prohibition of false testimony is counted as the eighth command (see Block, "Reading the Decalogue Right to Left," 56–60), the scholarly discussion of lying and deception in the OT predominantly follows the Anglican/Reformed/Eastern Orthodox numbering. Therefore, for simplicity of communication, I will use this latter numbering and refer to Exod 20:16 and Deut 5:20 as the "ninth command."

2. All versification will follow the MT. Where the MT differs from English versions, I will provide the English versification in brackets.

3. E.g., John Murray writes, "The Bible throughout requires veracity; we may never lie," and then quotes Exod 20:16; 23:1, 6 as support (*Principles of Conduct*, 132). See also Wayne Grudem, "Why It is Never Right to Lie," 783–84. However, Grudem rightly distinguishes between lying and deception and only appeals to the ninth command concerning the former. See chapter 2 for a critique of these interpretations.

4. Freund, "Lying and Deception," 45. See also Shemesh, "Lies By Prophets," 84.

5. Unless otherwise noted, all translations are my own.

boys. The narrator seemingly affirms their actions by commenting, "So God was good to the midwives" (Exod 1:20), and, "He gave them families" (Exod 1:21). After hiding the Hebrew spies, Rahab lied to her own king concerning the spies' whereabouts (Josh 2:4–6) and was rewarded by being spared in the destruction of Jericho. Subsequently she was so thoroughly incorporated into Israel (Josh 6:25) that she became an ancestress of King David and Jesus (Matt 1:5). The writer of Hebrews even lists her among Israel's models of obedient faith (Heb 11:31). These positive depictions[6] show that the issue of deception is complex and requires close analysis of legal, prescriptive, and narrative texts.

However, this situation raises many other questions. How should readers view an act of deception in a biblical narrative, especially when it involves lying? What situational characteristics are present when deception is depicted positively? Do these positive depictions of deception in biblical narratives cohere with the Bible's ethical prescriptions concerning lying and honesty? These and similar questions have been explored in several monographs on deception in the Pentateuch[7] as well as in studies of deception in the OT broadly.[8] However, even though the books of 1 and 2 Samuel contain the highest density of narrative episodes involving deception in the OT,[9] no full-length examination of the motif of deception in this corpus exists. This study seeks to fill this gap.

---

6. Many who conclude that deception is always wrong have argued that even though these deceivers were rewarded or praised, it does not follow that the deceptions themselves were approved (see, e.g., Kaiser, *Toward Old Testament Ethics*, 222–34, 271–74). Space prohibits a full analysis of such arguments concerning these particular narratives. It is sufficient to note that these narratives and many others *appear* to depict some deceptions positively, which should caution one against making sweeping statements before analyzing all the relevant data. The present work seeks to examine the deception episodes in the books of Samuel, many of which have not been adequately considered in the scholarly discussion.

7. Williams, *Deception in Genesis*; Nicholas, *Trickster Revisited*; Anderson, *Jacob and the Divine Trickster*.

8. Farmer, "Trickster Genre in the Old Testament"; Niditch, *Underdogs and Tricksters*; Prouser, "Phenomenology of the Lie."

9. Williams counts fifteen deception episodes in Genesis, which comprises fifty chapters (*Deception in Genesis*, 14–28). The present study counts twenty-eight deception episodes in the books of Samuel, which comprise fifty-five chapters. Thus while the deception-to-chapter ratio in Genesis is only 30 percent, in Samuel it is slightly over 50 percent.

Definition of Deception

Previous Definitions

Discussions of deception in biblical scholarship often lack a rigorous definition of the term. Many studies do not define the term at all,[10] which has led to subsequent methodological confusion.[11] Others have provided definitions, but in most cases they do not incorporate scholarly insight from philosophical studies on the phenomenology of deception, which results in imprecision.[12] For example, Gregory H. Harris writes, "Deception, at its core, is a lie in place of the truth."[13] This definition simply equates deception with lying, yet historically philosophers have distinguished between lying and deception; the former occurs when one communicates a falsehood and the latter occurs when one causes someone to believe a falsehood.[14] Although the goal of lying is to deceive and lying may result in deception, one may lie without deceiving (i.e., a lie may not be believed) and one may deceive without lying (i.e., through ambiguous language or physical motions rather than explicit communication). Thus deception is formally distinct from lying.

---

10. Hagan, "Deception as Motif," 301–26; Marcus, "David the Deceiver," 163–71; Roberts, "Does God Lie?" 211–20; Frontain, "The Trickster Tricked," 170–89; Bowen, "Role of Yhwh as Deceiver"; Chisholm, "Does God Deceive?" 11–28; Patterson, "Old Testament Use of an Archetype," 385–94; Esau, "Divine Deception in the Exodus Event?" 4–17.

11. For example, in postulating her reason for YHWH's alleged deception of Jeremiah in Jer 20:7–10 in promising protection but then not providing it, Bowen concludes that, among other potential possibilities, the "more likely possibility is that YHWH is *unable* to fulfill the promise" ("Role of Yhwh as Deceiver," 79, emphasis hers). However, a widely agreed upon characteristic of deception is *intentionality* on the part of the deceiver; an agent must intend to engender a false belief in another person to qualify as deceptive (see discussion below). Therefore, if the reason that YHWH failed to fulfill his promise of protection to Jeremiah was his *inability* to follow through, and thus not a lack of *intention* to follow through, we are not dealing with divine deception in this text but with divine *impotence*. If this were the case, as Bowen maintains, this passage would be misplaced in a study that seeks to understand the nature of divine deception.

12. As Vanhoozer wisely notes, "A biblical commentator would do well to consult the philosopher at this point in order to appreciate the fine conceptual distinctions between lying and deceiving" ("Ezekiel 14," 77).

13. Harris, "Does God Deceive?" 74.

14. See, e.g., Augustine, "Lying," 55–56; Mahon, "A Definition of Deceiving," 181; Carson, "Lying, Deception, and Related Concepts," 153–54.

In her study of lying and deception in biblical narrative, Ora Horn Prouser offers this definition:

> "Deception" entails communicating a message meant to mislead, making a receiver believe that which the deceiver does not. This can be done through gesture, disguise, actions, inaction or silence. Intention is a main ingredient of these definitions. False statements made by those who believe they are true are excluded.[15]

Prouser rightly emphasizes (1) that deception is necessarily *intentional* and (2) that it causes someone to believe something (in this case, "that which the deceiver does not [believe]"). However, according to this definition, a deception could theoretically result in the receiver believing something that is true. For example, if the soccer game begins at 4:00, but the deceiver (x) falsely believes the game begins at 3:00, and x tells the receiver (y) that the game begins at 4:00, intending to deceive y by making him believe something that x does not believe, and y shows up to the soccer game on time at 4:00, it cannot be said that x has deceived y. Certainly x has lied to y,[16] but he has not deceived him, since deception must involve y believing something false.[17]

In his study of deception in Genesis, Michael James Williams defines deception as follows:

> Deception takes place when an agent intentionally distorts, withholds, or otherwise manipulates information reaching some person(s) in order to stimulate in the person(s) a belief that the agent does not believe in order to serve the agent's purpose.[18]

Like Prouser's, Williams's definition could theoretically result in y adopting a true belief, since this definition only specifies that x does not hold the belief in question, not that the belief is actually false. Furthermore, this definition focuses only on the intention of x without specifying that y must actually adopt the false belief. However, if x does not succeed in causing y to believe something false, it cannot be said that a deception has occurred. As James Edwin Mahon notes, "deceiving necessarily has the result that another person either acquires a belief, or retains a belief, and that belief must be false."[19] For this reason, Mahon classifies deception as a perlocutionary

---

15. Prouser, "Phenomenology of the Lie," 1–2.
16. See, e.g., Fallis, "What is Lying?" 33; Mahon, "A Definition of Deceiving," 190.
17. Carson, "Lying, Deception, and Related Concepts," 154.
18. Williams, *Deception in Genesis*, 3. Williams's definition in a later article condenses this but does not change it in substance (see Williams, "Lies, Lies, I Tell You!" 11).
19. Mahon, "A Definition of Deceiving," 190.

act,[20] much like the acts of persuading or curing.[21] In addition to Williams's definition, neither the definitions of Yael Shemesh[22] nor John Anderson[23] include this aspect of deception.

Vanhoozer's Definition

Whereas critical elements in the phenomenology of deception are missing in each definition mentioned above, the definition proposed by Kevin Vanhoozer fully integrates the insights of the relevant philosophical discussion and provides the most succinct summary of the phenomenon. According to Vanhoozer, "'*x deceives y*' *means that x intentionally causes y to believe p, where p is false and x knows it to be so.*"[24] Thus for an action to be deceptive, the deceiver must (1) *intend* to cause another person to believe something false, (2) *know* that the belief in question is false, and (3) *successfully cause* the other person to adopt this false belief. This definition will govern the following study and direct which episodes in the Samuel narratives are selected for analysis.[25] As noted above, this understanding of deception is distinct from lying. Following the format provided by Vanhoozer, I summarize lying as follows: "*x lies to y*" *means that x believes p to be false, but intentionally and explicitly communicates to y that p is true.*[26] Therefore, of the

---

20. Ibid. Here Mahon categorizes deception in terms of the third class of speech act theory, the "perlocutionary act," which J. L. Austin defines as "what we bring about or achieve by saying something, such as convincing, persuading, deterring, and even, say, surprising or misleading" (*How to Do Things with Words*, 108). Later Austin notes that perlocutionary acts may achieve their response by "non-locutionary means," that is, non-verbally (ibid., 117–18). This is significant, since deception may be achieved by both verbal and non-verbal means.

21. Mahon, "Two Definitions of Lying," 211.

22. Shemesh's definition: "Deception . . . is the transmission of a message which the speaker believes to be false (even if it is actually—inadvertently—true), and moreover the speaker's intention is to mislead" ("Lies By Prophets," 82–83).

23. Anderson's definition, which he notes is streamlined from Williams's: "*Trickery or deception* . . . is what a trickster employs through any of various means of distorting, withholding, or manipulating information in order to serve or advance the trickster's own purposes and goals" (*Jacob and the Divine Trickster*, 46 [emphasis his]).

24. Vanhoozer, "Ezekiel 14," 77 (emphasis his).

25. This definition restricts the scope of this study to deceptions that actually occurred (i.e., the deceiver succeeded in causing the receiver to adopt the false belief). However, the ethical conclusions we draw from this study will logically apply to *attempted deceptions* as well (i.e., the deceiver failed to cause the receiver to adopt the false belief).

26. For a similar definition see Chisholm and Feehan, "The Intent to Deceive,"

three qualifications for deception summarized above, lying fulfills (1) but not necessarily (2) or (3). That is, like deception, lying must be *intentional*, but unlike the deceiver, the liar does not need to *know* but only *believe* that p is false (i.e., p may actually be true) and may or may not successfully cause y to believe p. Moreover, unlike deception, which can occur by ambiguous speech or physical actions that are neither true nor false, lying involves *explicit communication* of a falsehood, such as unequivocal speech or writing, or some other conventional means (e.g., nodding one's head to affirm or shaking one's head to deny).[27]

History of Research

Before investigating the motif of deception in the books of Samuel, it is necessary to survey views on the propriety of lying and deception, studies on deception in the OT generally, and the history of research of deception in Samuel specifically.

Views on the Propriety of Lying and Deception

In the history of thought, the discussion of the propriety of deception has usually revolved around the question of the legitimacy of lying. For many, such as Augustine and Immanuel Kant, it is never right to lie.[28] Others, such as Thomas Aquinas and Martin Luther, distinguished between different types of lies and evaluated them accordingly. Aquinas recognized three types of lies: (1) the *mischievous lie*, whereby one intends to injure another, (2) the *jocose lie*, whereby one intends to entertain another, and (3) the *officious lie*, whereby one intends to help another.[29] According to Aquinas, all three are sinful, though the officious is better than the jocose, and the jocose

---

152. It is important to highlight here that, although deception is a perlocutionary act, philosophers of language are generally agreed that lying is not an illocutionary act. A lie falls under the illocutionary category of *assertion*, though in this case the speaker does not believe that the assertion is true. See the discussion of Meibauer, "Lying and Falsely Implicating," 81–85, 111–14.

27. Kant also acknowledged that lying could occur through "the use of conventional signs" (see Mahon, "The Truth About Kant on Lies," 203).

28. See Augustine, "Lying," 66–69; Augustine, "Against Lying," 129–30; Kant, *The Metaphysics of Morals*, 182–83.

29. Aquinas, "Of Lying," 89. Although Aquinas's language here concerns "lies," the intentions of both the mischievous and the officious are to deceive; thus his tripartite scheme is a helpful illustration for the present discussion.

better than the mischievous.³⁰ Luther also acknowledged this threefold division, but he argued that the officious lie should be told, the jocose lie may be told, and the mischievous lie neither should nor may be told.³¹ Thus for Luther not all deception is wrong. This latter position coheres with the later articulation of Jeremy Bentham, who said,

> Falsehood, take it by itself, consider it as not being accompanied by any other material circumstances, nor therefore productive of any material effects, can never, upon the principle of utility, constitute any offense at all.³²

Therefore for Bentham, neither lying nor deception is right or wrong in itself, but depends upon the end for which it is employed. This utilitarian view represents the opposite end of the spectrum from the deontological position of Augustine and Kant. From this brief survey it is clear that the history of thought evidences a continuum of views concerning the propriety of lying and deception.

Deception in the Old Testament

Similarly, the history of research on deception in the OT is varied both in its scope and conclusions. Some studies have focused on the so-called "trickster genre," comparing various biblical episodes with trickster stories from other cultures.³³ Others have focused on the thorny issue of divine deception in the OT and how to reconcile it with the traditional understanding of the trustworthy character of God.³⁴ However, the studies most relevant for our purposes are those that have attempted to extrapolate from the OT broad conclusions concerning the ethics of deception. Three works in particular are most germane to the discussion. First, Martin Klopfenstein's *Die Lüge nach dem Alten Testament* offers an extensive analysis of the primary vocabulary used to describe lying in the OT. Klopfenstein concludes that the OT never

---

30. Ibid., 90–91.
31. See Plass, *What Luther Says*, 2:870.
32. Bentham, *Morals and Legislation*, 223.
33. Farmer, "Trickster Genre in the Old Testament"; Niditch, *Underdogs and Tricksters*; Nicholas, *Trickster Revisited*.
34. Roberts, "Does God Lie?" Bowen, "Role of Yhwh as Deceiver"; Chisholm, "Does God Deceive?" Patterson, "Old Testament Use of an Archetype"; Harris, "Does God Deceive?" Esau, "Divine Deception in the Exodus Event?" Block, "What Has Delphi to do with Samaria?" Anderson, *Jacob and the Divine Trickster*; Vanhoozer, "Ezekiel 14."

prohibits lying outright,[35] but still argues that all lying is wrong because it supposedly destroys one's relationship with God and is inimical to society.[36] Although Klopfenstein's study does not focus on the issue of deception by means other than lying, for him, to deceive by lying is clearly wrong.

Second, Prouser's dissertation examines a variety of narratives in which biblical characters tell lies. After summarizing the relevant vocabulary, she analyzes what she deems clear and ambiguous lies, the special relationship between women and deception, and narratives depicting divine deceit. Concerning the acceptability of deception, she concludes: "Biblical society condoned lying and any form of deception that allows an underdog to accomplish a positive goal he or she would not have been able to achieve by direct means."[37] Basically, as long as one deceives upward along the power scale and not for negative purposes, deception is acceptable biblically. She also argues that "those who lie in negative circumstances are unsuccessful,"[38] that is, they fail to deceive. Prouser believes that this pattern even accounts for depictions of divine deception, claiming that because YHWH allegedly failed to deceive Ahab in 1 Kings 22, "God's use of stratagems when in a position of strength is narratologically condemned as a misuse of power."[39]

Third, in a comparative treatment of deception in Genesis, Williams catalogues and analyzes fifteen deception episodes, compares them to various deceptions elsewhere in the Bible (including some in Samuel), explores how later Jewish tradition viewed these deceptions in Genesis, and then examines parallels from both ancient Near Eastern literature and folklore material. Williams finds that the depiction of deception in Genesis is unique among the biblical materials, concluding, "In Genesis, deception is justified when it is used by one previously wronged against the one who has done the wrong in order to restore *shalom*."[40] However, outside of Genesis, a different set of criteria is operative. According to Williams, in the rest of the OT, positively evaluated deception is that which either "benefits a third (Israelite) party by removing a threat to that party's physical or spiritual well-being" or "directly safeguards the physical well-being of the Israelite perpetrator(s)."[41] He suggests that the difference between these criteria may

---

35. Klopfenstein, *Die Lüge*, 322.

36. Ibid., 353.

37. Prouser, "Phenomenology of the Lie," 181.

38. Ibid.

39. Ibid., 198. Shemesh similarly argues that lying and deception was acceptable as a tool of the weak against the strong ("Lies By Prophets," 84).

40. Williams, *Deception in Genesis*, 55.

41. Ibid., 74.

be attributed to the social identity evident in national Israel as a covenantal community, which did not yet obtain during the time of the patriarchs.[42] This representative survey sets the stage for a fresh analysis of deception in the books of Samuel.

Deception in the Books of Samuel

The motif of deception in the books of Samuel has been explored in only four articles. Harry Hagan focuses his study on deception in the Succession Narrative and detects eighteen instances in this section alone.[43] However, since he does not define deception, he includes episodes that are questionable in light of the philosophical distinctions of deception discussed above.[44] Although Hagan sees deception as a theme in its own right, he also argues that it functions within the larger theme of fidelity and infidelity, especially in the relationship between a king and his subjects.[45] He analyzes the deceptions in these chapters under five headings, identified according to the characters involved: (1) David, Uriah, and Nathan, (2) Amnon and Absalom, (3) Absalom's rebellion, (4) Sheba, Amasa, Joab, and the Woman of Abel, and (5) Adonijah and Solomon. Hagan concludes that in each case deception was committed either to obtain a woman or the kingdom, and counter-deception was committed to restore the order.[46]

In his study of deception in the life of David, David Marcus observes two major trends: (1) when David was young and on the rise, he succeeded both in his own attempts at deception and in his responses to attempts at deception against him, but after his rise to power and the Bathsheba

---

42. Ibid., 75.

43. Hagan, "Deception as Motif," 302.

44. E.g., Hagan includes 2 Sam 10:1–8, where Hanun *believed himself deceived* by David's sympathy delegation (ibid., 303). However, the text suggests that David's intention was not to deceive but to show loyalty (10:2), and since intentionality is a prerequisite for deception, this episode should not be considered. He also includes 2 Sam 20:14–22, where the woman of Abel Beth Maacah led the citizens in killing Sheba and hurling his head over the city wall to Joab (ibid., 318). However, while Sheba was certainly *betrayed* by the people of the city, the text does not suggest that he was caused to believe a falsehood. Hagan admits that deception proper did not occur here, but that "rebellion and betrayal are members of the family of deception" (ibid.). Nevertheless, a rigorous definition would eliminate this episode, since the phenomena depicted therein were not deceptive.

45. Hagan, "Deception as Motif," 303.

46. Ibid., 322.

affair his fortunes in this area changed;[47] (2) the various instances of deception exhibit a pattern of "measure for measure." That is, the one who deceived often later became the victim of deception.[48] However, since, like Hagan, Marcus does not define deception, he includes episodes that do not belong in this category.[49]

Raymond-Jean Frontain also finds evidence throughout the David narrative for the first trend identified by Marcus: early in his career David was the trickster figure who successfully deceived, but as he rose in political power, and especially after the Bathsheba affair, he tended to become the dupe of deception.[50] Frontain sees David's changing social power as the significant variable in the narrative's changing perspective on his deceptive actions; with time, his deception turned from trickery to treachery.[51]

Lastly, Joe Barnhart argues that the characters' use of deception in the books of Samuel suggests that the author has fabricated many of the events depicted.[52] Although he concludes that many accounts in the David narrative are fictional, his exegetical engagement with the text is superficial, lacking serious effort to determine the author's disposition in the depiction of

---

47. Marcus, "David the Deceiver," 164.

48. Ibid., 165. He gives the examples of (1) Saul deceiving David with Merab and Michal (1 Sam 18:17–23), and then Michal deceiving Saul with the idol (1 Sam 19:12–17); (2) Amnon deceiving David about Tamar (2 Sam 13:6–7), and then Absalom deceiving David about Amnon (2 Sam 13:26–28); (3) Absalom deceiving David about going to Hebron for a vow (2 Sam 15:7–9), and David deceiving Absalom through Hushai's counsel (2 Sam 15:31; 17:7–14).

49. For example, Marcus includes David's appointing of Amasa to command the army in place of Joab (2 Sam 19:13) as a deception against Joab (ibid., 165). However, while David may have appointed Amasa without Joab's knowledge, this does not mean that he caused Joab to believe a falsehood. Marcus also suggests that David deceived Joab by leading him to believe falsely that he would reconcile with Absalom after the encounter with the Tekoite woman in 2 Sam 14:2–21. According to Marcus, by later declaring that he would not see Absalom's face (v. 24), David misled Joab (ibid., 165). However, David had simply instructed Joab to "bring back the young man Absalom" (v. 21). To suggest that David deceived Joab, one would have to show that (1) David intended Joab to believe falsely he would have a face-to-face encounter, and (2) Joab understood David's command to imply such. Since the narrative is vague concerning such details, this situation is best left out of consideration.

50. Frontain, "The Trickster Tricked," 182.

51. Ibid., 181.

52. Barnhart, "Acknowledged Fabrications," 231–36.

the deceptions.[53] He concludes that lies and deception were accepted during military conflict as necessary resources.[54]

While these studies provide helpful insights into some aspects of these deception episodes, they are all brief and thus necessarily partial treatments of the phenomenon. What is needed is a comprehensive investigation of the motif of deception that extends across both 1 and 2 Samuel. To fulfill this need, the present study will seek to (1) operate consistently from a philosophically rigorous definition of deception, (2) analyze the narratological depictions of all the deception episodes, (3) determine any observable trends in these positively and negatively depicted deceptions, and (4) compare these data to the explicit statements made concerning lying and deception in the OT's prescriptive material.

Method

A Literary-Synchronic Approach

The method I will use in this study is what Moshe Garsiel calls a "literary-synchronic approach."[55] This approach is *literary* in the sense that the object of interpretation is *literature*—the biblical text itself—and not the putative historical realities behind the text. V. Philips Long has compared biblical narratives to artistic portraiture; just as the latter is visual representational art, the former is verbal representational art.[56] Just as a portrait artist has a physical subject whom she must represent through visual means, so the implied author[57] of a biblical narrative has a historical subject that he must

---

53. Many of his conclusions seem to be based on his own perception of the unlikelihood or inexplicability of an event, or his own explicit conjecture. He writes: "*I suspect* the redactors of Samuel and Kings viewed some of their own fabrications as elements of good storytelling" (ibid., 232). Concerning Samuel's prophetic knowledge: "*We cannot help wondering* how they [the authors/redactors] would gain access to the content of those putative revelations" (ibid., 233); "*We may conjecture* that threads of both fiction and fact have been woven into the Samuel-Saul-David-Solomon narrative" (ibid., 233). Concerning Dagon falling before the ark: "This of course *has the ring of pure fabrication* for embroidering the explanation" (ibid., 235 [all emphases are mine]).

54. Ibid., 233.

55. Garsiel, *First Book of Samuel*, 16.

56. Long, *Art of Biblical History*, 63–68.

57. In literary theory, the "implied author" is the version of the author implied in and projected by the text and is responsible for the work as a whole. The narrator is the direct means by which the implied author communicates to the reader. See Booth, *Rhetoric of Fiction*, 71–76.

represent through verbal means. To accomplish this, both artist and author must make a variety of choices for how to depict their subject matter. The object of our study is this literary depiction in the biblical text. Therefore, by engaging in a close reading of the text and attending to its various shades of emphasis and reticence, we may glean great insight concerning the author's perspective on the events he depicts. This authorial perspective then provides the interpretive data from which we may draw theological conclusions. In addition, the approach taken here is *synchronic* as opposed to diachronic. Rather than focusing on the history of the text or any alleged sources behind the text, this analysis will examine the text as it stands in its final form. Although at certain points I will discuss textual variants or differences in the ancient versions where such items are especially relevant, the primary locus of study will be the Hebrew text as represented in *BHS*. This literary-synchronic approach to biblical narrative has blossomed over the last three decades and has been the subject of many fine theoretical treatments, most notably those of Robert Alter,[58] Adele Berlin,[59] Meir Sternberg,[60] Shimon Bar-Efrat,[61] and Jan Fokkelman.[62] The present study is greatly indebted to many interpretive insights found in these works.

In particular, this literary-synchronic approach pays special attention to narratological features such as plot, structure, characterization, point of view, repetition, allusion, narration time, narrated time,[63] direct and indirect discourse, and narration. Of special importance is the role of the so-called "omniscient narrator." As Sternberg writes, "Given the biblical narrator's access to privileged knowledge—the distant past, private scenes, the thoughts of the dramatis personae, from God down—he must speak from an omniscient position."[64] For this reason, the approach taken here views the narrator's (and God's) perspective on events within the narrative as supremely reliable, in contrast with the perspectives of the various characters, which may or may not be reliable.[65] Therefore, whenever a character's

---

58. Alter, *Art of Biblical Narrative*.

59. Berlin, *Poetics and Interpretation*.

60. Sternberg, *Poetics of Biblical Narrative*.

61. Bar-Efrat, *Narrative Art in the Bible*.

62. Fokkelman, *Reading Biblical Narrative*.

63. Narration time is the amount of space the narrator devotes to depicting a particular event; narrated time is the amount of time elapsed within the narrative itself. See the discussion in Bar-Efrat, *Narrative Art in the Bible*, 143–65.

64. Sternberg, *Poetics of Biblical Narrative*, 12. See also his later, extended discussion on pp. 84–99.

65. See also Bar-Efrat, *Narrative Art in the Bible*, 54; Berlin, *Poetics and Interpretation*, 55–56.

perspective differs from a narratorial description, the latter will carry more weight. If the two perspectives are contradictory, that is a sign that the implied author is depicting the character as wrong. Ultimately, our goal is to evaluate the action and actors by reference to the narrator's omniscient and reliable perspective.[66]

A Biblical-Theological Approach

In addition to being literary-synchronic, this study will also use a biblical-theological approach. Recognizing that the phrase "biblical theology" has become uncertain and unwieldy in recent decades,[67] it still seems to be an appropriate label for the method taken here. What I mean by a "biblical-theological approach" is a method of inquiry that seeks "to survey and synthesize the results of both OT and NT studies."[68] Although the books of Samuel are my primary corpus of study, these books do not exist in a vacuum, but have been canonized along with the rest of the OT and NT. Therefore when other biblical passages address issues relevant to the exegetical discussion of a particular text, I will view these other passages as assets to the interpretive task and seek to incorporate them accordingly. Although our interpretation of a particular text must be exegetical, in a biblical-theological approach our interpretations must also comport with the larger witness of the whole of Scripture. The underlying presupposition behind this is that the Bible is a coherent whole, the parts of which are mutually illuminating.

The Structure of this Study

This study will proceed in three major parts. First, in chapter 2, I will examine all the explicit, ethical statements concerning deception in the OT. Whereas ethical evaluations in biblical narrative are usually implicit, many passages in the Torah, Wisdom literature, Psalms, and Prophets provide explicit commentary on deceptive activity. The analysis of this material will provide a theological grid with which to compare the narrative depictions of deception in the books of Samuel. Second, in chapters 3–6, I will examine the narrative episodes involving deception in the books of Samuel.

66. Sternberg, *Poetics of Biblical Narrative*, 155.
67. See Barr, *Concept of Biblical Theology*.
68. Scobie, *Ways of Our God*, 77. This brief summary obviously does not exhaust the meaning of "biblical theology" (nor does it for Scobie), but it does provide a succinct summary of this particular aspect of biblical theology that is most relevant at this point in our discussion. For a fuller discussion see ibid., 46–79.

After summarizing each biblical episode, the study of each will include two parts. The first part, "Establishing the Deception," will ensure that the phenomenon being examined is rightly classified according to the definition of deception provided above. This part will identify (1) the deceiver, (2) the receiver, (3) the false belief, and (4) the evidence that the receiver adopted the false belief. The second part, "Analyzing the Deception," will examine the characteristics of each deception by answering the following questions:

1. What tactic did the deceiver use?
2. What was the motive for the deception?
3. Are there any significant features that contribute to the narrative art of the episode (e.g., irony, a hint of the truth, allusions to other episodes, etc.)?
4. Did the deceiver(s) achieve the goal(s) for which they deceived?
5. Did the deceiver(s) experience any negative consequences for their deception?
6. What is the implied author's evaluation of the deception?

Regarding this last element, since the narrator never gives an explicit evaluation of these deceptions, we must rely on more subtle literary indicators to determine how the author is depicting each deception. The conclusions regarding evaluation are therefore more subjective than the other elements of the account.[69] Where I cannot determine the evaluation of a deception confidently, I will seek to show how the author is characterizing the deceiver. Third, in chapter 7, I will conclude by analyzing the findings of chapters 3–6, comparing those findings with the theology of deception developed in chapter 2, interacting with various scholarly views on deception in the Bible, and testing my conclusions against deception as presented elsewhere in the canon.

---

69. Williams makes a similar qualification in his study (*Deception in Genesis*, 14).

2

Deception in the Explicit Statements of the Old Testament

THIS CHAPTER WILL EXAMINE all the explicit ethical statements concerning deception in the OT. To accomplish this I will first survey the semantics of the primary vocabulary denoting deception. This will provide a basis from which to study those texts that employ these words in a prescriptive manner. Next I will examine the sanctions concerning deception in the Torah, paying particular attention to the contexts in which and reasons why deception is prohibited. Lastly, I will survey briefly how deception is reflected upon in the Wisdom literature, the Psalms, and the Prophets.

The Vocabulary of Deception

Many words and idioms indicate deceptive activity in biblical Hebrew. However, since the goal of this chapter is to develop a theology of deception drawn from explicit statements, I will restrict this survey to the most common vocabulary used in contexts that make explicit ethical assessments concerning deception.

שקר

The root שקר occurs in the OT in both verbal and nominal forms. In half of its six verbal occurrences it contrasts with חסד (Gen 21:23; Ps 89:34–35 [33–34]; Isa 63:7–8), which is generally understood to mean faithfulness or loyalty in an interpersonal relationship.[1] Whereas חסד describes fidelity to

---

1. Stoebe, "חסד," 456; Baer and Gordon, "חסד," 211–18.

such a relationship, שקר is the breach of it.² The verbal action thus describes covenant violation (Ps 44:18 [17]), is something that YHWH does not do (1 Sam 15:29), and therefore is something that Israel is prohibited from doing to one another (Lev 19:11). The nominal form of שקר is used with similar meaning. In construction with עד it denotes a false witness in court,³ a situation in which one is socially obligated to testify truthfully. When linked to שבע it describes swearing false oaths;⁴ that is, a person officially binds himself to a course of action, but then breaks the self-imposed contract.

Although שקר seems to have originated in the context of covenant breaking, its meaning later expanded to include faithlessness in general.⁵ The prophets used שקר to describe false prophets and their prophecies,⁶ as well as the falseness of idols.⁷ שקר can also simply assert that a statement does not correspond to the facts (2 Kgs 9:12; Jer 37:14; 40:16). Klopfenstein argues that the nominal uses of שקר often connote an element of aggression or intention to bring harm to others, most clearly seen by the terms placed in parallel with it: חמס ("violence"; Deut 19:16 with v. 18; Ps 27:12; Mic 6:12), רעע ("evil"; Zech 8:17; Ps 52:5 [3]), שנא ("hate"; Prov 10:18; 26:28), רשע ("wickedness"; Ps 109:2; Prov 11:18; 29:12), און ("iniquity"; Isa 59:3; Zech 10:2; Ps 7:15 [14]), and פשע ("rebellion"; Isa 57:4).⁸ Thus the "deceiving spirit" (רוח שקר) sent from YHWH to entice Ahab went out to bring about the "disaster" (רעה) against him that YHWH had decreed (1 Kgs 22:22–23; 2 Chr 18:21–22).⁹ Therefore in its nominal uses שקר may be considered a falsehood that often intends to harm others.

שוא

The noun שוא shares some of its semantic range with שקר, most obviously in that it replaces the latter in the ninth command of the Deuteronomic Decalogue (Deut 5:20), and elsewhere occurs parallel to it (Zech 10:2; Ps 144:8, 11). Since the ninth command refers to a witness who testifies falsely

---

2. Klopfenstein, *Die Lüge*, 8.

3. Exod 20:16; Deut 19:18; Ps 27:12; Prov 6:19; 12:17; 14:5; 19:5, 9.

4. Lev 5:22 [6:3], 24 [6:5]; 19:12; Jer 5:2; 7:9; Zech 5:4.

5. Klopfenstein, *Die Lüge*, 17; Prouser, "Phenomenology of the Lie," 24.

6. Isa 9:14 [15]; Jer 5:31; 7:4, 8; 14:14; 20:6; 23:14, 25, 26, 32; 27:10, 14–16; 28:15; 29:9, 21, 23, 31; 43:2; Ezek 13:22; Mic 2:11; Zech 10:2; 13:3.

7. Jer 10:14; 13:25; 16:19; 51:17; Hab 2:18.

8. Klopfenstein, "שקר," 1400–1401.

9. See Chisholm, "Does God Deceive?" 12; Block, "What Has Delphi to do with Samaria?" 211.

with intent to condemn another unjustly,[10] שוא thus sometimes carries the same harmful nuance that שקר does.[11] Also like שקר it can refer to the falseness of idols (Jer 18:15; Jonah 2:9 [8]; Ps 31:7 [6]) and false prophecies and visions;[12] and like שקר it is associated with און (Isa 5:18; 59:4; Hos 12:12 [11]; Job 11:11). However, with שוא the semantic range includes the idea of futility or purposelessness.[13]

כחש

The verb כחש can refer to a false statement (1 Kgs 13:18; Jer 5:12), but more often it specifically describes a denial of truth, whether denying one's prior actions (Gen 18:15; Lev 5:21–22 [6:2–3]; Job 8:18) or denying God's right to obedience by rebelling against him.[14] Klopfenstein observes a range of meaning extending from denial (to say "no" regarding something that is true) to concealment (not to say anything regarding something that is true).[15] In many contexts כחש is associated with stealing (Lev 19:11; Josh 7:11; Hos 4:2), which follows logically, since a thief is likely either to deny his theft if questioned or conceal the stolen item if not questioned. The six nominal occurrences of כחש show its negative and harmful nuance, demonstrated by the terms in parallel with it: רעע ("evil"; Hos 7:3), רשע and עולה ("wickedness" and "injustice"; Hos 10:13); מרמה ("deceit"; Hos 11:12), and מרי ("rebellion"; Isa 30:9). Additionally, a "city of blood" is described as full of כחש (Nah 3:1), and it is said to be a "sin of the mouth" spoken by enemies (Ps 59:13 [12]). Therefore we may conclude that כחש has the particular nuance of deception through denial or concealment of what is true, though like שקר and שוא it also may connote deceptive activity that is done in the context of bringing wrong or harm to others.

כזב

The root כזב also occurs as both a verb and a noun. Verbally it may connote people saying they will do something, but then not doing it. Accordingly

---

10. See below for argumentation to substantiate this conclusion.

11. So also Klopfenstein, *Die Lüge*, 315.

12. Lam 2:14; Ezek 12:24; 13:6–9, 23; 21:34 [29]; 22:28.

13. Jer 2:30; 4:30; 6:29; 46:11; Mal 3:14; Ps 60:13 [11]; 108:13 [12]; 127:1–2; Job 7:3; 35:13. See also Prouser, "Phenomenology of the Lie," 61.

14. Josh 24:27; Isa 59:13; Job 31:28; Prov 30:9.

15. Klopfenstein, *Die Lüge*, 309.

it is outside the realm of God's actions (Num 23:19; cf. Ps 89:36 [35]). This sense is illustrated in the latter half of Num 23:19, which declares, "God is not man that he should lie (כזב), nor a son of man that he should relent," and then asks rhetorically, "Does he speak but then not act? Does he promise but then not fulfill?" The verb also refers to someone saying something will happen that then does not happen (2 Kgs 4:16; Hab 2:3). The sense of these uses suggests that כזב refers to saying something that does not transpire. Thus כזב can be the cause of injustice, as lies are told to convict the innocent and acquit the guilty (Ezek 13:19), and is considered the opposite of being in the right (Job 34:6). It is also associated with not remembering God in covenant faithfulness (Isa 57:11; Ps 78:34–37). In Psalm 78 especially, Israel sought God, repented, and remembered him (vv. 34–35), but then lied to him by not having their hearts firmly devoted to him and trusting in his covenant (vv. 36–37); that which they committed to do, they did not do.

Nominally כזב carries this same sense. Delilah twice chastised Samson for lying to her concerning how he may be bound; that which he said would happen did not happen (Judg 16:10, 13). כזב is also used in ways similar to שקר and שוא, particularly concerning legal witness and false prophecy. Proverbs describes the false witness (עד שקר) as one who "testifies lies" (יפיח כזבים, Prov 6:19; 14:5; 19:5, 9), something that a truthful witness does not do (Prov 14:5, 25). Such a witness can even be called a "witness of lies" (עד־כזבים, Prov 21:28). Ezekiel describes false prophets as those who have "futile" (שוא) visions accompanied by "lying" (כזב) divinations (Ezek 13:6–9; 21:34 [29]; 22:28). In addition to the harm associated with the "false witness," a harmful aspect of כזב is also illustrated by the words in parallel with it: שקר (Isa 28:15; Mic 2:11), שד ("destruction"; Hos 12:2 [1]), רשע ("wicked"; Ps 58:4 [3]), and איש־דמים ("men of blood"; Ps 5:7 [6]). Therefore, כזב particularly describes a statement that does not transpire,[16] while sharing the sense of causing harm present in the other terms.

רמה

The verb רמה is used eight times in the OT. Four of these occur in questions posed in direct discourse to deceivers by their victims after a deception in the form, "Why did you deceive me/us?" (Gen 29:25; Josh 9:22; 1 Sam 19:17; 28:12). Interestingly, all four episodes involve deception through misrepresentation by clothing.[17] In another occurrence, Mephibosheth defended

---

16. Klopfenstein summarizes כזב as something spoken that "does not arrive" ("nicht eintreffen," *Die Lüge*, 209).

17. That Jacob did not recognize Leah at their marriage is most likely due to the

his loyalty to David and claimed that Ziba "betrayed" him (2 Sam 19:27). In this instance the word does not mean "deceive"—for Mephibosheth was not caused to believe a falsehood—but rather "betray" or "misrepresent," as demonstrated by Mephibosheth's following words: "And he has slandered your servant to my lord the king" (v. 28, NIV). Thus רמה often connotes that the receiver expected loyalty from the deceiver, but received deceit/betrayal instead.[18] This sense of the word was present when David said that he would call upon God to judge the defectors from Benjamin and Judah if they "betrayed" him to his enemies (1 Chr 12:18 [17]). Similarly, in Lam 1:19 the writer bemoans that his allies "betrayed" him, evidently not describing deception but a failure to provide help during invasion. The verb is used in Prov 26:18-19 to describe an unspecified deceptive action that is compared to "deadly arrows." Therefore verbally רמה means either to deceive through misrepresentation of facts or to betray. In many cases the victim had expected loyalty from the deceiver/betrayer, and in each instance the act brought some type of advantage to the deceiver and/or disadvantage to the victim.[19]

This root also occurs in several nominal forms, the most prominent and relevant being מרמה. While used occasionally to describe deception in general (e.g., Gen 27:35) and dishonest commercial standards (Hos 12:8 [7]; Amos 8:5; Mic 6:11; Prov 11:1; 20:23), מרמה usually describes a deception where violence is involved.[20] This is also demonstrated by its associations with רע ("evil"; Ps 34:14 [13]; 50:19; Prov 12:20), און ("iniquity"; Ps 10:7; 36:4 [3]; Job 15:35), עולה ("injustice"; Ps 43:1), and those who are רשע ("wicked"; Ps 109:2; Prov 12:5). Similarly, those "devising words of deception" (דברי מרמות יחשבון) are those "not speaking peace" (לא שלום ידברו, Ps 35:20). In addition to מרמה, another nominal form used to describe deception is רמיה, which is also associated with violence (Mic 6:12; Ps 52:4 [2]; 120:2-3) and עולה ("injustice"; Job 13:7; 27:4). Similar to the nuance of the verb, these nominal forms involve a sense of advantaging the deceiver by disadvantaging the victim, while often adding an element of violence to the situation.

---

custom of veiling the bride before the husband (see Waltke, *Genesis*, 405). The ruse of the Gibeonites involved worn clothing (Josh 9:5); Michal covered the *teraphim* used to impersonate David with a garment (1 Sam 19:13); and Saul disguised himself with "other clothes" in order to visit the necromancer of Endor (1 Sam 28:8).

18. See also Prouser, "Phenomenology of the Lie," 39-41.
19. See also Klopfenstein, *Die Lüge*, 311.
20. Gen 34:13; Jer 9:7 [8]; Zeph 1:9; Ps 5:7 [6]; 38:13 [12]; 52:6 [4]; 55:12 [11], 24 [23]; Prov 14:25; 26:24; Dan 8:24-25.

Summary

The five terms surveyed above all have both peculiar and shared nuances. In their particularities, שקר emphasizes a breach of agreement or relational disloyalty; שוא emphasizes futility or purposelessness; כחש refers to a denial or concealment of what is true; כזב refers to something spoken that does not come true; and רמה refers to betrayal or self-advantage at the expense of disadvantaging another. None of these terms reflects untruth as an abstract principle, and all have negative social implications.[21]

Deception in the Prescriptive Material of the Pentateuch

Having looked at the primary vocabulary of deception, we now turn to the major body of material that legislates the ethics of deception: the prescriptions of the Torah. The Pentateuchal stipulations concerning deception occur in two types of contexts: the *judicial context* and the *economic/social context*.

Deception in the Judicial Context

Since truthfulness was especially important in the court, it is not surprising that the majority of stipulations concerning deception occur in the judicial context. Truth-telling in court was crucial because of the high significance placed on the testimony of witnesses; the condemnatory testimony of two or three witnesses could result in capital punishment for an accused person (Deut 17:6). This value placed on truthful testimony is also evident in the Code of Hammurabi, which begins by prescribing capital punishment for those who falsified witness in court.[22] In addition, judges could also be deceptive by pronouncing false judgments in legal cases. Thus the OT prescriptions concerning deception in the judicial context may be subdivided according to deception by *testimony* and deception by *judgment*.

Deception by Testimony

People could deceive by testimony in the judicial context in two ways: by giving *false testimony* and by *refusing to testify*.

---

21. See also Klopfenstein, *Die Lüge*, 321–22.
22. See Laws 2–3 in Roth, *Law Collections*, 81.

Prohibitions of False Testimony

Exodus 20:16

> לֹא־תַעֲנֶה בְרֵעֲךָ   16   You shall not testify against your neighbor
> עֵד שָׁקֶר   as a false witness.[23]

Deuteronomy 5:20

> לֹא־תַעֲנֶה בְרֵעֲךָ   20   You shall not testify against your neighbor
> עֵד שָׁוְא   as a false/vain witness.

Old Testament scholars generally agree that the ninth command proscribes giving false testimony as a witness in court,[24] primarily because the construction ענה with the preposition ב is used elsewhere in the Pentateuch to describe legal testimony (Num 35:30; Deut 19:16, 18).[25] When ענה is thus followed by ב, the testimony is usually condemnatory,[26] which suggests that

---

23. While עד can represent either the human witness or the testimony given, the construction עד שקר most likely refers to the former, since in virtually every other occurrence the phrase represents the person giving the false testimony (Deut 19:18; Ps 27:12; Prov 6:19; 12:17; 14:5; 19:5, 9). The only uncertain occurrence is in Prov 25:18, which is a verbal parallel to the Decalogue: "Like a club or a sword or a sharpened arrow is a man testifying against his neighbor as a false witness" (אִישׁ עֹנֶה בְרֵעֵהוּ עֵד שָׁקֶר). See Andrew, "Falsehood and Truth," 425; Weinfeld, *Deuteronomy 1–11*, 283; Baker, *Tight Fists*, 202.

24. See, e.g., Klopfenstein, *Die Lüge*, 19; Noth, *Exodus*, 166; Childs, *Exodus*, 424; Stamm and Andrew, *Ten Commandments*, 109; Phillips, *Ancient Israel's Criminal Law*, 142; Patrick, *Old Testament Law*, 56; Durham, *Exodus*, 295–96; Brueggemann, "Truth-Telling as Subversive Obedience," 291; Baker, *Tight Fists*, 202; Fretheim, *Exodus*, 236; Enns, *Exodus*, 423; Currid, *Exodus 19–40*, 48; Craigie, *Deuteronomy*, 162; Mayes, *Deuteronomy*, 171; Payne, *Deuteronomy*, 42–43; Miller, *Deuteronomy*, 93; Tigay, *Deuteronomy*, 71; McConville, *Deuteronomy*, 130; Block, *Deuteronomy*, 166.

25. Andrew, "Falsehood and Truth," 426; see also Klopfenstein, *Die Lüge*, 18; Childs, *Exodus*, 424; Durham, *Exodus*, 296; Mayes, *Deuteronomy*, 171.

26. Propp, *Exodus 19–40*, 180 (see, e.g., 1 Sam 12:3; 2 Sam 1:16; Isa 3:9; 59:12; Jer 14:7; Hos 5:5; 7:10; Mic 6:3). Bruce Wells argues that the construction specifically refers to the initial accusation (*Law of Testimony*, 46; see also Bovati, *Re-Establishing Justice*, 300). However, the construction does not always reflect damning testimony in general or the initial accusation in particular. In Job 15:6 Eliphaz says of Job, "Your mouth *condemns* you (יַרְשִׁיעֲךָ), not mine; your lips *testify against you* (יַעֲנוּ־בָךְ)." Eliphaz is not saying that Job is accusing himself, but rather that Job is testifying against himself in a condemnatory way. In a different use, Jacob employs the phrase in the

the false testimony prohibited in the ninth command is given with intent to condemn someone wrongfully of a crime. This conclusion is reinforced by Deut 19:16–19, which uses עד שקר interchangeably with עד חמס ("malicious witness") in describing someone who testifies falsely against an innocent person with intent to cause harm.

The Deuteronomic version of the ninth command differs from Exodus in one respect: the witness is described as a "vain witness" (עד שוא). Some scholars see significance in this change of terminology,[27] while others see no meaningful distinction between the two versions.[28] If the Deuteronomic version intends to exploit the additional meaning of שוא to connote "vain witness," this may expand the parameters of the injunction to include not only false but also pointless or empty testimony.[29] However, even this latter type of testimony does not serve the needs of justice in the courtroom,[30] so the overall concern of the command remains consistent. We may conclude therefore that the ninth command does not prohibit deception in general, but deception that intends to bring about an unjust verdict in the judicial context.

---

context of self-exoneration: "And my righteousness will *testify for me* (ענתה־בי) in the future, for when you come upon my wages before you, every one that is not speckled or spotted among the goats or brown among the lambs, it is stolen" (Gen 30:33). Moreover, in some of the passages Bovati cites to support his reading, it is not evident that an accusation specifically, as opposed to testimony generally, is in view (e.g., Exod 20:16; Deut 5:20; Prov 25:18). Nevertheless, the preponderance of occurrences suggests condemnatory testimony, which certainly includes the accusation, while not being limited to it.

27. Klopfenstein, *Die Lüge*, 18–21; Stamm and Andrew, *Ten Commandments*, 108–10; Ridderbos, *Deuteronomy*, 108; Weinfeld, *Deuteronomy 1–11*, 315.

28. Phillips, *Ancient Israel's Criminal Law*, 142; Merrill, *Deuteronomy*, 155; Mayes, *Deuteronomy*, 171; Wells, *Law of Testimony*, 136. Supporting the overall similarity of the versions, the LXX translates both passages identically, using ψευδής ("false") for both terms, whereas the translator(s) used μάταιος ("empty, vain") to translate שוא in its three other occurrences in the Torah (Exod 20:7; 23:1; Deut 5:11). This suggests that the LXX translators knew of the different semantic aspect of שוא, but here chose to render it the same way as שקר. While it is always possible that the LXX had a different *Vorlage* of Deut 5:20 that read שקר in place of שוא, this conjecture is unnecessary. Both שקר and שוא occur in Zech 10:2 and the LXX translates both with ψευδής, apparently viewing the terms synonymously in this context as well.

29. Block, *Deuteronomy*, 166–67; Miller, *Ten Commandments*, 351.

30. See Isa 59:4: "No one calls for justice (צדק), no one judges in faithfulness (אמונה). They trust in emptiness (תהו), and by vain words (דבר־שוא) they conceive trouble and beget iniquity."

Exodus 23:1-2

לא תשא שמע שוא	1a	You shall not take up a vain report.
אל־תשת ידך	1b	You shall not put your hand
עם־רשע		with a wicked person
להית עד חמס		in order to be a malicious witness.
לא־תהיה אחרי־רבים	2a	You shall not go after the crowd
לרעת		to do evil.
ולא־תענה	2b	And you shall not testify
על־רב		concerning a lawsuit
לנטת אחרי רבים		in order to turn aside after the crowd,
להטת		so that you cause [justice][31] to turn aside.

These verses are part of the larger pericope of Exod 23:1-9, which consists of two apodictic sections that address deception in the judicial context (23:1-3, 6-9), separated by two casuistic lines that exhort care for an enemy's animals (23:4-5). Source-oriented attempts to discern a structure in this section often involve revocalizing, emending, and/or rearranging the MT and usually end up dismissing the casuistic mid-section as a secondary intrusion that interrupts the flow between vv. 3 and 6.[32] However, these efforts rely on speculative reconstructions that cannot be substantiated textually and therefore lack a firm basis from which to begin examination.

In a literary approach, Joe Sprinkle observes that both apodictic sections in this pericope consist of five commands and thus balance each other on either side of the casuistic mid-section.[33] Sprinkle plausibly suggests that the casuistic lines of vv. 4-5 are purposefully placed between vv. 3 and 6 to illustrate the principle exhorted therein: let not your prejudices prevent you

---

31. The transitive Hiphil infinitive construct להטת presupposes an object. Since the Hiphil of the same root in 23:6 has משפט as its object and the LXX has the object κρίσιν as a plus in the present verse, it is probable that משפט is the intended object here as well, whether this was to be intuited from context or was originally present in the text, the latter for which Morgenstern argues ("Book of the Covenant," 91). A similar construction occurs in 1 Sam 8:3, which describes the wickedness of Samuel's sons: "They turned aside after (ויטו אחרי [Qal]) unjust gain and took bribes, and caused justice to turn aside (ויטו משפט [Hiphil])." Therefore, for the present discussion, משפט is understood as the object of להטת.

32. See Morgenstern, "Book of the Covenant," 59-105; McKay, "Exodus XXIII," 311-25; Halbe, "Gemeinschaft, die Welt unterbricht," 64-65.

33. Sprinkle, *Book of the Covenant*, 178.

from doing what is right, whether it involves giving a poor person justice in the courtroom or your enemies assistance with their animals.[34] Such an explanation makes the best sense of the text as it now stands.

The commands throughout these apodictic sections tend to fall into logical pairs.[35] Thus the prohibition to take up a false or vain[36] report in v. 1a is connected to the prohibition to align oneself with a wicked person as a malicious witness (עד חמס) in v. 1b. Since עד חמס refers to one who testifies against innocent persons with the intent of causing them harm (Deut 19:16-19; Ps 35:11-12), the connection between these two prohibitions suggests a scenario in which a wicked person brings charges against an innocent person and spreads a vain report to a third person in order to recruit a "second witness" as is required to convict (Num 35:30; Deut 17:6; 19:15).[37] Not only eyewitnesses but also "hearsay witnesses" could provide admissible testimony in Israel and throughout the ancient Near East.[38] If the "second witness" aligns with the wicked person, taking up the vain report and wrongfully testifying against the innocent, the witness has become a malicious witness, committing what Anthony Phillips refers to as "judicial murder."[39] Therefore the force of the overall injunction is clear: one is not to join the wicked in testifying falsely so that an innocent person is condemned unjustly.[40]

Just as v. 1 prohibits unjust testimony by aligning oneself with the wicked, so the second injunction in v. 2 prohibits unjust testimony as a

---

34. Ibid., 182.

35. Exodus 23:2 consists of two injunctions pertaining to the crowd; 23:3, 6 both concern justice for the poor; in 23:7 there is a logical connection between the two clauses in that a "false charge" (v. 7a) is that which causes an innocent person to be put to death (v. 7b). The connection between the two commands of 23:8-9 is more difficult to see. See also Sprinkle (*Book of the Covenant*, 179) and Morgenstern ("Book of the Covenant," 90), who also view these commands as divided into pairs.

36. Morgenstern argues that שוא here suggests an "unfounded, vain, fruitless" report ("Book of the Covenant," 89). This is plausible, but whether שוא here refers to an unsubstantiated report or an overtly false one, the broad sense of the injunction is the same: one is not to testify without positive knowledge of what is *true*. To take up a report known to be false would be all the more heinous.

37. See Van Seters, *Law Book*, 135.

38. Wells, *Law of Testimony*, 50.

39. Phillips, *Ancient Israel's Criminal Law*, 144.

40. *Contra* Sprinkle (*Book of the Covenant*, 179) and Enns (*Exodus*, 454), who suggest this verse prohibits allowing the wicked person to go unpunished. While this is certainly a concern of justice, the phrase עד חמס refers only to one testifying with unjust, *condemnatory* testimony that causes harm. So also Van Seters, *Law Book*, 135; Phillips, *Ancient Israel's Criminal Law*, 144-45.

result of majority influence. Verse 2a prohibits one from *joining* the crowd to do evil, while v. 2b prohibits one from being *enjoined* by the crowd to give false testimony in a lawsuit.⁴¹ In the present context of false witness, the evil of the crowd in the first half seems to be the same as that in the second—to influence a witness to testify falsely—though the language is too general to be certain. However, v. 2b explicitly proscribes testifying falsely in a way that perverts justice.⁴²

Leviticus 19:16

לא־תלך רכיל	¹⁶	You shall not walk as a slanderer
בעמיך		among your people.
לא תעמד על־דם		You shall not stand against the blood
רעך		of your neighbor.
אני יהוה		I am YHWH.

This prohibition against slander most likely refers not to false testimony *per se*, but to spreading false rumors that damage another's reputation and thus could lead to wrongful judicial action, including "judicial murder."⁴³ This is supported by later associations of "slander" (רכיל) with destruction and murder (Jer 6:28; Ezek 22:9) as well as the present context that connects it with "standing against/upon the blood of your neighbor." This latter phrase is unusual, and though some see it as a prohibition of bringing false capital charges against someone,⁴⁴ Jonathan Magonet has

---

41. Scholars have proposed many alterations to עַל־רִב ("concerning a lawsuit"). McKay suggests עַל־רֹב ("against the *crowd*"), which follows the LXX (μετὰ πλήθους) ("Exodus XXIII," 315). Morgenstern suggests עַל־רָב ("against a *litigant*") ("Book of the Covenant," 91). Van Seters suggests עַל־דָּם ("in a capital case" [lit. "against *blood*"]) (*Law Book*, 135–36). Although the text is difficult, as it stands it is clear enough, rendering hypothetical reconstructions unnecessary.

42. See the translation notes above for argument of the presence of משפט here conceptually.

43. Porter, *Leviticus*, 155; Wenham, *Leviticus*, 268; Gerstenberger, *Leviticus*, 270; Milgrom, *Leviticus 17–22*, 1645; Magonet, "Structure and Meaning of Leviticus 19," 157; Allbee, "Asymmetrical Continuity," 160. Due to the close connection of this prohibition to false testimony in the judicial context, I include it here rather than under deception in the social context.

44. Wenham, *Leviticus*, 268; Gerstenberger, *Leviticus*, 270; Allbee, "Asymmetrical Continuity," 161. If this understanding were correct, it would still support the contention that the slander in view causes harm against another.

persuasively argued on structural grounds that these two clauses of v. 16 present complementary prohibitions. The first prohibits slander that could bring your neighbor wrongful harm, and the second prohibits standing by when your neighbor is in danger of wrongful harm.[45] Therefore in this verse also the deception prohibited is that which brings unjust harm against one's neighbor.

Deuteronomy 19:16–21

כי־יקום עד־חמס	16a	If a malicious witness arises
באיש		against a man
לענות בו סרה	16b	to testify against him a crime,
ועמדו שני־האנשים	17a	the two men
אשר־להם הריב		in the lawsuit shall stand
לפני יהוה		before YHWH,
לפני הכהנים והשפטים	17b	before the priests and the judges
אשר יהיו בימים ההם		who will be in those days,
ודרשו השפטים היטב	18a	and the judges shall inquire thoroughly,
והנה עד־שקר העד	18b	and if the witness is a false witness,
שקר ענה באחיו		testifying falsely against his brother,
ועשיתם לו כאשר זמם	19a	then do to him just as he intended
לעשות לאחיו		to do to his brother;
ובערת הרע מקרבך	19b	you must purge the evil from your midst.
והנשארים	20a	Then the rest of the people
ישמעו ויראו		will hear and fear
ולא־יספו לעשות עוד	20b	and will never again do
כדבר הרע הזה בקרבך		such an evil thing in your midst.
ולא תחוס עינך	21a	And you shall not show pity:
נפש בנפש עין בעין שן בשן	21b	life for life, eye for eye, tooth for tooth,
יד ביד רגל ברגל		hand for hand, foot for foot.

---

45. Magonet, "Structure and Meaning of Leviticus 19," 157. So also Harrison, *Leviticus*, 198–99; Milgrom, *Leviticus 17–22*, 1645.

This passage prescribes the punishment for one who gives false testimony in court. Here a single "malicious witness" (עד חמס) brings condemnatory accusation against someone with intent to cause harm through an unjust verdict. The judges are to inquire into the veracity of the charges, and if proven false the malicious witness is to be punished according to the law of talion. This passage envisions a situation resembling that of Exod 23:1, except that in this case the accuser (the equivalent of the "wicked person" of Exod 23:1) does not recruit a second party to function as a second malicious witness.[46] Deuteronomy 19:18b refers to the witness as a "false witness" (עד שקר), and v. 19a emphasizes that this person *intends* to bring about an unjust and harmful verdict by his deceptive testimony: "Then do to him just as *he intended* (זמם) to do to his brother." Bruce Wells observes that זמם "conveys the idea of planning or plotting, sometimes carrying the specific connotation of planning evil (e.g., Ps 31:14 and 37:12)."[47] The present context supports this connotation here by the description of the witness as a "malicious witness" (עד חמס), that is, a witness seeking to cause violence through the judicial system. Thus, the false witnesses in view here are not genuinely mistaken in their testimony; rather, they intend to cause unjust harm through deception.

Deuteronomy 22:13–21

כי־יקח איש אשה	13a	If a man takes a wife
ובא אליה ושנאה	13b	and lies with her, but he dislikes her,
ושם לה עלילת דברים	14a	and charges her with shameful deeds
והוציא עליה שם רע		and gives her a bad reputation,
ואמר	14b	and says:
את־האשה הזאת לקחתי		"I took this woman,
ואקרב אליה ולא־מצאתי		but when I approached her I did not find
לה בתולים		tokens of her virginity,"

---

46. I am indebted to Van Seters (*Law Book*, 135) for this conceptual link between these two passages.

47. Wells, *Law of Testimony*, 147. To the passages cited by Wells we may add the negative connotation of זמם in Gen 11:6, where YHWH expressed concern that if the Babel builders were left as one people with one language "nothing *they intend* [יזמו] will be impossible for them to do," as well as Prov 30:32: "If you have been foolish and exalted yourself, or if *you have intended* [זמות], put your hand over your mouth." Although grammatically intransitive, the "intending" here in the latter passage is obviously negative.

ולקח אבי הנער ואמה	15a	the girl's[48] father and mother shall take
והוציאו את־בתולי הנער	15b	and bring out the girl's tokens of virginity
אל־זקני העיר השערה		to the elders of the city at the gate.
ואמר אבי הנער	16a	And the girl's father shall say
אל־הזקנים		to the elders,
את־בתי נתתי לאיש הזה	16b	"I gave my daughter to this man
לאשה וישנאה		for a wife, but he dislikes her.
והנה־הוא שם	17a	And behold, he charges
עלילת דברים		shameful deeds,
לאמר לא־מצאתי		saying, 'I did not find
לבתך בתולים		tokens of virginity for your daughter.'
ואלה בתולי		But these are the tokens of virginity
בתי		for my daughter."
ופרשו השמלה	17b	And they shall spread out the garment
לפני זקני העיר		before the elders of the city.
ולקחו זקני העיר־ההוא	18a	Then the elders of that city shall take
את־האיש ויסרו אתו	18b	the man and punish him.
וענשו אתו	19a	And they shall fine him
מאה כסף		one hundred (shekels) of silver
ונתנו לאבי הנערה		and give it to the girl's father
כי הוציא שם רע		because he gave a bad reputation
על בתולת ישראל		to a reputable young woman of Israel.
ולו־תהיה לאשה	19b	And she shall be his wife;
לא־יוכל לשלחה כל־ימיו		he may not divorce her all his days.
ואם־אמת היה הדבר הזה	20a	But if this charge is true;
לא־נמצאו בתולים	20b	tokens of virginity are not found
לנער		for the girl,
והוציאו את־הנער	21a	then they shall bring the girl
אל־פתח בית אביה		to the door of her father's house,
וסקלוה אנשי עירה		and the men of her city
באבנים ומתה		shall stone her to death,

48. Along with virtually all translations, I follow the *Qere* reading (הנערה) here and throughout this passage.

כי־עשׂתה נבלה	because she did a disgraceful thing
בישׂראל	in Israel
לזנות בית אביה	by being a harlot in her father's house;
ובערת הרע מקרבך ²¹ᵇ	you must purge the evil from your midst.

In this passage a man takes a wife, consummates the marriage, but then dislikes her and publicly accuses her of premarital infidelity.[49] However, it is not clear whether or not deception occurs here. Whether he accuses her genuinely or deceptively depends in part on how one understands the first clause of v. 14a, ושׂם לה עלילת דברים. Some translations interpret this as a deceptive accusation ("and slanders her" [NIV], "and makes up charges against her" [NRSV],[50] while others understand עלילת דברים to be the accusation itself ("and charges her with shameful deeds" [NASB], "and accuses her of misconduct" [ESV], "and charges her with shameful conduct" [NKJV]).[51] According to the first reading, the phrase explicitly describes the husband as deceptive. In the second reading he may or may not be acting deceptively. If the phrase describes the content of the accusation, it is possible that the husband brings this accusation of "shameful deeds" deceptively in vv. 13–19, or it could be that these verses describe the husband bringing this charge genuinely though mistakenly.

Supporting the first reading and the deceptive version of the second reading, Raymond Westbrook has argued that "dislike" (שׂנא) "expresses the fact that the divorce in this case is for purely subjective reasons, and the financial penalties, whether by contract or under the general law, will apply."[52] Thus for Westbrook, שׂנא suggests that the husband does not have legal grounds for divorcing his wife, without which he would have to return

---

49. Some understand the term בתולים to mean "tokens of virginity," a way of referring to the bloodied sheet from consummation (Wadsworth, "Is There a Hebrew Word for Virgin?" 162; Von Rad, *Deuteronomy*, 142; McConville, *Deuteronomy*, 335; Ridderbos, *Deuteronomy*, 225; Craigie, *Deuteronomy*, 292–93; Merrill, *Deuteronomy*, 302–3; Tigay, *Deuteronomy*, 204). However, Gordon Wenham has argued that the word meant "tokens of adolescence," referring to a bloodied menstrual cloth, the absence of which served as a positive pregnancy test ("$B^ETÛLĀH$ 'A Girl of Marriageable Age,'" 331; so also Phillips, "Another Look at Adultery," 7; Thompson, *Deuteronomy*, 236). Regardless of the specific referent, it is clear that extra-marital sexual sin was the issue at stake here (22:21).

50. So also Driver, *Deuteronomy*, 254; Von Rad, *Deuteronomy*, 142; McConville, *Deuteronomy*, 339; Mayes, *Deuteronomy*, 310.

51. So also Tigay, *Deuteronomy*, 204; Block, *Deuteronomy*, 521–22.

52. Westbrook, "Prohibition on Restoration of Marriage," 402; see also Wells, "Sex, Lies, and Virginal Rape," 60; McConville, *Deuteronomy*, 339.

her dowry. Therefore he slanders her by fabricating something about her that would justify his divorce legally, thereby allowing him to keep the dowry.[53] On this interpretation the husband is a false witness. However, this is problematic because the law of talion is not applied to the husband as prescribed for false witnesses in Deut 19:16–21.[54] In response, Wells suggests that the husband would have had the option of choosing which penalty to pursue against his wife in bringing his accusation. As Wells reconstructs the situation, in the first scenario (vv. 13–19) the husband is not seeking the wife's death when he accuses her, but wants to divorce her legally and thus benefit financially. Therefore, upon being discovered as a false witness, the punishments he receives actually follow talionic regulation.[55] Only in the second scenario (vv. 20–21) does the husband intend his charges to result in capital punishment. Wells bases this conclusion largely on comparative evidence from ancient Near Eastern judicial systems in which victims could typically exact full or partial penalties against their perpetrators.[56] While this solution is possible, nowhere does this passage suggest that the husband alters any aspect of the charge between the two scenarios. Therefore, deception on the husband's part in this passage may only be considered a possible reading.

On the other hand, the text itself provides compelling evidence that עלילת דברים describes the content of the accusation and that the husband is not being deceptive in vv. 13–19. First, according to the text, the difference between the two scenarios is not the husband's intention but the charge's veracity. The second scenario begins, "But if *this charge* is true" (ואם־אמת היה הדבר הזה, v. 20a). The only possible referent for "this charge" is the charge brought by the husband in v. 14. Since v. 20a indicates that "this charge" could be true, it follows that עלילת דברים in v. 14 may be true and therefore is not inherently deceptive. While this rules out the first reading noted above, we are still left with the possibility of the deceptive version of the second reading; that is, the phrase עלילת דברים means "shameful deeds" and the husband is bringing this accusation deceptively in vv. 13–19 but genuinely in vv. 20–21. However, as just noted, the text connects the charge of v. 20a with the charge of v. 14, and therefore the background information in v. 13 that gave rise to the charge of v. 14 also conveys the background to the situation

---

53. Such is the situation as reconstructed by Wells, "Sex, Lies, and Virginal Rape," 60; see also Westbrook, "Prohibition on Restoration of Marriage," 402.

54. See McConville, *Deuteronomy*, 339–40; Nelson, *Deuteronomy*, 270.

55. Wells, "Sex, Lies, and Virginal Rape," 56–63. Wells summarizes the husband's punitive intentions in vv. 13–19 as involving humiliation, money, and divorce; the punishments the husband receives correspond to these three intentions: flogging, fine, and inability to divorce.

56. Ibid., 63–71.

depicted in vv. 20–21. In both cases the man (1) takes a wife, (2) lies with her, (3) dislikes her, and (4) charges her with עלילת דברים; in vv. 13–19 this charge is not true, but in vv. 20–21 it is true. Against Westbrook, this suggests that שׂנא does not automatically implicate the husband as a deceiver.

Second, if the husband's accusation in vv. 13–19 is proven false, the absence of capital punishment according to the talion may have a simpler solution than that proposed by Wells. The absence of the talion may simply indicate that the husband is not viewed as a "false witness" (עד שׁקר), that is, one *intentionally* testifying deceptively with intent to cause harm. Rather, the husband is genuinely mistaken in his accusation, and therefore it is appropriate that his punishment is not talionic.[57] The absence in this passage of the vocabulary used to describe deception only strengthens this conclusion. In any case, even if vv. 13–19 describe an attempted judicial deception by the husband, it is a deception that seeks injustice against both the wife and her father and thus is consistent with our observations of prohibitions of deception so far.

While it seems unlikely that deception occurs in the first scenario of this text, in the second scenario a deception has clearly been perpetrated against the husband. The husband accuses his wife of not being a virgin when he approached her after taking her as his wife (v. 14). If this accusation is true, the wife, and possibly her father, had deceived the husband into believing falsely that she was a virgin up until the marriage—what Wells has labeled "pre-consummation sex plus deception."[58] In this deception the husband was wronged in that the woman for whom he paid the bride-price and took on marital responsibility turned out not to be a virgin. Here also the deception condemned is that which causes injustice against another person.

Prohibition of Refusing to Testify: Leviticus 5:1

ונפשׁ כי־תחטא	1	If a person sins
ושׁמעה קול אלה		in that he hears a call of adjuration,
והוא עד או ראה או ידע		and he is a witness or saw or knew,
אם־לוא יגיד ונשׂא עונו		but does not speak, then he bears his iniquity.

---

57. The fact that the husband may never divorce the wife becomes more reasonable once we conclude that he was genuinely mistaken. The wife is not decreed to live with a husband who deceptively attempted to have her divorced or killed, but with one who truly believed she had wronged him by committing a capital crime.

58. Wells, "Sex, Lies, and Virginal Rape," 49.

Whereas the prior passages have proscribed deception by giving false testimony, Lev 5:1 contains the only explicit prohibition of deception by omission of true testimony. Most agree that this verse envisions someone who is able to serve as a witness, and who hears a public adjuration to testify, but refuses to do so.[59] In this situation the lack of response to the public adjuration is a positive communicative action, creating the false belief that the person does not have pertinent testimony. Although this person does not engender whatever false belief prevails that his true testimony would clarify or overturn, the witness's silence perpetuates this false belief. Given the legal context of this statement, such an omission of true testimony would certainly have unjust and potentially deadly effects on those for whom it should be offered.

Deception by Judgment

Pentateuchal instructions not only prohibit witnesses from giving false testimony but also judges from pronouncing false judgments. A judgment is deceptive if it creates the belief that the guilty are innocent and the innocent are guilty. Whereas a "false witness" intends injustice to come to someone else, deceptive judges pronounce and carry out such injustice. Deception by judgment may be subdivided into three categories: false judgment based on *economic status*, *false charges*, and *bribery*.

FALSE JUDGMENT BASED ON ECONOMIC STATUS

Exodus 23:3, 6

ודל לא תהדר בריבו	3	But a poor man do not favor in his lawsuit.
לא תטה משפט	6	Do not cause justice to turn away
אבינך בריבו		from your needy person in his lawsuit.

---

59. Wells, *Law of Testimony*, 56–57; Kiuchi, *Purification Offering*, 30; Harrison, *Leviticus*, 68; Levine, *Leviticus*, 26; Milgrom, *Leviticus 1–16*, 295; Hartley, *Leviticus*, 68. Martin Noth views this passage as describing someone who overhears another utter an unlawful curse but fails to report it (*Leviticus*, 44). However, Kiuchi rightly points out that nothing in the text suggests that the curse here is unlawful (*Purification Offering*, 30).

This couplet commands people not to be prejudiced for or against the poor in lawsuits. Although some consider 23:3 to address witnesses,[60] the language employed suggests the injunction pertains to judging. This conclusion is reinforced by Lev 19:15, the only other occurrence of the proscription "Do not favor . . ." (לא תהדר), where the context explicitly involves the demand for righteousness in judging.[61] Some have suggested that "poor person" (דל) in 23:3 should be emended to "great person" (גדל),[62] while others have proposed that "your needy" (אבינך) in 23:6 actually means "your opponent."[63] However, neither alteration is convincing.[64] These verses prohibit people from making unjust judgments based on the poor economic status of a litigant. The purpose for this prohibition is explicitly stated in 23:6: that justice (משפט) might not be turned away.

Leviticus 19:15

לא־תעשו עול במשפט	15aα	You shall not do injustice in judgment.
לא־תשא	15aβ	You shall not be partial to

---

60. Patrick, *Old Testament Law*, 89; Sprinkle, *Book of the Covenant*, 183; Wells, *Law of Testimony*, 137.

61. See also Morgenstern, "Book of the Covenant," 92; Van Seters, *Law Book*, 136.

62. Auerbach, "Das Zehngebot," 263; Van Seters, *Law Book*, 137. McKay translates this verse with "poor one," but seems to favor the emended reading in his discussion ("Exod XXIII," 316–17).

63. Umberto Cassuto suggests that the word אבין here is a substantive found in other Semitic languages that means, "to refuse, be unwilling," thus rendering "your opponent" (*Exodus*, 298). For him it is thus a synonym for איב ("enemy") rather than a defective spelling of אביון.

64. In defense of emending דל to גדל, Van Seters asserts that the former reading "does not make sense, for the verb הדר has to do with honor and respect and is not appropriate for the 'poor'" (*Law Book*, 137). However, although the verb connotes this and is used concerning "the great" in Lev 19:15aγ, the sense of the proscription there is not to honor the great *unjustly* ("in righteousness you shall judge your neighbor" [v. 15b]). Therefore it is not clear why such unjust honor could not be applied to judgment for the poor, especially since the Levitical command pairs this proscription of unjustly honoring the great with another one prohibiting showing partiality to the poor (v. 15aβ). Concerning 23:6, Cassuto suggests that his reading of אבינך as "your opponent" connects 23:6 to 23:4–5, which discuss "your enemy" (איבך) and "the one who hates you" (שנאך) (*Exodus*, 298). While possible, this change removes the thematic connection between 23:6 and 23:3, which then disrupts the trend of couplets observed in this pericope and thus the structural connection between the second apodictic section (23:6–9) and the first (23:1–3) proposed above. Therefore while possible, Cassuto's proposal seems to create more problems than it solves.

פני־דל		the appearance of the poor.
ולא תהדר	15aγ	And you shall not favor
פני גדול		the appearance of the great;
בצדק תשפט	15b	in righteousness you shall judge
עמיתך		your neighbor.

Whereas the previous passage prohibits judgments based on prejudices for *or against* the poor, the current passage prohibits judgments based on prejudices for the poor *or the great*. Neither the poor nor the powerful are to be advantaged or disadvantaged in court based on their economic status. Jacob Milgrom argues that the final positive injunction ("in righteousness you shall judge") is not restricted to judges but applied to everyone, but his argument seems based on the false supposition that "your neighbor" (עמיתך) is the addressee to whom this command is given.[65] Nevertheless, it is clear that the second person plural commands throughout the chapter are addressed to all the people, since the chapter begins with YHWH instructing Moses to speak "to the whole assembly of Israel" (אל־כל־עדת בני־ישראל, vv. 1–2). The rationale for this prohibition is clearly stated in v. 15b: righteousness (צדק), rather than injustice (עול), is to be the guiding principle when judges make pronouncements in court.[66]

False Judgment Based on False Charges: Exodus 23:7

מדבר־שקר תרחק	7a	From a false charge keep far,
ונקי וצדיק	7bα	and the innocent and righteous
אל־תהרג		do not put to death,
כי לא־אצדיק רשע	7bβ	for I will not justify the wicked.

65. Milgrom writes: "In Deuteronomy [1:16; 16:18], the address is to the judges; here, it is to *ʿămîtekā* 'your fellow'—that is, to everyone—in all one's personal dealings" (*Leviticus 17–22*, 1643). On the contrary, Deut 16:18 is not addressed to judges, but to the people, and in Lev 19:15, "your fellow" is the direct object of "you shall judge."

66. As direct discourse recalling the prior giving of commands to judges, though not actually proclaiming the commands in context, Deut 1:17 could nevertheless be considered one of the explicit prescriptions concerning deceptive judging based on economic status. However, given its narrative setting and that it introduces no unique concepts, here I mention only that it provides support for the injunctions in this section: "Do not show partiality in judgment; hear both *the small* (קטן) and *the great* (גדל)."

This verse commands those with authority to "put to death"[67] to keep far from a false charge (מדבר־שקר). This use of דבר for "charge" or "accusation" is the same as that found in Deut 22:20 where the husband's "charge" (דבר) of premarital promiscuity against his wife is found true. Given the harmful intention often implicit in שקר, the second clause continues logically from the first: if judges accept a "false charge" (דבר־שקר), they unjustly convict the innocent or righteous, perhaps even sentencing them to death. In the final motive clause (v. 7bβ), the "wicked" (רשע) could refer to the one bringing the false charges, but more probably refers to the judges who convict based on those charges.[68] The former is possible because 23:1 describes the "wicked" (רשע) bringing a false accusation. However, that this injunction concerns false judgment suggests that the motive given for obedience pertains to judges: YHWH "will not justify the wicked" (i.e., wicked judges) who unjustly condemn the innocent.

False Judgment Based on Bribery

Exodus 23:8

ושחד לא תקח	8a	And a bribe you shall not accept,
כי השחד יעור פקחים	8bα	for a bribe blinds those who see
ויסלף דברי צדיקים	8bβ	and subverts the words of the righteous.

Deuteronomy 16:19

לא־תטה משפט	19aα	You shall not cause justice to turn away;
לא תכיר פנים	19aβ	you shall not show partiality;

---

67. This would include both judges and the elders of the city, which in some contexts seem to be distinguished from each other (Deut 21:2; Josh 8:33; 23:2; 24:1) but nevertheless had overlapping responsibilities, one of those being capital rulings (see Deut 22:13–21). Timothy M. Willis suggests that the "elders" adjudicated cases on the local level, while the "judges" did so on a regional level or when local cases became too difficult (*Elders of the City*, 83–86).

68. Judges are liable in such a situation presumably only if they know that the charges are false, yet make judgment based on that testimony. While judges were responsible to "inquire thoroughly" into the veracity of charges brought against someone (Deut 19:18), false witnesses could conceivably deceive them; in such cases the false witnesses alone would be considered "wicked."

ולא־תקח שחד	19bα	and you shall not accept a bribe,
כי השחד יעור עיני חכמים	19bβ	for a bribe blinds the eyes of the wise
ויסלף דברי צדיקם	19bγ	and subverts the words of the righteous.

Just as people were not to "cause justice to turn away" (לא־תטה משפט) by judging others based on their economic status (Exod 23:6), neither were they to "cause justice to turn away" (לא־תטה משפט) by having their judgments influenced by bribes (Deut 16:19aα).[69] The texts above declare that the bribe "blinds" those who otherwise would "see" (Exod 23:8bα) or be "wise" (Deut 16:19bβ). It also "subverts the words of the righteous" (Exod 23:8bβ; Deut 16:19bγ), which recalls the "righteous judgment" (משפט־צדק) that the judge is commanded to give according to Deut 16:18. Michael Goldberg has noted that while "gift giving" to judges in order to receive a favorable judgment was prevalent and morally acceptable elsewhere in the ancient Near East, Israel's Torah forbade it because YHWH himself "favors no person and takes no bribe" (Deut 10:17).[70] Indeed, when Jehoshaphat appointed judges, he reminded them that they judged in place of YHWH: "Consider what you are doing, because you are not judging on behalf of man but on behalf of YHWH, who is with you in declaring judgment" (2 Chr 19:6). Following this, he repeated the idea of Deut 10:17: "And now let the dread of YHWH be upon you; watch what you do, because with YHWH our God there is no injustice or partiality or taking of a bribe" (2 Chr 19:7). Since YHWH cannot be swayed to injustice through "gift giving," and since the human judge pronounced judgment in YHWH's stead, the human judge was not permitted to take a bribe that would cause him to twist his words and deceptively pronounce an unjust judgment. In the covenantal curse of Deut 27:25, this prohibition against deceptive judgment based on bribery is explicitly connected to a concern to prevent unjust harm: "Cursed is the one taking a bribe *in order to kill an innocent person*." This deception would cause injustice against YHWH, whom the judge represented, as well as the one wrongly condemned (and possibly killed) due to the deceptive judgment.

---

69. Peter Vogt has convincingly argued that Deut 16:19 addresses the community as a whole, not simply the judges mentioned in v. 18 (*Deuteronomic Theology*, 210). The second person plural verbs address the whole community in v. 18 and continue into v. 19 with no apparent shift in audience, while v. 18 refers to the judges in the third person. However, this community-wide program of refusing bribes and pursuing righteousness required that judges make just judgments.

70. Goldberg, "Story of the Moral," 24.

Deception in the Economic/Social Context

In addition to the judicial context, the Torah proscribed deception in the economic and social context. The texts that address economic deception may be subdivided into three categories: deception by *dishonest standards in commerce*, deception by *moving a boundary marker*, and deception by *lying about property*. The category of social deception consists of deception by *leading the blind astray*.

Deception by Dishonest Standards in Commerce

LEVITICUS 19:35–36

לא־תעשו עול במשפט	35a	You shall not do injustice in judgment
במדה במשקל ובמשורה	35b	by length, by weight, or by quantity.
מאזני צדק אבני צדק	36a	Just scales, just weights,
איפת צדק והין צדק		a just ephah, and a just hin
יהיה לכם		you shall use.
אני יהוה אלהיכם	36b	I am YHWH your God
אשר־הוצאתי אתכם		who brought you out
מארץ מצרים		from the land of Egypt.

DEUTERONOMY 25:13–16

לא־יהיה לך בכיסך	13a	You shall not have in your bag
אבן ואבן		two stones,
גדולה וקטנה	13b	a large one and a small one.
לא־יהיה לך בביתך	14a	You shall not have in your house
איפה ואיפה		two ephahs,
גדולה וקטנה	14b	a large one and a small one.
אבן שלמה וצדק יהיה־לך	15a	You shall have a complete and just stone,
איפה שלמה וצדק יהיה־לך		you shall have a complete and just ephah,
למען יאריכו ימיך	15b	that your days may be long
על האדמה		in the land
אשר־יהוה אלהיך נתן לך		that YHWH your God is giving to you.

כי תועבת יהוה אלהיך	16a	For an abomination to YHWH your God
כל־עשה אלה		is everyone who does these things,
כל־עשה עול	16b	everyone who does injustice.

Leviticus 19:35a is the same as Lev 19:15aα: "You shall not do injustice in judgment" (לא־תעשו עול במשפט). However, here the semantic range of משפט is exploited to refer to the "standard" of measurements used in commercial dealings.[71] The same flexible phrase thus refers both to judicial and economic contexts and in each case prohibits causing injustice by deception. The deception in question here is clarified by the corresponding prohibition in Deut 25:13–16. In order to advantage oneself in commerce, one would use two different weights or measures, a larger one for buying and a smaller one for selling, thereby acquiring more and selling less than the standard amount. The deception occurs when the other person falsely believes he is exchanging goods according to the standard amount, when in reality he is disadvantaged in the transaction. In short, this deception is a form of theft. Both passages demand that all types of weights and measures be "just" (צדק, Lev 19:36a; Deut 25:15a), with Deuteronomy further specifying that they are to be "complete" or "whole" (שלמה, Deut 25:15a). Both passages also refer to this deception as "injustice" (עול, Lev 19:35a; Deut 25:16b).

Deception by Moving a Boundary Marker: Deuteronomy 19:14

לא תסיג	14	Do not move
גבול רעך		your neighbor's boundary marker,
אשר גבלו ראשנים		which former ones set up
בנחלתך אשר תנחל		in your inheritance that you inherit
בארץ אשר יהוה		in the land that YHWH
אלהיך נתן לך לרשתה		your God is giving to you to possess.

This verse prohibits deception by moving a neighbor's boundary marker, which would unjustly enlarge one's own territory at the expense of

---

71. While משפט often means "decision" or "judgment" in the legal context, it may also mean "measure" or "standard" such as in Exod 26:30: "Erect the tabernacle *according to its standard* (כמשפטו), which you were shown on the mountain" (see *HALOT* 2:651). In the present economic context, the "standard" measurement is what is used to settle the commercial exchange.

another. For the Israelites in an agriculturally based society, the produce of the land was the source of sustenance and therefore central to one's livelihood. Furthermore, the type of land that was most susceptible to this crime was also that which was most productive: the open, arable pastureland without natural divisions or roads to delineate clear boundaries.[72] By moving a boundary marker, one causes his neighbor to have a false understanding of the amount of land owned and the deceiver receives the fruit of the land that actually belongs to his neighbor. Like deception by dishonest standards, this deception unjustly disadvantages another in order to advantage the deceiver and is a form of theft. The corresponding curse in Deut 27:17 against "the one who moves his neighbor's boundary marker" probably arises from the secrecy of such crimes and reflects the difficulty in detecting or proving them, calling for final justice to be exacted by YHWH himself.[73]

Deception by Lying About Property

LEVITICUS 5:20–26 [6:1–7]

וידבר יהוה אל־משה לאמר	20	And YHWH spoke to Moses, saying:
נפש כי תחטא ומעלה מעל ביהוה	21a	"If a person sins and is unfaithful to YHWH
וכחש בעמיתו	21b	and deceives his neighbor
בפקדון		concerning a deposit
או־בתשומת יד		or a pledge entrusted to him,
או בגזל		or by robbery,
או עשק את־עמיתו		or withholds from his neighbor,
או־מצא אבדה	22a	or he finds a lost item
וכחש בה		and deceives concerning it,
ונשבע על־שקר		and he swears falsely
על־אחת מכל	22b	concerning any of all
אשר־יעשה האדם		that a person might do
לחטא בהנה		and sin thereby,
והיה כי־יחטא ואשם	23a	it will be when he sins and feels guilty,
והשיב את־הגזלה		he will return the robbed item

---

72. McConville, *Deuteronomy*, 312.

73. Miller, *Deuteronomy*, 195; Thompson, *Deuteronomy*, 217; Tigay, *Deuteronomy*, 255.

אשר גזל		that he robbed,
או את־העשק אשר עשק		or the withheld item that he withheld,
או את־הפקדון		or the deposit
אשר הפקד אתו		that was deposited with him,
או את־האבדה אשר מצא	23b	or the lost item that he found.
או מכל אשר־ישבע	24a	or whatever he swore
עליו לשקר		falsely about.
ושלם אתו בראשו		He must restore its value
וחמשתיו יסף עליו		and add a fifth to it.
לאשר הוא לו	24b	To whomever it belongs
יתננו		he will give it to him
ביום אשמתו		on the day he feels his guilt.
ואת־אשמו	25a	And his guilt offering
יביא ליהוה		he shall bring to YHWH,
איל תמים מן־הצאן	25b	a clean ram from the flock,
בערכך		according to your valuation
לאשם		for a guilt offering,
אל־הכהן		to the priest.
וכפר עליו הכהן	26a	And the priest shall atone for him
לפני יהוה		before YHWH,
ונסלח לו		and it will be forgiven him,
על־אחת מכל אשר־יעשה	26b	concerning anything that he does
לאשמה בה		and is guilty by it."

In the absence of evidence or witnesses, when a dispute concerning someone's property arose, the one accused of misappropriating the property of another would have to swear his innocence before YHWH, and upon doing so the dispute would be considered settled (see Exod 22:10–11).[74] In the situation envisaged in Lev 5:20–26 [6:1–7], a person acquires the property of another,[75] but when questioned about it denies it (כחש) and

---

74. See also Phillips, "Undetectable Offender," 146–47.

75. Jacob Milgrom has argued at length that all the actions describing the acquisition of property in this passage show that the owner of the property is able to identify the perpetrator. Specifically, the presence of denial and swearing a false oath presuppose that an accusation was made (*Cult and Conscience*, 89–101). *Contra* Noth, *Leviticus*, 49.

swears falsely (ונשבע על־שקר) concerning it. Deception occurs in that the defendant causes the judiciary to believe falsely that he has not perpetrated the crime of which he is accused, which in turn causes injustice against the true owner of the property, who is left without legal claim to it after the oath is sworn. This deception also profanes YHWH's name, which is taken up falsely in order to perpetrate the crime.[76] This passage condemns such injustice through deception, but seeks to provide one who "feels guilty" an opportunity to repent and make amends with the owner (5:23-24 [6:4-5]) and YHWH (5:25-26 [6:6-7]).[77] Therefore in this passage the deception condemned is that which causes injustice against another and violates the sanctity of the divine name in doing so. This passage helps illuminate the next passage, which deals with the same type of deception.

Leviticus 19:11-12

לא תגנבו	11a	Do not steal,
ולא־תכחשו	11bα	and do not deny it,
ולא־תשקרו איש בעמיתו	11bβ	and do not deceive your neighbor,
ולא־תשבעו בשמי לשקר	12a	and do not swear falsely by my name
וחללת את־שם אלהיך	12b	and profane the name of your God.
אני יהוה		I am YHWH.

This passage shares much of its content with Lev 5:20-26 [6:1-7]: in both cases (1) some sort of misappropriation of property occurs (5:21-22 [6:2-3]) or is prohibited (גנב, 19:11a), (2) a denial occurs (כחש, 5:22a [6:3a]) or is prohibited (כחש, 19:11bα), (3) the offense occurs or is prohibited against a neighbor (בעמיתו, 5:21b [6:2b]; 19:11bβ); (4) a false oath follows the denial (לשקר . . . שבע, 5:24a [6:5a]) or is prohibited (לשקר . . . שבע, 19:12a); and (5) by such a crime YHWH is wronged (5:21a [6:2a]; 19:12b).

---

76. Wenham, *Leviticus*, 108; Rooker, *Leviticus*, 125; Von Rad, *Old Testament Theology*, 1:183-84.

77. Milgrom has argued persuasively that when the verbal form of אשם occurs intransitively it refers to psychological and not legal guilt, hence the translation "feels guilty" (*Cult and Conscience*, 7-12). This understanding explains the provision of atonement here for intentional sin, supposedly in contradiction of Num 15:30-31, where "high handed" sin is contrasted with unintentional sin, and no means of atonement is provided for the former. It appears that the "high handed" sin of Numbers 15 is intentional sin that is not followed by remorse and repentance; therefore it is distinct from the situation envisioned here.

Furthermore, Lev 19:13 shares other language with 5:21 [6:2] (עשׁק and גזל), further linking these two passages. All this suggests that Lev 19:11–12 proscribes apodictically what Lev 5:20–26 [6:1–7] describes casuistically: a wrongful acquisition of property followed by a deceptive denial of the act and a false oath in YHWH's name for legal vindication.[78] Therefore the prohibitions in this passage against denial (ולא־תכחשׁו) and deception (ולא־תשׁקרו) are not general prohibitions against all forms of untruth,[79] but contextually prohibit such activity that facilitates the crime of theft through false swearing.

Deception by Leading the Blind Astray: Deuteronomy 27:18

ארור משׁגה	18	"Cursed is the one who causes
עור בדרך		a blind person to err on the road."
ואמר כל־העם אמן		Then all the people will say, "Amen."

This passage prohibits deceiving the blind by causing them to believe they are being led properly along the road, when in fact they are being caused to err in some fashion. The text is unclear why one might commit such an act, but for our purposes we simply may observe that the deception in question causes some sort of disadvantage against the one deceived, whether economic or physical.[80]

---

78. So also observe Milgrom, *Cult and Conscience*, 86, 101–2; Allbee, "Asymmetrical Continuity," 153–54; Magonet, "Structure and Meaning of Leviticus 19," 161; Miller, *Ten Commandments*, 365.

79. *Contra* Harrison, *Leviticus*, 198.

80. Many note the affinity between this verse and Lev 19:14: "Do not curse the deaf, and before the blind do not put a stumbling block, but fear your God. I am YHWH" (Driver, *Deuteronomy*, 299; Merrill, *Deuteronomy*, 349; Craigie, *Deuteronomy*, 333; Tigay, *Deuteronomy*, 255; McConville, *Deuteronomy*, 393). This suggests that the "causing to err" of Deut 27:18 may be physical harm that would come from such a stumbling block. The Leviticus text is not considered here as a formal prohibition of deception because the scenario described does not involve causing the blind to believe something falsely, whereas the general and causative language of Deut 27:18 allows for such epistemic influence.

Summary

In the foregoing analysis we have seen that the prescriptive material of the Pentateuch never condemns deception outright. Yael Shemesh similarly observes, "It is perhaps surprising . . . that nowhere in the legal literature of the Bible is there any general injunction to refrain from telling lies."[81] This conclusion disagrees with the statement made by Williams:

> The legal material generally and specifically prohibits deception by word or deed. . . . *There is no indication that there are exceptions to this negative appraisal of deception.* An act of deception against a fellow member of the Israelite community is never described in favorable or even acceptable terms.[82]

While it is true that an act of deception against a fellow Israelite is never described favorably, it does not follow that deception of every kind is therefore prohibited. Rather, the prescriptive material of the Torah only prohibits deception that causes unjust harm or disadvantage to another person. Later Williams makes a similar observation:

> The deceptive practices proscribed in the legal material . . . benefit no other Israelite nor serve to preserve the life of any Israelite. Bearing false witness, perverting justice, lying, stealing, and fraud all serve instead to benefit the perpetrator at another's expense.[83]

This is the type of deception prohibited. As we have seen, this may take the form of legal injustice through deceptive testimony or false judgment; it may cause economic injustice by means of deceptive commercial standards, moving boundary markers, or taking false oaths to acquire another's property; or it may be as simple and cruel as deceiving a blind person to their harm and/or disadvantage. In the remainder of this chapter I will survey the explicit statements concerning deception made elsewhere in the OT to see how they compare with the Pentateuchal prohibitions. Given the large number of pertinent texts and the limitations of space, the following study of deception in the Wisdom literature, Psalms, and Prophets must be restricted to a broad survey rather than a close examination of each of the texts.

---

81. Shemesh, "Lies By Prophets," 83.
82. Williams, *Deception in Genesis*, 64 (emphasis mine).
83. Ibid., 74–75.

Deception in the Explicit Statements Outside the Pentateuch

Deception in the Wisdom Literature

The disposition toward deception in the Wisdom literature is similar to that of the Torah. The sages condemn deception by falsely testifying,[84] falsely judging (Prov 24:23–25)—including receiving bribes to pervert justice (Prov 17:23; cf. Job 15:34; Eccl 7:7)—and slander (Prov 11:13; 20:19). In economic contexts the sages repeatedly state that deception by dishonest standards is an abomination to YHWH (Prov 11:1; 20:10, 23), affirm the use of just (משפט) standards (Prov 16:11), and prohibit moving boundary markers (Prov 22:28; 23:10; Job 24:2) and deceptively acquiring money (Prov 11:18; 21:6) and food (Prov 20:17). The sages also discuss deception in contexts not explicitly addressed by the Pentateuch. Proverbs describes "one who conceals hatred" (מכסה שנאה) as having "lying lips" (שפתי־שקר, Prov 10:18). This figure is developed further in Prov 26:24–28, where the deceiver again is "one who hates" (שונא), disguises "with his lips" (בשפתו, 26:24), and "conceals hatred with guile" (תכסה שנאה במשאון, 26:26). Verse 28 adds that the "lying tongue hates its oppressed one" (לשון־שקר ישנא דכיו); elsewhere the object דך always refers to one who is wrongly oppressed and thus defended by YHWH (Pss 9:10 [9]; 10:18; 74:21).[85] Thus Proverbs correlates this deception to conceal hatred with the intention to oppress another. This is consistent with the description of the "liar" (שקר) as one who heeds a "tongue of destruction" (לשון הות) in Prov 17:4, as well as Prov 12:5–6, which chiastically contrasts the righteous and the wicked:

> The thoughts of the righteous are just (משפט)
>> The counsel of the wicked is *deceit* (מרמה)
>> The words of the wicked are an *ambush of blood* (ארב־דם)
> But the speech of the upright delivers them.

This text parallels deceptive counsel with causing physical harm and contrasts it with the "just" (משפט) actions of the "righteous" (צדיקים) that prevent harm. A similar contrast occurs in Job 34:5–6, where Elihu challenges Job's self-description as one who is "righteous" (צדק) and "just" (משפט), but wrongly considered a "liar" (כזב). Proverbs 26:18–19 compares deception to

---

84. Prov 6:19; 12:17; 14:5, 25; 19:5, 9, 28; 21:28; 24:28; 25:18.
85. Waltke, *Proverbs 15–31*, 366.

"a madman shooting firebrands, arrows, and death," which carries similar connotations of harm against others.

In contrast to righteous or just behavior, the sages denounce deception that gives rise to "evil" (רע, Prov 12:20) and parallel it with "iniquity" (און, Job 11:11; 15:35) and "injustice" (עולה, Job 27:4), all terms that imply harmful consequences for others.[86] In contrast, Prov 12:22 says, "Lying lips (שפתי־שקר) are an abomination to YHWH, but those who practice faithfulness (אמונה) are his delight." The noun אמונה connotes relational faithfulness demonstrated in action and is often used in conjunction with חסד[87] or צדק,[88] terms that also convey relational commitment and propriety.[89] Accordingly, this text suggests that the phrase שפתי־שקר refers to speech that is relationally unfaithful.[90] This agrees with the notion described above that שפתי־שקר belong to one who conceals hatred in order to oppress another. It also explains the use of the phrase in Prov 17:7: "Arrogant lips do not suit a fool; still less lying lips (שפתי־שקר) for a ruler." Since the ideal ruler—whether king or prince—rules in "righteousness" (צדק) and "justice" (משפט) (e.g., see Isa 32:1), speech that is relationally unfaithful and bent on carrying out deceptive oppression is categorically unfit for this office (cf. Prov 29:12). For this same reason, "A righteous person (צדיק) hates a false word (דבר־שקר)" (Prov 13:5), that is, falsity that promotes injustice.[91] Prov-

---

86. Regarding רע, Stoebe summarizes: "The concept of an inflicted injury or the resulting harmful situation underlies rā'" ("רעע," 1251; see also Baker, "רעע," 1154). Regarding און, Knierim understands the word to characterize "an event negatively as a dangerous power for disaster" ("און," 61) and thus simply renders it as "harm" (ibid., 60). Concerning עולה, Knierim observes: "In cases where the nature of the transgression is more nearly perceptible, it consistently involves crimes of a social, property, or commercial nature" ("עול," 850).

87. See, e.g., Pss 36:6 [5]; 88:12 [11]; 89:2-3 [1-2], 25 [24], 34 [33], 50 [49]; 92:3 [2]; 98:3; 100:5.

88. See, e.g., Isa 11:5; 59:4; Ps 96:13; 119:75, 138; Prov 12:17.

89. See Moberly ("אמן," 429-31), who also notes the frequent linking of אמונה with חסד and צדק. See the discussion above for the significance of חסד. Concerning the צדק word-group in Proverbs, Waltke concludes that it means "doing what is right *in a social relationship* as defined by God's standard of what is right behavior" ("Righteousness in Proverbs," 235 [emphasis mine]). See also Vogt, *Deuteronomic Theology*, 212-14.

90. In this context, most of the alternatives to deceptive speech are relationally positive: thoughts that are "just" (משפט, 12:5), speech that "delivers" (יצילם, 12:6), a tongue that brings "healing" (מרפא, 12:18), and being a promoter of "peace" (שלום, 12:20).

91. The singular construct chain דבר־שקר occurs only in Prov 13:5; 29:12, and in Exod 23:7, where it refers to a "false charge" to be avoided by a judge. If a judicial context was in mind for these proverbial passages as well, this would only strengthen the element of injustice in mind for the prohibition.

erbs 6:17 lists a "lying tongue" (לשון שקר) as one element among seven that YHWH hates. However, this phrase is part of a larger list that moves along the parts of the body and is followed by "hands that shed innocent blood, a heart that devises schemes of iniquity, feet that hasten to run to evil, a false witness who pours out lies, and a man causing strife between brothers" (Prov 6:17b–19). This context suggests that the "lying tongue" contributes to relational harm, which these subsequent clauses describe more specifically. Other passages in the Wisdom literature that denounce מרמה but offer less detail concerning the deception in view do not contradict this sense that injustice is the primary concern (Prov 14:8; Job 31:5–6).

A final passage to consider is Prov 30:8: "A deceitful lie (שוא ודבר־כזב)[92] keep far from me; give me neither poverty nor riches; feed me my quota of bread." The combination of שוא and כזב occurs elsewhere in the OT only in Ezekiel's diatribes against false prophecies (Ezek 13:6–9; 21:34 [29]; 22:28). The context of Prov 30:5–8 suggests that a related sense may be intended here as well:

> Every word of God is refined;
>   he is a shield for those taking refuge in him.
> *Do not add to his words,*
>   *lest he reprove you and you be found a liar* (כזב).
> Two things I ask from you;
>   do not withhold from me before I die:
> A deceitful lie (שוא ודבר־כזב) keep far from me;
>   give me neither poverty nor riches; feed me my quota of bread.

In context, the "deceitful lie" from which Agur prays to be spared in v. 8 seems to be falsely adding to the refined words of God, which in v. 6 is said to result in being found a "liar" (כזב).[93] To qualify as deception this action would need to be intentional. If it is intentional, the deceiver would be wronging YHWH, whose word he has purposefully misrepresented, and the people to whom he brought this false revelation, which, to use Ezekiel's words, would "cause [YHWH's] people to stray (הטעו את־עמי)" (Ezek 13:10).

---

92. This translation reads this phrase (lit. "deceit and a lying word") as a hendiadys. See Waltke, *Proverbs 15–31*, 458.

93. The allusions to Deuteronomy in Prov 30:4 ("Who has ascended to heaven and come down?" cf. Deut 30:12) and Prov 30:6 ("Do not add to his words . . ." cf. Deut 4:2) support this idea. The first Deuteronomy passage teaches that the word of God is to be obeyed and the second that it not be falsely expanded upon. According to Deuteronomy, Moses was a prophet (Deut 18:15; 34:10), and therefore to add falsely to his words in an unauthorized way would make one a false prophet.

From this survey we see that the Wisdom literature views deceitful words as improper, not simply because they do not correspond to reality, but because they bring unjust harm or disadvantage to another. This raises questions concerning the view that the sages rejected lies and deception altogether. According to Tremper Longman, "Lies are a specific form of foolish speech that the sages roundly condemn."[94] Michael Williams concludes similarly: "There is no indication in Proverbs that any type of deception is considered acceptable."[95] However, these conclusions seem too generalized. David Hubbard is closer to the mark when he writes: "Lies are regularly condemned in Proverbs for their disruptive impact on the social and especially judicial welfare of the community (6:19; 19:5, 9, 22)."[96] Indeed, a slight rewording of this statement summarizes well the conclusion here: deception *that disrupts the social and judicial welfare of the community* is regularly condemned.

Deception in the Psalms

A survey of the Psalms reveals a similar view of deception. Concerning deceptive testimony, Ps 27:12 describes "false witnesses" (עדי־שקר) as "breathing violence" (ויפח חמס) and Ps 35:11 laments "malicious witnesses" (עדי חמס), that is, witnesses that cause violence. In the context of judging falsely, Ps 58:2–4 [1–3] contrasts "speaking righteously" (צדק תדברון) and "judging uprightly" (מישרים תשפטו) with committing "injustices" (עולת) and dealing out "violence" (חמס); those guilty of the latter two are described as "speaking lies" (דברי כזב). Like the sages, the psalmists denounce taking bribes against the innocent (Ps 15:5; cf. 26:10). However, the most common contexts of deception in the Psalms involve oppression by enemies[97] and causing violence.[98] Several Psalms associate deception with "evil" (רע, רעה),[99] "evildoers" (רעע),[100] and "iniquity" (און),[101] roots noted above as having

---

94. Longman, *Proverbs*, 562.
95. Williams, *Deception in Genesis*, 68.
96. Hubbard, *Proverbs*, 461.
97. Pss 12:2–6 [1–5]; 31:18–19 [17–18]; 35:19–20; 38:13 [12]; 20–21 [19–20]; 41:6–7 [5–6]; 43:1; 59:13 [12]; 62:5 [4]; 63:11–12 [10–11]; 69:5 [4]; 89:23 [22]; 109:1–5; 120:1–7; 144:7–8, 11.
98. Pss 5:7 [6], 10 [9]; 10:7–8; 52:3–6 [1–4]; 55:12 [11], 21–24 [20–23].
99. Pss 15:3; 28:3; 34:14 [13]; 50:19.
100. Pss 26:4–5; 119:115–18 (Hiphil participles).
101. Pss 7:15 [14]; 32:2; 36:4–5 [3–4]; 49:6 [5]; 101:7–8.

connotations of bringing harm to others.[102] Psalm 28:3 typifies this association of deception and evil intentions: "Do not pull me with the wicked, with those committing iniquity (אוֹן), those speaking peace (שׁלוֹם) with their neighbor, but evil (רעה) is in their heart."

Psalm 116:11 hyperbolically accuses all humanity of deception (כל־האדם כזב), but in context YHWH has just delivered the psalmist from death (v. 8) and affliction (v. 10). This suggests that the deception condemned pertains to this personal harm that the psalmist had received (so similarly Ps 119:67-71). Psalm 119:161-163 condemns שׁקר in the context of unwarranted persecution from rulers. Elsewhere Psalm 119 rejects שׁקר because of the psalmist's commitment to YHWH's precepts (vv. 104, 128) and Torah (vv. 29-30). However, as observed above, the Torah prohibits שׁקר because of the injustice it brings upon others. In Ps 24:4 it is unclear whether the phrase ולא נשׁבע למרמה refers to swearing by an idol ("or swear by what is false" [NIV]; "or swear by a false god" [TNIV]) or swearing deceptively ("and does not swear deceitfully" [NRSV]; "and has not sworn deceitfully" [NASB]). The first seems less likely, since elsewhere מרמה never refers to idols. Rather, as Klopfenstein has shown, מרמה carries the sense of causing injury to one's neighbor.[103] Thus some sort of false oath to cause harm is most likely in view here.[104] Williams cites Ps 78:36 and 78:57 as instances of "deceit of the Israelites toward God."[105] Since his governing definition of deception does not require perlocutionary success, it is conceivable within such a framework that God could be the object of deceit. However, neither verse suggests that God believed a falsehood; rather, both suggest the crime in view is disloyalty to YHWH.[106] Therefore, according to our definition, no deception occurs in these verses.

---

102. Concerning the phrase פעלי און in Ps 101:8, Carpenter and Grisanti write: "These doers of evil represent individuals who, for their own advantage, harm innocent persons in precarious situations.... In most cases, the *pō ʿălê ʾāwen* depict those who want to harm a Yahweh worshiper by misusing their power, esp. by slander, cursing, false accusations, and other sins of the tongue (*TDOT* 1:147)" ("אָוֶן," 313).

103. Klopfenstein, *Die Lüge*, 311. Although in context he is discussing the verb רמה, he goes on to note that the features detected in the verb are also present in the noun מרמה (ibid., 312).

104. The plus in the LXX "to his neighbor" suggests a similar understanding: καὶ οὐκ ὤμοσεν ἐπὶ δόλῳ τῷ πλησίον αὐτοῦ.

105. Williams, *Deception in Genesis*, 68.

106. Psalm 78:37 adds, "their heart was not steadfast toward him; they were not faithful to his covenant"; Ps 78:56c-57a says, "his decrees they did not keep; and they turned back and were faithless like their fathers."

DECEPTION IN THE EXPLICIT STATEMENTS OF THE OLD TESTAMENT   49

Williams does see Ps 25:3 as "one possible hint that Psalms allows for occasions of justifiable deception."[107] This verse says, "Those acting treacherously without cause (הבוגדים ריקם) will be ashamed." Williams suggests that if the semantic range of בגד includes deceptive activity, this verse implies that situations may arise where one could act treacherously *with* cause.[108] He then goes on to say: "This dubious verse notwithstanding, the emphasis in the Psalms is on the unsatisfactory presence of deceitful men... and on the Psalmist's desired deliverance from them."[109] However, far from being dubious, Ps 25:3 illustrates the very concern underlying the last clause in Williams's statement: the psalmist desires deliverance from deceivers *because of the unjust effects of their deception against him* (i.e., they deceive without justifiable reason). Indeed, we may agree that the emphasis in the Psalms is on the unsatisfactory presence of deceivers; however, the reason the psalmists view the presence of deceivers as unsatisfactory is because their deceptions yield injustice.

Deception in the Prophets

The prophetic corpus reflects these same concerns regarding deception. Isaiah foresaw the time when deception would no longer be used to indict a person and justice would not be turned away (Isa 29:21). The prophets denounce deception by false swearing,[110] which elsewhere is always associated with falsely exonerating oneself from the charge of theft (Lev 5:20–26 [6:1–7]; 19:11–12).[111] They also condemn deception by slander (רכיל),

107. Williams, *Deception in Genesis*, 68.

108. Of the examples he adduces, Jer 12:6 best supports this term as reflecting deception: "Your brothers and the house of your father, even they have *acted treacherously* against you; they have called loudly after you; do not trust them, though they speak good words to you." This passage supports my thesis in that Jeremiah's family members evidently spoke good words deceptively in order to hide their malicious intentions. Williams also considers the possibility that ריקם ("without cause/reason") may mean "empty-handed" (BDB, 938), resulting in a translation, "Let the faithless be disappointed, empty-handed" (*Deception in Genesis*, 79). While most of the sixteen occurrences of ריקם carry this sense of "empty" or "empty-handed," the only other use in the Psalter supports the translation "without cause": "If I have returned evil to him who is at peace with me, or robbed my foe *without cause*...." (Ps 7:5 [4]).

109. Ibid., 68.

110. Jer 5:2; 7:9; Hos 10:4; Zech 5:3–4; Mal 3:5.

111. This link between theft and false oaths is explicit in Zech 5:3–4. In Mal 3:5 the reference to "those swearing falsely" is followed by "those oppressing the hired man of his wages," which is a form of theft. Jer 5:2 does not mention theft in its context, though those swearing falsely are contrasted with those who do "justice" (משפט) and

which is associated with "acting corruptly" (Jer 6:28) and "shedding blood" (Ezek 22:9). Zechariah implores the people to "judge in your gates in faithfulness, justice, and soundness" (Zech 8:16), and not to "plot evil against your neighbor in your heart and love to swear falsely" (Zech 8:17). Judging based on bribes is denounced and associated with intending to shed blood (Ezek 22:12), not defending the cause of the fatherless and widows (Isa 1:23), and denying justice to the righteous (Isa 5:23; cf. Isa 33:15; Mic 3:11; 7:3). The prophets condemn economic deception by dishonest standards (Ezek 45:9–10; Hos 12:8 [7]; Amos 8:5; Mic 6:11) and by moving boundary markers (Hos 5:10). Deception is directly associated with greed for unjust gain (Jer 6:13; 8:10), destroying the poor even when their plea is "just" (משפט, Isa 32:7), and intending to set a trap for one's neighbor (Jer 9:3–8 [4–9]). Jeremiah describes wicked men as "bird hunters" who set traps to capture men (Jer 5:26). He continues this avian imagery in describing their houses: "Like a cage full of birds, their houses are full of deceit (מרמה), therefore they have become great and rich" (Jer 5:27). Here Jeremiah refers to deceptive activity that disadvantages those deceitfully captured and wrongly advantages the deceiver, who benefits monetarily from his deception. In addition, like the sages and psalmists, the prophets parallel deception with violence,[112] associate it with "iniquity" (עון, Isa 5:18; 59:4), "evil" (רעה, Hos 7:3), and "injustice" (עולה, Hos 10:13; Zeph 3:13), and contrast it with "justice" and "righteousness" (משפט and צדקה, Isa 28:15–17; 59:12–15).

The prophets also use the language of deception to describe the activity of false prophets.[113] Sometimes false prophets seem to have been cognizant of the falsehoods they perpetrated. For example, concerning certain false prophets Zechariah says, "On that day each of the prophets will be ashamed of his vision when he prophesies; they will not wear a garment of hair *in order to deceive* (למען כחש)" (Zech 13:4). This element of intentionality qualifies such prophecies as deceptive. However, Ezekiel describes other false prophets as expecting their prophecies to come true: "They say, 'oracle of YHWH,' when YHWH has not sent them, yet they hope for their word to be fulfilled" (Ezek 13:6). This suggests that although these prophets were mistaken in their prophecies and thus culpable (see 13:8), they were sincere.[114] In this latter instance the false prophets' actions are not deceitful. Therefore,

---

seek "faithfulness" (אמונה), who cannot seem to be found in the city (5:1).

112. Isa 53:9; 59:3; Hos 12:2 [1]; Mic 6:12; Nah 3:1; Zeph 1:9.

113. Isa 9:14 [15]; Jer 5:12, 31; 14:14; 20:6; 23:14, 25–26, 32; 27:10, 14–16; 28:15; 29:8–9, 21, 23, 31; Lam 2:14; Ezek 13:6–9, 19–23; 21:34 [29]; 22:28; Mic 2:11; Zech 13:3–4; 10:2.

114. So also Greenberg, *Ezekiel 1–20*, 236; Zimmerli, *Ezekiel 1*, 293.

concerning false prophecy we must conclude that it was condemned not because it was deceptive, but because it misrepresented YHWH's word to the people—whether intentionally or not. This was Jeremiah's concern in his temple sermon in Jer 7:4-10:

> Do not trust in these false words (דברי השקר), saying, "The temple of YHWH, the temple of YHWH, the temple of YHWH." If you truly turn from your ways and your deeds; if you truly do justice (משפט) with one another—if you do not oppress the sojourner, fatherless, or widow, shed innocent blood in this place, or walk after other gods to your own harm—then I will cause you to dwell in this place forever and ever. Behold, you are trusting in false words (דברי השקר) that are of no profit. Will you steal, murder, commit adultery, swear falsely (והשבע לשקר), and burn incense to Baal, and walk after other gods that you do not know, and then come and stand before me in this house that is called by my name and say, "We are safe to do all these abominations?"

The "false words" YHWH condemns here are those that cause people to misplace trust in the temple and give them the illusion that they may disobey YHWH's word and act contrary to "justice" (משפט). Several believe that the litany of violations in v. 9 alludes to the Decalogue, where it seems that "swear falsely" refers to the ninth command.[115] A related sentiment is expressed in Hos 4:1-2, where instead of "faithfulness" (אמת) and "loyalty" (חסד) being found in the land, "cursing and lying (כחש) and murder and stealing and adultery" prevail and are associated with "bloodshed." Thus like the sages and psalmists, the prophets never simply condemn deception outright, but always do so in view of the injustice it brings to others.

Conclusion

From this analysis we have seen that in the prescriptive material of the Pentateuch, whenever deception is prohibited, it is the kind of deception that brings unjust harm or disadvantage to another person. This same emphasis is evident in the Wisdom literature, the Psalms, and the Prophets,

---

115. Bright, *Jeremiah*, 56; Craigie et al., *Jeremiah 1-25*, 121. Holladay suggests that the reference here and in Hos 4:2 is to the third command (*Jeremiah I*, 245). While this interpretation is possible, because there is no verbal link between these three texts (both versions of the third command use נשא with שוא, while Jeremiah uses והשבע לשקר and Hosea uses כחש), and since both lists in the prophets associate the phrase with murder, stealing, and adultery, which all come from the second half of the Decalogue, it is preferable to understand the false swearing here as a rendition of false testimony.

demonstrated conceptually by the types of deceptions denounced as well as by the frequent contrasting of such activity with terms like צדק and משפט.[116] We may conclude, therefore, that the OT never categorically condemns deception, which agrees with Klopfenstein's conclusion that the OT never categorically condemns lying.[117] Rather, the OT only condemns deception that causes injustice, where "justice" may be defined as "doing what is right in a social relationship as defined by God's standard of what is right behavior."[118] Since acts such as perjury, murder, and stealing are unjust, deception that facilitates these acts is therefore prohibited.

This concern for just or righteous living is evident throughout the OT, and its prominence in Israel's ethic is reflected most clearly in Deut 16:20: "Follow justice and justice alone, so that you may live and possess the land the LORD your God is giving you" (NIV).[119] Since this interpersonal ethic undergirds the OT's proscriptions of deception, Patrick Miller is correct to say that "the critical issue of truth and lies" in the OT is "how the well-being of others is affected by what one says about them."[120] Such a conclusion applies equally well to the theology of deception evident in the OT's explicit statements. With this theological background in place, we are now in a position to turn our attention to the books of Samuel and see how acts of deception are portrayed within that narrative.

---

116. That the LXX usually translates שקר with the ἀδικ* word-group further reinforces this (see Carpenter and Grisanti, "שׁקר," 248). See, e.g., Gen 21:23; Exod 23:7; Lev 5:22 [6:3], 24 [6:5]; 19:12; Deut 19:18; 2 Kgs 9:12; Isa 32:7; 59:13; Jer 5:31; 7:9; 27:15-16 [LXX 34:15-16]; 28:15 [LXX 35:15]; 29:9 [LXX 36:9]; Ezek 13:22; Pss 35:19 [LXX 34:19]; 38:20 [19; LXX 37:20]; Prov 6:17, 19; 11:18; 12:17, 19; 13:5 et al.

117. Klopfenstein, *Die Lüge*, 322. So also Ludwig Koehler, who notes that the Bible contains "no clear and simple statement" that explicitly prohibits lying (*Old Testament Theology*, 251, n. 155).

118. Waltke, "Righteousness in Proverbs," 235. See also the discussions of צדק in von Rad, *Old Testament Theology*, 1:370-83; Wright, *Old Testament Ethics*, 255-56; Goldingay, *Old Testament Theology: Israel's Faith*, 162.

119. In this context, "justice" (צדק) is not confined to the judicial sphere but pertains to all of life. For this reason, some suggest that "righteousness" better reflects this concept (see Vogt, *Deuteronomic Theology*, 212-14; Block, *Deuteronomy*, 399).

120. Miller, *Ten Commandments*, 344.

3

Deception Intended to Prevent Death or Harm in the Books of Samuel

SINCE THE EXPLICIT STATEMENTS concerning deception in the OT only prohibit deception that brings unjust harm or disadvantage to another person, we will examine the deceptions in the books of Samuel based on the *motives* for which they were committed. In the present chapter we will explore deception intended to prevent death or harm. This category includes both deceptions committed to protect oneself (the Jabeshites' deception of Nahash in 1 Sam 11:1-11 ["Deception A"]; Samuel's deception of the Bethlehemite elders in 1 Sam 16:1-5 ["Deception B"]; Michal's deception of Saul after David's escape in 1 Sam 19:17b ["Deception D"]; and David's first two deceptions of Achish in 1 Sam 21:11-16 [10-15] and 27:7-12 ["Deceptions F and G"]) and deceptions committed to protect someone else (Michal's deception of Saul's messengers in 1 Sam 19:11-17a ["Deception C"]; Jonathan's deception of Saul in 1 Sam 20:27-34 ["Deception E"]; and the woman of Bahurim's deception of Absalom's servants in 2 Sam 17:15-21a ["Deception H"]). At the end I will summarize the analyses of the characteristics of these deceptions.

Deception A: The Jabeshites' Deception of Nahash (1 Samuel 11:1–11)

In 1 Samuel 11, Nahash the Ammonite besieged the Transjordanian city of Jabesh Gilead. The Jabeshites offered to make a covenant with him, but Nahash agreed only on the condition that he be able to gouge out their right eyes and so "bring disgrace upon all Israel" (v. 2). The Jabeshites requested seven days to send messengers throughout Israel to seek out someone to deliver them and said that if one could not be found they would "go out" (יצא) to him, presumably to surrender. The messengers entered Gibeah, where Saul heard the message and rallied all Israel to deliver the Jabeshites. A huge army assembled and sent word to the Jabeshites that they would deliver them by the next day. The Jabeshites then sent word to Nahash saying that they would "go out" (יצא) to him the next day. During the morning watch, Saul's army entered the unsuspecting Ammonite camp and slaughtered them.

Establishing the Deception

Most agree that the Jabeshites deceived Nahash in v. 10 through the ambiguous use of the verb יצא.[1] In v. 3 they told Nahash, "If there is no one to deliver us, *then we will go out to you* (ויצאנו אליך)." The context of having "no one to deliver" suggests that יצא was meant to be understood as "going out to surrender."[2] After securing the help of Saul, in v. 10 the Jabeshites told Nahash, "Tomorrow *we will go out to you* (נצא אליכם), and you can do to us whatever is good in your eyes." Based on their statement in v. 3, this statement implied that they had not found a deliverer and therefore were "going out to surrender." However, in reality they had found a deliverer in Saul, and rather than surrendering they planned to "go out in battle." Therefore the Jabeshites deceived Nahash into believing falsely that they would surrender the next day, which left him unsuspecting of the early morning attack by Saul and his army.

However, one aspect of the text may call this interpretation into question. André Caquot and Philippe de Robert observe that the addressee in v. 10 is unstated and therefore ambiguous: the Jabeshites either could have been responding to the messengers sent from Saul's army or speaking to Nahash.[3] According to the first view, vv. 9b–10 would read: "And the messengers entered and told the men of Jabesh. And they [the Jabeshites] rejoiced and said [to the messengers]: 'Tomorrow we will go out to you, and you can do for us whatever is good in your eyes.'" According to Caquot and de Robert, on this reading the Jabeshites responded that they would go out to Saul's army and rely on them for the military strategy against the

---

1. Hertzberg, *I & II Samuel*, 93; Ackroyd, *First Book of Samuel*, 92; Eslinger, *Kingship of God in Crisis*, 370–71; Long, *Reign and Rejection*, 220; Wénin, *Samuel et l'instauration*, 355, n. 39; Baldwin, *1 & 2 Samuel*, 98; Edelman, *King Saul*, 63–64; Fokkelman, *Vow and Desire*, 474; Alter, *David Story*, 63; Tsumura, *First Book of Samuel*, 310; Firth, *1 & 2 Samuel*, 139; Vette, "Der letzte Richter?" 191–92.

2. Thus Josephus understood it (*Ant.* 6.5.1).

3. Caquot and de Robert, *Les Livres de Samuel*, 141.

Ammonites.[4] Supporting this reading are the second person plural pronominal suffixes (אליכם, בעיניכם) and the second person plural verb (ועשיתם) in the Jabeshites' statement, which would make sense if directed toward "the messengers" (המלאכים). If this reading were correct, there would be no deception in v. 10.

However, several factors suggest the Jabeshites' statement in v. 10 was directed to Nahash and the Ammonites. First, a response to Nahash moves the plot forward. A chart outlining the narrative structure illustrates this:

A: Problem: Nahash oppresses Jabesh (vv. 1–2)

   B: Jabesh sends word to Nahash requesting one week, and if no deliverer is found, they will "go out" (יצא) (v. 3)

      C: Jabesh sends word to Gibeah (v. 4)

         X: Saul assembles the army to deliver (vv. 5–8)

      C': Gibeah sends word to Jabesh (v. 9)

   B': Jabesh sends word to Nahash saying they will "go out" (יצא) (v. 10)

A': Solution: Saul and the army defeat Nahash (v. 11)

Only if the Jabeshites communicated with Nahash in B' does the narrative demonstrate a consistent plot development from problem to solution. A communication to the messengers in v. 10 does not contribute to the plot and thus is less preferable.[5] Second, a response to Nahash in v. 10 maintains balance in the narrative structure: a Jabesh-Nahash communication in B' balances the Jabesh-Nahash communication in B. Third, v. 3 also seems to record a deceptive communication between Jabesh and Nahash, which, based on the narrative structure, makes a deceptive communication to Nahash in v. 10 even more likely.

In v. 3 the Jabeshites said to Nahash: "Leave us alone for seven days so we can send messengers throughout Israel, and if there is no one to deliver us, we will go out to you." Two factors suggest that this initial request was deceptive. First, the Jabeshites' statement implied uncertainty concerning the existence of a deliverer, but the preceding chapter emphasized that "all the tribes of Israel" (כל־שבטי ישראל) were present at the public declaration of Saul as king (1 Sam 10:20). After Samuel had presented Saul, "*All the people* (כל־העם) shouted and said, 'Long the live the king'" (v. 24). Since all the tribes were represented at this occasion, it is probable that the elders of Jabesh Gilead knew about Saul's recent appointment. Since the people

---

4. Ibid.
5. Concerning plot structure, see Bar-Efrat, "Some Observations," 154–73.

had wanted a king so he could "lead us and *go out* (יצא) before us and fight our battles" (1 Sam 8:20), they almost certainly viewed Saul as this delivering king. The Jabeshites' implication of ignorance of this delivering king was therefore deceptive.[6]

Second, the Jabeshites further deceived by saying that they planned to send messengers "through all the territory of Israel" (בכל גבול ישראל). Verse 4 does not record a general dispersal of messengers throughout Israel, but only says, "Then the messengers went to Gibeah of Saul" (ויבאו המלאכים גבעת שאול). Although a temporal rendering of this phrase is grammatically possible ("*When* the messengers came to Gibeah of Saul" [e.g., NIV, NRSV]), which could imply that Gibeah was only one place among many to which the messengers traveled, as V. Philips Long points out, "apart from the dubious assumption that the elders of Jabesh have spoken candidly to Nahash, there is no reason to prefer the temporal rendering here."[7] Since the Hebrew *wayyiqtol* form most often describes temporal or logical succession,[8] the phrase could also be translated, "So/then the messengers went to Gibeah of Saul," suggesting that Gibeah was their intended destination. That this was the case is likely for two reasons. First, the description of the messengers going to Gibeah is articular (המלאכים), which suggests that the entire group of messengers mentioned in v. 3 went to Gibeah.[9] If the messengers were truly going "through all the territory of Israel" in seven days they probably would have split up. That the whole group went to Gibeah implies that they were not going throughout Israel as they claimed, but lied to Nahash to maintain the pretense of their uncertainty regarding the existence of a deliverer. Second, the toponym used by the narrator, "Gibeah *of Saul*," suggests that the messengers were seeking out Saul,[10] which also implies that Gibeah was their destination. This conclusion is reinforced by the LXX: "and the messengers went to Gibeah, *to Saul*" (καὶ ἔρχονται οἱ ἄγγελοι εἰς Γαβαα πρὸς Σαουλ).

Therefore it appears that in v. 3 the Jabeshites deceived Nahash into believing that they did not know if there was anyone to deliver them, when in reality they were aware of a new king who would go out and fight their battles. This deception set up Nahash for their second deception in which they utilized the ambiguity of the verb יצא to make him believe falsely that

---

6. So also Edelman, *King Saul*, 62; Fokkelman, *Vow and Desire*, 465.

7. Long, *Reign and Rejection*, 221.

8. *IBHS*, 547.

9. Wénin, *Samuel et l'instauration*, 355–56, n. 39; Edelman, *King Saul*, 62–63, n. 2; Long, *Reign and Rejection*, 222; Fokkelman, *Vow and Desire*, 465.

10. Hertzberg, *I & II Samuel*, 92; Fokkelman, *Vow and Desire*, 466.

they would go out to surrender the next day, when in reality they knew the Israelite army was going out to destroy the Ammonites. Nahash's willingness to allow the Jabeshite messengers to search for a deliverer and his apparent unpreparedness for the Israelite attack in v. 11 shows that their deception was successful.

Analyzing the Deception

The Jabeshites used two tactics to deceive Nahash: a lie (v. 3) and ambiguous language (v. 10). The episode begins by stating that Nahash "went up and camped against Jabesh Gilead" (v. 1), which establishes the overall motive of these deceptions as military self-defense. The first deception (v. 3) delayed Nahash from inflicting harm upon them until they could contact Saul for deliverance, and the second (v. 10) made Nahash unsuspecting of the upcoming Israelite attack. In both cases the Jabeshites achieved the goals for which they deceived. In the first case, they acquired the necessary time to notify Saul of their predicament, and in the second the Israelite army destroyed the Ammonites in battle. The Jabeshites experienced no negative consequences and the author offers no explicit evaluation of their deceptions, though he seems to characterize them negatively. The narrative begins with the Jabeshites' offer to become Nahash's vassal: "Make a covenant with us, and we will serve you" (v. 1b).[11] This initial offer of vassalage to a foreign king portrays the Jabeshites as disloyal to Israel and YHWH[12] and reflects the similar tribal disloyalty they demonstrated when they failed to assemble before YHWH at Mizpah in Judges 20–21, an event to which the present story alludes in multiple ways.[13] Only when Nahash expressed his

---

11. The substantial plus of 4QSam^a does not affect the inappropriateness of the Jabeshites' offer of vassalage in v. 1, although in its absence the immediacy of their offer is emphasized in the exposition, which characterizes them more explicitly as easily willing to betray Israelite loyalty. Interpreters are divided as to the plus's originality. McCarter argues for its originality based on the novelty of its content and its lack of apologetic motive (*1 Samuel*, 199). However, for convincing arguments that the plus is secondary, see Tsumura, *First Book of Samuel*, 302–3; Fokkelman, *Vow and Desire*, 459–61; Auld, *I & II Samuel*, 118.

12. Eslinger, *Kingship of God in Crisis*, 360–61.

13. In both Judges 19–21 and 1 Samuel 11 the cities of Gibeah and Jabesh Gilead play a significant role, and both narratives involve the dissevering of a person/animal in order to rally all Israel (Judg 19:29; 1 Sam 11:7). Furthermore, Saul's actions resemble those of the judges who delivered Israel from foreign oppression: the divine Spirit comes upon him (1 Sam 11:6; cf. Othniel [Judg 3:10], Gideon [Judg 6:34], Jephthah [Judg 11:29], and Samson [Judg 14:6, 19; 15:14]) and he divides his army into three companies (1 Sam 11:11; cf. Gideon [Judg 7:16–20] and Abimelech [Judg 9:43]). See

harsh terms for the covenant did the Jabeshites call upon Israel's king to save them. Nevertheless, Fokkelman argues that 1 Samuel 11 presents a redemptive contrast to the negative depictions of Gibeah and Jabesh Gilead in Judges 19-21; whereas Judges depicts these cities as an "unfavourable pair," each of which suffered great loss of life, 1 Samuel 11 describes the reversal of that prior tribal disharmony under the unified leadership of Saul.[14] However, Firth notes that these same links may be portraying Saul as a judge in order to question his role as king.[15] This latter position is supported by the negative depiction of Saul's kingship throughout 1 Samuel 9-15.[16] Although this narrative is ambiguous in many respects, the characterization of the Jabeshites seems negative.

Deception B: Samuel's Deception of the Bethlehemite Elders (1 Samuel 16:1–5)

After YHWH rejected Saul as king, he commanded Samuel to fill his horn with oil and go to Jesse of Bethlehem, saying, "I have chosen a king for myself from among his sons" (1 Sam 16:1). Samuel protested that if he went on such a mission "Saul will hear about it and kill me" (v. 2a), so YHWH replied, "Take a heifer with you and say, 'In order to sacrifice to YHWH I have come'" (v. 2b). It appears that YHWH instructed Samuel to deceive any inquirers, and thus Saul indirectly, by causing them to believe falsely that rather than going to Bethlehem to anoint a rival king, he was going to offer a sacrifice.

Establishing the Deception

While many see divinely ordained deception here,[17] others see no such element in YHWH's command.[18] For example, John Murray argues that rather than advocating any form of "untruth," YHWH only authorized Samuel to

---

McCarter, *I Samuel*, 204–5; Alter, *David Story*, 61; Vette, "Der letzte Richter?" 194).

14. Fokkelman, *Vow and Desire*, 477.
15. Firth, *1 & 2 Samuel*, 137.
16. Long, *Reign and Rejection*, 233.
17. Gunn, *Fate of King Saul*, 77; Polzin, *Samuel and the Deuteronomist*, 159; Brueggemann, *First and Second Samuel*, 121; Bergen, *1, 2 Samuel*, 178; Alter, *David Story*, 95; Cartledge, *1 & 2 Samuel*, 200; Leithart, *A Son to Me*, 104; Bodner, *1 Samuel*, 168; Van Seters, *Biblical Saga*, 133; Auld, *I & II Samuel*, 184.
18. Hertzberg, *Samuel*, 137, n. a; Youngblood, "1, 2 Samuel," 683; Firth, *1 & 2 Samuel*, 182.

engage in "concealment" or "evasion."[19] Similarly, Walter Kaiser sees this as a case of "concealment" and claims, "Samuel had no special prerogative to speak a falsehood."[20] Both scholars argue that although part of the truth was concealed, what Samuel actually spoke was true.[21] That is, Samuel said he was going to sacrifice, and since this sacrifice allegedly happened, his statement was true. However, Samuel did not simply conceal the true purpose of his visit by making another true statement. Regardless of whether or not a sacrifice subsequently took place, the deception concerned the communicated *purpose* of Samuel's visit.

In v. 1 YHWH told Samuel, "I am sending you to Jesse of Bethlehem, *for* (כי) I have chosen a king for myself from among his sons." According to this verse, the purpose of Samuel's trip was to anoint this new king. Only after Samuel protested did YHWH instruct him to say, "*In order to sacrifice* (לזבח) to YHWH I have come" (v. 2). Therefore Samuel's public communication was intended to convey that sacrifice, rather than anointing, was the *purpose* of his visit.[22] This communicated purpose would have averted any suspicions or danger that could have come from Saul. Since the purpose of Samuel's visit was not to offer sacrifice but to anoint a rival king, it follows that YHWH instructed the prophet to deceive by means of a lie. Furthermore, even if we were to concede the description of Samuel's action as not lying but only "concealing" part of the truth, his statement would still be deceitful. As Richard Patterson rightly notes, "were Saul to be told such a half-truth, he would assume that it was the whole truth."[23] Since the belief that such a half-truth is the whole truth is a false belief, under such circumstances Samuel would still be deceiving Saul in obedience to a divine command. Whether or not Samuel actually carried out the sacrifice is irrelevant;[24] the deception occurred when he caused others to believe falsely

---

19. Murray, *Principles of Conduct*, 139.

20. Kaiser, *Toward Old Testament Ethics*, 225–26.

21. Murray, *Principles of Conduct*, 140; Kaiser, *Toward Old Testament Ethics*, 226. See also Shemesh, "Lies By Prophets," 90.

22. So also observes Gunn, *Fate of King Saul*, 77; Bar-Efrat, *Das Erste Buch Samuel*, 227; Prouser, "Phenomenology of the Lie," 171; Cartledge, *1 & 2 Samuel*, 200; Van Seters, *Biblical Saga*, 133; *contra* Kaiser, who asserts: "As for Samuel's ultimate intentions, nothing is affirmed or denied" (*Toward Old Testament Ethics*, 226).

23. Patterson, "Old Testament Use of an Archetype," 394.

24. Murray seems to think that Samuel actually offered a sacrifice in Bethlehem, and that this vindicates his words as true (*Principles of Conduct*, 140). However, although the text says that Samuel invited Jesse and his sons to the sacrifice (v. 5), it never reports that it actually occurred.

concerning the *purpose* of his trip.²⁵ That Samuel received no opposition from Saul, which suggests that no one warned Saul of the purpose of his trip, shows that he deceived the Bethlehemites.

Analyzing the Deception

The tactic Samuel used to deceive the Bethlehemites was a lie. His motive was to avoid being killed by Saul (v. 2a). A significant feature of this deception is the irony of Samuel's lie in the aftermath of Saul's rejection. Robert Gordon observes that Samuel's lie ("*In order to sacrifice to YHWH* [לזבח ליהוה] I have come") ironically employs language from Saul's excuses to Samuel during his rejection in chapter 15.²⁶ When Samuel had confronted Saul about disobediently sparing sheep and cattle during the Amalekite raid, Saul twice claimed that the army spared the animals "*in order to sacrifice to YHWH*" (למען זבח ליהוה [15:15]; לזבח ליהוה [15:21]). In the present passage, Samuel used this same language to deceive the Bethlehemites in order to anoint Saul's royal replacement. Samuel achieved the goal for which he deceived by anointing David unharmed. Since YHWH commanded Samuel to deceive (v. 2b), the author's evaluation of this deception is positive.

Deceptions C and D: Michal's Deceptions of Saul's Messengers and Saul (1 Samuel 19:11–17)

First Samuel 19 describes David's escape from Saul's court. After eluding Saul's attempt to pin him to the wall with his spear, David went to his house. Saul sent messengers to David's house "to guard it and kill him in the morning" (v. 11a). Aware of this plan, Michal warned David and lowered him from the window, enabling him to escape (vv. 11b–12).²⁷ Apparently to al-

---

25. Thus Barbara Green's interpretation of God's command here misses the point. She argues that rather than advocating subterfuge, "the words make equal sense as the straightforward directions: Just 'go prepared to sacrifice' is my sense of it, rather than 'go pretending it is a sacrifice'" (*How Are the Mighty Fallen*, 281, n. 25). However, the issue is not whether or not Samuel was actually going to sacrifice or simply to pretend to sacrifice; the issue is the true purpose of the trip vs. the communicated purpose. Even the command "go prepared to sacrifice" does not make sacrifice the true purpose, and therefore her comment does not mitigate the presence of deception here.

26. Gordon, "Simplicity of the Highest Cunning," 30–31.

27. Thus the narrative emphasizes that Michal initiated this escape, with David depicted as following her lead, which will become important in considering Michal's response to Saul in v. 17 (see below). See Mommer, "David und Merab," 198; Exum, *Fragmented Women*, 49; Klein, "Michal, the Barren Wife," 39; Firth, *1 & 2 Samuel*, 217.

low more time for David to escape, Michal took a *teraphim*,²⁸ placed it in the bed, covered it with a garment, and put some goat's hair at the head. In so doing she created the false appearance that David was in the bed. When Saul's second set of messengers came to take David, Michal lied and said, "He is sick" (v. 14b). Saul then sent a third set of messengers to bring David to him so that he might kill him, but upon entering the room the messengers discovered the *teraphim* in the bed instead of David. Saul then asked Michal, "Why did you *deceive me* (רמיתני) like this and send my enemy away so that he escaped?" (v. 17a). Michal responded with what appears to be another lie: "He said to me, 'Send me away. Why should I kill you?'" (v. 17b).

Establishing the Deceptions

Two distinct deceptions occurred in this passage. Michal deceived (1) Saul's second set of messengers in vv. 13–16, and (2) Saul himself in v. 17.

Michal's Deception of Saul's Messengers (Deception C)

Michal deceived Saul's second set of messengers into believing falsely that David was sick in bed by two means: (1) the *teraphim* with the garment and goat's hair, and (2) a corresponding lie that David was sick. Many have suggested that this *teraphim* setup was intended to simulate a magical healing ritual whereby a figurine was placed in a bed as a substitute for a sick person.²⁹ According to Rouillard and Tropper, the normal ritual would involve the patient lying in the bed next to the figurine.³⁰ If this was what Michal intended to simulate, the second set of messengers may have seen the *teraphim* but believed that David was in the bed next to it, rather than mistaking the *teraphim* for David.³¹ However, this interpretation does not explain why Michal placed goat's hair at the head of the figurine, which suggests that she intended the *teraphim* to be mistaken for a person. Furthermore, this view

---

28. Scholars disagree on the appropriate referent of this word. It may refer to an "idol" (e.g., NIV, NRSV) or an "ancestor figurine" (see van der Toorn, "Nature of the Biblical Teraphim," 222). For a discussion of the various views see Lewis, "Teraphim," 844–50. Since the specific referent is not crucial to the deceptive function of this object, following common practice I will transliterate *teraphim* in the following discussion.

29. Willi-Plein, "Michal und die Anfänge des Königtums in Israel," 409–10; Willi-Plein, "1 Sam 18–19 und die Davidshausgeschichte," 152; Rouillard and Tropper, "*Trpym*," 346–51; Ackroyd, *First Book of Samuel*, 158; Bergen, *1, 2 Samuel*, 208.

30. Rouillard and Tropper, "*Trpym*," 347.

31. Thus claims Edelman, *King Saul*, 150; Ackroyd, *First Book of Samuel*, 158.

does not sufficiently account for the depiction of point of view regarding the third set of messengers and the *teraphim*.

Verse 16 describes the arrival of Saul's third set of messengers: "The messengers entered, *and behold* (והנה), *teraphim* in the bed." The particle הנה often indicates a shift from the narrator's point of view to a character's point of view.[32] As Adele Berlin notes, since the narrator has already informed the reader that the *teraphim* was in the bed in v. 13, this הנה of v. 16 indicates the point in the narrative when Saul's messengers saw the *teraphim* in the bed.[33] If the third set of messengers did not see the *teraphim* until they entered the room in v. 16, it is unlikely that the second set of messengers saw the *teraphim* in v. 14, for at least two reasons. First, since the depiction of point of view reflected in v. 16 precludes the messengers having prior knowledge of the *teraphim*, if the second and third sets of messengers consisted of the same individuals, they could not have seen the *teraphim* in v. 14. Second, even if these were distinct sets of messengers, only the third set entered the house, and only then did they see the *teraphim*. This makes it improbable that the second set of messengers saw the *teraphim* from a distance without entering. Therefore, it seems that the second set of messengers did not see the *teraphim*, which argues against the view that they recognized the *teraphim* and assumed that David was behind it, and instead suggests that they believed it to be David himself.

This analysis of point of view and attention to the narrative spatial descriptions addresses the objection that the *teraphim* was too small to serve as a realistic substitute for David. As many observe, this narrative recalls Rachel's deception of Laban after she stole his *teraphim* (Gen 31:19, 34–35).[34] Since Rachel is described as "sitting on them" during Laban's search (v. 34), Rouillard and Tropper posit that the *teraphim* in 1 Samuel 19 was probably small.[35] This then presents a problem: how could such a small figurine be mistaken for a human being? Yet this question assumes that *teraphim* were always uniform in size, an assumption rejected by some historians[36] and biblical scholars.[37] Rouillard and Tropper further argue that the *teraphim*

---

32. Bar-Efrat, *Narrative Art in the Bible*, 35.

33. Berlin, *Poetics and Interpretation*, 62.

34. Alter, *Art of Biblical Narrative*, 150; Frontain, "The Trickster Tricked," 176; Schäfer-Lichtenberger, "Michal—eine literarische Figur mit Vergangenheit," 97; Klein, *1 Samuel*, 197; Evans, *1 and 2 Samuel*, 90; Bergen, *1, 2 Samuel*, 208; Bodner, *1 Samuel*, 206.

35. Rouillard and Tropper, "*Trpym*," 340.

36. Hoffner, "Linguistic Origins of Teraphim," 232–33; King and Stager, *Life in Biblical Israel*, 10.

37. McCarter, *1 Samuel*, 326; Robinson, *Let Us Be Like the Nations*, 107; Tsumura,

DECEPTION INTENDED TO PREVENT DEATH OR HARM 63

was small and thus did not reasonably resemble David because the third set of messengers allegedly recognized it so quickly, citing v. 16 as support.[38]

Rouillard and Tropper do not explain why v. 16 implies that the messengers immediately recognized the *teraphim* as a ruse, but the הנה is the most likely element that could be used to support such a conclusion. However, if this were the case, this rationale would be inadequate. Berlin has shown that הנה indicates "suddenness in the *presentation of perception*, not suddenness in the occurrence of events."[39] Therefore, without further data, this verse does not imply that the *teraphim* was immediately recognized and thus could not have deceptively substituted for David. Verse 16 simply depicts the moment of the messengers' perception; it does not communicate a suddenness of recognition within the narrative.[40] Furthermore, this verse describes the third set of messengers and has no bearing upon the effective deception that occurred previously against the second set in v. 14. Therefore, it is sufficient to say that without entering the room to examine the details, the second set of messengers believed Michal's lie that David was sick in bed. Michal supported this lie by the *teraphim* in the bed, which they assumed to be David.[41]

Although this is the most probable scenario, even if the second set of messengers believed the *teraphim* to be next to David, they still believed falsely that David was in the bed. This is shown by Saul's command for the third set of messengers to "bring him up to me *in the bed* that I might kill him" (v. 15). The story is elliptical, but the second set of messengers who observed the contrived scene and heard Michal's corresponding lie in v. 14 must have communicated to Saul that David was in bed. Obviously Michal lied in v. 14, since her statement was intended to corroborate the fabricated sick scene, and she knew that David was not sick in bed.[42]

First Book of Samuel, 494; Campbell, *1 Samuel*, 204; Lewis, "Teraphim," 846.

38. They write, "the messengers have *hardly caught sight* of the object when they recognize the deception" ("à peine les émissaires avaient-ils entrevu le tableau qu'ils reconnurent la supercherie") (Rouillard and Tropper, "*Trpym*," 341, emphasis mine).

39. Berlin, *Poetics and Interpretation*, 93 (emphasis hers).

40. So also van der Toorn, "Nature of the Biblical Teraphim," 207.

41. Willi-Plein helpfully notes that it was sufficient for these messengers simply to have a general sense of a "sick room" from their perspective outside the room ("Michal und die Anfänge des Königtums in Israel," 410).

42. Furthermore, this corroborative sick scene means that her statement would be deceptive even if one were to conjecture that David, though on the run, actually was sick. In this case Michal's statement would not technically be false, but it still would be deceptive, since in context her statement implies, "He is sick *in bed*."

Michal's Deception of Saul (Deception D)

After the discovery of the *teraphim*, Saul asked Michal: "Why did you *deceive me* (רמיתני) like this and send my enemy away so that he escaped?" (v. 17a). The verb רמה suggests that Saul expected Michal to be loyal to him rather than David.[43] However, the author characterizes Michal as loyal to David in at least five ways: (1) the narrator twice reports that Michal "loved" David (1 Sam 18:20, 28); (2) the narrator refers to her as "his [David's] wife" (v. 11);[44] (3) Michal took the initiative and warned David of the upcoming danger (v. 11); (4) Michal deceived Saul's messengers in vv. 13–16 in David's absence; and (5) the allusion to the Rachel episode, which also depicts a married daughter siding with her husband against her father with a deception involving *teraphim*.[45] Therefore most interpret Michal's response to Saul's inquiry in v. 17b as a lie intended to exonerate her from his charge and protect her from the consequences of her betrayal.[46] Saul's later attempt to kill Jonathan for siding with David (20:33) supports the idea that Michal needed to protect her own life.

Despite these data, David J. A. Clines questions whether or not Michal lied to Saul here:

> We know that Michal's answer to the messengers, "He is sick" (19.14), is a lie, because we have just learned from the narrator that David is not in bed but out the window. We *assume* that Michal's answer to Saul, "He said to me, 'Let me go; why should I kill you?'" (19.17), is also a lie; but we do not *know* that; for there has been no report of David's speech against which we could check it. Perhaps she is lying to protect herself; or perhaps David had said such words.[47]

---

43. See the discussion of רמה in chapter 2.

44. For the contextual significance of this epithet, see Fokkelman, *Crossing Fates*, 263; Bowman, "Fortune of King David," 107. Contrast this characterization of Michal with that in 2 Sam 6:16, where in her critical opposition to David's celebration of the ark's entry to Jerusalem, she is identified as "daughter of Saul."

45. See the helpful discussion of Alter, *Art of Biblical Narrative*, 150.

46. Mauchline, *1 and 2 Samuel*, 143; Sternberg, *Poetics of Biblical Narrative*, 244; Berlin, *Poetics and Interpretation*, 25; Fokkelman, *Crossing Fates*, 268–69; Alter, *David Story*, 121; Klein, "Michal, the Barren Wife," 39; Bowman, "Fortune of King David," 107; Klein, *1 Samuel*, 198; McCarter, *1 Samuel*, 326; Willi-Plein, "Michal und die Anfänge des Königtums in Israel," 410.

47. Clines, "Michal Observed," 39 (emphasis his); see also Green, "Engaging Nuances of Genre," 155–56.

Admittedly, there is no reported speech of David against which to check this claim, but this is an argument from silence. Conversely, the characterization of Michal as loyal to David—especially the narratorial description of her initiating his escape (vv. 11–12)—supports the view that she voluntarily assisted him and thus lied to Saul in v. 17. In the absence of evidence to the contrary, this is the most natural reading of the narrative.

Furthermore, depending on how one understands Saul's question, Michal's answer is inconsistent with the order of events as depicted. Saul asked why she had "deceived" (רמה) him and "sent" David away. The word רמה could mean (1) "to betray," and refer to Michal sending David ("Why did you betray me like this *by sending* my enemy away?") or (2) "to deceive," and refer to the deception of the *teraphim* and corresponding lie in vv. 13–14, distinct from the previous act of sending ("Why did you deceive me like this *and send* my enemy away?"). According to the first interpretation, Michal deceived the second set of messengers and lied to Saul in v. 17 about her reason for *betraying* him (i.e., sending David away in vv. 11–12). On this reading her answer to Saul makes sense: she had to betray him and send David away because David threatened her life.

However, every other time the question "Why did you deceive (רמה) me/us?" occurs, it is posed by victims following deceptions that involve clothing.[48] This suggests that רמה refers not to the betrayal of vv. 11–12 but to the deception of vv. 13–14 (i.e., the disguised *teraphim* and lie). On this reading Michal's answer does not cohere with the order of events. By the time she deceived the messengers in vv. 13–14, David had already escaped (v. 12b), so it is difficult to see how she still would have feared a death threat that would have compelled her to deceive on David's behalf. Thus her answer to Saul, "He said to me, 'Send me away. Why should I kill you?'" does not adequately explain why she deceived the messengers after David was gone.[49] These discrepancies reinforce the view that Michal's imputed discourse for David was contrived and not the true reason why she helped him.

Diana Edelman argues that Michal's language in v. 11 emphasizes that David "must formulate his own plan for escape."[50] For Edelman this raises suspicions that David may have actually threatened Michal as she alleged in v. 17. According to Edelman's reconstruction, Michal initially warned David about the threat and implied that he must arrange his own escape, so David responded by threatening to kill Michal if she did not help him. For Edelman, this reconstruction suggests that Michal's excuse to Saul that

---

48. As noted in chapter 2 (Gen 29:25; Josh 9:22; 1 Sam 28:12).
49. So also notes Bar-Efrat, *Das Erste Buch Samuel*, 265.
50. Edelman, *King Saul*, 147.

she was simply following David's orders could be true.[51] However, this interpretation seems unlikely for at least two reasons. First, it is illogical that after David received warning of apparent danger from Michal, he would need to threaten her to assist him in escaping the very danger of which she had warned him. Based on the characterization of Michal in the narrative, it is improbable that she was willing to warn David but not to assist in his escape out of familial loyalty to Saul.

Second, in v. 11 Michal used a Piel participle of the root מלט in her exhortation for David to flee: "If you do not *get yourself to safety* ..." (אם־אינך ממלט את־נפשך). To Edelman this statement implies *how* David will save himself. However, the Piel stem emphasizes not the *means* of getting to safety but the resulting *state* of being safe.[52] Thus Michal's language pertained only to David's need to get to a safe place without implying anything about *how* he was to get there. Therefore Edelman's reconstruction, which relies largely upon this supposed implication, is unlikely.

To support her contention that Michal was telling the truth in v. 17, Edelman claims that nothing in the preceding passage with Jonathan or in the description of Michal's relationship with David allows the reader to determine whether or not she lied to Saul.[53] However, as noted above, the fivefold characterization of Michal as loyal to David suggests that she was willing to lie on his behalf to Saul. Furthermore, although the immediately preceding incident with Jonathan offers no parallel, a parallel does exist in the immediately succeeding narrative in which Jonathan explicitly lied to Saul on David's behalf (1 Sam 20:28–29). Thus context and characterization both support the view that Michal lied to Saul by fabricating a death threat by David in order to exonerate her actions.

The pericope ends with Michal's lie and without a corresponding response from Saul. After this, Michal appears in the Saul narrative only when he gives her in marriage to Palti son of Laish (1 Sam 25:24), which suggests that she suffered no negative effects from Saul and that he believed her deceptive excuse.

Analyzing the Deceptions

The tactics Michal used to deceive Saul's messengers were manipulating the environment with the *teraphim* and a lie; her tactic in deceiving Saul was a lie to cover up her first deception. Her motive for the first deception was

51. Ibid., 148.
52. *IBHS*, 400.
53. Edelman, *King Saul*, 149.

to save David's life (v. 11b); her motive for the second deception was apparently to save her own. A significant feature of her first deception is the relationship of the *teraphim* for Saul vis-à-vis David. After Saul failed to carry out YHWH's command through Samuel in 1 Samuel 15, the prophet responded:

> For rebellion is like the sin of divination
> and insubordination is like iniquity and *teraphim*,
> Because you have rejected the word of YHWH
> so he has rejected you as king (v. 23).

Immediately after this oracle, Samuel said that YHWH had torn (קרע) the kingdom from Saul and given it "to your neighbor (לרעך), one better than you" (v. 28). Since the word *teraphim* occurs in the books of Samuel only in these two passages, the presence of *teraphim* in 19:13–16 explicitly recalls the rejection of Saul and the election of David.[54] Thus in seeking to eliminate David, Saul was reminded of his own rejection and the promise of his replacement. A significant feature of Michal's second deception is Saul's question that precipitated it, "Why did you deceive me like this?" (למה ככה רמיתני). This question foreshadows the nearly identical question posed to Saul by the necromancer of Endor in 28:12: "Why did you deceive me?" (למה רמיתני). Significantly, this latter account describes the other occasion when Samuel repeated his prophetic denunciation of Saul's kingdom, that YHWH would "tear" (קרע) the kingdom from him and give it "to your neighbor" (לרעך). However, in this latter passage the vague description in 15:28 of "one better than you" is clarified as "David" (לדוד, 28:17). Therefore, elements of these deceptions in 19:11–17 correspond both retrospectively and prospectively to statements regarding the rejection of Saul and the election of David.

Michal achieved the goals for which she deceived, demonstrated by the fact that David escaped and she suffered no wrath from her father. At least one aspect of these deceptions suggests a positive evaluation. Meir Sternberg has argued that authors use the order of presentation in biblical narrative as a rhetorical device to persuade readers of their viewpoint. Specifically, the last word of an account is left "ringing in our ears and conditioning our response."[55] This account ends with Michal's lie to Saul and with no corresponding response from Saul, which suggests that the author is siding with her.[56] Supporting this conclusion, immediately after Michal

---

54. So also Bauck, "1 Samuel 19," 234; Rowe, *Michal's Moral Dilemma*, 198; Fokkelman, *Crossing Fates*, 274; Bodner, *1 Samuel*, 206.

55. Sternberg, *Poetics of Biblical Narrative*, 459.

56. Fokkelman, *Crossing Fates*, 269.

lied to Saul, v. 18 begins with a disjunctive clause: "But David fled and escaped" (ודוד ברח וימלט). The succession of the verbs ברח and מלט recalls v. 12, the only other place where they are used successively: "So Michal let David down through the window, and he went *and fled and escaped* (ויברח וימלט)." Thus immediately after Michal deceived Saul regarding the means of David's escape, the narrator disrupts the narrative syntax to remind the reader of the true circumstances of his escape: Michal enabled him to "flee and escape." This reinforces the sense that Michal was operating on David's behalf and contributes to her positive characterization in this episode and also to a positive evaluation of her deception.[57]

Deception E: Jonathan's Deception of Saul (1 Samuel 20:27–34)

In 1 Samuel 20, David went to Jonathan to ask why Saul was trying to kill him. Since Jonathan did not believe him, David devised a plan to help Jonathan determine Saul's intentions. David would skip the upcoming New Moon festival at the king's table, and when Saul asked about his whereabouts, Jonathan was to say that David requested permission to go to Bethlehem for an annual sacrifice. Saul's reaction would then reveal his disposition toward David (v. 7). The deception lies in the fact that David did not go to Bethlehem for a sacrifice, but waited in a field (v. 24). On the first night of the festival, Saul assumed David was absent because of ceremonial uncleanness, but when David missed the second night he asked Jonathan about it (v. 27). Jonathan responded with an expanded version of the lie composed by David (vv. 28–29), which triggered Saul's rage (vv. 30–31), proving to Jonathan his father's hostile disposition (vv. 32–33).

Establishing the Deception

No one questions whether or not Jonathan lied, though some argue that Saul did not believe Jonathan's lie.[58] However, although Saul was obviously upset with Jonathan when he heard his story, it is not clear that he was angry because he recognized the lie. Rather, it seems that Saul believed Jonathan's

---

57. Rowe also concludes that Michal is depicted positively here (*Michal's Moral Dilemma*, 203).

58. Klein, *1 Samuel*, 209; Brueggemann, *First and Second Samuel*, 151; Evans, *1 and 2 Samuel*, 94.

lie. As Table 1 shows, a comparison between David's instructions to Jonathan and what Jonathan actually said to Saul brings two reasons to light:

Table 1. David's Suggested Lie vs. Jonathan's Actual Lie

David's suggested lie (20:6)	Jonathan's actual lie (20:28–29)
"David earnestly asked me to run to Bethlehem, his city,	"David earnestly asked me [to go] to Bethlehem.
	He said, 'Send (שלח) me,
because an annual sacrifice is there for his whole clan."	because there is a clan sacrifice for us in the city and my brother commanded me.
	So now, *if I have found favor in your eyes*, let me escape (מלט) and see my brothers.' Therefore he has not come to the king's table."

This table shows that Jonathan added substantially to David's suggested lie, and these additions are what explain Saul's anger. The underlined words—שלח and מלט—allude to the previous deception involving Michal.[59] In that passage, these words occurred together when Saul confronted Michal in 19:17a: "Why did you deceive me like this and *send* (שלח) my enemy away so that he *escaped* (מלט)?" From Saul's perspective, Michal had committed two crimes: (1) she sent David away so that he escaped, and (2) she deceived Saul about it. Michal's second deception in v. 17b may have exonerated her in Saul's eyes from these grievances, but the fact that Saul considered it a grievance for her to "send" David so that he "escaped" explains his anger at Jonathan.[60]

---

59. So also Fokkelman, *Crossing Fates*, 332; Edelman, *King Saul*, 159; Alter, *David Story*, 128; Firth, *1 & 2 Samuel*, 227; Bar-Efrat, *Das Erste Buch Samuel*, 280.

60. The logic of this argument still holds even if we conclude that רמה in 19:17a carries the sense of "betray," a possible reading noted above. In this case Saul would view the sending of David as the betrayal, and Michal's second deception explained why she was forced to betray him. Thus in this reading also, Saul viewed "sending" David away from him as a crime.

In 20:29, Jonathan told Saul that David had asked him to "send" (שלח) him and let him "escape" (מלט) to see his brothers, which is why he was absent. This implies that Jonathan responded positively to David's request and therefore Saul was angry with Jonathan for the same reason he was previously angry with Michal: for "sending" David so that he "escaped." Since Saul himself had confronted Michal with these two verbs, it appears that hearing them on the lips of Jonathan enraged him. However, this scenario presupposes that Saul believed what Jonathan said, which means that he believed this lie and thus was deceived.[61]

The italicized phrase in the table above provides further reason for Saul to be angry with Jonathan without the need to assume he recognized the lie. According to Jonathan, David qualified his request to be "sent" with the condition: "If I have found favor in your eyes" (v. 29). From Saul's perspective, that Jonathan agreed to send David to Bethlehem confirmed that David had found favor in his eyes. However, according to David, it was Saul's knowledge of this fact that had kept him from revealing his murderous intentions to Jonathan. In v. 3 David had said, "Your father surely knows that *I have found favor in your eyes*, and he has said, 'Let not Jonathan know, lest he *be grieved* (יעצב).'" Presumably Saul was not concerned with Jonathan's feelings, but rather his proclivity to warn David of his intentions; being grieved would lead Jonathan to subvert Saul's plans. Indeed, this is exactly what happened when Jonathan discovered Saul's intentions: "And Jonathan rose from the table in fierce anger and ate no food the second day of the month, *for he was grieved for David* (כי נעצב אל־דוד),[62] because his father had disgraced him" (v. 34, ESV). Jonathan then met David and subverted Saul's plans by warning him (vv. 35–42).

This suggests that Saul associated David finding favor in Jonathan's eyes with Jonathan's loyalty to David over Saul. Although Saul had suspected this to be the case, in this narrative Jonathan confirmed this suspicion, precipitating Saul's exclamation: "Don't I know that you are choosing the son of Jesse . . ." (v. 30)? Thus Saul was angry not because he realized Jonathan was lying—something the text does not state—but because the crown prince had aligned himself with someone Saul viewed as a threat to his dynasty: "For all the days that the son of Jesse lives on the earth, neither you nor your kingdom will be established" (v. 31a).

---

61. Although it is logically conceivable that Saul could be angry because he recognized Jonathan's lie, such a reading is not textually demonstrable.

62. This rendering keeps the prepositional phrase אל־דוד in construction with the verb נעצב, supported by the *zāqēp qāṭōn* division (so also NRSV, NASB; *contra* NIV).

Analyzing the Deception

The tactic Jonathan used to deceive Saul was a lie. His motive was to confirm David's belief that Saul intended to kill him (20:1–7), and if so, for Jonathan to tell David and send him off in peace (20:9, 13). As in the previous interchange between Michal and Saul, Jonathan's lie and Saul's response hint at the themes of David's election and Saul's rejection. Particularly, four elements in the interchange recall David's anointing in chapter 16. First, the lie about a "sacrifice" (זבח) in Bethlehem recalls the similar lie Samuel told when he went to anoint David as king.[63] Second, Saul accused Jonathan of *choosing the son of Jesse* (בחר אתה לבן־ישי, 20:30). In 16:6–10, all Jesse's sons except David passed by Samuel, and thrice Samuel said, "YHWH has *not chosen*" him (לא־בחר יהוה). However, when David entered, YHWH instructed Samuel to anoint him as the chosen king (16:12). Jonathan's "choice" of this "son of Jesse" therefore recalls YHWH's "choice" of this "son of Jesse."[64] Third, Saul's command to Jonathan, "Send and take him" (שלח וקח אתו, 20:31), echoes Samuel's command to Jesse to have David brought in for his anointing (שלחה וקחנו, 16:11). Fourth, David's "brothers" are prominent in both passages. In chapter 16, all seven brothers passed by Samuel (v. 10) before he took the horn of oil and anointed David "in the presence of his brothers" (בקרב אחיו, v. 12). In chapter 20, Jonathan's expanded version of the lie to Saul included two references to David's "brothers." Jonathan described David as saying, "My brother has commanded me [to go to the sacrifice]," and "Now, let me escape and see my brothers" (v. 29). Thus Jonathan's lie and Saul's response hint at the theme of David's election, particularly to the scene of his anointing.

Saul's response to Jonathan's lie also hints at the theme of his rejection. In 20:31 Saul said, "For all the days that the son of Jesse lives on the earth, *neither you nor your kingdom will be established* (לא תכון אתה ומלכותך)." This phrase recalls 1 Sam 13:13, where Samuel rebuked Saul: "You have not kept the command of YHWH your God which he commanded you; for now *YHWH would have established your kingdom* (הכין יהוה את־ממלכתך) over

---

63. After the fourfold occurrence of זבח in 1 Sam 16:3, 5, David's instructions to Jonathan in 20:6 and Jonathan's lie in 20:29 are the next occurrences of this root in the narrative. See also the discussions of Edelman, *King Saul*, 159; Fokkelman, *Crossing Fates*, 337.

64. Fokkelman, *Crossing Fates*, 335; Edelman, *King Saul*, 159.

Israel for all time."[65] Thus the themes of David's election and Saul's rejection both occur as subtexts in this deceptive interchange as well.[66]

Jonathan achieved the goal for which he deceived by acquiring the requisite information to confirm David's knowledge of Saul's murderous intentions and sending David off in peace (20:35–42). Like Michal in chapter 19, Jonathan is characterized positively in this passage. He was willing to do anything for David (v. 4), risked his own life to sound out Saul on David's behalf (v. 33), and kept his word by notifying David of danger just as they arranged (vv. 35–42). Furthermore, as in Michal's confrontation with Saul, here the author gives Jonathan the last word. Jonathan asked Saul, "Why should he be put to death? What has he done?" (20:32). Since Saul never answered this question, but simply hurled his spear, Jonathan's question is left ringing in our ears and conditioning our response. The implied answer is that David had done nothing meriting death and Jonathan was right to defend him. In this way, Jonathan's perspective on Saul's guilt and David's innocence is the means by which the author reveals his own perspective. In addition, while Saul never mentioned David's name in this passage, but only referred to him as "the son of Jesse" (vv. 27, 30, 31), like the narrator (vv. 27, 33, 34) Jonathan called him by name (v. 28). Whereas Saul's label expressed contempt for David,[67] Jonathan's use of David's name further aligns him with the point of view of the narrator. Therefore, although the author does not provide specific data to assess confidently an evaluation of the deception, he characterizes the deceiver positively.

Deception F: David's First Deception of Achish (1 Samuel 21:11–16 [10–15])

First Samuel 21:11 [10] says that David fled from Saul to Achish, king of Gath. Upon David's arrival, Achish's servants recognized him and recalled the Israelite song inspired by his slaying of Goliath (1 Sam 18:6–7), the champion from Gath, whose sword he was evidently carrying with him (1 Sam 21:10 [9]). After being recognized, David "put these words in his heart and was very afraid of Achish king of Gath" (v. 13 [12]). He acted like a madman, scribbling on the doors of the gate and drooling on his beard,

---

65. These two verses are the only places in 1 Samuel where the verb כון is used with a noun for "kingdom."

66. So also Fokkelman, *Crossing Fates*, 336.

67. Polzin, *Samuel and the Deuteronomist*, 189–90; Fokkelman, *Crossing Fates*, 330.

thereby deceiving the Philistines into believing that he was insane and therefore not a threat to them.[68]

Establishing the Deception

For David to be deceptive here, he had to fake his insanity. All the major English translations understand David's actions this way—"he pretended to be mad" (NRSV); "feigned himself mad" (KJV); "pretended to be insane" (ESV, NIV); "acted insanely" (NASB)—as do the majority of commentators.[69] However, Frank Crüsemann objects and notes that, formally rendered, the first clause of v. 14 [13] says that David "changed his taste in their eyes" (וישנו את־טעמו בעיניהם). Crüsemann argues that since the verb שנה means "to change," not "to disguise," and since a similar Akkadian idiom, šanê ṭēmi, can designate "madness," David was therefore not pretending to be insane but actually went insane from his extreme fear of Achish.[70] This would suggest David was not being deceptive, since he was not intentionally causing false belief.

However, this conclusion does not sufficiently consider the point of view of David's actions. Although שנה means "to change," the critical element to understanding David's "change" is the qualifying prepositional phrase, "in their eyes" (בעיניהם). As Fokkelman points out, elsewhere בעיניהם always means "in their opinion" and here serves as a narratorial signal that David's madness was not real but simply a reality from the perspective of the Philistines.[71] Also supporting this interpretation is the fact that the Hithpael stem is consistently used to describe David's insanity (in contrast to the Pual that Achish used to describe the actual Philistine madmen in v. 16 [15]), which likely describes an imitative madness.[72] These data suggest that rather than actually going insane, David only feigned insanity.

Against this understanding, Peter Ackroyd suggests that David's madness was not feigned but rather induced by God, arguing that the Piel verb וַיְשַׁנּוֹ could be translated passively, "'his behaviour was altered,' the text

---

68. Firth, "Testimonies True (?) and False (?)," 22.

69. Fokkelman, *Crossing Fates*, 367–68; Miscall, *1 Samuel*, 133; Gunn, *Fate of King Saul*, 86; McCarter, *1 Samuel*, 357; Klein, *1 Samuel*, 217; Evans, *1 and 2 Samuel*, 98; Brueggemann, *First and Second Samuel*, 157; Firth, *1 & 2 Samuel*, 236; Bodner, *1 Samuel*, 229; Bergen, *1, 2 Samuel*, 224; Gass, "Achisch von Gat," 214.

70. Crüsemann, "Zwei alttestamentliche Witze," 221.

71. Fokkelman, *Crossing Fates*, 368; so also Gass, "Achisch von Gat," 214.

72. Fokkelman, *Crossing Fates*, 371; Edelman, *King Saul*, 169; Gass, "Achisch von Gat," 214–15.

perhaps meaning that God changed him and thereby enabled him to escape the danger."[73] However, it is unclear why a Piel of שנה should be construed this way; one would expect a Pual for a passive construction.[74] Furthermore, YHWH is never mentioned in this narrative, making Ackroyd's suggestion of a divine passive not only grammatically improbable but also contextually unlikely. In contrast, in 22:1 the narrator says that David went from Gath and "escaped (מלט) to the cave of Adullam." Elsewhere in the books of Samuel, the Niphal of מלט always describes someone intentionally leaving a dangerous situation;[75] therefore this verb seems inappropriate to describe David's departure from Gath if he was ejected due to actual madness, whether caused by fear or YHWH. Since Crüsemann views 21:11-16 [10-15] as an independent, non-historical tradition,[76] he does not admit 22:1 into his interpretation.[77] However, in its present arrangement, 22:1 suggests that David intentionally escaped from Philistine territory and thus supports the view that he deceived the Philistines by feigning insanity. Achish's exclamation in v. 15 [14]: "Look, the man is insane! Why bring him to me?" demonstrates that he succeeded.

Analyzing the Deception

The tactic David used to deceive Achish was nonverbal action. His motive was to avoid expected harm or death from Achish. Verse 13 [12] says David "greatly feared Achish king of Gath" after he realized that Achish's servants identified him as the subject of the Israelite song. Since the narrative associates this song with David's victory over Goliath, the champion from Gath (1 Sam 18:6-7), the Philistine servants' question suggests that David is a famous enemy of the Philistines. That David had fled from Saul and "went to Achish" (v. 11 [10]) implies that he was not initially afraid of Achish, but became so only after the Philistine servants uncovered his identity. All this

73. Ackroyd, *First Book of Samuel*, 173.

74. Chisholm, "שנה," 190.

75. 1 Sam 19:10, 12, 17, 18; 22:20; 23:13; 27:1; 30:17; 2 Sam 1:3; 4:6 (the Piel occurrences in 1 Sam 19:11 and 2 Sam 19:6, 10 convey the sense of "save," which is consistent with this observation). The one apparent exception for the Niphal is 1 Sam 20:29, where Jonathan deceptively quoted David to Saul as saying, "Let me *escape* (מלט) so I can see my brothers" for a sacrifice. However, as noted above, along with the verb שלח, Jonathan's use of מלט alludes to the Michal episode of 19:11-17, where Saul chastised his daughter for "sending" David so that he "escaped." Thus the ironic literary function of מלט in 1 Sam 20:29 presupposes the same meaning as its uses elsewhere.

76. Crüsemann, "Zwei alttestamentliche Witze," 218.

77. Ibid., 221.

suggests that David's flight to Achish was intended to be anonymous, but after his past military exploits against the Philistines had been publicized, he feared harmful or lethal repercussions.[78] He responded by faking insanity, which led Achish to believe that he was no threat.

David achieved the goal for which he deceived by leaving Gath safely and escaping to the cave of Adullam. The narrative evaluation of this deception is unclear, though David seems to be characterized positively. In v. 12a [11a] Achish's servants referred to David as "the king of the land" (מלך הארץ). From their perspective this statement probably referred to David's social and military prominence, though narratologically it also functions as an unwitting affirmation of his anointed status.[79] Similarly, in v. 12b [11b] these same servants also recalled the Israelite song celebrating David's victory over Goliath. Although this song certainly had negative connotations for the Philistines, for Israel it positively recalled David's decisive victory over Goliath and alluded to the song's first appearance in 18:6–7. In that context, David enjoyed the favor of Jonathan (18:3–4) and all the people (18:5). Thus narratologically these statements by Achish's servants characterize David positively. Unlike the two previous deceptions in which the deceivers had the last word, here the last word is given to the receiver: "Achish said to his servants, 'Look, the man is insane! Why bring him to me? Do I lack madmen that you bring this one to be crazy in front of me? Shall this one enter my house?'" (vv. 15–16). This outburst communicates both that Achish was fooled regarding David's mental state and that Gath was apparently full of madmen. Although the narrator gives the last word to Achish, this last word incriminates him as gullible (particularly in contrast to his servants' astuteness in v. 12) and the Philistines as generally insane. Therefore, although the author's evaluation of the deception is unclear, in this account the deceiver is characterized positively and the receiver is characterized negatively.[80]

Deception G: David's Second Deception of Achish (1 Samuel 27:7–12)

First Samuel 27:1 emphasizes the theme of David's "escape" from Saul by utilizing the verb מלט three times. David said, "There is nothing good for me except that *I certainly escape* (המלט אמלט) to the land of the Philistines. Saul will despair of searching for me any more throughout Israel, and *I will*

---

78. See Josephus, *Ant.*, 6.12.2.
79. Alter, *David Story*, 133; Bodner, *1 Samuel*, 229.
80. So also Arnold, *1 & 2 Samuel*, 311; Cartledge, *1 & 2 Samuel*, 260–61.

escape (ונמלטתי) from his hand." Therefore David again fled to Achish in Gath (vv. 2–4). However, instead of fearing the Philistine king as he had in 21:11–16 [10–15], David requested a place to live among the rural towns. Achish gave him Ziklag, and from this base David and his men spent sixteen months raiding the Geshurites, Girzites, and Amalekites, leaving no one alive to tell Achish. When Achish would ask David about his exploits, he would lie and say he raided the Negev of Judah, Jerahmeel, or the Kenites.

Establishing the Deception

It is clear that David deceived Achish. The narrator makes explicit the discrepancy between the objects of David's raids in v. 8 and his false reports to Achish in v. 10. Verse 12 provides the evidence of success: "Achish trusted David (ויאמן אכיש בדוד), saying, 'He has certainly become odious to his people in Israel and will be my servant forever.'" Achish believed falsely that David had been raiding the Israelites and thus had defected to the Philistines, which gave him a misplaced trust in David and belief that he would remain his loyal vassal.

Analyzing the Deception

Although it seems that David lied here, Peter Leithart argues that this was "not an outright lie," since

> verse 10 describes areas in the southern regions of Judah that David really did attack.... When David talked about attacking the "Negev," he did not actually say *whom* he was attacking in the Negev, but he deliberately left the false impression that he was "making himself odious" among Israelites.[81]

However, although the nomadic Amalekites could have dwelled in parts of the Negev of Judah, elsewhere the Geshurites are geographically associated with the Philistines (Josh 13:2), and the location of the Girzites is unknown. Since the Negev of the Jerahmeelites and the Negev of the Kenites were both east of the tribe of Simeon,[82] any claim to raid them could not have substituted ambiguously for Geshur, which was too far west; therefore a claim to have raided either of these regions when he raided Geshur would have been a lie. Moreover, if Gershon Galil is correct that the *waw* following

---

81. Leithart, *A Son to Me*, 150 (emphasis his).
82. Galil, "The Jerahmeelites and the Negeb of Judah," 38.

"the Negev of Judah" is a *waw-explicativum*, the regions of the Jerahmeelites and Kenites were being specified here as particular areas within the Negev of Judah that David claimed to raid.[83] This would mean that David never claimed to raid the western part of the Negev of Judah. If this were the case, none of the locations that David claimed to raid could have substituted for the Geshurites. Given these geographic discrepancies and the uncertainty concerning the location of the Girzites, it seems best to conclude that David used both ambiguous language and lies to deceive Achish.

David's motive for deceiving was to avoid negative (if not harmful) consequences from Achish. His settling in Gath "with Achish" (v. 3) indicates that he became his vassal.[84] This is demonstrated by David's self-description to Achish as "your servant" (עבדך, v. 5) and by the fact that after his raids from Ziklag he would return to Achish (v. 9), presumably to give him a portion of the booty.[85] Firth suggests that by placing David in Ziklag, Achish expected that he would raid Judah, given its geographic proximity.[86] However, David's loyalty to Saul and Israel, repeatedly demonstrated in chapters 24 and 26, posed a dilemma for this scenario. On the one hand, David could not raid Israel because of his loyalty to them. On the other hand, David could not let Achish know he was unwilling to raid Israel if he was to maintain his good standing as a Philistine vassal. In v. 12 Achish associated David's fidelity to him with his odiousness to Israel: "He has certainly become odious to his people in Israel *and will be my servant forever* (והיה לי לעבד עולם)." This suggests that Achish would have interpreted David's unwillingness to raid Israel as a breach of their master-vassal relationship. Indeed, in 28:1 Achish emphatically expected David to attack Israel on his behalf: "You *certainly know* (ידע תדע) that you will go out with me in the army [against Israel]." Thus if Achish were to learn that David was unwilling to raid Israel, one can only surmise what consequences this Philistine king would have exacted. David's motive for his deceptions was to avoid these repercussions.

David's deception exhibits several significant features. First, embedded in this deception is a hint of the truth. David's attacks against these nations, specifically the Amalekites, recall Saul's attack on the Amalekites in chapter 15 by the similar geographic description "from Shur to the land of Egypt"

---

83. Ibid., 40.

84. Tsumura, *First Book of Samuel*, 608; Firth, *1 & 2 Samuel*, 286; Alter, *David Story*, 168, 170.

85. Firth, *1 & 2 Samuel*, 286; Anderson, "David as a Biblical 'Good-Fella,'" 63.

86. Firth, *1 & 2 Samuel*, 286.

(v. 8; cf. 15:7).[87] However, the variation between YHWH's command to Saul in 15:3 and David's attacks in 27:9 is noteworthy, as Table 2 indicates:

Table 2: YHWH's Command to Saul vs. David's Attacks

YHWH's command to Saul (15:3)	David's attacks (27:9)
"Now go and strike (והכיתה) the Amalekites and totally destroy all that is theirs. Do not pity them, but put to death man and woman, *child and infant*, ox (שור) and sheep (שה), camel and donkey."	"And David struck (והכה) the land and did not let man or woman live, but he took sheep (צאן) and herd (בקר) and donkeys and camels and *clothes* and returned and went to Achish."

Aside from alterations in vocabulary for sheep and herd, the text replaces "child and infant" in the command to Saul with "clothes" in the description of David's raids. While Saul was commanded to destroy everything totally, David would bring the booty—including clothing—back to Achish. As Edelman notes, ancient clothing was regionally distinguishable and thus Achish should have discerned from the booty that David was lying.[88] Nevertheless, despite this evidence of the truth, Achish remained deceived and the narrator characterizes him as foolishly trusting David.

Second, by alluding to Saul's disobedience in his battle against the Amalekites, this account recalls his rejection. Whereas Saul spared Agag despite YHWH's command to "destroy totally" (והחרמתם) all the Amalekites (15:3), which was the catalyst for his rejection, twice chapter 27 states that David "did not leave a man or woman alive" (vv. 9, 11). Verse 11 specifies that this was to prevent his victims from revealing his lies to Achish; therefore his success in carrying out the ban (חרם) where Saul had failed facilitated his deception.[89] Some object that David did not carry out the ban here since he kept the booty instead of destroying it.[90] However, in Deut

---

87. Edelman, *King Saul*, 235; Bodner, *1 Samuel*, 287.

88. Edelman, *King Saul*, 236–37.

89. *Contra* Youngblood ("1, 2 Samuel," 775) and Van Seters (*Biblical Saga*, 203), who unnecessarily view this annihilation for the purpose of corroborating the deception as mutually exclusive with annihilation for religious purposes.

90. Hertzberg, *I & II Samuel*, 214; Miscall, *1 Samuel*, 164–65; Campbell, *1 Samuel*, 272; Leithart, *A Son to Me*, 150; cf. Brueggemann, *First and Second Samuel*, 190; Firth,

2:34–35 Moses recalled Israel's battle against Sihon in which they "totally destroyed" (ונחרם) all the people, yet carried off the booty for themselves.[91] Similarly, Josh 8:26 says that Joshua "totally destroyed (החרים) all the inhabitants of Ai," yet Israel carried off the booty according to YHWH's command (v. 27). Therefore, that David took the booty does not disqualify his raids as executions of the ban. Thus David's success in eradicating these peoples both supported his lies and recalled Saul's failure and rejection.

Supporting this conclusion, v. 8b begins with a deictic particle concerning David's victims: "Indeed (כי), these were *the inhabitants of the land* (ישבות הארץ) who were from ancient times . . . ." In the Torah and Former Prophets, the phrase ישבי הארץ refers almost exclusively to Canaanites, those whom Israel was to destroy in warfare.[92] Moreover, in 1 Sam 15:3 the Amalekites were explicitly identified as objects of the ban, and in Josh 13:1–2 YHWH described "all the regions of the Philistines *and all of the Geshurites*" as still remaining to be "dispossessed" (ירש) by Israel. Since the Girzites are not mentioned elsewhere in the OT, we have no evidence either way that they were previously objects of the ban. Nevertheless, the available evidence concerning David's victims indicates that they were previously objects of the ban, which supports the interpretation of David's raids as executions of the ban.

David achieved the goal for which he deceived, demonstrated by the fact that Achish never discovered his refusal to attack Israel and he therefore lived safely in Ziklag. As was the case in Deception F, the author's evaluation of this deception is unclear. After the description of David's practice of killing all the people so they would not expose his deception of Achish,

---

1 & 2 Samuel, 287.

91. Deuteronomy 3:6–7 records the same thing in Israel's battle against Og: they "totally destroyed" (ונחרם) all the people and kept the booty for themselves.

92. Genesis 34:30; 50:11; Exod 23:31; 34:12, 15; Num 14:14; 32:17; 33:52, 55; Josh 2:9, 24; 7:9; 9:24; 24:18; Judg 1:32, 33; 2:2; 2 Sam 5:6. There are three exceptions, though each case refers to a nation being dispossessed: Josh 13:21 refers to "Midianites" and Judg 11:21 refers to Transjordanian "Amorites," both of whom Israel dispossessed (Num 31:7–8 and 21:21–24, respectively), and Gen 36:20 refers to Horites, whom Edom dispossessed (Deut 2:22). Gass similarly sees this phrase as recalling the time of the conquest under Joshua ("Achisch von Gat," 221). Regarding the use of the feminine plural here (הנה ישבות הארץ), McCarter proposes that the original reading was והנה הארץ נשבת ("Though the land was inhabited"), a reading supported by the LXX (καὶ ἰδοὺ ἡ γῆ κατῳκεῖτο), which was later transposed to the received reading (*1 Samuel*, 413). However, as Driver observes, occasionally a nation or its population was construed as feminine (e.g., 1 Sam 17:21), so while unusual, the feminine plural here could refer to these three nations (Driver, *Samuel*, 163; so also Tsumura, *First Book of Samuel*, 610).

v. 11 ends with a narratorial comment: "And thus was *his practice* (משפטו) all the days he lived in the land of the Philistines." Fokkelman sees a double entendre in this language: this was not only David's "practice" but also his "quasi-administration of justice."[93] Erasmus Gass more specifically sees the choice of משפט as suggesting that the narrator views David's lies positively.[94] However, since משפט may describe a practice or custom without suggesting approval of it,[95] this datum alone does not indicate positive evaluation. Nevertheless, like Deception F, this episode characterizes the deceiver positively and the receiver negatively. In v. 6 the narrator says, "So on that day Achish gave Ziklag to him [David]; therefore Ziklag has belonged to the kings of Judah to this day." Previously, Ziklag had been allotted as part of Israel's inheritance for the tribe of Simeon (Josh 19:5; cf. 15:31), yet apparently Israel had not conquered it. If they had, they had not kept control of it, since it was now under Philistine rule. Therefore this narratorial comment emphasizes that David brought Ziklag under Israelite control, something that past generations of leaders had failed to do.[96] Moreover, as Alter observes, this narratorial comment about "the kings of Judah" foreshadows David's royal ascent: this fugitive and apparent Philistine vassal will eventually found the Judahite dynasty.[97] For these reasons, the characterization of David in this passage seems to be positive. As in Deception F, here also the author gives Achish the last word of the account. However, by a paronomastic infinitive construction Achish expressed certainty that David had become odious to Israel (הבאש הבאיש), which led him to conclude that he would be his servant forever (v. 12). This heightened certainty conveys even more forcefully how foolish Achish was in his perception of David, so that readers again leave the account with the impression of Achish's stupidity ringing in their ears. Similar to David's first deception of Achish, here also the receiver is characterized negatively.[98]

---

93. Fokkelman, *Crossing Fates*, 562.

94. Gass, "Achisch von Gat," 222.

95. E.g., 1 Sam 2:13 describes the "practice" (משפט) of Eli's sons in abusing their priestly duties; Samuel twice describes the negative "practice" (משפט) of the king whom the Israelites were wrongly requesting (1 Sam 8:9, 11).

96. See also Bergen, *1, 2 Samuel*, 261.

97. Alter, *David Story*, 169; see also Bodner, *1 Samuel*, 287.

98. See also Arnold, *1 & 2 Samuel*, 362.

Deception H: The Woman of Bahurim's Deception of Absalom's Servants (2 Samuel 17:15–21a)

After Hushai gave Absalom deceptive advice for how to defeat David in battle (2 Sam 17:7–14), he sent a message that Jonathan and Ahimaaz were to relay to David (vv. 15–17). A young man spotted Jonathan and Ahimaaz, who were known to be Davidic collaborators (v. 17b), and told Absalom, so the two hid in a well in the courtyard of a man in Bahurim. A woman put a covering over the well and spread grain[99] on it, thereby obscuring the presence of the well. When Absalom's servants came to the house and asked where Jonathan and Ahimaaz were, the woman lied and said they crossed over the brook. Absalom's servants searched but did not find them, so they returned to Jerusalem (v. 20), after which Jonathan and Ahimaaz went and informed David (v. 21).

Establishing the Deception

On the surface it seems clear that the woman deceived Absalom's men; however, the language is slightly ambiguous. It is clear that her statement in v. 20a ("They crossed over the brook of water") was a lie, since she had just hidden them in her well. However, after this statement, the narrator adds: "So they searched, but they did not find, so they returned to Jerusalem" (v. 20b). Grammatically it is unclear whether they searched the woman's premises or crossed over the brook and searched there. Youngblood asserts that Absalom's servants did not believe her,[100] though contextually it seems more likely that they were deceived and searched across the brook. They did not interrogate the woman further or take any action against her, which one would expect if they suspected she was lying to them.[101] The false belief was that Jonathan and Ahimaaz had fled across the brook and thus were not

---

99. The specific referent of הרפות is uncertain. Both McCarter (*II Samuel*, 389) and Anderson (*2 Samuel*, 215) argue that it probably refers to grains of sand, though both acknowledge its uncertainty. Others see it referring to grains of wheat (e.g., Hertzberg, *I & II Samuel*, 352). For our purposes the specific referent is not crucial. What is crucial is that the woman employed a visual disguise as reinforcement in her deception.

100. Youngblood, "1, 2 Samuel," 1013.

101. Evans suggests there was a societal assumption that women were incapable of deception (*1 and 2 Samuel*, 211), which made the woman an unlikely suspect in this situation. Yet the numerous examples of female deceivers in the OT argue against this suggestion. For further discussion see Prouser, "The Truth About Women and Lying," 15–28.

on the woman's property. The narratorial comment after the woman spread the grain over the covering of the well—"And nothing was known about it" (v. 19)—as well as the servants' search for the two men across the brook, shows that her deception succeeded.

Analyzing the Deception

The woman used two tactics to deceive Absalom's men: she manipulated the visual appearance of the courtyard by hiding the well, which reinforced her lie that the men were not there but had crossed over the brook. Her motive was to prevent Jonathan and Ahimaaz from being captured by Absalom's men, which, given the martial context of the narrative (vv. 12–14) probably would have resulted in either death or harm. Many see allusions to the narrative of Rahab in Joshua 2 in this account.[102] In both cases (1) scouts were identified by their enemies (Josh 2:2; 2 Sam 17:18), (2) entered a residence and were hidden by a woman (Josh 2:4a, 6; 2 Sam 17:19), (3) who lied to their pursuers (Josh 2:4b–5; 2 Sam 17:20a), and (4) sent the pursuers off in the wrong direction (Josh 2:5b, 7; 2 Sam 17:20b). This parallel to Rahab's deception also supports the conclusion above that Absalom's men searched across the brook, since in Joshua 2 the pursuers of the spies "pursued after them on the way to the Jordan" (v. 7).

The woman of Bahurim achieved the goal for which she deceived by successfully hiding Jonathan and Ahimaaz, who safely communicated their message to David (v. 21). The allusion to the Rahab narrative suggests a positive evaluation of this deception. In the book of Joshua, both Joshua (6:17) and the narrator (6:25) state that Rahab was spared in the destruction of Jericho "because she hid the spies" (כי החבאתה את־המלאכים). This implies that if she had not hidden the spies, she would not have been spared. Even without her lie, Rahab's act of hiding the spies was deceptive, since she intentionally manipulated the physical environment to cause the pursuers to believe falsely that the spies were not there. When the king of Jericho commanded Rahab to turn over the spies in 2:3, her lie was a necessary corroborating means to keep them hidden.[103] If she had responded

---

102. Gunn, *Story of King David*, 44–45; Ackroyd, *Second Book of Samuel*, 161; Gordon, *I & II Samuel*, 282; Robinson, *Let Us Be Like the Nations*, 242; Alter, *David Story*, 300; Firth, *1 & 2 Samuel*, 469; Cartledge, *1 & 2 Samuel*, 587; Caquot and de Robert, *Les Livres de Samuel*, 540; Stoebe, *Das Zweite Buch Samuelis*, 392.

103. Murray claims that this line of thinking presumes too much concerning God's providence and argues that God could have arranged a successful outcome for Rahab without her needing to lie (*Principles of Conduct*, 138–39). Although I affirm that YHWH's providence does not *depend* on human untruth, we have already seen that

truthfully to the king's command, she could not have hidden the spies and thus would have lacked grounds for being spared. If she had no grounds for being spared, she would have perished with the rest, and the writer of Hebrews could not have said, "By faith Rahab the harlot did not perish with those who disbelieved, having received the spies in peace" (Heb 11:31). This implies that Rahab's act of hiding the spies, which included lying, is portrayed as an act of faith.

The epistle of James says that Rahab was "considered righteous" (ἐδικαιώθη) for "receiving the spies and sending them out another way" (Jas 2:25). Murray acknowledges this verse, but then argues that James's approval of Rahab does not indicate approval of her deception.[104] Similarly, Kaiser claims that it was acceptable for Rahab to hide the spies and send them away, but that her lie was an "unnecessary accoutrement."[105] However, as I have argued above, Rahab's lie was necessary to keep the spies hidden once the king inquired about them. Unless Rahab continued to hide the spies when questioned, she would not have been able to "send them out another way," since they would have either escaped or been captured. In either case, her act of "sending them out another way" presupposes her lie. Therefore James could not have considered her righteous for receiving *and sending* the spies if she had not hidden the spies *and lied about it*. Thus James's approval of Rahab receiving and sending the spies logically includes approval of her deceptions on their behalf that enabled her to receive and send them.

David M. Howard Jr. also views Rahab's lie as sinful, but he bases his conclusion on (1) Murray's arguments that "truth-telling [is] in God's very nature";[106] (2) the assertion that "Lying is uniformly condemned in both Old and New Testaments (e.g., Lev 19:11; Prov 12:22; Eph 4:25)";[107] and (3) "Paul's arguments that the ends do not justify the means (Rom 3:7–8) and that God promises deliverance from the necessity of sinning (1 Cor 10:13)."[108] The first assertion is contradicted by our analysis of 1 Sam 16:1–5 and many other studies of divine deception in the Bible;[109] the second is contradicted

---

YHWH himself instructed Samuel to lie when going to anoint David as a protective means against the potential wrath of Saul (1 Sam 16:1–5). Since YHWH instructed Samuel to deceive, it is not presuming too much regarding God's providence to suggest that he chooses to use human untruth under certain circumstances.

104. Murray, *Principles of Conduct*, 138.

105. Kaiser, *Toward Old Testament Ethics*, 272.

106. Howard, *Joshua*, 110.

107. Ibid., 111.

108. Ibid.

109. See, e.g., Roberts, "Does God Lie?" 211–20; Prouser, "Phenomenology of the Lie," 152–81; Bowen, "Role of Yhwh as Deceiver"; Chisholm, "Does God Deceive?"

by our conclusion in chapter 2 that the OT never condemns lying or deception without qualification; and the third presumes the conclusion, that lying is inherently sinful, which is the very issue in question. On the contrary, rather than being sinful, Rahab's deceptions were the means by which she received and sent out the Israelite spies as a demonstration of her faith in YHWH's sovereignty over the land (v. 9). In vv. 9–11 she confessed this faith in thoroughly Deuteronomic language, contributing to an overall positive depiction of her as a character.[110] Since Rahab is characterized positively, by alluding to her parallel actions the author of Samuel is also characterizing the woman of Bahurim positively.

Summary

From this analysis we can make several observations concerning deception intended to prevent death or harm in the books of Samuel. First, in every episode the deceiver achieved the goal for which he or she deceived. Second, in every episode the tactic used to deceive involved a lie, except for Deception F, which used nonverbal action. Third, none of the deceivers experienced negative consequences for his or her deception. Fourth, in every episode the author either evaluates the deception positively or characterizes the deceiver positively, except for Deception A, in which the deceivers are characterized negatively.

11–28; Patterson, "Old Testament Use of an Archetype," 385–94; Esau, "Divine Deception in the Exodus Event?" 4–17; Anderson, *Jacob and the Divine Trickster*.

110. Matthews, "Female Voices," 9; Matties, "Reading Rahab's Story," 65–66; Stek, "Rahab of Canaan and Israel," 28–48; Sherwood, "A Leader's Misleading and a Prostitute's Profession," 60.

4

Deception Intended to Cause Death or Harm in the Books of Samuel

IN THE PREVIOUS CHAPTER we examined deception intended to prevent death or harm. In this chapter we will turn our attention to the opposite motive: deception intended to cause death or harm. Aside from Amnon's deception of David and Tamar in 2 Sam 13:1-22 ("Deception N"), in which Amnon deceived in order to rape Tamar, all deceptions in this chapter were committed with the intent of killing another person (Saul's deception of David in 1 Sam 18:20-27 ["Deception I"]; David's third deception of Achish in 1 Sam 28:1-2 and 29:1-11 ["Deception J"]; Joab's deception of Abner in 2 Sam 3:27 ["Deception K"]; Recab and Baanah's deception of Ishbosheth's palace guard in 2 Sam 4:6 ["Deception L"]; David's deception of Uriah in 2 Sam 11:7, 14-15 ["Deception M"]; Absalom's deception of David and Amnon in 2 Sam 13:23-39 ["Deception O"]; and Joab's deception of Amasa in 2 Sam 20:8-10 ["Deception P"]).

Deception I: Saul's Deception of David (1 Samuel 18:20–27)

First Samuel 18 describes Saul's growing jealousy of David after the latter's victory over Goliath and increasing popularity with the people. After failing to lure David into calamity by offering his oldest daughter Merab in marriage in exchange for military service (vv. 17-19), Saul learned that his younger daughter Michal loved David (v. 20). Seemingly speaking to himself, Saul said that he would give Michal to David so that "the hand of the Philistines might be against him" (v. 21). However, in the next verse Saul instructed his servants to tell David that the king "delights" in him, and thereby convince him to become the king's son-in-law. When David objected that he was too poor, Saul responded by saying that one hundred Philistine foreskins would suffice for the bride price. David accepted this offer, went out and killed two hundred Philistines, and brought their foreskins to Saul. His plan subverted by David's success, Saul gave Michal to David in marriage.

Establishing the Deception

The discrepancy between Saul's internal monologue and his communication to David through his servants shows that he lied. Verse 21 records Saul's internal monologue: "I will give her [Michal] to him, and she will be a snare to him, and the hand of the Philistines will be against him." The connection between Saul giving Michal to David in marriage and the hand of the Philistines being against him is clarified by observing that the phrase ותהי־בו יד־פלשתים is repeated from v. 17, where Saul had offered Merab in marriage on the condition that David be valiant and fight for him. Saul had then said to himself: "Let not my hand be against him, *but let the hand of the Philistines be against him* (ותהי־בו יד־פלשתים)" (v. 17b). Thus Saul had intended the first marriage offer to bring about David's death on the battlefield against the Philistines, and the repetition of this phrase in Saul's internal monologue in v. 21 suggests that he intended the offer of Michal to result in the same fatal end.

However, before giving similar conditions for this second offer, Saul instructed his servants to say to David, "Look, *the king delights in you* (חפץ בך המלך), and all his servants love you; now, become the king's son-in-law" (v. 22). Since Saul had just stated his harmful intentions in the previous verse, this communication through his servants was a lie.[1] Saul's use of the modifying phrase בלט to describe how the servants should speak to David in v. 22 supports this conclusion. Although some translate this phrase "in

---

1. André Wénin rightly observes that the "real Saul" is revealed through his interior monologue, whereas the discourse of the "apparent Saul" reveals his duplicity ("Marques linguistiques," 326). See also Polzin, *Samuel and the Deuteronomist*, 178; Firth, *1 & 2 Samuel*, 211–12; Willi-Plein, "Michal und die Anfänge des Königtums," 407; Birch, "First and Second Books of Samuel," 1122; *contra* Green, who postulates, "There is surely a part of Saul which is pleased with David" ("Engaging Nuances of Genre," 149; *How Are the Mighty Fallen*, 305). While Green later admits that Saul is "not unconflictedly pleased with David" (ibid.), it is unclear what part of Saul remains pleased with David at all at this point in the narrative. Although David initially found favor in Saul's eyes (16:22), after Saul heard the women's song elevating David's victories above his own (18:7) he became very angry (v. 8), kept his eye on David (v. 9), hurled his spear at him (v. 11), is twice described as "afraid" of him (vv. 12, 15), and tried to lure him to military death (v. 17).

private" (e.g., NRSV, ESV),² it is unclear why the servants would need to have a private conversation with David about the king's ostensible delight in him. Fokkelman argues that the phrase is better understood as meaning "discreetly," that is, "in such a way that the *origin* of their arguments remains concealed from David."³ This interpretation is reinforced by considering the three other adverbial occurrences of בלט.⁴

In Judg 4:21, when Sisera was sleeping in Jael's tent, she took a tent peg and hammer and "went to him *discreetly* (בלאט) and thrust the peg through his head." In 1 Sam 24:5, when Saul was in the cave relieving himself, "David arose and cut off the edge of Saul's robe *discreetly* (בלט)." In Ruth 3:7, after Boaz lay down on the grain pile, Ruth "approached *discreetly* (בלט), uncovered his feet, and lay down." In all three cases, knowledge of the verbal action that בלט modifies was withheld from the person to whom the action was directed: Sisera did not know that Jael was approaching with the tent peg; Saul did not know that David was cutting his robe; and Boaz did not know that Ruth was approaching the grain pile.⁵ Thus in 1 Sam 18:22, Saul's command, "*Speak* (דברו) to David *discreetly* (בלט)," suggests that knowledge of the verbal action was to be withheld *from David*, the person to whom the action was directed. However, unlike the three examples above, David was not kept ignorant of the verbal action itself but rather the *source* of the verbal action (i.e., that it was Saul who was truly speaking). In this way, Saul instructed his servants to deceive David into believing falsely that *they thought* Saul delighted in him in order to persuade him to accept Saul's conditions for marrying his daughter.

Whether or not David believed this lie is unclear. He responded with a rhetorical question (v. 23bα), which leaves room for uncertainty.⁶ He then objected that he was poor and little known (v. 23bβ), which, based on Saul's response in v. 25, suggests that he had no means to pay the bride price. Saul

---

2. McCarter similarly renders it as "privately" (*I Samuel*, 315).

3. Fokkelman, *Crossing Fates*, 237 (emphasis his); so also Alter, *David Story*, 116; Bar-Efrat, *Das Erste Buch Samuel*, 259.

4. Other than the three adverbial occurrences examined above, the phrase בלט only appears nominally three times in the Exodus narratives to describe the (attempted) mimicking of Moses' and Aaron's miracles by the Egyptian magicians "by their secret [arts] (בלטיהם)" (Exod 7:22; 8:3 [7], 14 [18]).

5. It was not until "the middle of the night" (בחצי הלילה) that Boaz woke up and noticed a woman sleeping at his feet (Ruth 3:8). Daniel I. Block observes that Ruth must have waited until Boaz fell asleep before she approached, otherwise he would have noticed immediately when she uncovered his feet (*Judges, Ruth*, 689).

6. Wénin, "Marques linguistiques," 328.

took this as his opportunity to send David to his death at the hand of the Philistines:

> Saul said, "Thus you shall say to David, 'The king *delights* (חפץ) in no other bride price except one hundred Philistine foreskins, to take revenge on the enemies of the king.'" But Saul planned to make David fall by the hand of the Philistines (v. 25).

This was Saul's second attempt to deceive through the mouths of his servants. Again he employed the root חפץ to communicate falsely what the king "delighted" in. This is clear from the narratorial comment in the last clause: Saul did not truly delight in one hundred Philistines foreskins, but planned to make David fall by the hand of the Philistines.[7]

In v. 26 the narrator provides the first glimpse into the inner life of David: "When [Saul's] servants reported these things to David, the matter was right in David's eyes to become the king's son-in-law (וישר הדבר בעיני דוד להתחתן במלך)." Tsumura suggests this phrase means that David accepted Saul's terms.[8] However, this is a narratorial description of David's inner thoughts, which on the level of the narrative discourse communicates more than simply an affirmative response. This phrase repeats the identical description of Saul's reaction to Michal's love for David in v. 20: "The matter was right in his eyes" (וישר הדבר בעיניו). Therefore, v. 26 describes David's *point of view* of "becoming the king's son-in-law." Earlier David had asked Saul's servants, "Is it small in your eyes to become the king's son-in-law (הנקלה בעיניכם התחתן במלך)? I am a poor man and little known" (v. 23b). David thus associated his low economic and social status with a "small" view of becoming the king's son-in-law. However, after receiving the offer of v. 25, David's view of becoming the king's son-in-law changed to being "right." This shows that David believed falsely that Saul valued the Philistine foreskins as a bride price, which would change David's economic and social status sufficiently to warrant his marriage to Michal.

Analyzing the Deception

The tactic Saul used to deceive David was a lie. His motive for deceiving was to cause David's death by the hand of the Philistines (vv. 21, 25). A significant feature of this deception is the irony in Saul's first lie. Saul instructed his servants to say to David, "Look, the king delights in you, *and all his servants love you*; now, become the king's son-in-law" (v. 22). The irony in this

---

7. Polzin, *Samuel and the Deuteronomist*, 178.
8. Tsumura, *First Book of Samuel*, 487.

statement is that Saul's servants probably did love David.[9] When Saul had put David over the army, "it was good in the eyes of all the people *and also in the eyes of Saul's servants* (וגם בעיני עבדי שאול)" (v. 5). Moreover, as David continued to succeed, Saul grew more and more afraid of him, "but all Israel and Judah *loved* (אהב) David, because he went out and entered before them" (v. 16). Assuming that Saul's servants were included in "all Israel and Judah," it follows that they too "loved" David.

Since David did not fall by the hand of the Philistines, Saul did not achieve the goal for which he deceived. Rather, David presented the full number of foreskins to Saul and received Michal in marriage. The characterization of Saul in this chapter is wholly negative. Three times the text declares, "YHWH was with David" (vv. 12, 14, 28), while an "evil spirit from God" (רוח אלהים רעה) rushed upon Saul (v. 10) and YHWH turned away from him (v. 12). Furthermore, Saul is repeatedly described as afraid of David (vv. 12, 15, 29), twice because he saw that YHWH was with David (vv. 12, 28–29), and once because he saw David's great success, which the previous verse associates with YHWH's presence with David (vv. 14–15). Since Saul is thus consistently depicted as at odds with YHWH and David, YHWH's man, he is characterized negatively, while David is characterized positively.

Deception J: David's Third Deception of Achish (1 Samuel 28:1–2; 29:1–11)[10]

First Samuel 28:1–2 calls David's feigned loyalty to Achish and true loyalty to Israel into question. Firmly trusting David as his "servant forever" (27:12), Achish called him to accompany the Philistines into battle against

---

9. So also Birch, "First and Second Books of Samuel," 1122.

10. These two passages are treated together since they concern the single event of David's call to join the Philistines in battle against Israel. Although Fokkelman contests that 28:1 introduces a new scene (*Crossing Fates*, 566), the subject matter in 28:1 clearly changes from David's raids against Israel's enemies to David accompanying Achish to battle. Edelman rightly notes that the temporal clause, ויהי בימים ההם, provides a link to the preceding scene while also introducing a new battle scene (*King Saul*, 238; see also Bodner, *1 Samuel*, 291; Tsumura, *First Book of Samuel*, 614). This new battle scene is abruptly interrupted in 28:3 by the circumstantial clause ושמואל מת, which introduces the story of Saul's séance of Samuel at Endor. In 29:1 the narrator resumes the battle scene by the near verbatim repetition of 28:1: ויקבצו פלשתים את־כל־מחניהם. Polzin notes that 28:3–25 interrupts the battle scene much like chapters 29–30 interrupt the prediction of Saul's fate in chapter 28 and its actualization in chapter 31 (*Samuel and the Deuteronomist*, 217). Thus these chapters display an "introduction A–introduction B–conclusion A–conclusion B" pattern to narrate both David and Saul's fates in relation to the Philistines.

Israel (28:1). David responded: "Therefore you will know what your servant does" (v. 2a). Achish interpreted this as an affirmation of loyalty and made David his bodyguard. After an interlude describing Saul's trip to the necromancer of Endor (28:3–25), 1 Samuel 29 picks up the narrative with David and his men marching with Achish to the Philistine camp at Aphek. The Philistine commanders questioned the propriety of having Hebrews in their midst and, despite Achish's apologetic for David, commanded that they be sent back (vv. 3–4a). The commanders' concern was that David would become their adversary during the battle (v. 4b). When Achish reported this to David, the latter protested his innocence and communicated his desire to fight against "the enemies of my lord the king" (v. 8b). Again, Achish interpreted this statement to mean that David wanted to fight against Israel, calling him "as good in my eyes as a messenger of God" (v. 9a). Nevertheless, he commanded David to turn back and not displease the Philistines. The scene ends with David and his men returning to Philistia.

Establishing the Deception

It is clear that Achish understood David's statements in 28:2a and 29:8b to mean that he wanted to fight against Israel. This is demonstrated by Achish's responses of making David his bodyguard (28:2b) and hyperbolically declaring his goodness (29:9a). Some have suggested that Achish was right, that David joined the Philistines sincerely and was willing to help them in their campaign against Saul.[11] This interpretation views David's statements in 28:2a and 29:8b as genuine affirmations of loyalty to Achish and therefore not deceptive. However, several factors suggest David was deceiving Achish through ambiguity, and that he did not intend to fight against Israel. Rather, if he had been allowed to accompany the Philistines, he intended to turn and fight against them.

First, after Achish told David, "You *certainly know* (ידע תדע) that you and your men will go out with me in the army" (v. 28:1b), David responded, "Therefore *you will know* what your servant does" (לכן אתה תדע את אשר־יעשה עבדך, 28:2a). Many recognize the ambiguity in this statement.[12] From Achish's perspective, what David "does" is attack the Negev of Judah (27:10), suggesting to him that David would fight against Israel. However, this un-

11. Jobling, "David and the Philistines," 83; Whitelam, *The Just King*, 105.

12. Shemesh, "David in the Service of King Achish of Gath," 83; Fokkelman, *Crossing Fates*, 567; Edelman, *King Saul*, 239; Gordon, *I & II Samuel*, 193; Evans, *1 and 2 Samuel*, 123; Alter, *David Story*, 171; Bodner, *1 Samuel*, 291; Firth, *1 & 2 Samuel*, 286; Gass, "Achisch von Gat," 223; Bar-Efrat, *Das Erste Buch Samuel*, 350.

derstanding is based on Achish's false belief engendered by David's lies in 1 Sam 27:8–12. In reality, what David "does" is attack Israel's enemies and deceive Achish about it. This is highlighted by the message David prevented his victims from communicating to Achish: "Thus David *did*" (כה־עשה דוד, 27:11). Therefore, although David's statement in 28:2a is ambiguous, the broader context suggests he was using this ambiguity to perpetuate Achish's false belief that he was willing to attack Israel. Simultaneously, to the reader who knows what David truly "does," this statement suggests that Achish will come to know what David does by being attacked by him.[13]

Second, Achish's response to David's ambiguous statement ironically supports the conclusion that David would attack him. In 28:2b Achish said, "Therefore I will make you *keeper of my head* (שמר לראשי) forever." Although Achish was apparently unaware of the implications of this statement, to the reader of 1 Samuel it is deeply ironic. In the past David had kept the head of a Philistine—after beheading Goliath he took his head with him back to Israel (1 Sam 17:54, 57).[14] Furthermore, in 29:4 the Philistine commanders protested David accompanying them in battle for fear that he would decapitate their soldiers: "By what could he please his master? *Is it not by the heads of these men* (הלוא בראשי האנשים ההם)?" This concern of the Philistine commanders sheds ironic light on Achish's promotion of David to "keeper of my head." Just as Achish's servants had correctly identified David in 21:12 [11] by the Israelite song associated with his slaying of Goliath, so the commanders identified him in 29:5 by this same song, suggesting that they also had a right perspective on David's true identity: a killer of Philistines.[15] Conversely, Achish had consistently misunderstood David's nature (21:15–16 [14–15]) and actions (27:10–12). Therefore, that Achish entrusted his head to David, while the commanders feared for the heads of the Philistines, subtly and ironically suggests that if given the opportunity, David would again "keep the heads" of the Philistines, including that of Achish.[16] However, rather than keeping Achish's head for protection, David would keep it the same way he kept the head of Goliath.

Third, in 29:3, when the Philistine commanders asked why the Hebrews were with them, Achish's response is unwittingly ironic and allusive. He initially responded, "Is this not David, servant of Saul (הלוא־זה דוד עבד

---

13. Edelman, *King Saul*, 239; Evans, *1 and 2 Samuel*, 123.

14. Shemesh, "David in the Service of King Achish of Gath," 85; Miscall, *1 Samuel*, 167; Bodner, *1 Samuel*, 292.

15. Shemesh, "David in the Service of King Achish of Gath," 88.

16. Fokkelman, *Crossing Fates*, 567, 574; Edelman, *King Saul*, 256–57; Klein, *1 Samuel*, 277; Miscall, *1 Samuel*, 167; Firth, *1 & 2 Samuel*, 299.

שאול), king of Israel?" The first part of this question, הלוא־זה דוד, occurs twice elsewhere in 1 Samuel, both times on the lips of Philistines recounting the Israelite song celebrating David's slaying of Goliath (21:12 [11]; 29:5). Thus by posing this question, Achish unwittingly alluded to David as a Philistine enemy. In the second part of this question, Achish referred to David as עבד שאול. Achish certainly meant that David was the "former servant of Saul," but his choice of words is again unwittingly ironic[17] and fits with the growing characterization of David as a Philistine enemy. After this question, Achish boasted about David's loyalty to him: "I have not found anything in him from the day of his desertion until this day" (v. 3b). However, this statement only highlights Achish's perpetual ignorance of David's true nature and actions: from the day of his desertion until that day David had been attacking Israel's enemies and deceiving Achish (27:8–11).[18] These ironies and subtleties further suggest that David's allegiance was with Saul and characterize him as a slayer of Philistines rather than their ally.

Fourth, in 29:8b David protested that he should be able to "fight against the enemies of my lord the king." Although many notice that the referent of "my lord the king" is ambiguous and thus *may* refer to Saul,[19] some have rightly noted that it is *likely* that Saul is the referent.[20] Elsewhere David never addressed Achish or referred to him as "my lord the king," but only used this phrase to address Saul in contexts in which he refrained from killing him (1 Sam 24:9 [8]; 26:17, 19; cf. 26:15). This suggests that the true referent of "my lord the king" in 29:8b was Saul, although David used the ambiguity of the locution to his advantage, knowing that his trusting Philistine master would assume it referred to him.

These data cumulatively suggest that David never intended to fight alongside the Philistines against Israel. Rather, he was using deceptive ambiguity to maintain Achish's trust in order to turn against the Philistines and kill them (Achish in particular) in the upcoming battle.

---

17. Shemesh, "David in the Service of King Achish of Gath," 83; Edelman, *King Saul*, 254; Alter, *David Story*, 180; Bodner, *1 Samuel*, 305.

18. Especially v. 11: "And thus was his practice [raiding and lying] *all the days* (כל־הימים) that he lived in the land of the Philistines."

19. Miscall, *1 Samuel*, 175; Alter, *David Story*, 181; Klein, *1 Samuel*, 277; Evans, *1 and 2 Samuel*, 127; Tsumura, *First Book of Samuel*, 636; Firth, *1 & 2 Samuel*, 300.

20. Shemesh, "David in the Service of King Achish of Gath," 83; see also McCarter, "The Apology of David," 501; Edelman, *King Saul*, 260.

Analyzing the Deception

The tactic David used to deceive Achish was ambiguous language. Nothing he said in 28:2a or 29:8 was a lie, but the ambiguity of his locutions set up Achish to interpret them falsely. David's motive for deceiving was to position himself so he could kill Philistines. Both statements to Achish in 28:2a ("Therefore you will know what your servant does") and 29:8b ("Why can't I fight against the enemies of my lord the king?") indicate that he intended to fight the Philistines. A significant feature of this deception is the irony of 29:8b; here David used a title that he repeatedly employed in contexts of refraining from fighting against Saul to make Achish believe he wanted to fight against Saul. David did not achieve the goal for which he deceived since he was dismissed from the Philistine ranks and was unable to kill the Philistines in battle. Although Fokkelman avers that David's release from battle was what he wanted,[21] the text does not state this. On the contrary, David's deceptions in this pericope were not designed to get him out of the battle but to keep him in it, which makes his dismissal in v. 11 a defeat of his goal. The consistent characterization of David as a Philistine killer supports this.

The evaluation of David's deception is unclear. Unlike the prior two episodes with Achish, this account does not end with Achish expressing his false belief, but with a narratorial comment in 29:11 describing David's return to the land of the Philistines. However, like the prior two episodes with Achish, it seems that David is characterized positively here as well. Like Achish's servants in 21:12 [11], in this passage the Philistine commanders recalled the Israelite song commemorating David's victory over Goliath (v. 5; cf. 18:6–7). As we saw in Deception F, although this song had negative connotations from a Philistine perspective, its positive narratological connotations (see 18:3–5) characterize David positively here. Moreover, the observations noted above concerning Achish's unwitting characterization of David as a Philistine enemy and "servant of Saul," in addition to David's covert affirmations of loyalty to Saul and Israel, further support a positive characterization of David.

Deception K: Joab's Deception of Abner (2 Samuel 3:27)

During the civil war between Israel and Judah, Ishbosheth accused Abner of sleeping with Saul's concubine Rizpah (2 Sam 3:7). This angered Abner, who then stated his intention to "transfer the kingdom from the house of

---

21. Fokkelman, *Crossing Fates*, 576.

Saul and establish the throne of David over Israel and Judah, from Dan to Beersheba" (v. 10). Abner asked David to make a covenant with him and traveled down to Hebron to inform David that Israel and Benjamin wanted to make him their king (vv. 17–19). At their meeting, Abner offered to assemble all Israel to make a covenant with David so that he might rule them, and David sent Abner off in peace (v. 21). When Joab arrived, he discovered that Abner had just left, accused Abner of coming to deceive David, and then sent messengers to call Abner back, without David knowing about it (vv. 22–26). When Abner returned to Hebron, Joab took him aside into the city gate as if to speak with him, and there stabbed him in the stomach and killed him "on account of the blood of Asahel his brother" (v. 27).

Establishing the Deception

That Joab killed Abner "on account of the blood of Asahel his brother" suggests that the murder was premeditated;[22] therefore the purpose clause "he took him aside *in order to speak with him* (לדבר אתו)" reflects the pretext for which Joab brought Abner into the gate.[23] The adverb בשלי, which modifies לדבר, is most often translated "privately."[24] Understood this way, Joab deceived Abner into believing falsely that he was bringing him into the city gate to speak with him privately, whereas in reality he was bringing him there to avenge his brother's death. However, Alter translates בשלי as "deceptively," arguing that this *hapax legomenon* could derive from the root שלה ("to delude") rather than שלו ("to be quiet").[25] Both readings cohere with the interpretation of the LXX, which renders בשלי as ἐνεδρεύων ("lying in wait for"). However, Alter's reading is further supported by the Lucianic recension, which modifies ἐνεδρεύων with ἐν παραλογισμῷ ("in deception,

---

22. Although some assert that this final clause of v. 27 is a secondary addition (Haelewyck, "La Mort d'Abner," 185; Stoebe, *Das Zweite Buch Samuelis*, 138; Robinson, *Let Us Be Like the Nations*, 167), without manuscript support this is conjectural. Robinson argues that vv. 27 and 30 contradict one another, since the former attributes the murder to Joab alone while the latter to both Joab and Abishai (*Let Us Be Like the Nations*, 167). However, these verses can be reconciled if Abishai conspired with Joab in retrieving Abner and in orchestrating the murder, even if he did not actually wield the knife.

23. Fokkelman, *Throne and City*, 103; Anderson, *2 Samuel*, 61.

24. So NIV, ESV, NRSV, NASB, NKJV.

25. Alter, *David Story*, 213. Alter's preference for the former root seems to be because of the "small leap of semantic inference" that is required to arrive at "privately" from a verb meaning, "to be quiet" (ibid.).

on false pretenses").²⁶ Nevertheless, no matter how one translates בשלי, it is clear that Joab brought Abner into a secluded area in such a way that caused him to believe falsely that he wanted to speak with him. That Abner went into the gate with Joab shows he was deceived, since he would not have done so if he had suspected that Joab was going to kill him.

Analyzing the Deception

The tactic Joab used to deceive Abner was nonverbal action. Although it is conceivable that he may have lied or used ambiguous language to turn Abner aside into the gate, no statement is reported. Joab's motive for deceiving was to kill Abner as revenge for the death of Asahel at the battle at Gibeon. A significant feature of this deception is that it alludes to that previous episode. At the battle at Gibeon, Asahel chased Abner and would not "turn aside (נטה) to go to the right or to the left" (2:19), even when Abner advised him to "turn aside" (נטה) (2:21). Since Asahel would not do so, in 2:23 Abner struck him (ויכהו) in the stomach (החמש) so that he died (וימת). In 3:27 Joab "turned [Abner] aside" (Hiphil of נטה) into the city gate and struck him (ויכהו) in the stomach (החמש) so that he died (וימת). Thus not only does the narrator state that Abner's killing of Asahel was the reason Joab killed Abner, the description of the deception and murder also alludes to this event.²⁷

Joab achieved the goal for which he deceived by killing Abner. However, although he achieved this immediate goal, he ultimately paid for this deceptive action with his life. On his deathbed David reminded Solomon of what Joab had done:

> And you yourself know what Joab son of Zeruiah did to me, that which he did to the two commanders of Israel's army—to Abner son of Ner and to Amasa son of Jether. He killed them and shed the blood of war during peacetime. . . . Act according to your wisdom, but do not let his gray head go down to the grave in peace (1 Kgs 2:5–6).

Solomon subsequently had Benaiah kill Joab for these deceptive murders (vv. 28–34). The text suggests that the author evaluates Joab's deception negatively. First, the narrator goes to great lengths to distance David from Joab's

---

26. See McCarter, *II Samuel*, 109.

27. So also Polzin, *David and the Deuteronomist*, 37; Fokkelman, *Throne and City*, 103; Alter, *David Story*, 213; Bodner, *David Observed*, 43; Bar-Efrat, *Das Zweite Buch Samuel*, 44.

actions, which presupposes that he viewed them negatively.[28] It is thrice mentioned that Abner left David "in peace" (בשלום, vv. 21, 22, 23); thus David is depicted as having no reason to kill him. After Joab sent messengers to bring Abner back, the narrator highlights David's ignorance by a disjunctive clause (ודוד לא ידע, v. 26). Furthermore, after David cursed Joab, lamented Abner's death, and swore to fast for the remainder of the day, the narrator comments, "All the people and all Israel knew on that day that it was not from the king to kill Abner son of Ner" (v. 37). Thus from the narrator's point of view, David was not involved in Abner's death,[29] and this effort to exonerate David simultaneously indicts Joab and his deceptive action.

28. VanderKam, "Davidic Complicity," 533. Although VanderKam correctly identifies "the zeal of the editor to exonerate David," it does not follow, as he suggests, that this therefore "leads one to suspect him [David] as a conspirator in Abner's death." For a response to skeptical readings of this text, see Gordon, "Covenant and Apology in 2 Samuel 3," 38–46.

29. Bodner employs Bakhtin's concept of "pseudo-objective motivation" to suggest that, despite appearances, vv. 36–37 reflect the people's point of view but not the narrator's (*David Observed*, 38–66). However, his conclusion is grounded in unduly skeptical reading. Bodner's suggestion that Abner is characterized as deceptive in this chapter is based largely on gaps in the story rather than positive evidence. For example, along with McCarter he suggests that because Abner's quotation of divine speech in vv. 17–18 has no "verifiable antecedent" it is best viewed as a "diplomatic invention" (ibid., 51–52). He admits that it coheres with the concerns of the broader Deuteronomistic narrative, but he asserts that in the immediate context this aspect of Abner's speech is inadvertent. However, in these verses Abner also quotes the elders of Israel whom he is addressing without a "verifiable antecedent": "For a while you have been seeking David to be king over you" (v. 17b). Applying the same skepticism to this unverified quotation would suggest that Abner was inventing discourse for the people to whom he was speaking, which is a most implausible situation. Thus principled skepticism of Abner's speech in vv. 17–18 cannot be sustained consistently throughout the narrative. Just as the veracity of his quotation of the elders should be given the benefit of the doubt, so should his repetition of divine speech.

Elsewhere Bodner suggests, "the triple repetition of 'peace' may actually be an example of narrational overstatement to indicate that all is not tranquil" (ibid., 52). Yet he provides no rationale for *why* such an inversion should be read in the text. On the other hand, Fokkelman analyzes vv. 20–25 and identifies four chiasms consisting of "coming, sending, and going" sections, with each chiasm centering on the "going" of Abner (*Throne and City*, 95). The first three chiasms center on the three narratorial comments that Abner "went in peace" (וילך בשלום, vv. 21, 22, 23). However, while the fourth chiasm similarly centers on Abner's going, the speaker is no longer the narrator but Joab, who angrily exclaims, "Now he's gone!" (וילך הלוך, v. 24). Fokkelman notes the disappearance of the element of "peace" here (ibid., 96), which subtly depicts Joab's perspective on Abner's departure as quite different than the narrator's. Therefore, rather than being "narrational overstatement," the narrator's threefold perspective of Abner's peaceful departure is set in sharp contrast against Joab's exclamation and subsequent hostile actions.

Second, the threefold description of peace also emphasizes that the civil war was over; thus Joab's action should be evaluated according to the laws governing peacetime.[30] Second Samuel 2 emphasizes that Abner killed Asahel reluctantly and in self-defense during battle; therefore he should not have been the object of blood vengeance.[31] However, even if Abner had been a candidate for blood vengeance, according to the Torah he could have fled to a city of refuge for protection (Deut 19:1–10), and only if he left the city of refuge could the blood avenger lawfully kill him (Num 35:26–27). Joshua 20 further specifies that such a person should go and "stand at the entrance of the city gate" to find protection (v. 4), and then identifies Hebron as one such city of refuge (v. 7). Thus Joab wrongfully exacted blood vengeance on Abner within the bounds of a city of refuge at the very location where one was assured of protection against such blood vengeance. Joab is therefore depicted as a Torah violator.[32]

Third, the interpretation of Joab's actions in the LXX supports the view that he is depicted as a Torah violator. As mentioned above, the LXX says that Joab took Abner into the gate, "lying in wait for [him]" (ἐνεδρεύων). According to Deut 19:11–13, one who "hates his neighbor, *lies in wait for him* (וארב לו; LXX: καὶ ἐνεδρεύσῃ αὐτόν), and rises up against him and kills him" is not to be protected if he flees to a city of refuge. Therefore, not only did Joab wrongfully kill Abner in a place of protection, but the LXX portrays him doing so in a manner that was not worthy of such protection in a city of refuge. All these factors suggest that the author's evaluation of Joab's deception is negative.

Deception L: Recab and Baanah's Deception of Ishbosheth's Palace Guard (2 Samuel 4:6)

After Abner's death, Saul's son Ishbosheth and all Israel were frightened. Two Beerothite brothers, Recab and Baanah, went to Ishbosheth's house in the middle of the day while he was taking a nap. Pretending to be wheat carriers, they deceptively entered the house, stabbed Ishbosheth in the

---

30. Fokkelman, *Throne and City*, 104. Gunn opines that even though Abner left in peace from David's perspective, Joab may have had a different perspective, having just recently come from a context of battle against Israel (Chapter 2; 3:1) and raiding (3:22) ("David and the Gift of the Kingdom," 17). However, v. 23 explicitly states that Joab was informed (ויגדו ליואב) that Abner had left in peace.

31. Wong, "Ehud and Joab," 408–9; Gordon, *I & II Samuel*, 221; Evans, *1 and 2 Samuel*, 153; Firth, *1 & 2 Samuel*, 350.

32. Bergen, *1, 2 Samuel*, 312; Leithart, *A Son to Me*, 193.

stomach, cut off his head, and carried it overnight to Hebron. Apparently hoping to receive a reward, they presented Ishbosheth's head to David, only to be executed by David for "killing a righteous man in his house, upon his bed" (2 Sam 4:11).

Establishing the Deception

Two different readings of this episode exist, which substantially affect how one understands Recab and Baanah's deceptive activity. First we will look at the reading adopted by the majority of scholars, and then we will survey an alternative reading proposed by Emmanuel Mastéy.

The Majority Reading

The majority of scholars understand Recab and Baanah as entering Ishbosheth's residence with the intent of killing him. However, the MT and LXX record two distinct versions of this episode, with deception occurring only in the former. In the latter version, rather than posing as wheat carriers, Recab and Baanah approached Ishbosheth's[33] house and saw a female doorkeeper cleaning wheat; she became drowsy and fell asleep, enabling them to slip past her unnoticed and thus non-deceptively. Many prefer this version of the account, viewing v. 6 in the MT as "incomprehensible"[34] or "simply not viable."[35] However, Fokkelman prefers the LXX for narratological reasons. He argues that the female doorkeeper of v. 6 serves a complementary role to Mephibosheth's nurse in v. 4; just as one unnamed woman dropped and crippled Mephibosheth, so did another fail to protect Ishbosheth.[36] Although this reading has much to commend it, compelling reasons exist for holding to the literary integrity of the MT.

Only the MT describes the assassins as stabbing Ishbosheth in "the stomach" (החמש).[37] This significant descriptive element links Ishbosheth's murder with both the parenthetical comment about Mephibosheth in v. 4 and the prior murders of Asahel and Abner. Verse 4 says that Mephibosheth was "stricken in the feet" (נכה רגלים) when he was "five years old" (בן־חמש). This not only reveals that Mephibosheth was physically incapable of rul-

---

33. LXX reads Μεμφιβοσθε.
34. Hertzberg, *I & II Samuel*, 264.
35. Alter, *David Story*, 218.
36. Fokkelman, *Throne and City*, 126.
37. Bodner, "Crime Scene Investigation," 16.

ing—thus heightening the drama, since if the frightened Ishbosheth falls, Israel will be without a fitting Saulide ruler—but it does so by lexically linking Mephibosheth's fall with Ishbosheth's: the former was "stricken" (נכה) when he was "five" (חמש), while the latter was "struck" (נכה) in "the stomach" (החמש; literally "the fifth rib").[38]

This mention of החמש also connects Ishbosheth's death with the two previous killings in 2 Samuel 2–3, where both Asahel and Abner were "struck" (נכה) in "the stomach" (החמש),[39] a connection that is absent in the LXX. Fokkelman views the striking of Ishbosheth in "the stomach" in the MT as inspired by these prior two killings, but insists that this "mars the concentration on 'his head' which is quite authentic in this chapter."[40] However, there is no reason that only one physiological description can have narratological significance. Furthermore, this reference to החמש occurs in the midst of a broader set of verbal parallels with Joab's deceptive murder of Abner, which argues for the literary integrity of the MT. First, Joab and Recab and Baanah are all described as "raiding" (גדוד). In 3:22 Joab had just returned "from a raid" (מהגדוד), and in 4:2 Recab and Baanah are identified as "captains of raiding bands" (שרי־גדודים).[41] Second, as Table 3 highlights, there is a significant structural similarity in the MT between the descriptions of the two murders:

---

38. While both vv. 4 and 6 utilize the same root (נכה), I translate the adjective נָכֵה in v. 4 as "stricken" and the verb וַיַּכֻּהוּ in v. 6 as "struck" to reflect the different parts of speech.

39. Polzin, *David and the Deuteronomist*, 50; Firth, *1 & 2 Samuel*, 355, 357. Haelewyck also observes this connection, though he draws the unnecessary conclusion that Recab and Baanah were therefore acting on orders from Joab ("L'assassinat d'Ishbaal," 151).

40. Fokkelman, *Throne and City*, 125.

41. So also Bodner, "Crime Scene Investigation," 6.

Table 3: Structural Comparison of 2 Samuel 3:27 and 2 Samuel 4:6

2 Samuel 3:27	2 Samuel 4:6
"Joab turned him aside *into the midst* (אל־תוך) of the gate *to speak with him deceptively* (לדבר אתו בשלי), and he *struck him* (ויכהו) there in *the stomach* (החמש), and he died on account of Asahel *his brother* (אחיו)."	"They entered *to the midst* (עד־תוך) of the house *carrying wheat* (לקחי חטים), and they *struck him* (ויכהו) in *the stomach* (החמש), and Recab and Baanah *his brother* (אחיו) escaped."

Both accounts describe (1) a murder that occurred in the "midst" of a physical structure, (2) followed by a description of the deceptive tactic by which the murder was perpetrated, (3) followed by a description of the murderer "striking" the victim in "the stomach," and (4) end with the mention of a "brother." These parallels of theme and vocabulary suggest that, rather than being "incomprehensible" or "simply not viable," the narrator of MT is inviting the reader to read 2 Sam 4:6 in light of the earlier murder.[42] Third, although some see the redundancy of v. 7 in the MT as evidence that multiple accounts have been conflated,[43] others rightly observe that such repetition in biblical narrative is normal.[44] Moreover, the reprise of v. 7 also corresponds to the murder of Abner, since 3:30 is a reprise of Abner's murder that was first reported in 3:27.

Lastly, Bodner suggests that the two sets of brothers in 2 Samuel 3–4 committed their murders for parallel twofold reasons.[45] In chapter 3 the narrator reports that Joab and Abishai murdered Abner because he had killed Asahel (vv. 27, 30). It is also likely that Joab was motivated to kill Abner because he posed a threat to his position as commander of David's army. After all, Joab would later "strike" (נכה) Amasa in "the stomach" (החמש) after David made Amasa commander of the army in his place (2 Sam 20:10;

---

42. Youngblood also notes several of these parallels ("1, 2 Samuel," 845).

43. Haelewyck, "L'assassinat d'Ishbaal," 149; Caquot and de Robert, *Les Livres de Samuel*, 396.

44. Bergen, *1, 2 Samuel*, 316, n. 23; Cartledge, *1 & 2 Samuel*, 403.

45. Bodner, "Crime Scene Investigation," 4–7.

cf. 19:14).[46] Thus two motives plausibly explain the murder of Abner: revenge for a past killing and politico-military self-advancement. These two motives are also evident in Recab and Baanah's murder of Ishbosheth. The narrator provides the patrilineage of these brothers, identifying them as "sons of Rimmon, the Beerothite, from the Benjaminites (for Beeroth is considered part of Benjamin)" (2 Sam 4:2). The Beerothites were of Gibeonite stock and thus had a peace treaty with Israel (see Josh 9:17–18), yet Saul had put the Gibeonites to death in an attempt to annihilate them (2 Sam 21:1–2). Since 4:3 mentions that "the Beerothites had *fled* (ברח) to Gittaim," it is plausible that Saul's Gibeonite persecution was the cause of this flight. Therefore some conclude that Recab and Baanah were motivated by blood vengeance against Saul for his slaughter of their kinsmen.[47] Supporting this is the narrator's omission of Ishbosheth's name in the opening verses where he gives the patrilineage of Recab and Baanah. Instead, he refers to him twice as the "son of Saul" (vv. 1–2), emphasizing his Saulide patrilineage. Further supporting this is the narrator's repetition of the epithet, "the sons of Rimmon the Beerothite," when describing Recab and Baanah entering Ishbosheth's house (v. 5). When David later asked the Gibeonites what he could do to make amends for Saul's persecution, they demanded the death of seven of Saul's male descendents (2 Sam 21:5–6), which confirms that these victims of Saul's persecution wanted vengeance against his offspring. Collectively these data make it likely that one of Recab and Baanah's motives for killing Ishbosheth was blood vengeance for Saul's prior killing of their Gibeonite kinsmen.

Recab and Baanah also seem to have been motivated by the prospect of a reward from David, since they traveled all night to present Ishbosheth's head to him. David implied this when he referred to what he "gave" (נתן) to the Amalekite for his "good news" (v. 10). Since Recab and Baanah were captains of raiding bands, it appears that the reward they expected for slaying David's "enemy" (v. 8) was some sort of politico-military advancement in David's growing army. Therefore Recab and Baanah seem to have had the same two motives as Joab and Abishai.[48] All these parallels suggest that the two sons of Rimmon and their deception are depicted like the two sons of Zeruiah and their deception, reinforcing on narratological grounds the

---

46. Shemesh, "Measure for Measure in the David Stories," 96, n. 25; see also Birch, "First and Second Books of Samuel," 1225.

47. Bodner, "Crime Scene Investigation," 6–7; Leithart, *A Son to Me*, 197; Caquot and de Robert, *Les Livres de Samuel*, 395.

48. Bodner, "Crime Scene Investigation," 7.

conclusion that, though grammatically difficult, the MT is comprehensible and has its own literary integrity.[49]

Recab and Baanah deceived Ishbosheth's household into believing falsely that they were entering the house as wheat carriers. The rendering of לקחי חטים in most translations implies that Recab and Baanah were not actually carrying wheat, but were acting "as if" they were getting wheat.[50] However, some doubt that the participle לקחי could connote simply the intention to take wheat.[51] Firth suggests they were actually gathering wheat.[52] Either way, by their actions they engendered the false belief that "wheat carrying" was their *purpose* for entering the premises, which enabled them to enter without suspicion. That they entered the house without any opposition and murdered Ishbosheth is evidence of their deception's success.

Mastéy's Reading

In a fascinating essay, Emmanuel Mastéy offers an alternative reading of this text.[53] He argues that since the pronoun הֵנָּה is feminine, it cannot be the subject of v. 6, and thus הנה should either be understood as the adverb "here" (also vocalized as הֵנָּה; e.g., Gen 45:8) or be revocalized as הִנֵּה, "behold" (with LXX). He further suggests that לקחי חטים is best understood substantivally ("robbers of grain") as the subject of the verbs באו and ויכהו. This leads him to translate v. 6 as follows:

> And behold, there were grain robbers that had come into the midst of the house, and they struck Ish-Bosheth in the belly, and Rechab and Baanah [who had just arrived, as we were told at the end of the previous verse] turned around and fled.[54]

On this reading, Recab and Baanah did not enter Ishbosheth's palace deceptively. Mastéy argues that the verbal tenses in v. 6 support this as a pluperfect clause; the *qatal* באו interrupts the main storyline to introduce the past action of the robbers, and the *qatal* נמלטו returns the action to the point when Recab and Baanah encountered the robbers and fled.[55] Verse 7

---

49. So also Firth, *1 & 2 Samuel*, 354.

50. "as if to get some wheat" (NIV); "as if to get wheat" (NASB, ESV); "as though to take wheat" (NRSV, NKJV).

51. Anderson, *2 Samuel*, 68; Firth, *1 & 2 Samuel*, 354.

52. Ibid., 357.

53. Mastéy, "A Linguistic Inquiry," 82–103.

54. Ibid., 94.

55. Ibid., 96.

is thus not redundant to v. 6, but describes Recab and Baanah returning to Ishbosheth's house, giving him the *coup de grâce*, and taking his head as they left. According to Mastéy, Recab and Baanah's original intent in entering Ishbosheth's residence was not to kill him but to see how they could take advantage of the power vacuum that existed after Abner's death. However, after seeing Ishbosheth's mortal situation, they changed their plan, killed him, and brought his head to David. This suggests that the murder was not deceptive, but that Recab and Baanah deceived David into believing falsely that they had intentionally killed Ishbosheth out of allegiance to him.[56] If this reading is correct, this episode would belong in chapter 6, "Deception Intended to Benefit the Deceiver," since Recab and Baanah did not deceive in order to cause death or harm.

However, although Mastéy's reading is grammatically plausible, it does not seem preferable narratologically. On this reading, the structural similarity between 2 Sam 3:27 and 4:6 is lost, since the latter verse does not describe a deceptive murder. Moreover, since this reading suggests that Recab and Baanah did not enter Ishbosheth's house for blood vengeance, it does not account for the repeated epithets of Ishbosheth as "Saul's son" (vv. 1–2) and Recab and Baanah as "the sons of Rimmon the Beerothite" (vv. 2, 5). Although the הנה of v. 6 is difficult, it can be interpreted adverbially, and thus our analysis will follow the majority reading.[57]

Analyzing the Deception

The tactic Recab and Baanah used to deceive Ishbosheth's palace guard was nonverbal action. Their motive was to gain access to Ishbosheth so they could kill him. As mentioned above, a significant feature of this deception is that it recalls Joab's deceptive murder of Abner. Recab and Baanah achieved the goal for which they deceived by murdering Ishbosheth. However, although they achieved this immediate goal, they were subsequently

---

56. Ibid., 100.

57. Even if one adopted Mastéy's reading, it would not affect the overall conclusions of the present study. According to Mastéy, Recab and Baanah's deception was analogous to the Amalekite's deception in 2 Samuel 1 ("A Linguistic Inquiry," 100). In the latter episode, the Amalekite caused David to believe falsely that he had finished off Saul with the hope that he would receive a reward from David (see Deception X in chapter 6). On Mastéy's reading, in the present passage Recab and Baanah caused David to believe falsely that they had assassinated Ishbosheth "out of pro-Davidic ideological motives" (ibid.), seemingly for the similar motive of a reward (see 2 Sam 4:9–11). Thus in both cases the deceivers acted to benefit themselves, and in both cases they received negative consequences and a negative evaluation.

condemned and killed by David for this act (v. 12). By depicting this deception like Joab's deceptive murder of Abner, the author seems to evaluate it negatively. David's evaluation of their actions in 4:11, where he refers to Ishbosheth as a "righteous man" (איש־צדיק) and to Recab and Baanah as "wicked men" (אנשים רשעים), supports this negative evaluation.

Deception M: David's Deception of Uriah (2 Samuel 11:7, 14–15)

In 2 Samuel 11 David sent Joab and the Israelite army to besiege the Ammonites, while he remained in Jerusalem. After sleeping with and impregnating Bathsheba, the wife of one of his soldiers, Uriah the Hittite, David brought Uriah back to Jerusalem on the pretext of asking for a battle update (v. 7). He then suggested that Uriah spend the night at home, with the apparent hope that Uriah would sleep with Bathsheba and thus obscure David's paternity. However, Uriah slept at the palace gate. When David asked him why he did not go home, Uriah answered that his solidarity with his fellow soldiers prohibited him from enjoying domestic pleasures while his comrades were camped in the open field. David then got Uriah drunk, evidently in order to reduce his inhibitions, but Uriah again refused to go home. The next day David sent a letter to Joab by Uriah's hand, instructing Joab to arrange for Uriah to die on the battlefield, a charge that Joab fulfilled.

Establishing the Deception

Although Hagan summarizes the motif of deception in 2 Samuel 11–12 as "sin by deception in ch. 11 and reconciliation by counter-deception in ch. 12,"[58] he never specifically identifies a deception in chapter 11. He correctly notes that in vv. 8–13 David thrice "attempts to bring about this deception" that Uriah fathered the expected child,[59] but an attempted deception that fails is no deception at all. Therefore it is unclear to what action Hagan refers in his conclusion when he describes the deception of Uriah that made him like a "sheep led to slaughter."[60] However, despite the ambiguity in Hagan's study, it is clear that David deceived Uriah into believing falsely that the purpose of his trip from Rabbah to Jerusalem was to serve as a military courier.[61]

---

58. Hagan, "Deception as Motif," 303.

59. Ibid., 304.

60. Ibid., 323.

61. Ackroyd, *Second Book of Samuel*, 101; McCarter, *II Samuel*, 288; Cartledge,

In v. 7 the narrator says, "When Uriah came to him, David asked how Joab and the people fared, and how the war was going" (NRSV). Against Sternberg, who sees David here chatting with Uriah "politely but to no purpose,"[62] David's questions in v. 7 served the critical and deceptive function of providing Uriah with a false reason for his callback: to update the king on the battle.[63] By thus deceiving Uriah upon his arrival, David made it natural for him to carry a message back to Joab in v. 14, which would be the cause of Uriah's demise.

For David to sustain this deception throughout Uriah's stay, the latter must have remained ignorant of David's affair with Bathsheba. If Uriah acquired such knowledge he would have plausibly concluded that courier work was not the true reason David brought him back, and interpreters have posited a variety of arguments that this was in fact the case. Some speculate that Uriah learned about the affair from the guards with whom he spent the night in vv. 9 and 13.[64] George Nicol further conjectures that David's disposition may have revealed the true situation.[65] However, these speculations are based on gaps in the narrative and cannot be substantiated.

David Marcus concludes that Uriah knew about the affair and that his refusal to go home was a "brilliant coup" against David's attempt to pin the paternity on him.[66] However, Marcus bases this reading on an *a priori* view that deception functions according to a measure-for-measure principle[67] rather than an analysis of Uriah's actual words and actions. Marcus supports this reading by claiming that Uriah's statement in v. 11 was intended to be transparent, but he concludes this simply because "Uriah's choice of words deal [sic] a stinging rebuke to the man who has actually been 'eating, drinking, and sleeping with [his] wife.'"[68] However, based on the sexual implications of David's instruction in v. 8 ("Go down to your house and wash your

---

1 & 2 Samuel, 501; Firth, *1 & 2 Samuel*, 419–20.

62. Sternberg, *Poetics of Biblical Narrative*, 201.

63. Yee, "Fraught with Background," 248; Arnold, *1 & 2 Samuel*, 528; Bar-Efrat, *Das Zweite Buch Samuel*, 108.

64. Sternberg, *Poetics of Biblical Narrative*, 202; Garsiel, "Story of David and Bathsheba," 257; Nicol, "David, Abigail, and Bathsheba," 141; Prouser, "Phenomenology of the Lie," 104.

65. Nicol, "David, Abigail, and Bathsheba," 141.

66. Marcus, "David the Deceiver," 166.

67. Marcus writes, "Recognizing the importance of retributive deception in the David stories *inclines one* to interpret the actions of Uriah in a certain direction" (ibid.,165 [emphasis mine]).

68. Ibid., 166.

feet" [רד לביתך ורחץ רגליך]),[69] David's question in v. 10 ("Why did you not go down to your house?" [מדוע לא־ירדת אל־ביתך]) was implicitly asking why Uriah did not go down *and have sex*. Therefore Uriah's response in v. 11 was a simple decline of such pleasure and contextually provides no hint that he was aware of the affair. Furthermore, the text nowhere records David eating and drinking with Bathsheba, which militates against Marcus's claim that Uriah's words intimated that David had done so.

Marcus and others also claim that, despite Uriah's statement, there was no ban on sex during battle, which they use to support their contention that Uriah knew about the affair and was not being forthright.[70] However, as Anderson observes, Deut 23:11 states that if a soldier encamped against enemies had a nocturnal emission, he was unclean and had to depart the camp.[71] Since the emission of semen made a man unclean (Lev 15:16), sexual intercourse similarly brought uncleanness (Lev 15:18) and thus would have logically applied to encamped soldiers. First Samuel 21:6 [5] corroborates this by emphasizing that David's soldiers abstained from sex while on duty.[72] This supports the validity of Uriah's claim that sexual abstinence for cultic-military propriety was the reason he refrained from going home.

Sternberg describes Uriah's pious behavior as "strange and unrealistic" and "*too* heroic to be true."[73] However, his skepticism that someone could not hold religious convictions above physical desires is unwarranted. Moreover, both Sternberg and Nicol believe that Uriah knew about the affair and thus suspected the letter, but still accepted his fate "with an awe-inspiring dignity,"[74] demonstrating a "loyalty married to a stern and uncompromising morality."[75] However, if Uriah could be so dignified and loyal to David that

---

69. Most understand David's instruction that Uriah go down and "wash his feet" as a euphemism for sex, since רגלים can refer to the male reproductive organ (McCarter, *II Samuel*, 286; Brueggemann, *First and Second Samuel*, 274; Arnold, *1 & 2 Samuel*, 501; Birch, "First and Second Books of Samuel," 1286; Nicol, "David, Abigail, and Bathsheba," 138; Yee, "Fraught with Background," 245; Firth, "David and Uriah," 313, 317–18; *contra* Garsiel, "Story of David and Bathsheba," 257).

70. Marcus, "David the Deceiver," 166; Garsiel, "Story of David and Bathsheba," 257; Nicol, "David, Abigail, and Bathsheba," 140–41.

71. Anderson, *2 Samuel*, 154.

72. Admittedly, in this verse David testified that his soldiers abstained from sex on missions in the midst of deceiving Ahimelech about being on a mission from Saul (see Deception V). However, the fact that Ahimelech agreed to give David holy bread after hearing this (1 Sam 21:7 [6]) shows that he viewed this practice of sexual abstinence during military excursions as reasonable.

73. Sternberg, *Poetics of Biblical Narrative*, 206 (emphasis his).

74. Ibid.

75. Nicol, "David, Abigail, and Bathsheba," 142.

he would go to his grave without publicizing what David had done, it is not unrealistic that he could demonstrate such loyalty to YHWH and his comrades by adhering to Israel's military code of conduct. Neither Sternberg nor Nicol explains why the former type of loyalty is more likely than the latter. Against their interpretation, Uriah's actions and reported speech characterize him as upright and loyal to YHWH and his fellow soldiers[76] and do not indicate that he was aware of the affair. Furthermore, as Richard G. Smith observes, Bathsheba's ritual bathing similarly characterizes her as religiously pious,[77] portraying the two as a faithful Yahwistic couple. Collectively this supports the view that Uriah knew nothing about the affair and believed falsely that he had been brought to Jerusalem to convey information between the king and Joab. That he transmitted David's letter to Joab without any indication of suspicion shows that the deception succeeded.

Analyzing the Deception

The tactics David used to deceive Uriah were misleading requests and actions. David did not lie to Uriah by asking him about the welfare of the people and the battle, but his questions created the false impression that Uriah was called back to give a battle update. David reinforced this initial false impression when he entrusted Uriah with a message for Joab in v. 14. David's initial motive for deceiving was to get Uriah back to Jerusalem in the hopes that he would sleep with his wife and thus obscure David's paternity.[78] When this effort failed, David utilized Uriah's false belief that he was functioning as a courier and sent his death warrant back to Joab by his own hand; thus David's final motive in deceiving Uriah was to have him killed.

76. In v. 11 Uriah first mentioned concern for "the ark," which reveals his religious loyalty, and then "Israel and Judah . . . my master Joab, and the servants of my master," which reveals his national-military loyalty. See Fokkelman, *King David*, 54, 56; Firth, "David and Uriah," 313; Van der Bergh, "Narratological Analysis of Time," 509; Halpern, *David's Secret Demons*, 36; Van Seters, *Biblical Saga*, 297.

77. Smith, *Fate of Justice and Righteousness*, 124.

78. This is the traditional understanding of David's intentions in vv. 6–13 (see e.g., Fischer, "David und Batseba," 51; Marcus, "David the Deceiver," 165; Hertzberg, *I & II Samuel*, 310; Robinson, *Let Us Be Like the Nations*, 208). However, Firth contends that when 2 Samuel 11 is read with the relevant prolepses and analepses in the books of Samuel, the sexual taking of a woman is an attack on her husband; therefore by taking Bathsheba, David was attacking Uriah, possibly because he saw him as a threat. If sex during war was a crime, which Firth affirms, then David's recall of Uriah and encouragement for him to sleep with Bathsheba was an attempt to entrap him into a capital offense (Firth, "David and Uriah," 310–28). On this interpretation, David's initial motive for deceiving Uriah in v. 7 was to kill him.

David achieved the goal for which he deceived, demonstrated by the fact that Uriah carried the death warrant back to Joab and was subsequently killed in battle. However, although David achieved this immediate goal, he failed in his ultimate goal of obscuring his paternity, since YHWH sent Nathan to confront him and expose his sin. David experienced negative consequences when YHWH put to death his son because of his offense "by this thing" (בדבר הזה, 12:14), which likely referred to David's deceptive murder (see below).

The author's evaluation of David's deception is negative. In v. 27b the narrator says explicitly, "But the thing that David did was evil in the eyes of YHWH" (וירע הדבר אשר־עשה דוד בעיני יהוה). Although the referent of "the thing" (הדבר) likely includes the adultery, several factors suggest that David's deceptive murder of Uriah is primarily in view. First, this divine evaluation alludes to and contrasts with David's encouragement to Joab, "Let not *this thing* be evil in your eyes" (אל־ירע בעיניך את־הדבר הזה).[79] Since David was responding to Joab's message, "Uriah the Hittite is dead" (v. 24b), the referent of "this thing" in v. 25 is Uriah's death. Since v. 27b alludes to v. 25, YHWH's negative evaluation of "the thing that David did" probably referred to Uriah's murder as well. Second, the distribution of narrative time focuses on David's interactions with Uriah, which suggests that his death and the events leading up to it (i.e., the deception and attempted deceptions) are the author's primary concern.[80] Third, David's murder of Uriah was primary in Nathan's prophetic rebuke of him.[81] This is explicit in 12:9, where Nathan says:

> Why did you despise the word of YHWH by doing *evil in his eyes* (הרע בעינו)?
> Uriah the Hittite you struck down (את אוריה החתי הכית) with the sword,
> and his wife you took (ואת־אשתו לקחת) for yourself as a wife,
> and him you killed (ואתו הרגת) by the sword of the Ammonites.

Here Nathan defined what was evil in YHWH's eyes by twice referencing Uriah's murder, both times fronting Uriah as the object for emphasis. He referred to the adultery only once, and even then the grievance was still

---

79. Fischer, "David und Batseba," 56; Brueggemann, *David's Truth*, 57; Bar-Efrat, *Das Zweite Buch Samuel*, 113.

80. Bar-Efrat, "Some Observations," 173; Van der Bergh, "Narratological Analysis of Time," 506, 510; Stoebe, "David und Uria," 388.

81. So also Stone, *Sex, Honor, and Power*, 98.

described in relation to Uriah ("his wife [ואת־אשתו] you took"). Therefore the author's evaluation of David's deception is negative.[82]

Deception N: Amnon's Deception of David and Tamar (2 Samuel 13:1–22)

Second Samuel 13:1 describes Amnon as in love with his beautiful half-sister, Tamar. However, Amnon was frustrated because he was unable "to do anything to her" (v. 2), since she was a reputable young woman (בתולה) and therefore likely chaperoned constantly.[83] Amnon's cousin Jonadab suggested that he pretend to be sick and ask David to send for Tamar so she might feed him. Amnon complied, and believing falsely that Amnon was ill, David sent Tamar to his house, where she prepared food for him. Amnon refused to eat it, sent everyone out except Tamar, and then asked her to come into his bedroom and feed him. When Tamar came to Amnon, he seized her and demanded that she have sex with him. Tamar refused, so Amnon raped her and ejected her from the house. Tamar tore her robe, which symbolized her reputable status, and fled to the house of Absalom, her full brother, to live there as a "desolate woman" (v. 20).

Establishing the Deception

Amnon deceived both David and Tamar into believing falsely that he was so sick that he needed special food for nourishment. Although the narrator describes Amnon as "sick" (להתחלות) on account of Tamar (v. 2), Jonadab's advice ("Lie on your bed and [pretend to] *be sick*" [שכב על־משכבך והתחל], v. 5) was for Amnon to "play up this condition by pretending to be dangerously ill and in need of special ministrations."[84] This is supported by Jonadab's instruction that Amnon request that Tamar make him הבריה, which likely referred to food designed to bring special nourishment and healing to a sick or weak person.[85] However, when Amnon spoke to David, rather than using the term הבריה he substituted לבבות—variously translated as "heart-

---

82. *Contra* Prouser ("Phenomenology of the Lie," 104), who sees ambiguity in the author's evaluation of David because he later repented in chapter 12. However, repentance does not imply that the sin that precipitated that repentance or the deception that facilitated that sin should be reevaluated.

83. Josephus, *Ant.*, 7.8.1; Trible, *Texts of Terror*, 38.

84. Alter, *David Story*, 266. See also Ridout, "The Rape of Tamar," 78.

85. Bledstein, "Habbiryâ," 15–31; Bar-Efrat, *Narrative Art in the Bible*, 254; Alter, *David Story*, 266.

shaped cakes,"[86] "heart-shaped dumplings,"[87] "hearty dumplings,"[88] "heart-cakes,"[89] "heart loaves"[90]—along with the cognate verb לבב (v. 6). Although other connotations may be present in this repeated use of the root לבב (see below), David could have understood this as a request for "enheartening" or "invigorating" food,[91] a connotation that overlaps semantically with הבריה. That David understood Amnon's request this way is supported by his instruction to Tamar, "Go to the house of Amnon your brother and make *healing food* (הבריה) for him" (v. 7).

That David sent Tamar to Amnon's house to make him הבריה shows that he was deceived into believing that Amnon was sick. Tamar's obedience to David's instructions shows that she was also deceived, as does the circumstantial clause at the end of v. 8: "So Tamar went to the house of Amnon her brother. *And he was lying down* (והוא שכב)." Since the narrator has already stated that Amnon was lying down (וישכב אמנון, v. 6), it is best to understand the circumstantial clause in v. 8, which is interjected among verbal clauses with Tamar as the subject, as a description of *Tamar's point of view* when she entered the house.[92] Tamar entered, saw Amnon lying on his bed, and then prepared the healing food for him. This indicates that she falsely believed Amnon to be as sick as he claimed.

Against this interpretation, Pamela Tamarkin Reis argues that rather than being ignorant of Amnon's intentions, Tamar complied in arranging their private meeting and thus their subsequent sex was consensual.[93] According to Reis, since the narrator describes Tamar as making "heart-loaves" (לבבות, v. 8), even though David had instructed her to make "healing food" (הבריה, v. 7), this reveals that Tamar was seeking to arouse Amnon. However, as we have seen, the "invigorating" connotation of ותלבב ... את־הלבבות overlaps with הבריה and therefore the narrator's use of this phrase need not suggest that Tamar was purposefully arousing Amnon. Although the Piel of לבב can have sexual overtones (cf. Song 4:9),[94] it is more consistent nar-

---

86. Smith, *Samuel*, 328; *IBHS*, 412.
87. Alter, *David Story*, 267.
88. McCarter, *II Samuel*, 314.
89. Reis, "Cupidity and Stupidity," 46.
90. Bledstein, *Habbiryâ*, 16.
91. McCarter, *II Samuel*, 322; Bledstein, *Habbiryâ*, 18. See also Bar-Efrat, *Das Zweite Buch Samuel*, 128.
92. Conroy, *Absalom Absalom*, 22; Fokkelman, *King David*, 105.
93. Reis, "Cupidity and Stupidity," 47–49.
94. Fokkelman, *King David*, 106; McCarter, *II Samuel*, 322; Anderson, *2 Samuel*, 174.

ratologically to recognize its polysemy and conclude that different hearers recognized different meanings in its two occurrences in this narrative.

When Amnon asked David to send Tamar to "make" (לבב) him some "heart-loaves" (לבבות, v. 6), based on his sickly appearance David heard the invigorating connotation rather than the sexual one, which he demonstrated by transmitting Amnon's request as being for הבריה (v. 7). However, having been informed of Amnon's "love" for Tamar (v. 1) and the feigned nature of his sickness (v. 5), the reader is equipped to hear the sexual connotation implicit in Amnon's request. Similarly, since David instructed Tamar to make הבריה (v. 7), when the narrator reports that Tamar "made" (לבב) Amnon the "heart-loaves" (לבבות, v. 8), it is most consistent narratologically that Tamar thought she was making "invigorating food" (i.e., the meaning that overlaps with הבריה). However, the narrator utilizes the polysemy of the phrase to communicate something more to the reader. Equipped with the knowledge of Amnon's true feelings of which Tamar was ignorant, the reader once again hears the sexual connotation implicit in the narrator's description. Although Tamar falsely believed she was making "invigorating food," in reality she was inadvertently arousing him. Amnon perpetuated this deception by asking Tamar to bring the "healing food" (הבריה) into the bedroom (v. 10). That she complied with this request shows that the deception succeeded.

Analyzing the Deception

The tactics Amnon used to deceive David and Tamar were nonverbal actions (lying in bed as if sick) and misleading requests. Although Amnon initially attempted to solicit Tamar's consent for intercourse (v. 11), his subsequent rape revealed that his intention for the deception was to have sex with her one way or another. Since the Torah prohibited sexual intercourse with one's half-sister (Lev 18:9, 11; 20:17; Deut 27:22), Amnon's desire and subsequent actions should be viewed negatively.

Many argue that marriage between half-siblings was not prohibited at this time, and therefore this was a case of rape rather than incest. Usually this is based on Tamar's statement in v. 13 that David would not refuse giving her to Amnon[95] or on the precedent of Abraham and Sarah being half-siblings (Gen 20:12).[96] Regarding the first argument, Tamar's appeal does not show that half-sibling marriage was approved during this time;

---

95. Gressmann, "The Oldest History Writing in Israel," 31; Bar-Efrat, *Narrative Art in the Bible*, 239–40; Caquot and de Robert, *Les Livres de Samuel*, 496.

96. Hertzberg, *I & II Samuel*, 322; Mauchline, *1 and 2 Samuel*, 260; Anderson, *2 Samuel*, 172; Fokkelman, *King David*, 103.

it merely reflects *her belief* that David would agree to their marriage[97] or was a desperate attempt to buy time.[98] Regarding the second argument, the existence of half-sibling marriage during the patriarchal period does not indicate that half-sibling marriage was authorized after the promulgation of the Sinai covenant, which prohibited such unions. Therefore, from a biblical-theological standpoint, Amnon's desire to have sex with Tamar was incestuous and prohibited. The repeated familial labels "brother" and "sister" throughout the narrative reinforce this interpretation.[99]

A significant feature of this deception is the hint of the truth in Amnon's request for לבבות (v. 6). As already noted, Amnon's use of לבבות with the cognate verb introduced a sexual connotation that was not present in Jonadab's suggested use of הבריה and thus hinted at his intentions.[100] Amnon achieved the goal for which he deceived by arranging the private meeting with Tamar and having sex with her. However, although he achieved this immediate goal, two years later Absalom killed him for it (vv. 23–29). The characterization of Amnon in this narrative is negative. Structurally, the narrative forms a chiasm that centers on vv. 14b–15a, which describe the rape itself and Amnon's subsequent intense hatred.[101] In v. 14b the succession of verbs suggests a violent altercation: "He overpowered her and oppressed her and laid her" (ויחזק ממנה ויענה וישכב אתה). The transitive use of the verb שכב—"he laid her" (וישכב אתה)—depicts the act as a violent sexual violation, in contrast to the regular prepositional construction, "he lay *with* her."[102]

In addition to Amnon's rape of Tamar being incestuous, he further violated the Torah after the rape by sending her away. The Torah required a man who had sex with a reputable young woman (בתולה) to pay a bride price and marry her; he could not send her away (לא־יוכל שלחה, Deut 22:28–29; see also Exod 22:15-16). However, after raping Tamar, Amnon violated this law by commanding his servant, "Send this [woman] away from me" (שלחו־נא

---

97. Reis, "Cupidity and Stupidity," 50.

98. Alter, *David Story*, 268.

99. Propp, "Kinship in 2 Samuel 13," 43; Smith, "Discourse Structure," 26; McCarter, *II Samuel*, 328; Smith, *Fate of Justice and Righteousness*, 149.

100. So also Ackerman, "Knowing Good and Evil," 45; Fokkelman, *King David*, 105; Bar-Efrat, *Narrative Art in the Bible*, 254; Baldwin, *1 & 2 Samuel*, 248; Youngblood, "1, 2 Samuel," 959; Bledstein, *Habbiryâ*, 26; van Dijk-Hemmes, "Tamar and the Limits of Patriarchy," 73.

101. See Ridout, "The Rape of Tamar," 81; Fokkelman, *King David*, 100.

102. Gray, "Amnon: A Chip off the Old Block?" 48; Driver, *Samuel*, 230; Fokkelman, *King David*, 105; Sternberg, *Poetics of Biblical Narrative*, 446; Bar-Efrat, *Narrative Art in the Bible*, 265; Trible, *Texts of Terror*, 46; Caquot and de Robert, *Les Livres de Samuel*, 498; Alter, *David Story*, 269.

את־זאת מעלי, v. 17b). Furthermore, the narrator highlights Tamar's violated status and thus the heinous nature of Amnon's actions by describing her long robe (כתנת פסים) that symbolized her status as a "reputable daughter of the king" (v. 18a) between Amnon's command that his servant eject her (v. 17b) and the servant's ejection of her (v. 18b).[103] For these reasons, the characterization of Amnon in this narrative is negative.

Deception O: Absalom's Deception of David and Amnon (2 Samuel 13:23–39)

Two years after Amnon raped Tamar, Absalom hosted a sheep-shearing festival and asked David and his servants to attend (v. 24). Despite Absalom's urging, David refused, so Absalom requested that Amnon attend instead. After more urging, David finally agreed and sent Amnon and the rest of his sons. Absalom then told his servants that when Amnon became intoxicated, at his command they should strike him down (v. 28). The murder went according to plan, and Absalom fled to Geshur, where his maternal grandfather was king (cf. 2 Sam 3:3), staying there for three years (vv. 37–38).

Establishing the Deception

Absalom deceived David (and Amnon) into believing falsely that he wanted Amnon to celebrate with him at the sheep-shearing festival in David's place, when in reality he wanted to kill him. That Absalom's primary goal in this narrative was to kill Amnon is evident from two details. First, the temporal notice in v. 23 (ויהי לשנתים ימים) depicts the events that follow as a continuation of the narrative of Amnon's rape of Tamar. By ending the prior scene with a description of Absalom's hatred of Amnon (v. 22), the narrator has set up the present scene as Absalom's hateful response to Amnon. Second, the description of Absalom inviting "all the sons of the king" (כל־בני המלך) in v. 23 is best viewed as a proleptic summary of the ensuing action rather than as preceding Absalom's invitation of David in v. 24.[104] This coheres with the first datum and in conjunction with it suggests that Absalom's primary goal was to get the princes—particularly Amnon—away from Jerusalem. Therefore, Amnon's initial invitation of David was merely a strategic step in the process rather than his primary goal. This argues against the view that

---

103. Hammond, "Michal, Tamar, Abigail," 66; Bar-Efrat, *Narrative Art in the Bible*, 269–70.

104. So also Fokkelman, *King David*, 115.

Absalom primarily wanted David to attend, and that his request for Amnon was secondary to his original plan.[105]

By initially requesting David and his servants to attend, Absalom strategically asked for too much (see David's response in v. 25: "Let not *all of us* go" [אל־נא נלך כלנו]) and thus (1) put David in a position where he was more likely to comply with a lesser request,[106] and (2) reduced suspicion concerning his request for Amnon specifically.[107] After David declined, Absalom said, "If not, let Amnon my brother go with us" (v. 26a). This created the false impression that Absalom was requesting Amnon to attend the festival in place of David, possibly because as the eldest son Amnon would have been regarded as the king's representative in his absence.[108] Furthermore, when Absalom requested Amnon he referred to him as "my brother." Only here does Absalom refer to Amnon this way, probably to create the impression of filial intimacy in order to assuage any concerns of David. David asked why Amnon should go (v. 26b), suggesting he may have been suspicious, but Absalom convinced him with his urging (v. 27a). That David sent Amnon with Absalom shows that the deception succeeded (v. 27b).

Analyzing the Deception

The tactic Absalom used to deceive David was a misleading request (v. 26a). His motive was to kill Amnon (v. 28). Dominic Rudman has identified a significant feature of this deception by showing that it replays the circumstances of Amnon's rape of Tamar.[109] Rudman identifies five major parallels between Tamar's rape and Amnon's murder. First, both stories involve transgression of a family bond: just as Amnon referred to Tamar as "my sister" before raping her (v. 11), so Absalom referred to Amnon as "my brother" before killing him (v. 26a). Second, both stories involve transgression of a hospitality bond: Amnon invited Tamar to his house in order to have sex with her, while Absalom invited Amnon to his festival in order to kill him. Third, Amnon and Absalom each involved their servants in carrying out their sin; the former commanded his servant to eject Tamar from

---

105. *Contra* Yamada, *Configurations of Rape*, 127.

106. Fokkelman, *King David*, 115–16; Gordon, *I & II Samuel*, 264–65; Bergen, *1, 2 Samuel*, 384; Esler, *Sex, Wives, and Warriors*, 354.

107. Anderson, *2 Samuel*, 180; Alter, *David Story*, 272; Bar-Efrat, *Das Zweite Buch Samuel*, 136.

108. Ackroyd, *Second Book of Samuel*, 125; Baldwin, *1 & 2 Samuel*, 250; Robinson, *Let Us Be Like the Nations*, 223.

109. Rudman, "Reliving the Rape of Tamar," 326–39.

the house (v. 17), and the latter commanded his servants to strike Amnon down (v. 28). Fourth, and especially pertinent to the present study, David's role in the two stories is similar: in both cases his son deceived him into unwittingly sending one of his children to their harm. Fifth, the stories have significant parallels in the descriptions of mourning after the crimes.[110] Therefore Absalom's deception alludes to Amnon's deception as part of a larger structural parallel to that prior narrative.

Absalom achieved the goal for which he deceived by convincing David to send Amnon to the sheep-shearing festival and then having Amnon killed. The characterization of Absalom in this episode is tied up with the evaluation of his killing of Amnon. Richard Smith argues that Absalom's execution of Amnon was legitimate, since he understands Lev 20:17 as declaring that "one guilty of incestuous rape should be publicly executed before the sons of the clan."[111] However, Lev 20:17 speaks only about the incestuous couple being "cut off" (ונכרתו), which does not necessarily indicate execution, since a person could avoid execution yet still be "cut off" (see Lev 20:4–5). Moreover, Leviticus 20 repeatedly prescribes capital punishment by saying that the person(s) "must surely be put to death" (מות יומת).[112] Therefore, whatever being "cut off" may signify, it does not seem to refer to execution.[113] Thus the Torah provides no support for Amnon's execution, which suggests that by killing him Absalom committed a capital offense. This is supported by the fact that Joab acquired no bloodguilt for killing Absalom. When condemning Joab in 1 Kgs 2:5–6, David denounced him for murdering Abner and Amasa, but conspicuously omitted his killing of Absalom. This suggests that, whereas Joab acquired bloodguilt for his murders of Abner and Amasa—neither of whom deserved to die—he did not acquire bloodguilt for killing Absalom. A plausible explanation for this is that Absalom's murder of Amnon made him guilty of a capital offense

---

110. After Tamar's rape Amnon ordered her, "Get up and go" (קומי לכי, v. 15), and she "tore" (קרעה) her robe, "went" (ותלך הלוך), and "cried out" (וזעקה, v. 19). After Amnon's murder, all the king's sons "got up" (ויקמו) and fled" (v. 29); David also "got up" (ויקם) and "tore" (ויקרע) his garments (v. 31), and later the king's sons are described as "going" (הלכים, v. 34) and "lifting up their voice" (וישאו קולם, v. 36). See Rudman, "Reliving the Rape of Tamar," 335–37.

111. Smith, *Fate of Justice and Righteousness*, 155.

112. See Lev 20:2, 9, 10, 11, 12, 13, 15, 16, 27.

113. Jacob Milgrom suggests that being "cut off" refers either to being denied offspring (one's lineage is cut off) or not being gathered to one's ancestors at death (one is cut off from their kin) (*Leviticus: A Book of Ritual and Ethics*, 66). Wenham suggests that it indicates "a threat of direct punishment by God usually in the form of premature death" (*Leviticus*, 285). Either way, YHWH is the one who "cuts off."

and thus deserving of execution.[114] For this reason, and because Absalom's actions are depicted as a replaying of Amnon's earlier actions, the characterization of Absalom in this narrative is negative.

Deception P: Joab's Deception of Amasa (2 Samuel 20:8–10)

After Joab killed Absalom, David appointed Amasa over the army in place of Joab (2 Sam 19:14). As David returned to Jerusalem, the men of Judah and Israel quarreled concerning who had a greater claim to solidarity with David (19:41–44). Sheba, son of Bicri, began a revolt and all the men of Israel went with him (20:1–2). David sent Amasa to gather the Judahites for battle, but when Amasa took longer than the prescribed time, David dispatched Abishai, who pursued Sheba along with "Joab's men" and the Kerethites and Pelethites. Amasa met up with this group at Gibeon, and as Joab walked out to greet him, his dagger dropped from its sheath. Joab asked Amasa if he was well, and as he grasped Amasa's beard with his right hand to kiss him, he stabbed him in the stomach, spilling his intestines and leaving him for dead.

Establishing the Deception

Joab deceived Amasa into believing falsely that he was greeting him peacefully, when in reality he intended to kill him. This is demonstrated by (1) Joab's manipulation of his dagger, (2) his verbal greeting, and (3) his grasping of Amasa's beard with his right hand as if he intended to kiss him. First, although it is unclear how Joab's dagger fell and how he obscured his intention with it,[115] the text is clear that "Amasa was not on his guard

---

114. For further discussion, see Propp, "Kinship in 2 Samuel 13," 48–53.

115. The absence of a prepositional phrase following the verb ותפל creates ambiguity. Some think Joab's sword fell into the folds of his military garment and thus was obscured from Amasa's vision (Hertzberg, *I & II Samuel*, 372; Anderson, *2 Samuel*, 240). This is supported by the extensive description of Joab's attire, which seems to suggest that his clothing should play some element in the plot (Cartledge, *1 & 2 Samuel*, 625). Following Josephus (*Ant.* 7.11.7), others suggest Joab's sword fell to the ground, thus looking like an accident, and therefore Amasa did not think anything of Joab picking it up (Neiderhiser, "2 Samuel 20:8–10: A Note for a Commentary," 210; Gordon, *I & II Samuel*, 294; Alter, *David Story*, 323). Still others posit a "two-sword theory" in which Joab let one sword fall to the ground, making it appear that he was unarmed, and then stabbed Amasa with a second sword (Robinson, *Let Us Be Like the Nations*, 260). In another interpretation, the Syriac version sees the subject of ותפל as Joab's

against the sword that was in Joab's hand" (v. 10aα). Although Joab's hostile intentions become evident as the narrative unfolds, by some means he put his dagger in striking position without arousing Amasa's suspicion. Second, while ready to strike, Joab greeted Amasa kindly by asking, "Is it well with you, my brother?" (השלום אתה אחי, v. 9a). This greeting falsely implied that Joab cared about Amasa's well-being (שלום) and employed familial language (אחי) to suggest relational harmony between them. Third, Joab grasped Amasa's beard with his "right hand" (יד־ימין, v. 9b). Since weapons were normally wielded with the right hand, this seems to have put Amasa at ease.[116] Moreover, v. 9b also describes Joab as grasping Amasa's beard "in order to kiss him" (לנשק־לו). As in modern times, in the ancient Near East a kiss connoted relational harmony and affection.[117] These three actions caused Amasa to believe falsely that Joab was not a threat but was giving him a friendly greeting, when in reality Joab was gaining access to him in order to stab him. That Amasa was not on his guard against the dagger in Joab's hand (v. 10aα), and that Joab successfully stabbed and killed him (v. 10aβ), shows that the deception succeeded.

Analyzing the Deception

The tactics Joab used to deceive Amasa were nonverbal actions (manipulating his dagger, grasping Amasa's beard) and a misleading question. Joab's motive was to kill Amasa. A significant feature of this deception is that it alludes back to the three prior killings of Asahel, Abner, and Ishbosheth. Including the present pericope, these are the only four places in the OT where someone "strikes" (ויכהו) another person in the "stomach" (החמש) so that he "dies" (וימת). The location of Gibeon further alludes to Asahel's killing, which occurred at the same place (2:12), while the pretense of engaging in a harmless action ("to kiss him" [לנשק־לו]) in order to kill parallels the pretenses in the killings of Abner ("to speak with him" [לדבר אתו]) and Ishbosheth ("carrying wheat" [לקחי חטים]).[118]

"hand" (יד); thus his hand "fell" over the sword, thereby concealing it (see Cartledge, *1 & 2 Samuel*, 626). All these interpretations have difficulties; however, due to the narratological significance it gives to Joab's garment I am inclined toward the first.

116. Bergen, *1 & 2 Samuel*, 436; Firth, *1 & 2 Samuel*, 496.

117. Long, "1 and 2 Samuel," 472.

118. This deception also has parallels with Ehud's deceptive killing of Eglon in Judg 3:15–22. See the discussions of Wong, "Ehud and Joab," 411; Chisholm, "Ehud: Assessing an Assassin," 274–82.

Joab achieved the goal for which he deceived by killing Amasa, who had approached him unsuspectingly. However, although Joab achieved this immediate goal, he ultimately paid for it with his life. As noted above, because of his deceptive killings of Abner and Amasa, David later instructed Solomon to put Joab to death (1 Kgs 2:5-6). The author's evaluation of this deception is negative. Of the three other "stomach-striking" passages, many see this killing of Amasa as most explicitly alluding to Joab's previous killing of Abner.[119] That these are connected in David's charge to Solomon in 1 Kgs 2:5-6 supports this, as do further parallels between the two passages. In both cases: (1) Joab was the perpetrator, who (2) used deception (3) to murder (4) someone who was a threat to his position as military commander (5) under the guise of "peace." In 2 Samuel 3 the narrator thrice repeats that Abner left David "in peace" (בשלום, vv. 21, 22, 23), which likely explains his willingness to return at Joab's request. Similarly, in 2 Sam 20:9 Joab approached Amasa and asked about his "peace" (השלום אתה אחי). David specifically recalled this aspect of Joab's deceptions, condemning him for "shedding the blood of war *during peacetime* (בשלם)" (1 Kgs 2:5). Like his evaluation of Joab's deception of Abner, these parallels suggest that the author evaluates this deception of Amasa negatively.

This evaluation is further supported by the narrator's emphasis on Joab's "girdle" (חגור) in the present passage. In a circumstantial clause the narrator says, "Now Joab was *girded* (חגור) with his military garment, and over it was *a girdle* (חגור) with a dagger attached to *his loins* (מתניו) in its sheath" (20:8b). The only other place in the Former Prophets where the nouns "girdle" (חגור) and "loins" (מתנים) appear together is 1 Kgs 2:5.[120] There David condemned Joab's deceptive murders of Abner and Amasa, saying, "he put the blood of war *on his girdle* (בחגרתו) that is on *his loins* (מתניו)." By emphasizing Joab's attire with this rare language in 2 Sam 20:8, the narrator is subtly aligning his point of view concerning Joab's deceptive killing with David's explicitly negative evaluation in 1 Kgs 2:5.

---

119. Ackroyd, *Second Book of Samuel*, 189; Gordon, *I & II Samuel*, 295; Fokkelman, *King David*, 327; Brueggemann, *First and Second Samuel*, 331; Firth, *1 & 2 Samuel*, 496. However, see also the discussion of Polzin (*David and the Deuteronomist*, 199), who views 2 Samuel 2 as having the most affinities with 2 Samuel 20. Polzin's observations concerning the literary parallels between these two chapters are significant and convincing, though they do not detract from the simultaneous parallels to 3:27.

120. In 2 Sam 20:8 the noun "girdle" is masculine (חגור) and in 1 Kgs 2:5 it is feminine (חגורה). Fokkelman also sees this connection to 1 Kgs 2:5 (*King David*, 328).

Summary

From this analysis we can make several observations concerning deception intended to cause death or harm in the books of Samuel. First, in two deceptions (I and J) the deceiver did not achieve the goal for which he deceived. Second, only Deception I used a lie as the tactic; all the others used ambiguous language, misleading requests, or nonverbal actions. Third, with the exception of Deceptions I and J, all the deceivers experienced negative consequences for their deceptions. Fourth, in all these episodes either the deception is evaluated negatively or the deceiver is characterized negatively, except for Deception J, in which the deceiver is characterized positively.

5

Deception Intended to Benefit Someone Else in the Books of Samuel

IN THIS CHAPTER WE will focus on deception committed to benefit someone else, where preventing or causing death or harm was not the central concern. Four episodes fall into this category. First, we will look at Nathan's deception of David by his parable of the ewe lamb, which was in the interests of YHWH, who sent Nathan to bring judgment against David after the Uriah incident (2 Sam 12:1–7 ["Deception Q"]). Second, we will examine Joab and the Tekoite woman's deception of David by her pretending to be a widow trying to ensure the safety of her fratricidal son, which served the interest of "the people of God," who seemingly would have suffered if David had not restored his fratricidal son, Absalom (2 Sam 14:1–21 ["Deception R"]).[1] Third and fourth, we will analyze Hushai's two deceptions of Absalom, both of which he committed in David's interests during Absalom's revolt. By his first deception (2 Sam 16:16–19 ["Deception S"]) Hushai convinced Absalom that he was loyal to him rather than David, and by his second deception (2 Sam 17:5–14 ["Deception T"]) he convinced Absalom and his men that his counsel was better than Ahithophel's, thereby delaying

---

1. In 2 Sam 14:13, the Tekoite applied David's judgment back against him by asking, "Why then have you devised a thing like this *against the people of God*? (עַל־עַם אֱלֹהִים)?" Jeanne Marie Leonard argues that this statement implies that, without a king, other nations could occupy the land and deport the people to serve other gods ("La Femme de Teqoa," 138). However, since David had other sons at this time (2 Sam 3:2–5), it is difficult to see how Absalom's continued exile would have left Israel without a king-elect. Nevertheless, the reason given in the text pertains in some way to the welfare of the nation.

an attack against David and enabling him and his people to regroup and recover from their weariness.²

Deception Q: Nathan's Deception of David (2 Samuel 12:1–7)

After David's adultery with Bathsheba and murder of Uriah in 2 Samuel 11, YHWH "sent" (שלח) Nathan the prophet to David (12:1). By using the *Leitwort* שלח from chapter 11,³ the narrator depicts YHWH sending Nathan as the divine response to David's sin: "But the thing that David did was evil in the eyes of YHWH, so YHWH sent Nathan to David" (11:27b—12:1a). Nathan told David a parable about two men, one rich and one poor. The rich man had many sheep and cattle, but the poor man had only one ewe lamb that was like a child to him. A traveler came to the rich man, and rather than feed him from his own flock, the rich man took the poor man's ewe lamb, killed it, and fed it to the traveler. After hearing the story David became angry and exclaimed, "The man who did this is a son of death" (v. 5),⁴ and then declared that the man must make fourfold restitution (v. 6). After David pronounced judgment on the man, Nathan revealed the true significance of the parable, telling David: "You are the man" (v. 7). This led David to confess his guilt (v. 13).

---

2. Arguably this last deception could be included in chapter 3, since Hushai deceived in order to delay an attack and thus to prevent death or harm. However, I include it here because Hushai's goal was not simply to prevent death or harm against David and his men but to "defeat Ahithophel's counsel" (2 Sam 15:34; 17:14) and ultimately to restore the kingship to David. Moreover, immediately after Hushai deceived Absalom and all the men of Israel, in a circumstantial clause the narrator informs us that YHWH orchestrated this "to bring disaster (הרעה) upon Absalom" (2 Sam 17:14), which is quite the opposite of preventing death or harm. In contrast, the deceptions analyzed in chapter 3 all have prevention of death or harm as their immediate and ultimate goal.

3. Among other occurrences, David "sent" for Bathsheba to commit adultery with her (11:4); he "sent" Uriah's death warrant by his own hand (11:14); and after Uriah's death he "sent" for Bathsheba to become his wife (11:27a).

4. Scholars disagree on the meaning of this phrase. Although some conclude that David is pronouncing a death sentence (e.g., Fokkelman, *King David*, 76), most view it as an exclamation that the man deserves to die while recognizing that there is no legal precedent for execution (Phillips, "Interpretation of 2 Samuel 12:5–6," 243; Simon, "Poor Man's Ewe-Lamb," 230; Ackroyd, *Second Book of Samuel*, 109; Gordon, *I & II Samuel*, 257; Anderson, *2 Samuel*, 162; Bergen, *1, 2 Samuel*, 370).

Establishing the Deception

Nathan deceived David into believing falsely that the rich man in the parable referred to a third party, when in reality it referred to David himself. To demonstrate this, we must inquire both to whom Nathan intended the characters to refer and to whom David was falsely led to believe they referred. The traditional reading of this parable identifies the characters as follows:

Rich man = David

Poor man = Uriah

Ewe lamb = Bathsheba

However, some have suggested that in this reading the characters do not adequately correspond to the events of the prior chapter. Lienhard Delekat argues that the slaughtered lamb better represents Uriah rather than Bathsheba.[5] Randall Bailey sees three dissimilarities between the parable and the previous chapter: (1) evidence of adultery and murder is absent from the parable; only theft is mentioned; (2) the rich man's actions issued from not wanting to use his own possessions, while David's motive was personal gain and desire; and (3) the parable evokes readers' sympathy for the ewe lamb, which is incongruous as a representative of Bathsheba, who must have cooperated to some degree with David in the adultery. Thus Bailey concludes that the parable does not fit the situation it purportedly describes.[6]

However, these criticisms press the details of the parable beyond their limits. While not every aspect of the parable carries directly over to the prior chapter, the correspondence need only be sufficient to serve Nathan's prophetic needs. As many have argued, such a parable likely had one major point of comparison with the situation to which it referred, removing the need to force every detail to match the narrative of chapter 11.[7] Rather, Nathan's prophetic purpose in telling the parable should direct our interpretation. Since 11:27b—12:1a identifies "the thing that David did" as the reason that "YHWH sent Nathan to David," it follows that the point of the parable primarily concerned the issue of David's sin, and the most significant point of comparison between David's sinful actions and the parable is the abuse of

---

5. Delekat, "Tendenz und Theologie," 33.

6. Bailey, *David in Love and War*, 105–6.

7. Jones, *Nathan Narratives*, 98. See also Hoftijzer, "David and the Tekoite Woman," 423; Pyper, *David as Reader*, 100; Eynikel, "The Parable of Nathan," 86; Van Seters, *Biblical Saga*, 299.

power.[8] In both chapters, the person with power took what was not his and killed: David "took" (לקח) Bathsheba (11:4) and killed Uriah (11:14–17), while the rich man "took" (לקח) the ewe lamb and killed it (12:4). Moreover, these actions of David were precisely those condemned by Nathan: "Uriah the Hittite you *struck down* with the sword, and his wife you *took* (לקח) to be a wife for you" (12:9). That the rich man took and killed the same object (the ewe lamb), while David took one object (Bathsheba) and killed another (Uriah), is not a problem once the deceptive function of the parable is taken into account.

Uriel Simon has proposed that the genre of Nathan's story fits into a category he calls the "juridical parable":

> The juridical parable constitutes a realistic story about a violation of the law, related to someone who had committed a similar offence with the purpose of leading the unsuspecting hearer to pass judgement on himself. The offender will only be caught in the trap set for him if he truly believes that the story told him actually happened, and only if he does not detect prematurely the similarity between the offence in the story and the one he himself has committed.[9]

Although some have questioned certain aspects of Simon's description of this genre,[10] he rightly observes that this type of parable is "based on a delicate relationship of closeness and remoteness towards the object of its application."[11] Indeed, the rhetorical efficacy of Nathan's parable was contingent upon David being deceived concerning its referents. Thus we should not be surprised that the details between David's actions and the rich man's do not correspond in every respect. This lack of correspondence advanced the deception by partially obscuring the connection between the rich man and David. Nevertheless, the rich man's and David's actions were sufficiently congruous for Nathan to use David's condemnation against him. Therefore

---

8. Seebass "Nathan und David in II Sam 12," 205–6; Whitelam, *The Just King*, 126; Jones, *Nathan Narratives*, 100; Eynikel, "The Parable of Nathan," 86.

9. Simon, "Poor Man's Ewe-Lamb," 220–21.

10. Subsequent studies have attempted to clarify Simon's label by calling this type of discourse "judgement eliciting parables" (Gunn, "Traditional Composition," 218–19; Jones, *Nathan Narratives*, 97) or "oath-provoking stories" (Pyper, *David as Reader*, 109). Despite these different labels, the general parabolic design is clear: the deceiver describes a situation to the receiver with the intention that the latter will acknowledge that a certain response is warranted. Once this response is voiced, the deceiver reveals that the parable applies to the receiver, thereby showing that the response given should be applied to the receiver's situation.

11. Simon, "Poor Man's Ewe-Lamb," 223.

the traditional identification of the parable's intended referents is tenable, with David most importantly identified as "the [rich] man" (12:7).[12]

In order to deceive David, Nathan must have caused him to believe falsely that the rich man did not refer to him. Nathan accomplished this by presenting sufficiently vague circumstances ("two men were in a certain city" [v. 1b]) and by having an animal be the object taken rather than a woman. That "David burned with anger greatly against the man" (12:5) and then cast judgment upon him demonstrates that Nathan succeeded in deceiving him. The text does not say whether David believed he was hearing a real or hypothetical judicial case. Either way, Simon's conclusion that the hearer must believe that the story "actually happened" in order for it to be effective is unnecessary. Even if the hearer believes the story is hypothetical, if he condemns the actions within the story, the one presenting it may logically reapply that condemnation back against him. Thus it is unnecessary to conclude firmly whether[13] or not[14] David believed the parable referred to a real situation. The deception was successful because David was led to believe that the parable was *not about him*.[15]

Analyzing the Deception

The tactic Nathan used to deceive David was ambiguous language. His motive was to get David unwittingly to condemn his own sinful actions. A

---

12. Polzin suggests a tripartite referential scheme for the application of the phrase, "You are the man," to David's entire career that corresponds to Nathan's indictment of vv. 7–12. According to Polzin, (1) early on David was "the man who comes" (i.e., the traveler), to whom the rich man (God) gave the kingdom (the ewe lamb) after taking it from Saul (the poor man) (vv. 7–8); (2) in the present situation David is the rich man (vv. 9–10); and (3) in the future he will become the poor man when God punishes him and his house (vv. 11–12) (*David and the Deuteronomist*, 123–26). Jeremy Schipper argues that when David heard the parable, he understood that it concerned the death of Uriah, but he mistakenly identified Joab as the rich man, Uriah as the ewe lamb, Bathsheba as the poor man, and himself as the traveler. By condemning the rich man, David believed he was condemning Joab and thereby distancing himself from the murder. Nathan then revealed that the true referent of the rich man was David himself (*Parables and Conflict*, 48–49). To engage these theories fully is beyond the scope of this study. Suffice it to say that, even if one accepts Polzin's or Schipper's view, David would still be deceived concerning the identity of the rich man.

13. As do Lasine, "Melodrama as Parable," 106–7; Vorster, "Reader-Response, Redescription, and Reference," 103; Marcus, "David the Deceiver," 165.

14. As do Lategan, "Reference: Reception, Redescription, and Reality," 81; Schipper, *Parables and Conflict*, 50.

15. So also Pyper, *David as Reader*, 90.

significant feature of this deception is the hint of the truth within it. As many have noted, Nathan said that the ewe lamb "ate" (אכל) from the poor man's food, "drank" (שתה) from his cup, and "lay" (שכב) in his bosom (12:3).[16] This chain of verbs recalls Uriah's response to David's encouragements for him to go down to his house and "wash his feet" in 2 Sam 11:11:

> And Uriah said to David, "The ark and Israel and Judah are staying in tents, and my lord Joab and the servants of my lord are camping over the face of the field. So shall I enter into my house to *eat* (אכל) and to *drink* (שתה) and to *lie* (שכב) with my wife? As you live and as your soul lives, I will not do this thing."

Nathan subtly depicted the relationship between the poor man and the ewe lamb in the same terms used by Uriah to describe the marital intimacy with Bathsheba that he was foregoing because of loyalty to his fellow soldiers. Furthermore, in his final description of the relationship between the poor man and the ewe lamb, Nathan said of the lamb, "She was *like a daughter* (כבת) to him." The noun בת is also the first part of Bathsheba's name, בת־שבע, thus serving as a play-on-words that further links the parable to the events to which it referred.[17]

Nathan achieved the goal for which he deceived, demonstrated by the fact that David condemned the man in the parable and thus inadvertently condemned himself. Nathan experienced no negative consequences for his deception. Since YHWH sent Nathan to David (v. 1), and since immediately after the parable Nathan employed the messenger formula (כה־אמר יהוה) to communicate YHWH's condemnation of David's actions (v. 7b), the deception is depicted as part of Nathan's prophetic mission and therefore the author's evaluative viewpoint of it is positive.

Deception R: Joab and The Tekoite Woman's Deception of David (2 Samuel 14:1–21)

After luring Amnon to his death, Absalom fled to Geshur, where he stayed for three years (2 Sam 13:38). In order to restore Absalom to David,[18] Joab

---

16. Coxon, "A Note on 'Bathsheba' in 2 Samuel 12:1–16," 249; Fokkelman, *King David*, 79; Polzin, *David and the Deuteronomist*, 123; Alter, *David Story*, 258; Pyper, *David as Reader*, 101; Keith Bodner, "Nathan: Prophet, Politician and Novelist?" 48; Schipper, *Parables and Conflict*, 47–48; Bar-Efrat, *Das Zweite Buch Samuel*, 116.

17. Fokkelman, *King David*, 79; Polzin, *David and the Deuteronomist*, 123; Auld, *I & II Samuel*, 465.

18. Scholars disagree whether 2 Sam 13:39—14:1 describes David longing to be reconciled with Absalom (e.g., Camp, "Wise Women of 2 Samuel," 15; Nicol, "Wisdom

commissioned a "wise woman from Tekoa" to go to David and pretend to be mourning. She told David that she was a widow, that her two sons had fought and one had killed the other, and now her clan wanted to execute her other son (vv. 5–7a). She appealed to David for help, since the death of her remaining son would leave her without anyone to support her, and her dead husband would be left without an heir (v. 7b). David twice attempted to assure the woman's well-being while not commenting on her son's fate (vv. 8, 10), but she pressed him to assure protection for her son by an oath (v. 11a). Finally, David swore by YHWH that not one hair of her son's head would fall to the ground (v. 11b). Like Nathan in chapter 12, at that point she turned David's response back upon his own situation: "In speaking this word, the king is like a guilty person, for the king has not brought back his banished one" (v. 13). David asked if Joab was behind this charade, which she affirmed, so David commanded Joab to bring Absalom back from Geshur (vv. 18–21).

Establishing the Deception

Although the Tekoite woman spoke with David, ultimately Joab was the perpetrator of this deception. The pericope begins and ends with reference to Joab and David (vv. 1, 19–21),[19] with the Tekoite serving as Joab's mouthpiece (v. 3; cf. v. 19). For this reason, some have argued that the "wisdom" of

---

of Joab," 97; Bellefontaine, "Customary Law and Chieftainship," 48) or as "against" Absalom (e.g., Fokkelman, *King David*, 126–27; Smith, *Fate of Justice and Righteousness*, 163–64; Anderson, *2 Samuel*, 182, 187). Fokkelman observes that if David were favorably disposed toward Absalom, Joab's ruse would have been unnecessary and David's subsequent refusal to see Absalom (14:24) would not make sense (*King David*, 126; see also McCarter, *II Samuel*, 344). Furthermore, Lyke notes that the language of 14:1 (כי־לב המלך על־אבשלום) is similar to 1 Sam 25:25 (אל־נא ישים אדני את־לבו אל־איש הבליעל הזה על נבל), in which Abigail requested that David not attack Nabal, which suggests that David was negatively disposed toward Absalom as he was toward Nabal (*King David with the Wise Woman of Tekoa*, 114). Although Lyke later suggests that David may have longed to be reconciled with Absalom and that Joab's ruse "might be employed to get for David what he is afraid to do on his own or in public" (ibid., 162, n. 65), this does not explain why David refused to see Absalom after he was restored. It is also possible that the ambiguity of the preposition על purposefully indicates David's ambivalence toward Absalom (see Polzin, *David and the Deuteronomist*, 139–40; Alter, *David Story*, 275; Cartledge, *1 & 2 Samuel*, 548).

19. Leonard sees ידע as the key word connecting Joab and David: at the beginning of the passage Joab "knew" (ידע) David's intentions (v. 1) and at the end David "knew" (ידע) Joab's intentions (v. 20) ("La Femme de Teqoa," 143–44). See also Alonso-Schökel, "David y la mujer de Tecua," 193.

this chapter belongs to Joab and not the Tekoite.[20] However, although Joab was shrewd in orchestrating this charade, it is also clear that the Tekoite exercised wisdom in applying his deceptive scheme in her conversation with David, with its many contingencies and uncertainties.[21]

Although it seems clear that the Tekoite deceived David into believing falsely that she was mourning and needed help (vv. 8, 10, 11), two theories call into question the presence of deception here. First, Patricia K. Willey argues that, through the Tekoite, Joab used the phrase "this thing" (הדבר הזה) to allude to David's murder of Uriah in order to coerce his response.[22] Willey observes that the phrase הדבר הזה is highly concentrated in 2 Samuel 11–14,[23] beginning with Uriah's refusal to do "this thing," that is, sleep with Bathsheba while on duty (2 Sam 11:11), and then referring several times to Uriah's death (11:25; 12:6, 14). According to Willey, by using this phrase repeatedly in the conversation with David,[24] through the Tekoite, Joab subtly blackmailed him with his past sin in order to produce Joab's desired response. For David to be coerced like this, he must have understood the subtext of the Tekoite's communication and thus not have been deceived by her story, as Willey acknowledges.[25] However, while הדבר הזה may be a key phrase throughout these chapters, it seems improbable that the allusion to the Uriah affair coerced David to comply for fear of his sin being revealed. Nathan had already uncovered David's sin concerning Uriah and Bathsheba in 12:9. Although knowledge of David's orchestration of Uriah's death may not have been publicized at this point, this is a narrative gap and thus a tenuous anchor for interpreting the present passage.

Second, Jeremy Schipper argues that, rather than trying to trick David into passing a judgment, Joab and the Tekoite wanted him to acknowledge his inability to resolve the family conflict and his need to allow Joab to take

---

20. Whybray, *Succession Narrative*, 59; Ackroyd, *Second Book of Samuel*, 130; Nicol, "The Wisdom of Joab," 97.

21. See Alonso-Schökel, "David y la mujer de Tecua," 194; Hoftijzer, "David and the Tekoite Woman," 444.

22. Willey, "Importunate Woman of Tekoa," 126–27.

23. Willey incorrectly counts thirteen occurrences in chapters 11–14 and only eight in the rest of 1–2 Samuel (ibid., 126). There are actually twelve occurrences in chapters 11–14 (11:11, 25; 12:6, 12, 14, 21; 13:20; 14:3, 13, 15, 20, 21) and fifteen elsewhere in 1–2 Samuel (1 Sam 9:21; 17:27, 30; 18:8; 20:2; 24:7; 26:16; 28:10, 18; 30:24; 2 Sam 2:6; 15:6; 17:6; 19:43; 24:3). Nevertheless, even this latter count shows a high concentration in 2 Samuel 11–14.

24. See vv. 13, 15, 20; in slightly modified form in vv. 12, 15, 17, 19, 20.

25. Ibid., 122.

charge of the situation with Absalom.[26] Schipper suggests that subtleties in the conversation show that the Tekoite was trying to be transparent and that David understood the subtext as referring to Absalom.[27] However, although Schipper claims that Joab achieved this goal and that David "simply allows Joab to take charge of the situation,"[28] the subsequent narrative does not support this conclusion. Although David allowed Absalom to return, he prohibited him from entering his presence, using a third-person command regarding Absalom that was seemingly addressed to Joab (2 Sam 14:24, cf. v. 23). Moreover, after living in Jerusalem for two years and not seeing the king's face, Absalom summoned Joab, who, rather than taking charge himself, "went to the king and told him this" (v. 33aα). David then permitted Absalom to enter his presence (v. 33aβ). Furthermore, during Absalom's revolt, David did not put Joab in charge of dealing with Absalom but "commanded" (צוה) him to deal gently with him (18:5a). All the troops heard this (18:5b), which was the reason an unnamed soldier refused to kill Absalom (18:12). All this suggests that David did not put Joab in charge of dealing with Absalom. Since Joab declared that David had granted his request after the Tekoite's deception (14:22), it follows that Joab's goal was not to receive charge over Absalom.

The most plausible interpretation is that Joab and the Tekoite deceived David into believing falsely that her story was true so that he would issue a decision that they could apply back to his situation with Absalom.[29] Like Nathan's parable, the Tekoite's story was both similar and dissimilar to David's situation, serving respectively to legitimate her later application of his response to his situation and to keep him from suspecting her true motives.[30] That she deceived David is evident from his assurance of protection for both her (vv. 8, 10) and her son (v. 11).

Analyzing the Deception

The tactics Joab and the Tekoite used to deceive David were nonverbal actions (she wore "mourning clothes" and did not anoint herself with oil [v. 2]) and lies (vv. 5b–7). The motive was "to change the present situation"

26. Schipper, *Parables and Conflict*, 57–73.
27. Ibid., 68–70.
28. Ibid., 72.
29. See, e.g., Hoftijzer, "David and the Tekoite Woman," 420; Gunn, "Traditional Composition," 219; Bellefontaine, "Customary Law and Chieftainship," 48; Camp, "Wise Women of 2 Samuel," 21; Lyke, *King David with the Wise Woman of Tekoa*, 13.
30. Hoftijzer, "David and the Tekoite Woman," 421.

(v. 20, NIV), that is, to get David to restore Absalom from exile. That David instructed Joab to do this (v. 21) shows that Joab and the Tekoite achieved the goal for which they deceived. Neither of the deceivers experienced any negative consequences for their deception. Although the author's evaluation of the deception itself is difficult to determine, he seems to characterize the Tekoite positively. In addition to exercising great care in her interactions with David, both in the politeness of her speech[31] and in her tact of not mentioning Absalom by name,[32] several elements in the text recall the account involving Abigail in 1 Samuel 25.[33]

Table 4: Abigail and the Tekoite's Audiences with David

	Abigail and David	Tekoite and David
Description of David's adverse relationship with another man	Abigail asked David not to set his "heart" (לב) "against Nabal" (על־נבל) (1 Sam 25:25).	Joab knew that David's "heart" (לב) was "against Absalom" (על־אבשלום) (2 Sam 14:1)[34]
The woman "fell on her face"	ותפל לאפי דוד על־פניה (1 Sam 25:23)	ותפל על־אפיה (2 Sam 14:4)
The woman prostrated herself	ותשתחו (1 Sam 25:23)	ותשתחו (2 Sam 14:4)
The woman suggested that the iniquity be laid upon her	בי־אני אדני העון (1 Sam 25:24)	עלי אדני המלך העון (2 Sam 14:9)
The woman requested permission to speak, referring to herself as "your maidservant"	ותדבר־נא אמתך (1 Sam 25:24)	תדבר־נא שפחתך (2 Sam 14:12)

---

31. Bar-Efrat, *Narrative Art in the Bible*, 66.

32. Alter, *David Story*, 278.

33. For insight to these parallels I am indebted primarily to Gunn, "Traditional Composition," 221–22; see also Lyke, *King David with the Wise Woman of Tekoa*, 114; Youngblood, "1, 2 Samuel," 758.

34. See n. 18 above for discussion of the potential nuances of the preposition in the case of Absalom.

| David responded by telling the woman to "go to her house." | עלי לשלום לביתך (1 Sam 25:35) | לכי לביתך (2 Sam 14:8) |

Although some of these elements are common for any interaction between an inferior and a superior (e.g., prostration), their accumulation in these parallel contexts of a woman interceding with David on behalf of another man suggests that the Tekoite is being depicted similarly to Abigail. Since the narrator clearly characterizes Abigail positively,[35] it seems the Tekoite is characterized positively as well.

Deception 5: Hushai's First Deception of Absalom (2 Samuel 16:16–19)

When Absalom revolted, David, his family, and his officials fled Jerusalem. During his flight, after hearing that his counselor Ahithophel had joined Absalom's revolt, David met Hushai the Arkite and asked him to return to Jerusalem and lie to Absalom by telling him that he would be his servant (2 Sam 15:34). By doing so, Hushai could defeat Ahithophel's counsel and relay any plans he heard back to David (2 Sam 15:35–36). When Hushai came to Absalom, he greeted him, "Long live the king! Long live the king!" (2 Sam 16:16). Absalom interpreted this to refer to himself and inquired about Hushai's loyalty to David (v. 17). Hushai responded that he would serve the one chosen by YHWH and the people—implying that this was Absalom (vv. 18-19).

Establishing the Deception

Hushai deceived Absalom into believing falsely that he was loyal to him rather than to David. At the beginning of their encounter, the narrator describes Hushai as "David's friend" (רעה דוד, v. 16)[36] for a second time (cf.

---

35. In 1 Sam 25:3 the narrator describes Abigail as "of good understanding and beautiful of form" (טובת־שׂכל ויפת תאר). As Sternberg notes, multiple epithets like this are "the most perceptible form of judgment" the narrator provides by which to shape our response to a character (*Poetics of Biblical Narrative*, 476). Indeed Abigail's actions throughout the narrative support this initial characterization. See also Berlin, *Poetics and Interpretation*, 31; Birch, "First and Second Books of Samuel," 1170–71.

36. Most agree that the title "David's friend" denoted not simply a social acquaintance but an official position in the royal cabinet, probably a high-ranking counselor

2 Sam 15:37), emphasizing his true loyalty. Hushai's prior planning (2 Sam 15:32–37) and subsequent carrying out (2 Sam 17:7–16) of espionage on David's behalf further demonstrated his true allegiance. However, Hushai's greeting to Absalom ("Long live the king! Long live the king!") was not simply a wish for long life but an expression of allegiance and acknowledgement of royal authority.[37] Absalom's response in v. 17 shows that he understood Hushai's statement of loyalty to be directed at him and thus falsely believed that Hushai was defecting from David. Hushai reinforced this false belief by stating that his loyalties lay with "the one chosen by YHWH" and the dynasty, not David particularly (vv. 18–19). Although no response from Absalom is recorded, that he falsely believed Hushai was loyal to him is shown in that he later called upon him for tactical advice against David and accepted it.[38]

Analyzing the Deception

The tactic Hushai used to deceive Absalom was ambiguous language. Although David had told Hushai to lie ("Say to Absalom, '*I will be your servant* [אהיה ... עבדך אני], O king. Your father's servant I was then, *but now I am your servant* [ועתה ואני עבדך]'" [15:34]), Hushai's communication to Absalom was more subtle and employed ambiguity rather than lies. His greeting ("Long live the king! Long live the king!") did not specify to which "king" he was giving allegiance. This ambiguity invited Absalom to assume it referred to him, though the reader can see the hidden loyalty to David expressed below the surface. Moreover, in contrast to David's instructions, Hushai never addressed Absalom as "O king," which further suggests that he did not consider Absalom to be king and thus was expressing allegiance to the true king, David.[39]

Absalom then asked two questions: "Is this your loyalty to your friend? Why did you not go with your friend?" (v. 17). Hushai responded with more

(Payne, *I & II Samuel*, 232; Anderson, *2 Samuel*, 205; Firth, *1 & 2 Samuel*, 458; Arnold, *1 & 2 Samuel*, 582, n. 22; Youngblood, "1, 2 Samuel," 998; Long, "1 and 2 Samuel," 466). This is substantiated by the occurrence of "the king's friend" in lists of royal officials (see 1 Kgs 4:5; 1 Chr 27:33).

37. Mettinger, *King and Messiah*, 131–37; McCarter, *II Samuel*, 384; Arnold, *1 & 2 Samuel*, 586; Cartledge, *1 & 2 Samuel*, 581.

38. Bar-Efrat, *Narrative Art in the Bible*, 72. Although Antony Campbell claims that even when Absalom summoned Hushai for advice, it is still not clear that Hushai himself had been accepted (*2 Samuel*, 152), that Absalom accepted *Hushai's advice* presupposes that he falsely believed Hushai was advising in his interests.

39. Anderson, *2 Samuel*, 213; Brueggemann, *First and Second Samuel*, 309.

ambiguous language along with a hint of the truth. First he replied, "No" (לֹא, v. 18). Since Absalom's second question did not call for a "yes or no" answer (לָמָּה), it seems that this negation was a response to the first question. Since Absalom believed falsely that Hushai had expressed allegiance to him, his question, "Is *this* your loyalty to your friend?" was sarcastic, meaning, "Do you show loyalty to David *by giving allegiance to me*?" Hushai's first word denied this, but by doing so he actually described the true situation: Hushai was *not* showing loyalty to David by giving allegiance to Absalom (the misinterpretation of "Long live the king!") but by covertly working in David's interests (the true meaning of "Long live the king!").[40] Therefore this negative response hinted at the truth, though Absalom was blinded to it by his misinterpretation of Hushai's initial greeting.

Hushai followed this negation with more ambiguity: "For the one YHWH has chosen, and this people, and every man in Israel, his I will be and with him I will remain" (v. 18). Hushai claimed not to be disloyal to David but loyal to YHWH's chosen, another ambiguous statement that Absalom assumed referred to him.[41] However, while the OT never refers to Absalom as YHWH's chosen, it is replete with references to David as YHWH's chosen.[42] Therefore, in conjunction with the characterization of Hushai as loyal to David, the true sense of his reply in v. 18 was, "No, I do not show my loyalty to David by giving allegiance to you. Rather, I am loyal to YHWH's chosen, who is David, and with him I will remain." However, misinterpreting the ambiguity, Absalom falsely believed that Hushai was saying, "No, I am not disloyal to David but loyal to YHWH's chosen, which used to be David but now is you."

Rendered woodenly, Hushai's last statement was, "Secondly, whom shall I serve? Shall I not (serve) in the presence of his son? Just as I served in your father's presence, thus will I be in your presence" (v. 19). Concerning this statement Birch says that "even clever phrases must give way to the bold lie that allows Hushai access to the inner councils of Absalom: 'I will serve you,' he lies."[43] However, a careful examination reveals that Hushai never said, "I will serve you," and while his language here was deceptive, he did not lie. First, Hushai asked rhetorically, "Whom shall I serve?" (לְמִי אֲנִי אֶעֱבֹד). Contextually the implied answer is the subject of the previous verse, "the one YHWH has chosen," since Hushai had said, "with him I will

---

40. See also Bar-Efrat, *Das Zweite Buch Samuel*, 168–69.

41. Brueggemann, *First and Second Samuel*, 310; Bergen, *1, 2 Samuel*, 410.

42. 1 Sam 16:8–13; 2 Sam 6:21; 1 Kgs 8:16; 11:34; 1 Chr 28:4; 2 Chr 6:5–6; Ps 78:70. See also Bergen, *1, 2 Samuel*, 410; Youngblood, "1, 2 Samuel," 1006.

43. Birch, "First and Second Books of Samuel," 1331.

remain." Then Hushai asked elliptically, "Shall I not (serve) in the presence of his son?" (הלוא לפני בנו). Although some translations render this question as if "son" were the object of the verb "to serve" (עבד),⁴⁴ this verbless clause uses the complex preposition לפני, which elsewhere never indicates the object of עבד. Most often a direct object follows עבד,⁴⁵ and occasionally the preposition ל marks its object (as it does in v. 19a: למי אני אעבד).⁴⁶ However, the construction לפני + עבד is unique to this verse. It occurs elliptically in the first half (הלוא לפני בנו) and explicitly in the second (כאשר עבדתי לפני אביך). This irregularity suggests that לפני does not mark the object of service but the *location*,⁴⁷ which conforms to its common function of indicating a spatial relationship.⁴⁸ Therefore the true meaning of Hushai's words in v. 19a was: "Whom shall I serve? (The one YHWH has chosen [i.e., David]). Shall I not (serve him) in the presence of his son?" Remaining loyal to David, Hushai would serve his interests in the presence of Absalom. However, building off Absalom's previous false belief, the elliptical nature of this statement created ambiguity by which Absalom misinterpreted Hushai as saying: "Whom shall I serve? (The one YHWH has chosen [i.e., you, Absalom]). Shall I not (serve) in the presence of his (i.e., my friend's) son?" That is, Absalom believed Hushai would remain loyal to the dynasty by serving its interests in the presence of his "friend's" son. Whereas for Hushai, the pronoun "his" referred to "The one YHWH has chosen" (v. 18), from Absalom's perspective it referred to "your friend" (v. 17).⁴⁹

Hushai's last statement continued the ambiguity: "Just as I served in your father's presence, thus will I be in your presence" (כאשר עבדתי לפני אביך כן אהיה לפניך, v. 19b). Again, rather than explicitly saying that he would "serve *you* [Absalom],"⁵⁰ Hushai used לפני in both clauses to describe the *location* of his service.⁵¹ Building off his prior deceptive allegiance, he implied

---

44. E.g., "Should I not serve the son?" (NIV); "Moreover, whom should I serve? Should it not be his son?" (NRSV); "And again, whom should I serve? Should it not be his son?" (ESV). The NLT paraphrases the first half of the verse as, "And anyway, why shouldn't I serve you?"

45. E.g., 1 Sam 7:3, 4; 8:8; 11:1; 12:10 (2x), 14, 20, 24; 17:9; 26:19; 2 Sam 9:10; 10:19; 15:8; 22:44.

46. See also Judg 2:13; 1 Sam 4:9 (2x); Jer 44:3.

47. This is how the NASB translates it ("Besides, whom should I serve? *Should I not serve* in the presence of his son?") as well as the KJV ("And again, whom should I serve? Should I not serve in the presence of his son?").

48. *IBHS*, 221.

49. On this sort of ambiguity, see Block, "What Has Delphi to do with Samaria?"

50. *Contra* NIV, NRSV, ESV, which all render the final clause, "so I will serve you."

51. So NASB ("As I have served in your father's presence, so I will be in your

that just as his service in David's presence was in David's interests, so would his service in Absalom's presence be in Absalom's interests. However, for the reader who knows Hushai's true loyalties, the ambiguity in his language suggests something different: "Just as I served in your father's presence (in his interests), thus will I be (serving his interests) in your presence."[52] Therefore Hushai's tactic in deceiving Absalom was ambiguous language, not lies.

Hushai's motive for deceiving was to gain Absalom's confidence in order to defeat Ahithophel's advice (cf. 15:34). That Absalom later called upon Hushai to offer tactical advice against David and accepted it shows that he achieved his goal. Hushai experienced no negative consequences for his deception. Since this deception was the first step in Hushai's defeat of Ahithophel's counsel, and since the narrator later says that YHWH had "decreed to defeat the good counsel of Ahithophel" (17:14), the author evaluates this deception positively.

Deception T: Hushai's Second Deception of Absalom (2 Samuel 17:5–14)

After Hushai entered Absalom's court, Absalom asked Ahithophel for counsel (2 Sam 16:20). Ahithophel advised Absalom to lie with David's concubines, which he did (16:21–22). Ahithophel then advised Absalom to let him pursue David that night with twelve thousand men, strike him down while he was weak, and thereby return David's forces to Absalom's control (17:1–3). This plan seemed good to Absalom and the elders, but Absalom summoned Hushai for a second opinion. Hushai entered, claimed that this time Ahithophel's counsel was "not good" (v. 7), argued that David's military expertise invalidated the wisdom of Ahithophel's plan, and instead suggested that Absalom gather "all Israel" and lead them into battle and thereby defeat David by superior numbers (vv. 11–13). Absalom and the men of Israel declared that Hushai's counsel was better than Ahithophel's, but in a disjunctive clause the narrator notes that this was because "YHWH had decreed to defeat the good counsel of Ahithophel, so that YHWH might bring disaster upon Absalom" (v. 14b).

---

presence") and KJV ("as I have served in thy father's presence, so will I be in thy presence").

52. For further discussion, see Fokkelman, *King David*, 208.

Establishing the Deception

Hushai deceived Absalom and all the men of Israel into believing falsely that his counsel was better than Ahithophel's. The narrator explicitly states that Ahithophel's counsel was "good" (v. 14b), and the narratorial descriptions of David as "barefoot" (15:30) and "weary" (16:2, 14) support Ahithophel's tactical wisdom.[53] However, that Absalom and all the men of Israel responded, "the counsel of Hushai the Arkite is better than the counsel of Ahithophel" (v. 14a), suggests that Hushai deceived them. Nevertheless, some argue that the subsequent events reveal that ultimately Absalom followed Ahithophel's counsel, in which case Absalom was not deceived. Caquot and de Robert argue this based on the urgency with which Hushai instructed Zadok and Abiathar to send word to David ("And now, send quickly and tell David . . ." [v. 16aα]) and the content of his message ("Do not spend the night at the fords in the desert" [v. 16aβ]), both of which seem to presume an imminent attack.[54] Since Jonathan and Ahimaaz advised David to cross the Jordan because of Ahithophel's counsel (v. 21), Ackroyd suggests that Ahithophel's plan was about to be implemented.[55] Moreover, Anderson cites v. 24, where "Absalom crossed the Jordan, he and all the men of Israel with him," concludes that Absalom followed Ahithophel's counsel, and suggests that Hushai's counsel may be explained as a redactional addition.[56]

However, aside from postulating competing redactional layers, these arguments do not account for Absalom's stated acceptance of Hushai's counsel (v. 14a) or Ahithophel's suicide, which the narrator says happened because "he saw that his counsel was not followed" (v. 23). To explain these discrepancies, some have suggested that although Hushai's counsel prevailed, he encouraged David to move quickly out of precaution, since Ahithophel had correctly identified David's current position as weak and vulnerable,[57] and there was always the possibility that Absalom might change his mind.[58] Therefore, despite Hushai's victorious counsel, quick action was prudent. Although this accounts for Hushai's urgency in light of his victory and Ahithophel's suicide, it does not explain why (1) Hushai recounted both

---

53. Ahithophel counseled, "I would pursue after David tonight. I would come upon him, for he is weak and weary" (17:1b–2a). See also Fokkelman, *King David*, 222; Arnold, *1 & 2 Samuel*, 588.

54. Caquot and de Robert, *Les Livres de Samuel*, 539.

55. Ackroyd, *Second Book of Samuel*, 161.

56. Anderson, *2 Samuel*, 213; see also Birch, "First and Second Books of Samuel," 1332.

57. McCarter, *II Samuel*, 387; Cartledge, *1 & 2 Samuel*, 586.

58. Mauchline, *1 and 2 Samuel*, 280; Baldwin, *1 & 2 Samuel*, 267.

his and Ahithophel's advice to Zadok and Abiathar *without saying whose was accepted* (v. 15), and (2) Jonathan and Ahimaaz only reported to David what Ahithophel had counseled (v. 21).

The interpretation that accounts for these last two observations best is that, after making his speech, Hushai was excused from the council and therefore did not know whose advice Absalom accepted.[59] Since Hushai was not originally in the council when Ahithophel gave his advice, but was summoned afterward (v. 5) and informed what Ahithophel had said (v. 6), it is plausible that he would have been excused after offering his counsel and before a decision was made. Therefore Hushai reported both his and Ahithophel's counsel to Zadok and Abiathar without knowing whose was accepted (v. 15), and instructed them to communicate to David quickly and tell him to plan for the worst in case Absalom followed Ahithophel's counsel (v. 16). When Jonathan and Ahimaaz came to David, they only reported what Ahithophel had advised, since the potential for an imminent attack required immediate action (v. 21). Even if Jonathan and Ahimaaz had given David hope by reporting Hushai's counsel as well, it would not have changed his response since they did not know what Absalom would do. None of this indicates that Absalom followed Ahithophel's counsel, but only that Hushai and David's espionage network *did not know* whose counsel Absalom would follow. This explains why they reacted in haste, while also accounting for Absalom's acceptance of Hushai's counsel and Ahithophel's suicide.

Furthermore, that Absalom crossed the Jordan in v. 24 does not show that he was following Ahithophel's counsel, as Anderson maintains. Rather, a young man had spotted Jonathan and Ahimaaz in En Rogel and informed Absalom (v. 18a), who sent his servants to search for them in Bahurim (v. 18b–20).[60] When these servants returned unsuccessful, it seems that Absalom crossed the Jordan in pursuit. Moreover, Ahithophel had advised Absalom to let him pursue David "tonight" (הלילה, v. 1), yet in v. 22 the narrator states that by "the light of the morning" (אור הבקר) everyone in David's company had crossed the Jordan. Since this happened before Absalom crossed over in v. 24, this shows both that Absalom was not following Ahithophel's counsel to pursue David that night and that Hushai's deceptive counsel successfully gained David the requisite time to retreat and regroup. That Absalom, rather than Ahithophel, led the pursuit in v. 24 also shows that Absalom was not following Ahithophel's counsel.[61] All this indicates

---

59. Gordon, *I & II Samuel*, 281; Smith, *Justice and Righteousness*, 188.
60. See Deception H in chapter 3.
61. Cartledge, *1 & 2 Samuel*, 586.

that Hushai had deceived Absalom and all the men of Israel into believing falsely that his counsel was better than Ahithophel's.

Analyzing the Deception

The tactics Hushai used to deceive Absalom were lies, rhetoric, and possibly ambiguity. When summoned for his analysis of Ahithophel's counsel, Hushai said, "The counsel that Ahithophel has given is *not good* (לא־טובה) this time" (v. 7). This statement starkly opposes the narrator's evaluation in v. 14, where he refers to "the good counsel of Ahithophel" (את־עצת אחיתפל הטובה). Since Hushai's task was to defeat Ahithophel's counsel (15:34), and in light of Ahithophel's good reputation and the evident tactical wisdom in his plan noted above, Hushai probably did not believe that Ahithophel's counsel was not good. Therefore this statement seems to be a lie.

However, several have noted that Hushai did not specify *for whom* Ahithophel's counsel was "not good"; although it was good for Absalom, it certainly was "not good" for David.[62] On this reading, Hushai did not lie, but employed ambiguity that invited misinterpretation as he did in Deception S. However, although this statement may or may not be construed as a lie, it seems probable that Hushai did lie when he said, "He [David] will not stay overnight with the people. See, now he has hidden himself (עתה הוא־נחבא) in one of the pits or in one of the places" (vv. 8b–9a). Since the last place Hushai saw David was at "the summit" (הראש) of the Mount of Olives (15:32), which is the very opposite of a "pit" (פחת), at best this latter statement seems speculative. However, Hushai's emphatic description of David's location, using both a time adjunct (עתה) and the grammatically unnecessary subject pronoun (הוא), implies a certainty beyond speculation, suggesting that Hushai was making a definitive statement and therefore was lying to Absalom. This is supported by the fact that, although Hushai asserted that David would not stay overnight "with the people" (את־העם) (v. 8b), the narrator has already informed us that David "and all the people" (וכל־העם) had arrived at their destination (16:14). Furthermore, immediately after receiving Hushai's message from Jonathan and Ahimaaz, "David *and all the people* (וכל־העם) with him arose and crossed over the Jordan" (17:21). All this shows that David was with "all the people" throughout the narrative and thus negates the validity of Hushai's assertion in v. 8b.

In addition to this, the fundamental means by which Hushai deceived in this episode was his rhetoric. Hushai succeeded in having his counsel accepted

---

62. Conroy, *Absalom Absalom*, 114; McCarter, *II Samuel* 386; Brueggemann, *First and Second Samuel*, 311; Cartledge, *1 & 2 Samuel*, 584.

over Ahithophel's not because of what he said, but because of how he said it.⁶³ By means of multiple similes and hyperboles, Hushai criticized Ahithophel's counsel and promulgated his own. To counter Ahithophel's plan he described the ferocity of David and his men "like a bear robbed of her young in the field" (v. 8) and hyperbolically stated that any initial attack by David would be interpreted as a "slaughter" (מגפה)⁶⁴ and melt the heart of even the bravest soldier "whose heart was like the heart of a lion" (v. 10). To promote his own plan, Hushai described the benefit of gathering all Israel "like the sand on the seashore" (v. 11) and falling on David "like the dew that falls upon the ground" (v. 12). If David should withdraw to a city, Hushai again used hyperbole to suggest that "all Israel" would take ropes and drag the city into the valley "until not even a pebble is to be found there" (v. 13, NRSV).

Furthermore, in Hushai's description of David's military might he alluded to his legendary exploits against lions and bears (cf. 1 Sam 17:34-37).⁶⁵ By using such rhetoric and emphasizing Absalom's knowledge of David's famous military prowess ("*You know* [אתה ידעת] your father and his men, that they are warriors" [2 Sam 17:8]), Hushai suggested that Absalom should recognize the (seeming) deficiencies in Ahithophel's plan. Moreover, whereas Ahithophel's speech was full of first person verbs, stating that he would lead the nighttime attack against David,⁶⁶ Hushai advocated that Absalom lead the attack, "that all Israel, from Dan to Beersheba, be gathered *to you* . . . and that *you* go to battle in person" (v. 11, NRSV). Although many view this as an appeal to Absalom's vanity,⁶⁷ Stoebe has plausibly suggested that this was intended for Absalom to meet the ideal by which a ruler was legitimized by demonstrating his leadership in battle.⁶⁸ Either way, by his rhetoric Hushai painted a flattering picture, glorifying Absalom and

---

63. For full analyses of Hushai's rhetoric, see Bar-Efrat, *Narrative Art in the Bible*, 223-37; Park, "Frustration of Wisdom," 453-63.

64. This term often referred to a "plague" (Num 16:48-50; 25:8-9, 18-19; 31:16; 2 Sam 24:21, 25; 1 Chr 21:17, 22; Ps 106:29-30; Zech 14:12, 15, 18) or a military victory (1 Sam 4:17; 2 Sam 18:7) that involved heavy loss of life.

65. See Alter, *David Story*, 297; Bar-Efrat, *Narrative Art in the Bible*, 231-32; Fokkelman, *King David*, 217; Park, "Frustration of Wisdom," 458.

66. "Let *me* choose (אבחרה) . . . and *I* will arise and pursue (ואקומה וארדפה) . . . and *I* will come upon him (ואבוא עליו) . . . and *I* will cause him to tremble (והחרדתי אתו) . . . and *I* will strike down (והכיתי) the king . . . and *I* will bring back (ואשיבה) all the people to you" (vv. 1-3).

67. Ackroyd, *Second Book of Samuel*, 160; Evans, *1 and 2 Samuel*, 210; Fokkelman, *King David*, 219; Bodner, *David Observed*, 134; Firth, *1 & 2 Samuel*, 468.

68. Stoebe, *Das Zweite Buch Samuelis*, 388; Long, *Art of Biblical History*, 209-10.

predicting victory in battle, which contributed to Absalom's false belief that Hushai's counsel was superior.

Hushai's motive for deceiving was to defeat Ahithophel's counsel and gain time for David and his people to regroup and recover from their weariness.[69] Hushai achieved the goal for which he deceived by gaining enough time for David and the people to cross the Jordan safely (17:22) and receive food for nourishment (17:27–29). Hushai experienced no negative consequences for his deception. After Absalom and all the men of Israel expressed their false belief that Hushai's counsel was better than Ahithophel's, the narrator interjects, "For YHWH had decreed to defeat the good counsel of Ahithophel" (v. 14). Since Hushai's deception was the means by which YHWH carried out this decree, the author's evaluation of this deception is positive.

Summary

From this analysis we can make several observations concerning deception intended to benefit someone else in the books of Samuel. First, in each deception the deceiver achieved his or her goal. Second, whereas deceptions committed to prevent death or harm used lies almost exclusively as the tactic (seven out of eight), and inversely those committed to cause death or harm usually did not use lies (only one out of eight) but employed other subtler means (ambiguity, misleading requests, and nonverbal actions), the distribution of deceptive tactics in the present category is evenly split: two used lies along with either nonverbal action (Deception R) or rhetoric (Deception T), while the other two used only ambiguous language and no lies (Deceptions Q and S). Third, none of the deceivers experienced negative consequences for their deceptions. Fourth, none of these deceptions are depicted negatively. Rather, every account presents either a positive evaluation of the deception or a positive characterization of the deceiver.

---

69. Hertzberg, *I & II Samuel*, 351; McCarter, *II Samuel*, 386; Fokkelman, *King David*, 222. The extensive description of the supplies that Shobi, Makir, and Barzellai brought to David in 17:28–29 emphasizes this need narratologically.

6

Deception Intended to Benefit the Deceiver in the Books of Samuel

IN THE PREVIOUS CHAPTER we examined deception intended to benefit someone else. In this chapter we turn our attention to the remaining deceptions in the books of Samuel, all of which were committed to benefit the deceiver in situations where death or harm was not in view. Eight deceptions fall into this category: (1) Saul deceived his uncle in order to keep his recent anointing secret (1 Sam 10:14–16 ["Deception U"]); (2) David deceived Ahimelech in order to get provisions as he fled (1 Sam 21:2–10 [1–9] ["Deception V"]); (3) Saul deceived the necromancer in order to receive illegal and divinely prohibited necromantic services (1 Sam 28:3–25 ["Deception W"]); (4) the Amalekite deceived David in order to receive a reward for allegedly killing Saul (2 Sam 1:1–16 ["Deception X"]); (5) Absalom deceived the men of Israel in order to create discontent with David and present himself as an ideal leader (2 Sam 15:1–6 ["Deception Y"]); (6) Absalom deceived David and two hundred Jerusalemites in order to initiate his revolt in Hebron (2 Sam 15:7–12 ["Deception Z"]); (7) Ziba deceived David in order to receive a reward by making Mephibosheth look like a traitor (2 Sam 16:1–4; 19:25–31 [24–30] ["Deception α"]); and (8) Ahimaaz deceived David in order to receive a reward for bringing good news of victory in battle (2 Sam 18:19–30 ["Deception β"]).

Deception U: Saul's Deception of His Uncle[1]
(1 Samuel 10:14–16)

In 1 Samuel 8, the people asked Samuel to appoint a king to lead them like all the nations (v. 5). YHWH told Samuel that this request reflected their rejection of divine kingship (v. 7) and instructed him to warn the people about what such a king would do. Despite Samuel's warnings, the people persisted in their request, so YHWH told Samuel, "Listen to their voice and set a king over them" (v. 22, NRSV). Chapter 9 introduces Saul, who embarked on a journey to find his father's lost donkeys. Unable to locate the donkeys, Saul and his servant went to visit Samuel, hoping to receive some prophetic insight. Meanwhile, YHWH had revealed to Samuel that he would anoint a Benjamite as "leader" (נגיד) over Israel, and when Saul approached, YHWH told Samuel that he was the one (9:17). After eating together at the high place, Samuel told Saul to send his servant ahead, and Samuel anointed Saul as "leader" (נגיד) over Israel (10:1). Samuel told Saul that three signs would follow this anointing (vv. 2–6), after which he would enjoy God's presence (v. 7). The narrator tells us that "all these signs occurred that day" (v. 9), but only records the fulfillment of the third sign, in which the Spirit came upon Saul in power and he joined a procession of prophets in prophesying (vv. 10–13).

Verses 14–16 then record a brief conversation between Saul and his uncle. The uncle asked Saul and his servant where they had been, and Saul told him how they had searched for the donkeys and went to Samuel when they could not find them (v. 14). Saul's uncle then asked what Samuel said to them (v. 15). Verse 16 records Saul's response, followed by a narratorial comment, "Saul said to his uncle, 'He surely told us that the donkeys had

---

1. Scholars disagree over the identity and significance of this person. Depending on how one interprets 1 Sam 14:50–51 and 1 Chr 8:33; 9:39, Saul's uncle may have been either Abner or Ner. However, others posit that דוד does not mean "uncle" but refers to a "Philistine ruler" (Ap-Thomas, "Saul's Uncle," 241–45) or simply a "trusted friend" (Stoebe, *Das Erste Buch Samuelis*, 212). Peter Leithart suggests that "uncle" represents Saul's father Kish, who was symbolically replaced as Saul's father by Samuel when Saul entered the company of the prophets (*A Son to Me*, 79). Barbara Green, followed by Keith Bodner, sees a play-on-words between דוד ("uncle") and דוד ("David") and posits that this figure may be some sort of usurper or opponent (*How Are the Mighty Fallen*, 210; see also Bodner, *1 Samuel*, 98). For the purposes of this study we need not decide firmly between these different theories, though the pun on David's name seems especially appropriate given the many allusions to David's kingship in the deceptions of chapter 3. Since it is plausible that Saul had this conversation with the brother of one of his parents, and since 1 Sam 14:50 refers to a דוד in the context of discussing Saul's family members, I will refer to this character as his "uncle" throughout this section.

been found.' But the matter of the kingship, of which Samuel had spoken, he did not tell him."

Establishing the Deception

By omitting "the matter of the kingship" from this conversation, Saul caused his uncle to believe falsely that the location of the donkeys was all he discussed with Samuel. The text highlights this omission in two ways. First, after the uncle asked what Samuel said to him, Saul responded, "He *surely told us* [הגד הגיד] that the donkeys had been found" (v. 16a). The paronomastic infinitive construction emphasizes the certainty of the action described—in this case, what Samuel told them—and thus calls attention to Saul's silence about *what else Samuel told him*.[2] Second, the narrator emphasizes Saul's omission by a disjunctive clause, which uses the verb נגד that Saul used in the infinitive construction above: "But the matter of the kingship, of which Samuel had spoken, he did not tell him" (ואת־דבר המלוכה לא־הגיד לו אשר עמר שמואל, v. 16b). These emphases show that Saul deceived his uncle, which is further supported by the fact that his uncle did not ask any more questions.

Analyzing the Deception

The tactic Saul used to deceive his uncle was omitting information. His motive for deceiving was to keep knowledge of his anointing secret. Many conclude that, just as Samuel sent the servant ahead in 9:27 so he could anoint Saul in secret, so Saul refrained from mentioning the anointing to his uncle to preserve this secrecy.[3] This is possible, though it is unclear why such secrecy was needed. To support this view, Fokkelman argues that the final clause of v. 16 (אשר אמר שמואל) should be understood as a causal clause rather than a relative clause. He argues that because three words separate אשר from the object clause (ואת־דבר המלוכה), it is improbable that אשר modifies it as a relative pronoun. Rather, he thinks it more likely that the אשר clause modifies the immediately preceding verbal clause (לא־הגיד לו). This would result in a causal reading: "But concerning the matter of the kingship he did not tell him, *as Samuel had said*."[4] According to this

---

2. Tsumura, *First Book of Samuel*, 295; Bar-Efrat, *Das Erste Buch Samuel*, 166.

3. Birch, *Rise of the Israelite Monarchy*, 41; Baldwin, *1 & 2 Samuel*, 92; Klein, *1 Samuel*, 93; Alter, *David Story*, 57; Arnold, *1 & 2 Samuel*, 166.

4. Fokkelman, *Vow and Desire*, 434–35.

interpretation, Samuel had instructed Saul to be silent about the kingship,[5] which implies that Saul's omission of this subject was legitimate, or at least obedient. In addition to this, Fokkelman argues that interpreting אשר אמר שמואל as a relative clause makes it redundant ("the matter of the kingship ... *of which Samuel had spoken*").[6]

However, Fokkelman's rationale for interpreting the אשר clause as modifying the immediately preceding verbal clause rather than the object clause is faulty. Robert Holmstedt has shown that the phenomenon of extraposition—placing a constituent near the end of a clause—is common with biblical Hebrew relative clauses, which results in the separation of the relative clause from its antecedent.[7] Therefore, that three words separate אשר אמר שמואל from its most natural antecedent (ואת־דבר המלוכה) does not militate against it modifying this phrase as a relative clause. On the contrary, Holmstedt argues that relative clauses were extraposed in order to receive focused attention, since they cannot be moved to the front of a sentence— like a noun in a circumstantial clause—because they cannot precede their antecedents.[8] If this analysis is correct, this would mean that rather than being redundant, the relative clause in v. 16 has been extraposed to emphasize *Samuel's role* in mediating "the matter of the kingship." As we will see below, this passage depicts Samuel's words as trustworthy, but Saul did not trust or obey them. The emphasis of this extraposition coheres with this larger context and makes Fokkelman's causal interpretation unwarranted.

Saul achieved the goal for which he deceived, demonstrated by the fact that his uncle did not ask any more questions about his interaction with Samuel. Although Saul did not experience any negative consequences for this deception, the author evaluates it negatively. One cannot prove that Saul had no legitimate reason for secrecy, but nothing in the text states that he was obligated to keep the anointing secret.[9] On the contrary, as V. Philips Long has shown, the context suggests that Saul's silence was part

---

5. See also Eslinger, *Kingship of God in Crisis*, 335–36; Bar-Efrat, *Das Erste Buch Samuel*, 166.

6. Fokkelman, *Vow and Desire*, 434–35.

7. Holmstedt, "Relative Clause in Biblical Hebrew," 290–307.

8. Ibid., 304. Holmstedt gives Gen 24:15 as an example: "And behold Rebekah was coming out [יצאת], who [אשר] *was the daughter of Bethuel, the son of Milcah, the wife of Nahor, the brother of Abraham ....*" Noting that the verb יצאת separates אשר from its clear antecedent, "Rebekah," Holmstedt rightly observes that the important point in this narrative is not that Rebekah was coming out, but that she was related to Abraham and thus fulfilled Abraham's requirements for Isaac's wife (cf. Gen 24:2–4). He cites 1 Sam 10:16 as another example of relative clause extraposition (ibid., 301, n. 31).

9. So also Campbell, *1 Samuel*, 106.

of a larger pattern of ineptitude, reluctance, and faithlessness despite divine calling and confirmation.[10] Although Kish had charged Saul to find the lost donkeys (1 Sam 9:3), it was *Saul's servant* who advocated persistence in their search, knew about the man of God (9:6), and had the means to pay him to provide direction (9:8). In contrast, Saul appears quicker to give up on their search (9:5) and unprepared to overcome obstacles along the way (9:7). Interestingly for our purposes, Saul's servant said of the man of God, "everything he says certainly comes true" (כל אשר־ידבר בוא יבוא, v. 6a). This faithful perspective concerning Samuel's words contrasts sharply with Saul's later silence concerning "what Samuel said" (10:16). After Samuel anointed Saul (10:1),[11] he told him that several signs would follow (10:2–6), and the narrator notes that "all these signs were fulfilled that day" (v. 9). This immediate fulfillment demonstrated the reliability of Samuel's words, which the servant had previously confessed, and should have convinced Saul that God was with him in his new calling (see v. 7).

Specifically, Samuel instructed Saul, "When these signs are fulfilled, do what your hand finds to do, for God is with you" (v. 7). Long argues that the mention of the "Philistine outpost" at "Gibeah of God" (v. 5), the site where YHWH's Spirit was to come on Saul in power, provides a hint as to the meaning of the cryptic instruction, "do what your hand finds to do."[12] That is, Samuel implied that after the Spirit came upon Saul, he was to attack this Philistine outpost, after which he was to go down to Gilgal and wait for Samuel (10:7–8).[13] It seems that Saul understood this to be his charge, since

10. This discussion is greatly indebted to Long, *Reign and Rejection*, 200–218. His reading contrasts with traditional source-critical interpretations, which have generally viewed 9:1—10:16 as depicting Saul positively (see, e.g., Wellhausen, *Prolegomena to the History of Israel*, 251–54; Birch, *Rise of the Israelite Monarchy*, 29; Klein, *1 Samuel*, 93).

11. It is noteworthy that Samuel did not anoint Saul with the "horn" (קרן) of which Hannah spoke (1 Sam 2:10) and as he will when anointing David (1 Sam 16:1, 13). Rather, he used a "vial" (פך, 1 Sam 10:1). Such a departure from the expected method raises questions concerning the significance of this anointing. In line with this, when describing Saul's anointing, the narrator says that Samuel "poured" (יצק) the oil on his head, whereas for David's anointing he uses the verb "anoint" (משח), which Daniel Block suggests reveals the narrator's bias against Saul ("Empowered by the Spirit of God," 52). Furthermore, when anointing Saul, rather than making a statement, Samuel actually asked a question: "Has not YHWH anointed you over his inheritance as a leader?" (10:1). This seems to insert a further element of ambiguity into the anointing. See also the discussions of Miscall, *1 Samuel*, 59; Edelman, *King Saul*, 51–52; Bodner, *1 Samuel*, 92–93.

12. Long, *Reign and Rejection*, 207.

13. This reading explains the relationship between vv. 7 and 8, which many see in tension with one another, since Samuel instructed Saul to take the initiative in v. 7 but then to wait in v. 8 (see, e.g., Miller, "Saul's Rise to Power," 161; Klein, *1 Samuel*, 92;

after Jonathan later attacked the Philistine outpost at "Geba" (13:3)—which was seemingly the same as the one at "Gibeah of God" (10:5)[14]—the people were immediately summoned to join Saul at Gilgal (13:4b). This movement to Gilgal after the attack on the Philistine outpost indicates that Saul was following Samuel's instructions for where he should go after doing "what his hand found to do" (10:7-8),[15] even though, significantly, it was *Jonathan* and not Saul who attacked the Philistine outpost. All this reveals that in chapter 10, after all three signs were fulfilled and the Spirit had come upon Saul, he failed to "do what his hand found to do." Instead, he went to the "high place,"[16] where he deceived his uncle regarding what Samuel said (vv. 13b-16). On this reading, Saul's deceptive silence was not a matter of secrecy or humility, but reflected his faithlessness and failure to obey "what Samuel said," despite the trustworthiness of Samuel's words demonstrated in the fulfillment of the three signs.

This is reinforced by the succeeding episode in which Saul hid during the lot-casting ceremony (vv. 17-25). Although some have posited that Saul hid due to humility[17] or bashfulness,[18] it is more probable that his hiding reflected his reluctance to accept his new, divinely ordained position.[19] Supporting this is the overall negative depiction of the lot-casting ceremony. Samuel gathered the people at Mizpah and delivered a speech that followed the typical structure of an oracle of judgment, recalling God's past deliverances (v. 18) and Israel's unfaithful response (v. 19a). However, whereas an announcement of judgment would normally follow the transition "and now" (ועתה, v. 19b),[20] instead Samuel assembled the nation by tribes and clans for the lot-casting ceremony (vv. 20-24). Through this format, the lot-casting ceremony is depicted as God's judgment upon the nation.[21] This is

---

Robinson, *Let Us Be Like the Nations*, 60; Campbell, *1 Samuel*, 108).

14. For discussion that the references to "Gibeah" (גבעה) and "Geba" (גבה) are plausibly the same, see Miller, "Geba/Gibeah of Benjamin," 145-66.

15. Long, *Reign and Rejection*, 209.

16. Long argues that 10:13b should read that Saul went "home" (הביתה) rather than to the "high place" (הבמה), which would more clearly depict him as neglecting his new calling (ibid.). However, even without this emendation, Saul is still depicted as failing to follow through and attacking the Philistine outpost after the Spirit came upon him.

17. Edelman, *King Saul*, 57.

18. Gordon, *I & II Samuel*, 121.

19. Long, *Reign and Rejection*, 218; Arnold, *1 & 2 Samuel*, 167; Tsumura, *First Book of Samuel*, 298.

20. See McCarter, *1 Samuel*, 191.

21. Fokkelman, *Vow and Desire*, 443; Long, *Reign and Rejection*, 216; Cartledge,

supported by the two other passages in which similar lot-casting ceremonies occur, both of which were performed in order to identify someone who was guilty of a crime (Josh 7:14–26; 1 Sam 14:38–44).[22] McCarter acknowledges the negative implication of these parallel passages, but tempers the parallels by saying, "it would be overstating the case to say that all of this means Saul is guilty of something."[23] However, as Long argues, that Saul failed to obey Samuel's word and "do what his hand found to do," but instead kept quiet about the kingship and did nothing, suggests that he was guilty of something.[24] All this contributes to a negative evaluation of Saul's deception concerning "what Samuel said."

Deception V: David's Deception of Ahimelech (1 Samuel 21:2–10 [1–9])

After Jonathan discovered Saul's murderous intentions toward David (1 Samuel 20), David left and went to Ahimelech the priest in Nob. When Ahimelech asked why David was alone, he claimed that he was on a secret mission for the king and was to rendezvous with his men later (1 Sam 21:3 [2]). David requested bread, and Ahimelech said he only had consecrated bread, which the men could have only if they had "kept themselves from women" (v. 5 [4]). When David assured Ahimelech that his men had done so, Ahimelech gave him the bread of the Presence. In v. 8 [7] the narrator interjects a circumstantial clause noting the presence of one of Saul's servants, Doeg the Edomite. David told Ahimelech that the urgency of the king's request did not give him time to bring his weapon, and asked if Ahimelech had a spear or sword. Ahimelech gave him Goliath's sword, which had been stored behind the ephod.

---

1 & 2 Samuel, 142; Arnold, *1 & 2 Samuel*, 167. *Contra* Bruce Birch, who argues that vv. 20–24 present an "extremely positive view of the king" ("The Choosing of Saul at Mizpah," 454). He supports this by noting that not all prophetic speeches have judgment in the announcement, and argues instead that the scene in vv. 20–24 "redeems" the people's rejection of YHWH (ibid.). However, Birch admits that the "most common form" of prophetic speech involved an announcement of judgment after an accusation like that made in v. 19a (ibid.).

22. McCarter, *1 Samuel*, 196; Miscall, *1 Samuel*, 64; Fokkelman, *Vow and Desire*, 443–44; Polzin, *Samuel and the Deuteronomist*, 103.

23. McCarter, *1 Samuel*, 196.

24. Long, *Reign and Rejection*, 216–17.

Establishing the Deception

Although deception clearly occurred in this episode, scholars differ regarding who deceived whom. Most believe that David's claims to be on a secret mission and have a rendezvous with his men were lies, since he was obviously not on official business from Saul and was seemingly alone when he left Gibeah in the previous chapter (1 Sam 20:42) and when he fled to Gath in the next section (1 Sam 21:11–16 [10–15]).[25] However, it is possible that David had an entourage that was not visible in this part of the narrative, so his reference to them may not have been a lie.[26] Regarding David's claim that "the king charged me with a matter" (v. 3 [2]), several argue that since "the king" is unspecified here, it is unclear whether this referred to Saul or YHWH.[27] If YHWH had sent David as he claimed, then David was not lying but using ambiguity to deceive, since Ahimelech probably would have assumed that "the king" referred to Saul. However, the evidence for this is inconclusive. Therefore, although the means are open to discussion, most agree that David deceived Ahimelech in v. 3 [2].

Others have suggested that, not only did David deceive Ahimelech, but Ahimelech also deceived David. Several disbelieve Ahimelech's claim that he had no ordinary bread (v. 5 [4]), maintaining that the city of Nob was sufficiently large and thus there must have been *some* ordinary bread there.[28] If this line of reasoning were correct, Ahimelech lied to David and seemingly deceived him regarding the availability of ordinary bread. However, two observations argue against this. First, Ahimelech did not claim that there was no ordinary bread in all of Nob, but only that he currently did not possess any (אֵין־לֶחֶם חֹל אֶל־תַּחַת יָדִי [v. 5 (4)]). Therefore arguments about the size of Nob and the unrealism of no ordinary bread being there are irrelevant. Since the consecrated bread was set apart for the priests (Lev 24:8–9), it is possible that this was Ahimelech's primary source of sustenance at the sanctuary, and thus it is plausible that he would not have had ordinary bread on hand.

---

25. E.g., Conrad, "Davids Königtum als Paradoxie," 414; Miscall, *1 Samuel*, 132; Robinson, *Let Us Be Like the Nations*, 115; Birch, "First and Second Books of Samuel," 1139; Cartledge, *1 & 2 Samuel*, 252; Campbell, *1 Samuel*, 225; Bar-Efrat, *Das Erste Buch Samuel*, 285.

26. Brueggemann, *First and Second Samuel*, 154. This would also cohere with Jesus' interpretation of the narrative in the NT, which seems to presume that David had companions (see Matt 12:1–8; Mark 2:23–28; Luke 6:1–5).

27. Fokkelman, *Crossing Fates*, 355; Polzin, *Samuel and the Deuteronomist*, 195; Edelman, *King Saul*, 163; Green, *How Are the Mighty Fallen*, 348; Youngblood, "1, 2 Samuel," 727; Bergen, *1, 2 Samuel*, 221; Firth, *1 & 2 Samuel*, 234.

28. Fokkelman, *Crossing Fates*, 352; Ackroyd, *First Book of Samuel*, 170; Green, *How Are the Mighty Fallen*, 348.

Second, and more importantly, not only did Ahimelech claim there was no ordinary bread, but the narrator confirms this: "So the priest gave him the holy bread, *for there was no bread there except the bread of the Presence*" (v. 7 [6]). Since the narrator is omniscient and reliable, it follows that there was no ordinary bread available, and therefore Ahimelech was not lying.

Against the views that David deceived Ahimelech or vice versa, Pamela Tamarkin Reis has argued that David and Ahimelech were colluding together to deceive Doeg.[29] According to Reis, when David entered the sanctuary, Ahimelech was trembling because he knew that David was on the run from Saul and that Saul's servant Doeg was present. Reis claims that by overemphasizing David's solitude in his initial questions (v. 2 [1]), Ahimelech subtly tipped David off that they were not alone.[30] She then argues that David picked up this subtle hint and colluded with Ahimelech by pretending to be on a secret mission from Saul, hoping to divert any suspicions Doeg may have had.[31] Reis suggests that David's request for "five loaves" (v. 4 [3]) alluded to the five smooth stones by which he killed Goliath. By this allusion David intended to encourage Ahimelech regarding his ability to succeed in this dangerous situation.[32] Reis also claims that their discussion of Goliath's sword, in which Ahimelech mentioned that David killed Goliath, was meant to intimidate Doeg by recalling David's famous military feat.[33] Keith Bodner has expanded Reis's theory by arguing that the narrator introduces Doeg in v. 8 [7] by a technique of "delayed exposition," whereby his late introduction casts his shadow back upon the entire preceding narrative and shows that his presence influenced David and Ahimelech's whole conversation.[34] Bodner further argues for Ahimelech's collusion with David by viewing it as part of a larger "motif of deceptive alliances" that began with Michal in chapter 19 and continued with Jonathan in chapter 20.[35]

Although creative, Reis's theory is unlikely for several reasons. First, her explanation of Ahimelech's trembling in contrast to that of the Bethlehemite elders in 1 Samuel 16 is unpersuasive. She notes the parallels between these two passages and then opines that if Ahimelech was truly afraid of David as the Bethlehemites were of Samuel, he would have asked if David came peaceably rather than inquiring into his solitude. Reis writes, "Only

---

29. Reis, "Collusion at Nob," 59–73.
30. Ibid., 64.
31. Ibid., 65.
32. Ibid., 66.
33. Ibid., 68.
34. Bodner, *David Observed*, 27; Bodner, *1 Samuel*, 227.
35. Bodner, *David Observed*, 37. See chapter 3, Deceptions C, D, and E.

the same question as that in the earlier passage, or one similar, would indicate such a trepidation."[36] According to her reasoning, if Ahimelech did not fear David, this would increase the probability that he was colluding with him. However, Reis does not explain why only the same type of question as that asked by the Bethlehemite elders could reflect such fear, and thus her argument is unfounded.

Second, Bodner argues that Ahimelech purposefully interjected his first question before David had time to say anything, since during David's prior two trips to see Samuel and Jonathan he had immediately expressed grief over Saul's oppression of him (see 19:18; 20:1). According to Bodner, if David had spoken first, he may have revealed his fugitive status, which would have endangered him with Doeg in the room; therefore Ahimelech interjected in order to tip David off.[37] However, unlike the reader, Ahimelech had no way of knowing that David had been so quick to blurt out his plight with Saul. Moreover, as Mauchline notes, as the king's son-in-law and captain of the army, David would normally be accompanied by a detachment of soldiers,[38] which more naturally explains Ahimelech's inquiry. Others observe that Ahimelech could have known about Saul and David's fluctuating relationship, which at this point had been publicized on more than one occasion (see 1 Sam 19:1, 11, 19–20; 20:30–33), and thus David's solitary arrival may have given him the appearance of a fugitive (which was in fact the truth).[39] With a paranoid, spear-wielding king on the throne, the arrival of a potential fugitive would have been reason enough for Ahimelech to tremble and question why David came alone. It is more plausible that Ahimelech's questions regarding David's solitude expressed his fearful response to this seemingly unstable political situation, rather than being an extremely subtle way of ironically hinting that he and David were not alone. This is analogous to the Bethlehemites' response to Samuel's arrival in 1 Samuel 16, which also happened in the context of political instability. Miscall observes that both passages involved (1) deception, (2) the receiver(s) trembling at the arrival of the deceiver, (3) consecration, and (4) sacrificial food.[40] Furthermore, in these two incidents both Samuel and David had recently had multiple conflicts with Saul,[41] which further supports the view

36. Reis, "Collusion at Nob," 63.
37. Bodner, *David Observed*, 27, n. 7.
38. Mauchline, *1 and 2 Samuel*, 150.
39. Fokkelman, *Crossing Fates*, 353; Alter, *David Story*, 131; Cartledge, *1 & 2 Samuel*, 252.
40. Miscall, *1 Samuel*, 131.
41. Samuel in 1 Sam 13:10–14; 15:10–35; David in 1 Sam 19:1, 11, 19–20; 20:30–33.

that in both cases fear of becoming a casualty of political instability caused the trembling and the initial questions.

Third, Reis's claim that David's request for "five loaves" alluded to the five smooth stones from his battle with Goliath seems improbable. This presumes both that the number of stones David picked up in 1 Samuel 17 was common knowledge at that time and that Ahimelech would correctly understand such a subtle allusion, with only the number "five" as an indicator. Rather than weighing the merits of such non-demonstrable speculations, Alter's observation that in biblical Hebrew the number five was sometimes used idiomatically to mean "a few" explains David's request for "five" loaves more easily and naturally.[42] Similarly, instead of viewing Ahimelech's mention of David's slaying of Goliath as intended to intimidate Doeg, this statement is more easily and naturally explained simply as part of Ahimelech's description of the sword that he had on hand.

Fourth, although Bodner suggests that the literary technique of "delayed exposition" explains Doeg's introduction in v. 8 [7], the narrator's presentation of Doeg in this verse does not comport with this technique. Quoting *The Concise Dictionary of Literary Terms*, Bodner defines "delayed exposition" as

> a form of dischronologizing "by which some of the events of a story are related at a point in the narrative after later story-events have already been recounted. Commonly referred to as retrospection or flashback," such a device "enables a storyteller to fill in background information about characters and events."[43]

Bodner subsequently elaborates, "As defined here, *delayed exposition* deals with a new divulgence of a past action in the narrative sequencing, *after* it has happened in the story."[44] In these statements, Bodner emphasizes that this technique involves divulging a past *action* or *event*. However, in 1 Sam 21:8 [7] the narrator introduces Doeg in a circumstantial clause that presents no narrative action or events. Therefore, based on Bodner's own definition, this is not an example of delayed exposition.[45]

---

42. Alter, *David Story*, 131. See also Philip P. Jenson, who describes חמש as "a small, 'round' number (Lev 26:8; Isa 30:17), perhaps related to the use of five fingers for a 'handful'" ("חמש," 191).

43. Bodner, *David Observed*, 28–29; quoting Baldick, *Concise Dictionary*, 9.

44. Bodner, *David Observed*, 29, n. 13 (emphasis his).

45. Bodner also refers to Sternberg's discussion of temporal discontinuity (*Poetics of Biblical Narrative*, 264–320) to support his argument (*David Observed*, 29, n. 13). However, Sternberg only mentions "delayed exposition" when discussing the circumstantial clause in Judg 4:11 that recounts the migration of Heber the Kenite (*Poetics of*

Fifth, Bodner's suggestion that David's deceptive alliances with Michal and Jonathan in the previous two chapters initiate a motif that extends to the present passage reflects only one possible interpretation. One could also argue that David's solitary deception of Ahimelech and Doeg matches his solitary deception of Achish and the Philistines in the immediately subsequent pericope (vv. 11–16 [10–15]). For all these reasons, Reis's and Bodner's interpretation of this passage is unconvincing.

Lastly, Reis and Bodner posit that Doeg's later claim in 22:10 that Ahimelech had inquired of God for David was a lie and thus a deception of Saul.[46] Alter argues that the narrator would not have elided such a significant event from 21:2–10 [1–9] had it actually happened.[47] However, whether or not Ahimelech inquired of God for David depends significantly upon how one interprets Ahimelech's statement in 22:15. After being interrogated by Saul concerning his assistance to David, Ahimelech responded, "Did I just begin to inquire of God for him today? Far be it from me" (היום החלתי לשאול-לו באלהים חלילה לי, NASB). This statement is ambiguous. It could mean that this was not the first time Ahimelech had inquired of God for David, since he had done so previously, or it could mean that Ahimelech had never inquired of God for David, so why would he begin now?[48] Alter prefers the second reading,[49] but this makes Ahimelech's overall discourse confused. In v. 14 Ahimelech had just praised David's highly trusted and honored status within Saul's house. It makes little sense for him to follow this praise by immediately emphasizing how he had never inquired of God for David, and how outlandish the thought of him beginning today would be. However, it fits well within Ahimelech's self-defense if he was arguing that because David was so trusted and honored, he had inquired of God for him many times, including this most recent one. Therefore it seems best to conclude that Ahimelech admitted to inquiring of God for David, and thus Doeg did not deceive Saul.[50]

Biblical Narrative, 280). Unlike 1 Sam 21:8 [7], Judg 4:11 fits the category of delayed exposition since it uses a *wayyiqtol* verb (ויט) to describe a prior *action*: Heber had "pitched" his tent near Kedesh prior to the Israelite battle with Jabin.

46. Reis, "Collusion at Nob," 70; Bodner, *David Observed*, 33.

47. Alter, *David Story*, 137; see also Brueggemann, *First and Second Samuel*, 159.

48. Firth, *1 & 2 Samuel*, 239–40; Long, "1 and 2 Samuel," 360; Taggar-Cohen, "Political Loyalty," 262.

49. Alter, *David Story*, 138.

50. As Cartledge observes, in the next two episodes after Saul's slaughter at Nob, David inquired of the Lord before taking action (23:1–5, 6–14), which shows it was not unusual for him to seek YHWH (*1 & 2 Samuel*, 265).

To summarize: David deceived Ahimelech (and indirectly Doeg) into believing falsely that he was on a secret mission for Saul, and possibly that he was on his way to meet his men. That Ahimelech gave David the consecrated bread and Saul's sword shows that David successfully deceived him.

Analyzing the Deception

The tactic David used to deceive Ahimelech was a lie. His motive for deceiving was to acquire provisions as he fled from Saul's presence (cf. 1 Sam 20:13; 21:11). David achieved the goal for which he deceived by acquiring these provisions. Although David did not personally experience negative consequences for this deception, because of his actions Saul later commanded Doeg to slaughter all the priests of Nob, so Doeg killed the priests and all the men, women, children, infants, cattle, donkey, and sheep; only Abiathar escaped (1 Sam 22:17-20). After hearing about this slaughter from Abiathar, David evaluated his own actions negatively: "I knew on that day that Doeg the Edomite was there, that he would surely inform Saul. I am responsible for every person in your father's house" (22:22). Hertzberg claims that David condemned himself not because he deceived Ahimelech but because he was careless.[51] However, David located his guilt in his knowledge that Doeg would "surely inform" (הגד יגיד) Saul. Since David's goal in deceiving was to get Ahimelech's assistance, which is precisely what Doeg informed Saul about (22:9-10), it follows that David knew that his deception was putting Ahimelech at risk.[52] Therefore David's negative evaluation applied directly to his deception and suggests that the author's evaluation of this deception is negative as well.

Deception W: Saul's Deception of the Necromancer at Endor (1 Samuel 28:3–25)

In 1 Samuel 28 the Philistines set up camp in Shunem, making Saul greatly afraid (vv. 4-5). After unsuccessfully inquiring of YHWH by legitimate means, Saul disguised himself and sought out a female necromancer (אשת בעלת־אוב),[53] a type of practitioner he had previously banished from the land

---

51. Hertzberg, *I & II Samuel*, 179.
52. So also Payne, *I & II Samuel*, 111.
53. For theories regarding the etymology and meaning of אוב, see Hoffner, "Second Millennium Antecedents," 385-401; Lust, "On Wizards and Prophets," 133-42; Nihan, "1 Samuel 28," 29-30. Depending on the context, אוב seems to have referred either to

(v. 8; cf. v. 3). With his identity obscured and after allaying the woman's fears about the illegality of her actions, Saul instructed her to conjure up the spirit of Samuel. Upon seeing Samuel, the woman recognized Saul and asked why he deceived her (v. 12). Once again, Saul assured her that she was safe and asked her to continue the séance. After Saul explained to Samuel his military plight and lack of response from YHWH, Samuel reiterated YHWH's rejection of him, identified David as the one to whom the kingdom was being given, and declared that the next day YHWH would hand Saul over to the Philistines unto his death (vv. 17–19). Saul fell to the ground, and after the woman and his men convinced him to eat, she prepared them food, and they ate and left.

Establishing the Deception

Saul deceived the necromancer into believing falsely that he was someone else. This is evident for three reasons. First, when recalling Saul's prohibition of necromancy, the woman referred to Saul in the third person (v. 9a), which implies that she did not believe she was speaking to him. Second, the woman expressed fear for her life when asked to practice necromancy (v. 9b), but engaged in it eventually (vv. 11–12a), which she surely would not have done if she had known her inquirer was Saul. Third, after recognizing Saul, the woman confessed that she had been deceived: "Why did you *deceive me* (רמיתני)? You are Saul" (v. 12b).

Analyzing the Deception

The tactic Saul used to deceive the necromancer was a disguise, as v. 8a says: "Saul disguised himself and put on other clothes" (NRSV). His motive was to receive illegal necromantic services. Additionally, many have suggested that because Endor was northeast of the Philistine camp at Shunem, coming from Gilboa Saul would have had to sneak past the Philistines to reach the necromancer; thus his disguise was also designed to hide him from them.[54] While this may be true, Saul's disguise also served a symbolic, narratological function. Ora Horn Prouser has highlighted the symbolic significance attached to clothing throughout the books of Samuel, where putting on

---

a deceased spirit or metonymically to the necromantic cult (see Arnold, "Necromancy and Cleromancy," 201; Van Pelt and Kaiser, "אוב," 303).

54. Ackroyd, *First Book of Samuel*, 213; McCarter, *1 Samuel*, 271; Fokkelman, *Crossing Fates*, 600; Klein, *1 Samuel*, 271; Gordon, *I & II Samuel*, 195; Blenkinsopp, "Saul and the Mistress of the Spirits," 52.

garments is generally depicted positively and losing them is depicted negatively.⁵⁵ For example, in contrast to Eli's wicked sons (1 Sam 2:12–17), the narrator depicts Samuel positively as ministering before YHWH "wearing a linen ephod" (v. 18), and Samuel's mother would bring her faithful son a "little robe" annually (v. 19).⁵⁶ When Saul tore the edge off Samuel's robe, Samuel declared that YHWH had similarly torn the kingdom from Saul (1 Sam 15:27–28). During David's rise, Jonathan gave his robe, tunic, sword, bow, and belt to David (1 Sam 18:4), and Michal used a garment to deceive Saul's messengers and thus protect David (1 Sam 19:13); in both cases Saul's children are depicted as helping David against Saul's wishes. However, immediately after this, Saul pursued David, but the Spirit of God came upon him in such a way that he "stripped off his garments" and lay naked all day and night (1 Sam 19:24). This survey offers only a representative sampling, and as Prouser argues, although each example may not seem significant by itself, viewed collectively they reveal a pattern that corresponds to the characters' changing positions in the story.⁵⁷ Therefore some have plausibly concluded that Saul's disguise in 1 Samuel 28, which involved "wearing other clothes" and thus the removal of his royal clothes, had negative overtones representing the removal of his kingship.⁵⁸

Saul achieved the goal for which he deceived, demonstrated by the fact that the woman conjured up Samuel for him (even though she recognized Saul before doing so). However, although Saul achieved this immediate goal, when Samuel appeared, rather than telling Saul what to do in the upcoming battle, the prophet reiterated YHWH's rejection of his kingship and prophesied his death in battle the following day (vv. 17–19). The author's evaluation of Saul's deception is negative. The Torah condemned the "medium and spiritist" (אוב וידעני), saying that Israel would be defiled by them (Lev 19:31), that YHWH would cut off anyone who turned to them (Lev 20:6), and that they must be stoned to death (Lev 20:27). Although Saul had originally expelled these practitioners from the land, he deceived in order to engage in this sinful practice. Furthermore, Saul's deception of the woman began with the request: "Divine a spirit for me" (קסומי־נא לי באוב, v. 8). Significantly, the root קסם recalls Samuel's prophetic denunciation in 15:23:

---

55. Prouser, "Suited to the Throne," 27–37.

56. Significantly, both of these latter two verses are disjunctive. The first contrasts Samuel with Eli's sons (ושמואל משרת את־פני יהוה), and the latter fronts the object of the "little robe" that Hannah would bring to Samuel annually (ומעיל קטן תעשה־לו).

57. Prouser, "Suited to the Throne," 34.

58. Fokkelman, *Crossing Fates*, 600; Alter, *David Story*, 173; Green, *How Are the Mighty Fallen*, 427–28; Craig, "Rhetorical Aspects," 229, 243.

> For rebellion is like the sin of *divination* (קסם)
> and insubordination is like iniquity and *teraphim*,
> Because you have rejected the word of YHWH
> so he has rejected you as king.

Other than a reference to Philistine "diviners" (קסמים) in 1 Sam 6:2, these are the only two occurrences of the root קסם in the books of Samuel. In addition, Saul's only use of the divine name in this narrative was to swear by YHWH that no harm would come to the necromancer (v. 10). As Leithart notes, since Deut 18:10 commanded that no one who "practices divination" (קסם קסמים) was allowed in the land, Saul was "swearing in the Lord's name that he would not obey the Lord's word!"[59] Thus it is not surprising that the Chronicler identified this event as one of the reasons YHWH "put him to death and caused the kingdom to turn to David son of Jesse" (1 Chr 10:13–14). Therefore the author's evaluation of Saul's deception in this narrative is negative.

Deception X: The Amalekite's Deception of David (2 Samuel 1:1–16)

First Samuel 31 tells the story of Saul's last battle against the Philistines at Mount Gilboa. According to that account, after being critically wounded and failing to convince his armor bearer to kill him so that the Philistines would not torture him, Saul committed suicide by falling on his sword. However, 2 Sam 1:1–16 reports a seemingly contradictory version of Saul's demise. In this latter account, three days after Saul's death, an Amalekite entered David's camp in Ziklag and told David that he was on Mount Gilboa during Saul's last moments. According to the Amalekite, while Saul was leaning on his spear and suffering in agony, he asked the Amalekite to give him the *coup de grâce*. Seeing that Saul could not survive, the Amalekite complied and brought Saul's crown and armlet to David. After mourning Saul's death, David had the Amalekite put to death for killing the Lord's anointed.

Establishing the Deception

Several explanations have been offered to account for these different versions of Saul's death. Mauchline acknowledges the discrepancy between these two versions and argues that the Amalekite's story "rings true."[60] However, this

---

59. Leithart, *A Son to Me*, 155.
60. Mauchline, *1 and 2 Samuel*, 196–97.

would mean that the narrator's account in 1 Samuel 31 is inaccurate, which is unacceptable narratologically. Some explain the discrepancy on source-critical grounds, arguing that these two chapters reflect alternative traditions.[61] Others have sought to harmonize the two accounts. For example, Josephus suggested that after his armor bearer refused to kill him, Saul tried to fall on his sword, but was unable to pierce himself with it. Saul then asked the Amalekite, who obliged his request and killed him, took his royal items, and fled. After Saul's armor bearer saw that Saul was dead, he killed himself.[62] Thus Josephus attempts to fit the Amalekite's version in a gap he perceives between vv. 4 and 5 of chapter 31. The problem with this view is that 31:4 says, "Saul took his sword *and fell on it*" (ויקח שאול את־החרב ויפל עליה), whereas in Josephus's reconstruction Saul only attempted to fall on it.

Shimon Bar-Efrat has provided a more sophisticated harmonization by arguing that Saul actually fell on his sword in 31:4, and that the first clause of v. 5 reports, not that the armor bearer saw that Saul was dead, but that he was *dying*.[63] Upon seeing this, the armor bearer fell on his own sword and evidently died first,[64] after which the dying Saul asked the Amalekite to kill him. Thus Bar-Efrat attempts to fit the Amalekite's account between vv. 5 and 6 of chapter 31. However, v. 5 presents a problem for this reconstruction, which I translate here with Bar-Efrat's imperfective aspect in the first occurrence of מות: "And the armor bearer saw that Saul *was dying*, so he also fell on his sword, *and he died/was dying with him* (וימת עמו)." In Bar-Efrat's reconstruction, if this latter occurrence of מות is understood perfectively, the armor bearer died before Saul, which is an unnatural reading of the phrase, "he died *with* him," especially in a context in which the armor bearer is depicted as following in Saul's footsteps. However, to understand this latter occurrence of מות imperfectively creates an equally awkward reading, with v. 5 describing Saul and his armor bearer both in the process of dying, but with no concomitant action. Therefore Arnold is correct in stating that "any harmonization that forces the Amalekite's actions of vv. 7–10 into the

---

61. Klopfenstein, *Die Lüge*, 327; Ackroyd, *Second Book of Samuel*, 20; Robinson, *Let Us Be Like the Nations*, 150. For a discussion of the inadequacies of source-critical explanations, see Arnold, "Amalekite's Report," 290–94.

62. *Ant.* 6.14.7.

63. Bar-Efrat, "Death of King Saul," 276. Bar-Efrat supports this by noting other instances where מות describes someone in the process of dying (e.g., Gen 35:18; 1 Sam 4:20).

64. Bar-Efrat does not specifically say this in his reconstruction, though this would seem to be the necessary conclusion from this point.

account of 1 Samuel 31 . . . does a fundamental injustice to the literary unity of that account."[65]

However, neither source-critical hypotheses nor reconstructive harmonizations are necessary if one does not assume that the Amalekite was telling the truth. Accordingly, many conclude that since the narrator's version is reliable and authoritative, and since the Amalekite's version differs from this authoritative version, the Amalekite must have been lying.[66] Several elements in the text support this interpretation. First, three times the narrator refers to the Amalekite as "the young man who was telling him" (הנער המגיד לו, vv. 5, 6, 13). By this description the author characterizes the Amalekite as a "talker" and thus invites the reader to question the reliability of his report.[67] Second, the Amalekite began his report by claiming that he "*surely chanced* (נקרא נקריתי) upon Mount Gilboa" (v. 6a). The paronomastic infinitive construction depicts the man as forcefully asserting that he was

65. Arnold, "Amalekite's Report," 295. Bar-Efrat adduces other data to support his argument ("Death of King Saul," 276–77), but several are non-sequiturs regarding the veracity of the Amalekite's report and none justify the awkward reading of 31:5 that results from his reconstruction. He notes that the Amalekite's possession of the royal items shows that he was actually on Mount Gilboa; but this does not mean that the Amalekite's account of what happened there was truthful. Bar-Efrat also claims it is significant that David believed the Amalekite. However, believing a communication to be true does not indicate that it is true; otherwise deception would not exist. Lastly, Bar-Efrat claims that when biblical characters lie, typically the narrator or a character identifies it (ibid., 277). In support he cites Gen 27:35, where Isaac described Jacob's actions as done "with deceit" (במרמה), and 1 Kgs 13:18, where the narrator comments that the old prophet of Bethel "was lying to him" (כחש לו). However, in light of the present study we must dispute the assertion that such comments are normal where lying occurs (see, e.g., 1 Sam 11:1–11; 16:1–5; 20:27–34; 21:2–10 [1–9]; 27:7–12; 2 Sam 14:2–21; 17:5–14, 15–21a). Bar-Efrat also cites 2 Sam 19:25 [24], where "the narrator makes it clear that Ziba lied by informing us that Mephibosheth gave expression to his grief 'from the day the king left until the day that he returned safe'" (ibid.). However, by this same logic we may conclude that the narrator makes it clear that the Amalekite lied by informing us that Saul committed suicide in the prior chapter.

66. Fokkelman, *Crossing Fates*, 639; Edelman, *King Saul*, 303; Polzin, *David and the Deuteronomist*, 3; Payne, *I & II Samuel*, 157; Reis, "Killing the Messenger," 170–71. *Contra* Brueggemann, who claims that we cannot adjudicate between these two accounts. He says, "The important point for interpretation is not the issue of facticity. What claims our attention is the intention of the narrative. The Amalekite account must be taken on its own terms" (*First and Second Samuel*, 213). However, the question here is not one of facticity outside the narrative but of factual coherence within the narrative. The "intention of the narrative" surely includes the data reported by the *narrator*, without whom we do not even know which character is saying which line. Thus to question the reliability of the narrator is to read contrary to the intention of the narrative.

67. Fokkelman, *Crossing Fates*, 636; Alter, *David Story*, 195.

on Mount Gilboa unintentionally that day. In context this raises suspicions concerning the tale he was telling. Third, in v. 6b the man employed two הנה clauses successively to describe what he saw when he chanced upon Mount Gilboa. Berlin has pointed out that הנה clauses usually occur one at a time, except in dream reports, where they are compounded; thus the repeated occurrences here reflect the fictional nature of his account.[68] Fourth, in v. 8 the man finally revealed his Amalekite nationality, which only makes him more suspicious. Every reference to Amalekites in the books of Samuel puts them in a wholly negative light as Israel's enemies. Therefore it would be odd for an Amalekite to give Israel's king a merciful death, especially since Saul had previously killed a great number of Amalekites (1 Sam 15:7–8). In light of the narrator's alternative report in the preceding chapter and these hints in the text, it is best to view the Amalekite as lying. That David had the Amalekite executed for "killing the Lord's anointed" (v. 16) shows that he believed the lie and thus was deceived.

Analyzing the Deception

The tactics the Amalekite used to deceive David were lies and nonverbal action. In addition to lying about his role in Saul's death, when the Amalekite arrived at David's camp he had torn his clothes and put dirt on his head (2 Sam 1:2), which were common signs of grief and sorrow in the ancient Near East. Polzin calls these signs a "behavioral lie,"[69] intending to convey solemnity and mourning concerning the battle and the recent deaths. By appearing this way he presented himself as a loyal sojourner in order to increase his chances of receiving a reward from David, which was evidently his motive (see 2 Sam 4:10). The Amalekite did not achieve the goal for which he deceived since, rather than rewarding him, David ordered that he be killed (v. 16). The narrator characterizes this deceiver negatively by emphasizing his Amalekite nationality. The chapter begins with a circumstantial clause noting that David had just returned from destroying the

---

68. Berlin, *Poetics and Interpretation*, 81; so also Edelman, *King Saul*, 301; Gordon, *I & II Samuel*, 208. Reis rejects Berlin's argument, saying, "Berlin's argument is weakened by her 'usually' and by the fact that the Bible does not regard dreams as falsehoods but as conduits of divine truths" ("Killing the Messenger," 171, n. 10). Regarding the first criticism, Berlin says that הנה clauses "usually" occur singly *because of the exception of dream reports*; therefore her use of "usually" does not weaken her argument. Regarding Reis's second criticism, although YHWH communicates truth through dreams, it is also true that dreams are distinct from events that occur in reality, and the Amalekite claimed to represent an event that occurred in reality.

69. Polzin, *David and the Deuteronomist*, 7; see also McCarter, *II Samuel*, 58.

Amalekites (v. 1), reminding the reader of the Amalekites' raid on Ziklag in 1 Sam 30:1–2. Moreover, the man's Amalekite nationality is mentioned twice in this narrative (vv. 8, 13). Since Amalekites are always depicted negatively elsewhere in the books of Samuel, it is best to view the characterization of this Amalekite deceiver as negative as well.

Deception Y: Absalom's Deception of the Men of Israel (2 Samuel 15:1–6)

After 2 Samuel 14 recounts Absalom's restoration to David from exile in Geshur, 15:1–6 describes how Absalom began his revolt. He would rise early in the morning and intercept those who came to David with disputes seeking justice. Absalom would ask the people about themselves (v. 2b), assure them that their claims were "good and right" (v. 3a), and then tell them that there was no one to listen to them on behalf of the king (v. 3b). Absalom then expressed that if he were appointed judge in the land, everyone would bring their disputes to him and he would give them justice (v. 4). Additionally, if a person came and bowed to him, Absalom would take hold of him and kiss him (v. 5). The narrator summarizes the result of all of this: "Absalom behaved like this toward all the Israelites who came to the king for justice; and so Absalom stole the hearts of the men of Israel" (v. 6).[70]

---

70. The phrase "the men of Israel" (אנשי ישראל) is best understood as referring to people from the whole nation, including Judah. Some understand "the tribes of Israel" (שבטי־ישראל) in vv. 2 and 10 to refer to the northern tribes only (e.g., Hertzberg, *I & II Samuel*, 336; Evans, *1 and 2 Samuel*, 201). However, although the phrase "the tribes of Israel" sometimes denotes only the northern tribes in the books of Samuel (e.g., 2 Sam 5:1), on other occasions it clearly refers to both Israel and Judah (e.g., 1 Sam 2:28; 10:20; and especially 2 Sam 24:2 ["from Dan to Beersheba"]), and thus context must determine its referent here. After describing Absalom's conversations with people from "the tribes of Israel" (v. 2), the narrator concludes that, "Absalom stole the hearts of the men of Israel" (ויגנב אבשלום את־לב אנשי ישראל, v. 6), connecting these two phrases. Then, after Absalom inaugurated his revolt, a messenger informed David that "the hearts of the men of Israel" (לב־איש ישראל) were with Absalom (v. 13). Since the rebellious declaration was that "Absalom is king *in Hebron*" (v. 10), and since "two hundred men from Jerusalem went with Absalom" (v. 11), giving the appearance of Jerusalemite support (see below), from this messenger's perspective the revolt included a southern component. All this suggests that both "the tribes of Israel" (vv. 2, 10) and "the men of Israel" (vv. 6, 13) referred to people from all throughout the nation (see also Firth, *1 & 2 Samuel*, 455; Arnold, *1 & 2 Samuel*, 574, n. 7).

Establishing the Deception

Absalom deceived the Israelites in two ways. First, he told the people who came that their claims were "good and right" (טובים ונכחים, v. 3a), and the narrator tells us that he did this to all Israel (ויעש אבשלום כדבר הזה לכל־ישראל, v. 6). Unless we assume that every single person who came for justice actually had a claim that was "good and right," it seems that Absalom deceived some people into believing falsely that their claims were valid when they were not. Second, Absalom caused the people to believe falsely that they could not get justice from David. Although some conclude from vv. 3–4 that Absalom was simply capitalizing on already-existing public discontent with David's administration of justice,[71] it is more likely that Absalom was deceiving them concerning their opportunity for a hearing. Supporting this is the fact that Absalom would "rise early" in order to intercept people at the gate, before they reached the king (v. 2). As Elizabeth Bellefontaine argues, if Absalom's statements were true, it would have been better for him to meet these people after they sought justice from David and returned dissatisfied.[72] Furthermore, as others have noted, the preceding narrative about David's encounter with the Tekoite woman shows that he was available to hear legal disputes and issue judgments (see 2 Sam 14:8, 10, 11b).[73] Although it is conceivable that David's availability in this regard may have changed in the intervening period, aside from Absalom's assertions nothing in the narrative indicates this. Since this chapter begins with a description of the chariots, horses, and runners that Absalom provided for himself (v. 1)—which are widely understood as showing pretension to the throne[74]—Absalom's claims about the inadequacy of David's administration of justice are better understood as lies by a royal pretender intended to disgruntle the populace concerning the current monarch.

It is clear that Absalom deceived the men of Israel, since the narrator summarizes this section by saying, "Absalom *stole the hearts* (ויגנב אבשלום

---

71. Brueggemann, *First and Second Samuel*, 301; Garsiel, *First Book of Samuel*, 72; Robinson, *Let Us Be Like the Nations*, 228; Alter, *David Story*, 283; Campbell, *2 Samuel*, 145. Jacob Weingreen suggests that public bitterness toward David existed because of his ruthlessness in war and his affair with Bathsheba ("Rebellion of Absalom," 264–66), but nothing in the narrative supports this supposition.

72. Bellefontaine, "Customary Law and Chieftainship," 59; see also Cartledge, *1 & 2 Samuel*, 559.

73. Fokkelman, *King David*, 168; Baldwin, *1 & 2 Samuel*, 257; Cartledge, *1 & 2 Samuel*, 559; Leithart, *A Son to Me*, 265; Firth, *1 & 2 Samuel*, 455.

74. Ackroyd, *Second Book of Samuel*, 138; Fokkelman, *King David*, 166; McCarter, *II Samuel*, 356; Youngblood, "1, 2 Samuel," 988; Stoebe, *Das Zweite Buch Samuelis*, 358; Caquot and de Robert, *Les Livres de Samuel*, 526.

אֶת־לֵב) of the men of Israel" (v. 6). The only other place in the OT where the idiom "steal the heart" occurs is Genesis 31. In that episode, the narrator says, "Jacob *stole the heart* of Laban the Aramean (ויגנב יעקב את־לב לבן הארמי) by not telling him that he was fleeing" (v. 20). When Laban caught up to Jacob, his questions further clarify this idiom:

> Laban said to Jacob, "What have you done? You have deceived me (lit: "You have stolen my heart" [ותגנב את־לבבי]), and carried away my daughters like captives of the sword. *Why did you flee secretly and deceive me* (lit: "steal me" [ותגנב אתי]) *and not tell me? I would have sent you away with mirth and songs, with tambourine and lyre* (vv. 26–27, NRSV).

From Laban's perspective, Jacob's act of "stealing his heart" was not simply leaving with his daughters, *but leaving secretly* (i.e., giving Laban the false impression that they were still in Paddan Aram). This agrees with the narrator's description in v. 20 that Jacob "stole his heart" by not telling him of their departure. For this reason, this construction is widely considered an idiom implying deception.[75]

Analyzing the Deception

The tactic Absalom used to deceive the men of Israel was telling lies. His assertions that every Israelite's case was "good and right" (v. 3a) and that they would get no legal hearing from David (v. 3b) were not true. His motive for deceiving was to create discontent with David's rule and present himself as a worthy alternative (v. 4), thereby making the political environment fertile for his upcoming *coup d'état*. Absalom achieved the goal for which he deceived since he successfully inaugurated his revolt with the allegiance of "the men of Israel" (v. 13). However, although Absalom achieved this immediate goal, the revolt he began here eventuated in his death (2 Sam 18:14–15).

The author evaluates this deception negatively. As Bergen observes, from Exodus up to this point in 2 Samuel, the biblical writers have consistently portrayed the use of horses and chariots negatively and associated them only with the failed attempts of Israel's enemies to overtake her.[76] Thus

---

75. Anderson, *Jacob and the Divine Trickster*, 123.

76. Bergen, *1, 2 Samuel*, 396. He cites Exod 14:9—15:21; Deut 11:4; Josh 11:4–9; 24:6; Judg 4:15; 5:19–22; 2 Sam 8:4; 10:18. To these we may add Gen 49:17, in which Dan is described as a "serpent by the road" that "bites the heels of the horse (סוס) so that its rider (רכב) falls back," and Deut 20:1, which describes the "horse and chariot" (סוס ורכב) of enemy armies that Israel was not to fear, for YHWH would give her victory (v. 4).

Absalom's acquisition of horses and chariots characterizes him as an enemy of God's people. Moreover, the narratorial comment that Absalom "stole the hearts" of the men of Israel (v. 6) has negative connotations, demonstrated by Gen 31:26, in which Laban used the phrase in a condemnatory manner; from his perspective, Jacob had wronged him.[77]

Deception Z: Absalom's Deception of David and the Men of Jerusalem (2 Samuel 15:7–12)

After Absalom deceived the men of Israel in 2 Sam 15:1–6,[78] he asked David for permission to go to Hebron and fulfill a vow that he allegedly made while in Geshur (vv. 7b–8). David granted him permission, so Absalom went to Hebron (v. 9). From there Absalom sent spies throughout Israel, telling the people to proclaim him king in Hebron when they heard the trumpet blast (v. 10). Verse 11 notes that two hundred men from Jerusalem accompanied Absalom to Hebron as invitees, but that they did not know all that Absalom was doing. The account ends with the narrator's summary: "And so the conspiracy was strong, and the people with Absalom kept increasing" (v. 12b).

Establishing the Deception

Absalom deceived both David and the two hundred men from Jerusalem into believing falsely that he was going to Hebron to "worship YHWH" (v. 8), when in reality his primary objective was to begin the revolt he had

---

77. So also Fokkelman, *King David*, 169; Caquot and de Robert, *Les Livres de Samuel*, 527; Arnold, *1 & 2 Samuel*, 575; Auld, *I & II Samuel*, 501.

78. MT says that Absalom went to David at the end of "forty years" (ארבעים שנה, 2 Sam 15:7). Almost all translators and commentators agree that this reading is problematic. Some suggest that it should be modified to read "four years," along with some LXX manuscripts and Josephus (e.g., Budde, *Samuel*, 342; Gordon, *I & II Samuel*, 271; Campbell, *2 Samuel*, 141), while others suggest it could have originally read "forty days" (e.g., McCarter, *II Samuel*, 355). Robert Althann argues that the number "forty" could have been elliptical, with the referent supplied by the context. If שנה is then read as a verb ("to repeat, do again") and placed after the *athnach*, the verse would have the sense of, "At the end of forty days Absalom spoke insistently to the king . . ." ("The Meaning of ארבעים שנה," 250–52). Leithart suggests that "forty" refers to the fortieth year of David's reign (*A Son to Me*, 263–64). However, elsewhere in the OT the construction שנה + number + ויהי מקץ always refers to an intervening period of time, never to an absolute chronology (see Gen 41:1; Exod 12:41; 1 Kgs 2:39; Isa 23:17; 2 Chr 8:1). In the end, Conroy's conclusion seems wisest: "As matters stand, it seems better to register the uncertainty and not to build further conclusions (chronological or structural) on a doubtful text" (*Absalom Absalom*, 106–7, n. 40).

been preparing in vv. 1–6. This interpretation is supported by Absalom's first recorded action in Hebron, which was sending spies to organize his revolt (v. 10).[79] Since David sent Absalom to Hebron in peace, Absalom obviously succeeded in deceiving him. Since the two hundred men from Israel accompanied Absalom to Hebron with "integrity" (תמם) and "did not know anything about the matter" (v. 11), it is clear that Absalom succeeded in deceiving them as well.

Analyzing the Deception

The tactic Absalom used to deceive David and the men of Jerusalem was misleading requests. His request of David in vv. 7b–8 implied that the purpose of his trip was to fulfill a vow to worship YHWH in Hebron. If Absalom never made this vow in Geshur, v. 8 would be a lie, but since the narrator does not tell us whether or not Absalom made it we may not conclude this firmly.[80] The narrator also does not tell us the content of Absalom's request for the two hundred men from Jerusalem to join him; all we know is they were "invited" (קראים, v. 11). Nevertheless, since the implied purpose of Absalom's trip was to fulfill a vow to worship, and since the narrator emphasizes that these men from Jerusalem went with "integrity" (תמם) and "did not know anything about the matter" (ולא ידעו כל־דבר, v. 11), it follows that they did not know about the revolt and probably believed that worship was the purpose of this gathering in Hebron.[81] Absalom's motive for deceiving David was to get permission to travel to Hebron, from where he planned to begin his revolt. His motive for deceiving the two hundred men from Jerusalem was probably to create the false impression of strong Jerusalemite support for his revolt.[82]

A significant feature of this deception is its resemblance to Absalom's previous deception of David and Amnon in 2 Sam 13:23–39 ("Deception

---

79. So also Mauchline, *1 and 2 Samuel*, 270; Birch, "First and Second Books of Samuel," 1319.

80. Bergen argues that since Deut 23:21 demanded that vows be fulfilled quickly, "Absalom's slackness in this matter should have raised questions about his true devotion to the Lord" (*1, 2 Samuel*, 398). However, while such delay should have reflected his laxity, it does not follow that he never made the vow.

81. Payne, *I & II Samuel*, 228. *Contra* Stoebe, who opines that the two hundred men were not unsuspecting extras but partisans of the revolt (*Das Zweite Buch Samuelis*, 361). To conclude this, however, Stoebe explicitly reads against the editorial "retouching" ("Retuschen") that he sees in v. 11 (ibid.).

82. Gordon, *I & II Samuel*, 271–72; Birch, "First and Second Books of Samuel," 1320; Leithart, *A Son to Me*, 267; Firth, *1 & 2 Samuel*, 455.

O"). Fokkelman has highlighted five common elements in these two episodes. In both cases: (1) Absalom waited a long time before striking (13:23; 15:7a);[83] (2) Absalom made a request to the king; (3) the content of this request concerned going elsewhere for a festive meeting (13:23–24; 15:7b–8); (4) Absalom's instructions to others are introduced by לאמר and begin with a כ + infinitive time adjunct (13:28 [כטוב לב־אמנון]; 15:10 [כשמעכם]); and (5) Absalom "invited" (קרא) a group of unsuspecting guests who accompanied him (13:23; 15:11).[84] To these we may add that in both cases (6) Absalom used the request to deceive David in order to carry out his underhanded action. Absalom achieved the goal for which he deceived David by successfully inaugurating his revolt in Hebron (v. 9). That David and his servants fled Jerusalem immediately upon hearing of this revolt (vv. 13–14) shows that Absalom achieved the goal for which he deceived the two hundred men from Jerusalem as well; the presence of these men seemingly gave the appearance of significant support for Absalom from the capital city.[85] However, although Absalom achieved these immediate goals, as mentioned above, the revolt that he began here eventuated in his death (2 Sam 18:14–15).

The author evaluates this deception negatively. In v. 12 the narrator says, "When he was offering sacrifices, Absalom sent for Ahithophel the Gilonite, David's *counselor* (יועץ), from his city Giloh. And so the *conspiracy* (קשר) was strong, and the people with Absalom kept increasing." Outside this chapter, the only other occurrence of קשר with the sense of "conspire/conspiracy" in the books of Samuel is when Saul used it to accuse the Benjamites and Ahimelech of "conspiring" against him (1 Sam 22:8, 13).[86] The negative connotation in Saul's use suggests a similarly negative connotation in the narrator's parallel use here.[87] Moreover, the mention of Ahithophel in this verse connects it to v. 31, where David was informed of Ahithophel's

---

83. This parallel is slightly weakened from the textual uncertainty at 15:7 (see n. 78 above), though two of the three possible readings reflect an extended period of time ("forty years" and "four years").

84. Fokkelman, *King David*, 170; see also Birch, "First and Second Books of Samuel," 1319; Cartledge, *1 & 2 Samuel*, 560.

85. The narrator highlights the presence of the two hundred men with Absalom by the disjunctive nature of v. 11, in which the prepositional phrase ואת־אבשלום ("and with Absalom") is fronted.

86. Aside from this, the root only occurs in 1 Sam 18:1, in which the narrator says that "the soul of Jonathan *was bound* (נקשרה [Niphal]) with the soul of David," but this relational use does not carry the same political connotations as the other uses.

87. See Brueggemann, *First and Second Samuel*, 302; Hagan, "Deception as Motif," 314.

defection: "Now David had been told, 'Ahithophel is among the *conspirators* (קשרים) with Absalom.' So David said, 'YHWH, turn Ahithophel's *counsel* (עצה, from the root יעץ) into foolishness.'" This is the next reference to Ahithophel in the narrative, and the only other occurrence of קשר in 2 Samuel. Since YHWH answered David's prayer and frustrated Ahithophel's counsel and thus Absalom's conspiracy, it follows that 15:12 reflects a negative evaluation of these events by the author.

Deception α: Ziba's Deception of David (2 Samuel 16:1–4; 19:25–31 [24–30])

In 2 Sam 16:1–4, as David was fleeing Jerusalem because of Absalom's revolt, he encountered Ziba, the servant of Mephibosheth, who was waiting beyond the summit of the Mount of Olives with donkeys and a set of supplies. After inquiring into the purpose of these supplies, David asked where Mephibosheth was. Ziba replied that Mephibosheth was waiting in Jerusalem with the hope that the Saulide kingdom would revert to him. In response to this news, David declared that all of Mephibosheth's property now belonged to Ziba. However, after Absalom's revolt failed and David returned, Mephibosheth met David and defended himself (19:25–31 [24–30]). This pericope begins with the narrator noting that Mephibosheth had neither cared for his personal hygiene nor washed his clothes "from the day the king left until the day he entered in peace" (v. 25 [24]). When David asked Mephibosheth why he did not accompany him, Mephibosheth claimed that Ziba had betrayed him. He said that he had intended to saddle his donkey and go with the king, since his lameness prohibited him from going on foot, but evidently Ziba took his donkey and then slandered him to David. Mephibosheth then highlighted the fact that his household deserved nothing from David, yet David had given him a seat at his table (cf. 2 Sam 9:7), so he had no right to make further appeals (19:28 [27]). In response, David revised his earlier judgment and declared that Ziba and Mephibosheth would divide the field. Mephibosheth replied that Ziba could take all of it, now that David had returned in peace (v. 31 [30]).

Establishing the Deception

Since Ziba and Mephibosheth gave conflicting accounts of what happened, one of them was lying. Although some maintain that the narrative does not clearly indicate who was telling the truth,[88] several elements suggest that Ziba lied about Mephibosheth's actions. The first and most important indicator is the narratorial comment in 19:25 [24]:

> Now Mephibosheth, son of Saul, went down to greet the king. He had not cared for his feet or his mustache, nor had he washed his clothes, from the day the king left until the day he entered in peace.

As many observe, this verse reveals that Mephibosheth had mourned throughout David's absence, demonstrating that he was not aspiring to take back the Saulide throne as Ziba had claimed.[89] Questioning this conclusion, Ackroyd compares Mephibosheth to the Gibeonites in Joshua 9, who disheveled their appearance for deceptive purposes, and questions whether Mephibosheth was doing the same thing.[90] However, this comparison is faulty, since the narrator of Joshua explicitly states that the Gibeonites "acted craftily" (בערמה, v. 4, NASB) and were Israel's "neighbors" and "lived in their midst" (v. 16), rather than living far away as they claimed and as their appearance suggested. In contrast, in 2 Sam 19:25 [24] the narrator says that Mephibosheth began showing signs of grief and mourning "the day the king left." To conclude that Mephibosheth was deceptive, one must posit that, upon David's flight, he hoped for David's defeat as he aspired for the Saulide throne, yet simultaneously began showing signs of grief to give himself a cover in case David was victorious and his aspirations went unrealized.[91] Although this is logically possible, it does not seem probable narratologically. If the narrator intended to depict Mephibosheth as deceptive, it seems unlikely that he would provide this extensive comment on his physical condition, which supports Mephibosheth's testimony, without noting its "craftiness" or something similar. Without such a qualification, it is better to conclude that, by inserting this circumstantial clause at the

---

88. Ackroyd, *Second Book of Samuel*, 181; Conroy, *Absalom Absalom*, 106; Anderson, *2 Samuel*, 238; Birch, "First and Second Books of Samuel," 1347; Campbell, *2 Samuel*, 149; Schipper, "Why Do You Still Speak of Your Affairs?" 346; Frontain, "The Trickster Tricked," 188.

89. Hertzberg, *I & II Samuel*, 366; Gordon, *I & II Samuel*, 277; Sternberg, *Poetics of Biblical Narrative*, 380; Marcus, "David the Deceiver," 169, n. 20; Garsiel, *First Book of Samuel*, 71; Halpern, *David's Secret Demons*, 50; Van Seters, *Biblical Saga*, 285.

90. Ackroyd, *Second Book of Samuel*, 181; see also Schipper, "Why Do You Still Speak of Your Affairs?" 345; Firth, *1 & 2 Samuel*, 488.

91. So also notes Lasine, "Judicial Narratives," 61.

beginning of Mephibosheth's defense, the narrator is substantiating his claim to innocence.[92]

The second reason not to believe Ziba is the improbability that Mephibosheth would view Absalom's coup as an opportunity for his own political advancement. Rather than raising the likelihood of Mephibosheth acquiring the Saulide throne, Absalom's rise to power put Mephibosheth in a more precarious position because he had no covenant with Absalom as he did with David (see 1 Sam 20:14–17; 2 Sam 9:1).[93] Third, after David decided to divide the estate between the two men, Mephibosheth suggested that David give the entire estate to Ziba: "Let him take everything, now that my lord the king has entered his house in peace" (v. 31 [30]). This further characterizes Mephibosheth as loyal to David and thus supports his innocence.[94]

92. Thus Gros Louis is mistaken when he claims that "the *narrative* tells us" that Mephibosheth hoped to get back the Saulide kingdom ("Difficulty of Ruling Well," 26 [emphasis mine]). On the contrary, one character *claimed* that Mephibosheth hoped for this, whereas the narrator has chosen to reveal evidence against this claim. Similarly, contrary to the narrator's depiction, Veijola claims that these verses show that Mephibosheth repented of his behavior ("David und Meribaal," 352). However, if Mephibosheth's physical signs reflected repentance, one would have to conclude that he had been repenting since "the day the king left," which would have left him no time for any disloyal behavior during Absalom's revolt.

93. Klopfenstein, *Die Lüge*, 327; Mauchline, *1 and 2 Samuel*, 275; Hertzberg, *I & II Samuel*, 345; Gordon, *I & II Samuel*, 276–77; Birch, "First and Second Books of Samuel," 1325; Van Seters, *Biblical Saga*, 283.

94. McCarter, *II Samuel*, 422; Birch, "First and Second Books of Samuel," 1347. Schipper argues that the phrase בשלום may mean "safely," which would suggest that Mephibosheth was concerned for David, or it could mean "peaceably," which would suggest that Mephibosheth was "expressing relief that David is not eliminating his political enemies upon his return" ("Why Do You Still Speak of Your Affairs?" 350–51). This latter interpretation implies that Mephibosheth viewed himself as a political enemy of David, which presupposes that he had not been loyal during David's exile and therefore was being deceptive. However, this latter meaning of בשלום cannot be sustained in this context. In v. 31 [30] Mephibosheth said, "Let him take everything, *now that my lord the king has entered his house in peace* (אחרי אשר־בא אדני המלך בשלום אל־ביתו)." In parallel language the narrator has already noted that Mephibosheth expressed grief "from the day the king left until the day *he entered in peace* (אשר־בא בשלום)" (v. 25 [24]). This parallel language suggests that the narrator is aligning Mephibosheth's viewpoint with his own (so also Lasine, "Judicial Narratives," 61). Furthermore, in the narratorial comment it does not make sense for בשלום to mean "peaceably." This would result in a situation in which David's *exile* engendered Mephibosheth's expressions of grief—which implies that Mephibosheth cared about David—yet upon David's return Mephibosheth expressed relief that David was not hostile to his enemies, which implies that Mephibosheth viewed himself as an enemy. Such a reading of v. 25 [24] is illogical. However, to understand the narrator's use of בשלום as meaning "safely" yields a consistent and reasonable scenario in which, upon

Against this, Hagan suggests that Mephibosheth's offer might imply that he still "entertained some preposterous thought of grandeur."[95] However, it is unclear how Mephibosheth's offer supports such a conclusion. Rather, that Mephibosheth was willing to give up his half of the estate to demonstrate that David's safe return was his fundamental concern is consistent both with his stated loyalty to David (v. 27 [26]) and the narrator's comment on his mourning during David's absence (v. 25 [24]).[96]

Some have argued that Mephibosheth's comment that David was "like a messenger of God" (כמלאך האלהים, v. 28 [27]) suggests that he was deceptive, since in 2 Samuel 14 the Tekoite woman used this same phrase in a context of deception.[97] In that narrative, the Tekoite compared David to a divine messenger in both vv. 17 and 20, yet interestingly, both Lasine and Schipper cite only v. 20 as support that Mephibosheth's use of the phrase implies he was deceptive. However, by v. 20 the Tekoite had finished deceiving and was telling the truth: "In order to change the present situation your servant Joab did this. But my lord has wisdom like the wisdom of the messenger of God (מלאך האלהים) to know everything that is in the land." Since this later use of the phrase was not deceptive, one may not conclude that Mephibosheth was being deceptive simply because he used it. Moreover, in 1 Sam 29:9 the phrase "like a messenger of God" (כמלאך אלהים) appears again in a context of deception.[98] However, in this narrative, it was Achish, *the victim of deception*, who used it to describe David. Therefore, since in two of the three other instances in which someone compared David to a "messenger of God" (1 Sam 29:9; 2 Sam 14:20) the phrase was not used to deceive,[99] one cannot conclude that Mephibosheth was deceptive because he used it. Rather, in each case the person using the phrase simply expressed confidence in

---

David's departure, Mephibosheth expressed grief due to his fidelity to the king, and he ceased such expressions upon the king's safe return. Since this is the best understanding of the narrator's use of בשלום, and since the narrator aligns his comment with Mephibosheth's in v. 31 [30], it follows that the most consistent understanding of בשלום in v. 31 [30] is "safely," which argues for Mephibosheth's fidelity and thus his truthfulness.

95. Hagan, "Deception as Motif," 318.

96. So also Lasine, "Judicial Narratives," 61.

97. Hagan, "Deception as Motif," 318; Lasine, "Judicial Narratives," 61–62; Schipper, "Why Do You Still Speak of Your Affairs?" 350.

98. See Deception J in chapter 4.

99. Both Pyper (*David as Reader*, 125–26) and Schipper ("Why Do You Still Speak of Your Affairs?" 350, n. 16) include 2 Sam 24:16 in this discussion, but this verse simply describes "the messenger of YHWH" (מלאך יהוה) bringing God's judgment against the people; nothing in it clarifies the situations in which someone compares David to a "messenger of God" (מלאך אלהים).

David, whether in his "goodness" (1 Sam 29:9), his ability "to discern good and evil" (2 Sam 14:17), or his "wisdom" (2 Sam 14:20). Mephibosheth's use also fits this pattern: he expressed confidence in David's ability to decide, saying, "Do what is good in your eyes" (19:28 [27]).

For all these reasons, it is best to conclude that Ziba deceived David into believing falsely that Mephibosheth remained in Jerusalem with the hope that the Saulide throne would revert to him (2 Sam 16:3). That David gave all of Mephibosheth's estate to Ziba (16:4) shows that his deception succeeded.

Analyzing the Deception

The tactic Ziba used to deceive David was a lie. His motive for deceiving seemingly was to receive a reward from David and to find favor in his eyes (16:4). Ziba achieved the goal for which he deceived, demonstrated by the fact that David initially gave him the entire Saulide estate. However, although Ziba achieved this immediate goal, David modified his judgment later and divided the estate between the men, so Ziba ended up with only a partial reward. Although Ziba experienced no negative consequences for this deception, the author seems to evaluate it negatively. Alter has noted the general symmetry and chiastic relationship between David's encounters on his departure from Jerusalem and those on his return:

Departure

Ittai the Gittite (insisted on going across the Jordan [15:19–22]) → loyal

   Ziba (denounced Mephibosheth [16:1–4]) → **ambiguous**

   Shimei (expressed hostility [16:5–14]) → disloyal

Return

   Shimei (expressed contrition [19:17–24]; → disloyal
   Ziba interjected [v. 18])

   Mephibosheth (defended himself [19:25–31]) → ambiguous

Barzillai the Gileadite → loyal[100]
(insisted on returning across the Jordan [19:32–40])

---

100. This arrangement is adapted from Alter's observations (*David Story*, 315). To conserve space I have only provided MT versification here.

Since David's departure also involved encounters with Zadok and Abiathar (15:24-29) and Hushai (15:30-37), this symmetry is imprecise. However, the general correspondence between these elements is apparent, as is the descending scale of loyalty among the encounters during David's departure, which is mirrored in an ascending manner during his return. From David's perspective, during his exile, Ittai and Barzillai showed the clearest loyalty (2 Sam 15:19-22; 19:32-40 [31-39]); Ziba and Mephibosheth's loyalty was ambiguous, demonstrated by David's division of the estate (19:30 [29]);[101] and Shimei clearly had been disloyal (16:11-12).[102] However, in the return section the narrator associates Ziba with Shimei:

> Shimei son of Gera, the Benjamite from Bahurim, hurried and went down with the men of Judah to meet King David. Now, one thousand men from Benjamin were with him, *and Ziba the servant of the house of Saul, and his fifteen sons and twenty servants with him*. And they rushed to the Jordan before the king. They crossed the ford to bring across the king's house and to do good in his eyes. And Shimei son of Gera fell before the king when he crossed over the Jordan (2 Sam 19:17-19 [16-18]).

Both Youngblood and Firth acknowledge that this reference to Ziba interrupts the account of Shimei,[103] but neither explains why this is placed here. However, by interjecting this disjunctive clause mentioning Ziba in the midst of the story of Shimei, the narrator is associating these two characters. In terms of the chart above, in so doing the narrator subtly shifts Ziba from the category of ambiguity to the category of disloyalty. Furthermore, in Mephibosheth's defense, which immediately follows, the narrator provides another disjunctive clause that subtly shifts Mephibosheth from the category of ambiguity to the category of loyalty (v. 25 [24]). Therefore, although from David's perspective Ziba's and Mephibosheth's loyalties were still ambiguous upon his return, by these two disjunctive clauses the narrator clarifies for the reader where their true loyalties lay. Since the narrator associates Ziba with Shimei, he seems to be depicting Ziba's actions negatively along with Shimei's. That the narrator gives Mephibosheth the last word in this episode (19:31 [30]) supports this conclusion. As we have already seen, this suggests that the narrator is sympathetic toward Mephibosheth and therefore likely critical of Ziba.

---

101. See Gordon, *I & II Samuel*, 291.

102. David's departure encounters with Zadok, Abiathar, and Hushai also fit within this movement of loyalty → ambiguity → disloyalty, since they all were loyal to David and came between Ittai the Gittite (loyal) and Ziba (ambiguous) (15:24-37).

103. Youngblood, "1, 2 Samuel," 1035; Firth, *1 & 2 Samuel*, 487.

Deception β: Ahimaaz's Deception of David (2 Samuel 18:19–30)

After Joab and his armor bearers killed Absalom and ended the revolt, Ahimaaz requested of Joab, "Let me run and tell the king that YHWH has delivered him from the hand of his enemies" (2 Sam 18:19). Joab told Ahimaaz that he would not take the news that day, and instead sent a Cushite to inform David of what happened. Ahimaaz continued to petition Joab until he finally dispatched him as well (v. 23). Ahimaaz outran the Cushite, arrived first, and told David that YHWH had delivered him (v. 28). However, when David asked if Absalom was safe, Ahimaaz gave an unclear response: "When Joab sent the king's servant, and your servant, I saw a great tumult, but I did not know what it was" (v. 29, NASB).

Establishing the Deception

Most believe that Ahimaaz's answer in v. 29 was evasive, thereby deceiving David into believing falsely that he did not know whether or not Absalom was safe.[104] A common explanation of this evasiveness is Ahimaaz's supposed fear of a violent response from David, which also explains why Joab hesitated to send him.[105] In v. 20 Joab had told Ahimaaz, "You are not a bearer of news today; you may bring news another day, but today you will not bring news, *for the king's son is dead.*" According to this interpretation, the final clause in Joab's speech proves that Ahimaaz knew about Absalom's fate, and although initially he was eager to bring news to David, upon arriving he had second thoughts and nervously bumbled his deceptive words.[106] However, McCarter has provided an alternate reading, arguing that the final clause of v. 20 is a narratorial comment rather than part of Joab's speech to Ahimaaz.[107] If this is correct, Ahimaaz may not have known what happened to Absalom, and therefore his statement in v. 29 may have been truthful.

---

104. Mauchline, *1 and 2 Samuel*, 289; Ackroyd, *Second Book of Samuel*, 172; Hertzberg, *I & II Samuel*, 361; Conroy, *Absalom Absalom*, 73; Fokkelman, *King David*, 257; Bar-Efrat, *Narrative Art in the Bible*, 62–63; Baldwin, *1 & 2 Samuel*, 272; Robinson, *Let Us Be Like the Nations*, 249; Firth, *1 & 2 Samuel*, 379; Cartledge, *1 & 2 Samuel*, 604; Auld, *I & II Samuel*, 545; Reis, "Killing the Messenger," 183–84.

105. See, e.g., Polzin, *David and the Deuteronomist*, 190.

106. As Conroy states, "the contorted syntax mirrors the speaker's unease" (*Absalom Absalom*, 73).

107. McCarter, *II Samuel*, 408.

A benefit of this interpretation is that it easily explains Ahimaaz's eagerness to go, since he may not have known about Absalom. Nevertheless, Ahimaaz's two statements, "Come what may" (ויהי מה, vv. 22, 23) present a difficulty for McCarter's reading. These two statements indicate that Ahimaaz had some uncertainty concerning David's response to this news.[108] This suggests that the last clause of v. 20 was part of Joab's direct discourse and not a narratorial comment. Otherwise, Ahimaaz's answer in v. 22 ("Come what may") would have been in response to Joab's abbreviated statement, "You are not a bearer of news today; you may bring news another day, but today you will not bring news" (v. 20). Ahimaaz's answer does not follow this well dialogically. This abbreviated statement of Joab does not imply any reason for uncertainty about David's response, which Ahimaaz's answer in v. 22 seems to presume; Joab simply prohibited Ahimaaz from going. However, if Joab was discouraging Ahimaaz from going because David's son was dead, Ahimaaz's response in v. 22 makes sense. This last observation raises doubts about McCarter's reading. It seems best to conclude that Ahimaaz knew about Absalom's death, yet lied to David and said he did not know. That David believed this lie and was deceived is clear since he did not press Ahimaaz for more information, but told him to stand aside as he waited for the Cushite to arrive (v. 30).

Analyzing the Deception

The tactic Ahimaaz used to deceive David was a lie. The final clause of v. 29 ("but I don't know what [it was] [ולא ידעתי מה]") was false, since Ahimaaz was responding to David's concern about Absalom's welfare. To determine Ahimaaz's motive for deceiving, we must first determine why he insisted on taking news to David if he knew that Absalom's death would upset him. It is possible that simple zeal motivated Ahimaaz and that initially he did not realize how devastating the news of Absalom's death would be for David, but when he arrived and David expressed concern about Absalom, he changed his mind and deceived him. As noted above, based on David's reactions to the Amalekite (2 Samuel 1) and Recab and Baanah (2 Samuel 4), some have posited that fear of a violent response motivated this change in Ahimaaz. However, others have observed that those messengers who received a deadly response from David were implicated in the deaths they reported, which differentiates them from Ahimaaz.[109] In the end, this interpretation must view Ahimaaz as strangely inconsistent, first desperately wanting to

---

108. So also Brueggemann, *First and Second Samuel*, 321.
109. Anderson, *2 Samuel*, 226; Firth, *1 & 2 Samuel*, 478.

bring news to David, but then changing his mind when the moment came for fear of negative consequences that do not follow logically from past messengers' experiences. This reading also makes Ahimaaz initially quite obtuse regarding David's likely response to the death of his son.[110] Although this is logically possible, it does not seem to be the best solution.

However, that Ahimaaz hoped for a reward explains both his eagerness to go and his deception when he arrived, without needing to ascribe to him any inconsistency or obtuse thinking regarding David. Verse 22b suggests that reward may have been Ahimaaz's motivation: "But Joab said, 'Why would you run, my son, *since you will have no reward for going* (ולכה אין־בשׂורה מצאת)?'" (NASB). As Driver observes, this last phrase is strange, but probably means "'no message *finding* or *attaining* (aught),' i.e., no message that will secure you a reward."[111] The LXX supports this interpretation, rendering this phrase, "by going you have no good tidings *for gain*" (οὐκ ἔστιν σοι εὐαγγελία εἰς ὠφέλειαν πορευομένῳ, NETS). Furthermore, the noun בשׂרה ("news"),[112] which occurs four times in this passage (vv. 20, 22, 25, 27), only occurs once elsewhere in the books of Samuel (2 Sam 4:10). In that verse, David reminded Recab and Baanah of his previous interaction with the Amalekite, saying, "[W]hen the one who told me, 'See, Saul is dead,' thought he was bringing good news, I seized him and killed him at Ziklag—*this was the reward I gave him for his news*" (אשׁר לתתי־לו בשׂרה, NRSV). This other occurrence of בשׂרה associates it with the hope of reward for the one bringing news and therefore supports the idea that reward motivated Ahimaaz here.

This reading also accounts for Ahimaaz's twofold qualification, "Come what may," since the second occurrence of this phrase (v. 23) was in direct response to Joab's statement that Ahimaaz would receive no reward (v. 22b). Therefore it is plausible that in their first exchange (vv. 20, 22a), Joab's unstated reason for prohibiting Ahimaaz from going was because there was

---

110. For example, concerning Ahimaaz's initial request to run, Yairah Amit claims that Ahimaaz thought that David viewed Absalom as just another enemy, and thus Ahimaaz did not realize that Absalom's death would be devastating for him (*Reading Biblical Narratives*, 41). However, since David had commanded the captains to deal gently with Absalom—and the text explicitly adds that "the entire army heard the command of the king" (וכל־העם שׁמעו בצות המלך, v. 5; see also v. 12)—it is difficult to believe that Ahimaaz would have thought that David viewed Absalom this way.

111. Driver, *Samuel*, 255 (emphasis his).

112. Although the forms of the root בשׂר usually connote "good news" (e.g., 2 Kgs 7:9; Isa 41:27; 52:7; 60:6; 61:1), this is not always the case. Since in 1 Sam 4:17 בשׂר does not connote "good news" but "bad news," I translate the nominal form here with the nondescript, "news." See also Mauchline, *1 and 2 Samuel*, 288; Conroy, *Absalom Absalom*, 68, n. 97.

no prospect of reward, since the king's son was dead. Joab made this reason clear in his second attempt to dissuade Ahimaaz (v. 22b). However, to both of these Ahimaaz responded, "Come what may, let me run" (i.e., "I realize I may not receive a reward, but still allow me to run"). It is plausible that Ahimaaz still wanted to run because he planned to deceive David concerning his knowledge of Absalom's welfare in order to maintain his chances of receiving a reward. Although none of this proves that the prospect of reward motivated Ahimaaz, this scenario best explains all the data in the text.

A significant feature of this deception is that it alludes to the Amalekite's deception in 2 Samuel 1 by means of 2 Sam 4:10, as referred to above. In both cases (1) a man brings "news" (בשרה) to David (2) that is deceptive (3) concerning a death (4) that is intended to bring him a reward. However, whereas the Amalekite deceived David into believing falsely that he killed Saul, Ahimaaz deceived David into believing falsely that he did not know about Absalom's death. Like the Amalekite, Ahimaaz did not achieve the goal for which he deceived since he received no reward from David. However, unlike the Amalekite, he did not receive any negative consequences for his deception.

The author's evaluation of this deception is unclear, as is his characterization of Ahimaaz. On the one hand, the allusion to the Amalekite could suggest a negative characterization of Ahimaaz, though as just noted, the latter was not punished as the former was. On the other hand, David referred to Ahimaaz as a "good man" (איש־טוב), from which he concluded that he must have been bringing "good news" (בשורה טובה, v. 27). This parallels Adonijah's later statement that Jonathan was a "worthy man" (איש חיל) and thus must be bringing "good news" (וטוב תבשר, 1 Kgs 1:42). However, as Bar-Efrat notes, the point of these character statements in these two passages is not to characterize the two messengers but to reflect the speakers' hopes concerning the news they carried.[113] Indeed, from 2 Sam 18:19—19:8 the narration time slows considerably to focus on David's reception of and response to the news of Absalom's death. Ahimaaz's deception thus functions narratologically to retard the process of David hearing about Absalom's death, after which Ahimaaz is never mentioned again in the books of Samuel. For these reasons, the author's evaluation of this deception is unclear.

Summary

From this analysis we can make several observations concerning deception intended to benefit the deceiver. First, in all but two deceptions (X and β)

---

113. Bar-Efrat, *Narrative Art in the Bible*, 56.

the deceiver achieved his intended goal. Second, as was the case in chapter 5, no consistent tactic of deception was used in this category: five episodes involved lying (V, X, Y, α, and β), whereas three used other means (U [omitting information], W [disguise], and Z [misleading requests]).[114] Third, only one deceiver experienced negative consequences for his deception (the Amalekite in Deception X). Fourth, in all these episodes, the author either evaluates the deception negatively or characterizes the deceiver negatively, except for Deception β, in which the evaluation is unclear.

---

114. Deception X used nonverbal action in addition to a lie.

7
Conclusion

HAVING EXAMINED THE DECEPTION episodes in the books of Samuel, we are now in a position to look back over all the material and synthesize the results. In this chapter I will first summarize the findings of chapters 3–6, seeking to highlight trends in the narrative evaluations and thereby determine the author's rationale for the depictions of deception. Second, I will compare these findings with the theology of deception evident in the explicit statements of the OT in chapter 2, where I concluded that deception is only proscribed when it brings unjust harm or disadvantage to another person. Third, I will compare the conclusions developed from these narrative and prescriptive materials to the scholarly views of deception surveyed in chapter 1. Fourth, I will survey deception elsewhere in the Bible to see if these conclusions cohere with the other narrative depictions and explicit statements. At the end, I will offer some concluding remarks concerning the overall results of the study and how they contribute to our understanding of a theology of deception.

Summary of Deception in the Books of Samuel

Of the twenty-eight episodes studied, twelve were depicted positively (whether the deception received a positive evaluation [B, C, D, Q, S, T] or the deceiver a positive characterization [E, F, G, H, J, R]), fifteen were depicted negatively (whether the deception received a negative evaluation [K, L, M, P, U, V, W, Y, Z, α] or the deceiver a negative characterization [A, I, N, O, X]), and one was unclear (β).[1] In this section I will first summarize

---

1. In some episodes I was not able to determine confidently the author's evaluation of the deception, so I analyzed the characterization of the deceiver instead. In this

the significant features observed in the episodes to see what contributions these deceptions make to the literary artistry of the narratives. Then I will compare the narrative evaluations against the various characteristics observed in each deception (tactic, motive, achievement of goals, and negative consequences) to see if any trends emerge. Since Deception β is unclear, it will not be included in the following discussion.

Significant Features

The significant features observed in these deception episodes contribute to the literary artistry of the narrative in a variety of ways. Most prominent are the many deceptions that recalled Saul's rejection and/or David's election (B, C, D, E, G, W). In fact, every deception involving Saul, whether as deceiver or receiver, recalled his rejection, except for Deceptions I and U. However, even these latter two episodes fit this pattern indirectly. In Deception I, Saul instructed his servants to tell David that they "loved" him (1 Sam 18:22), which we saw was ironically true (cf. vv. 5, 16). Since the verb "to love" (אהב) is widely attested in the ancient Near East as connoting political loyalty,[2] the unwitting irony in this deception pointed to the changing political situation that would result in David assuming the throne and Saul being rejected from it. Similarly, in Deception U, Saul deceived his uncle by failing to mention "the matter of the kingship" (1 Sam 10:16). As we saw in our discussion there, this omission was part of a larger pattern of Saul failing to embrace his recently anointed status as leader, which cast an ominous shadow over his subsequent reign. Many have argued that a major function of the books of Samuel was to legitimate the Davidic dynasty,[3] and these multiple recollections of Saul's rejection in the deception episodes support this rhetorical goal. Other significant features included several hints of the truth in the midst of deception (G, N, Q, S), allusions to other deception episodes (H, K, L, O, P, Z, β), and irony (I, J). Collectively, these features illustrate how the author of Samuel depicted these deceptions in an artistically sophisticated

---

section I am combining these episodes and referring to them collectively as "positive deceptions" and "negative deceptions." However, since not every action of a character necessarily reflects their overall characterization, the evaluation of deception in episodes that rely on characterization is less certain than the others. Nevertheless, in the absence of reliable indicators concerning deception evaluation, deceiver characterization is the next best narratological datum.

2. See Moran, "Ancient Near Eastern Background," 77–87; Thompson, "Significance of the Verb *Love*," 334–38.

3. E.g., see the discussions of McCarter, "Apology of David," 493–99; Bergen, *1, 2 Samuel*, 37–42.

manner, portraying these events to serve his larger rhetorical purposes, yet doing so in a way that is entertaining and narratologically complex.

Tactic and Evaluation

In comparing the narrative evaluations to the deception characteristics we will first explore the relationship between the tactic of deception and the corresponding evaluations. To clarify this and the subsequent relationships explored below, the following tables group the deceptions according to their narrative evaluation.

Table 5. Tactic and Evaluation

Ref	Deceiver-Receiver	Tactic	Evaluation
B	Samuel-Bethlehemites	Lie	Positive evaluation
C	Michal-Messengers	Lie, manipulation of environment	Positive evaluation
D	Michal-Saul	Lie	Positive evaluation
Q	Nathan-David	Ambiguous language	Positive evaluation
S	Hushai-Absalom 1	Ambiguous language	Positive evaluation
T	Hushai-Absalom 2	Lie, rhetoric	Positive evaluation
E	Jonathan-Saul	Lie	Positive characterization
F	David-Achish 1	Nonverbal action	Positive characterization
G	David-Achish 2	Lie	Positive characterization
H	Bahurim-Servants	Lie, manipulation of environment	Positive characterization
J	David-Achish 3	Ambiguous language	Positive characterization

Ref	Deceiver-Receiver	Tactic	Evaluation
R	Joab/Tekoite-David	Lie, nonverbal action	Positive characterization
K	Joab-Abner	Nonverbal action	Negative evaluation
L	Recab/Baanah-Palace	Nonverbal action	Negative evaluation
M	David-Uriah	Misleading requests and actions	Negative evaluation
P	Joab-Amasa	Nonverbal action, misleading question	Negative evaluation
U	Saul-Uncle	Omitting information	Negative evaluation
V	David-Ahimelech	Lie	Negative evaluation
W	Saul-Necromancer	Disguise	Negative evaluation
Y	Absalom-Men of Israel	Lies	Negative evaluation
Z	Absalom-David	Misleading requests	Negative evaluation
α	Ziba-David	Lie	Negative evaluation
A	Jabeshites-Nahash	Lie, ambiguous language	Negative characterization
I	Saul-David	Lie	Negative characterization
N	Amnon-David/Tamar	Nonverbal actions, misleading requests	Negative characterization
O	Absalom-David/Amnon	Misleading request	Negative characterization
X	Amalekite-David	Lie, nonverbal action	Negative characterization
β	Ahimaaz-David	Lie	Unclear

As this table shows, the deceivers used a variety of tactics, and often multiple tactics in the same episode. Most noteworthy is the relationship of lies to narrative evaluation. Eight of the twelve positive deceptions used a lie as one of the tactics (B, C, D, E, G, H, R, T); the other four positive deceptions used either ambiguous language (J, Q, S) or nonverbal action (F). In contrast, only six of the fifteen negative deceptions used lies (A, I, V, X, Y, α); the majority of the negative deceptions used other, usually more equivocal, means (ambiguous language, nonverbal actions, misleading requests, omission of information, disguise). These data suggest that the tactic of deception has no apparent bearing on the narrative evaluation. Specifically, whether or not a deceiver lied does not issue in a negative or positive evaluation respectively.

Motive and Evaluation

Next we will consider the relationship between the deceivers' motives and the corresponding narrative evaluations.

Table 6. Motive and Evaluation

Ref	Deceiver-Receiver	Motive	Evaluation
B	Samuel-Bethlehemites	Prevent Death/Harm	Positive evaluation
C	Michal-Messengers	Prevent Death/Harm	Positive evaluation
D	Michal-Saul	Prevent Death/Harm	Positive evaluation
Q	Nathan-David	Benefit Someone Else	Positive evaluation
S	Hushai-Absalom 1	Benefit Someone Else	Positive evaluation
T	Hushai-Absalom 2	Benefit Someone Else	Positive evaluation
E	Jonathan-Saul	Prevent Death/Harm	Positive characterization

Ref	Deceiver-Receiver	Motive	Evaluation
F	David-Achish 1	Prevent Death/Harm	Positive characterization
G	David-Achish 2	Prevent Death/Harm	Positive characterization
H	Bahurim-Servants	Prevent Death/Harm	Positive characterization
J	David-Achish 3	Cause Death/Harm	Positive characterization
R	Joab/Tekoite-David	Benefit Someone Else	Positive characterization
K	Joab-Abner	Cause Death/Harm	Negative evaluation
L	Recab/Baanah-Palace	Cause Death/Harm	Negative evaluation
M	David-Uriah	Cause Death/Harm	Negative evaluation
P	Joab-Amasa	Cause Death/Harm	Negative evaluation
U	Saul-Uncle	Benefit the Deceiver	Negative evaluation
V	David-Ahimelech	Benefit the Deceiver	Negative evaluation
W	Saul-Necromancer	Benefit the Deceiver	Negative evaluation
Y	Absalom-Men of Israel	Benefit the Deceiver	Negative evaluation
Z	Absalom-David	Benefit the Deceiver	Negative evaluation
α	Ziba-David	Benefit the Deceiver	Negative evaluation
A	Jabeshites-Nahash	Prevent Death/Harm	Negative characterization
I	Saul-David	Cause Death/Harm	Negative characterization

Ref	Deceiver-Receiver	Motive	Evaluation
N	Amnon-David/Tamar	Cause Death/Harm	Negative characterization
O	Absalom-David/Amnon	Cause Death/Harm	Negative characterization
X	Amalekite-David	Benefit the Deceiver	Negative characterization
β	Ahimaaz-David	Benefit the Deceiver	Unclear

As this table indicates, the positive and negative deceptions are almost completely distinct in terms of the motives of the deceivers. Every positive deception was committed either to prevent death or harm or to benefit someone else, except Deception J, which was intended to cause death or harm. Inversely, every negative deception was committed either to cause death or harm or to benefit the deceiver, except Deception A, which was intended to prevent death or harm. These data reveal an apparent relationship between a deceiver's motive and the corresponding evaluation and therefore suggest that motive is a criterion by which deception is evaluated. However, since Deceptions J and A are outliers, any theory concerning the relationship between motive and evaluation must explain these two anomalies. This observation that motive is the criterion for deception evaluation agrees with Williams's work on deception in Genesis.[4]

Achievement of Goals and Evaluation

The third comparison to consider is the relationship between the deceivers' success in achieving their goals and narrative evaluation.

---

4. Williams, *Deception in Genesis*, 53–55. See also Williams, "Lies, Lies, I Tell You!" 14.

Table 7. Achievement of Goals and Evaluation

Ref	Deceiver-Receiver	Achieved goal?	Evaluation
B	Samuel-Bethlehemites	Yes	Positive evaluation
C	Michal-Messengers	Yes	Positive evaluation
D	Michal-Saul	Yes	Positive evaluation
Q	Nathan-David	Yes	Positive evaluation
S	Hushai-Absalom 1	Yes	Positive evaluation
T	Hushai-Absalom 2	Yes	Positive evaluation
E	Jonathan-Saul	Yes	Positive characterization
F	David-Achish 1	Yes	Positive characterization
G	David-Achish 2	Yes	Positive characterization
H	Bahurim-Servants	Yes	Positive characterization
J	David-Achish 3	No	Positive characterization
R	Joab/Tekoite-David	Yes	Positive characterization
K	Joab-Abner	Yes	Negative evaluation
L	Recab/Baanah-Palace	Yes	Negative evaluation
M	David-Uriah	Yes	Negative evaluation
P	Joab-Amasa	Yes	Negative evaluation
U	Saul-Uncle	Yes	Negative evaluation

Ref	Deceiver-Receiver	Achieved goal?	Evaluation
V	David-Ahimelech	Yes	Negative evaluation
W	Saul-Necromancer	Yes	Negative evaluation
Y	Absalom-Men of Israel	Yes	Negative evaluation
Z	Absalom-David	Yes	Negative evaluation
α	Ziba-David	Yes	Negative evaluation
A	Jabeshites-Nahash	Yes	Negative characterization
I	Saul-David	No	Negative characterization
N	Amnon-David/Tamar	Yes	Negative characterization
O	Absalom-David/Amnon	Yes	Negative characterization
X	Amalekite-David	No	Negative characterization
β	Ahimaaz-David	No	Unclear

Among the positive deceptions, every deceiver achieved their goal, except in Deception J. Similarly, in the negative deceptions the deceivers almost always achieved their goals, except in two cases (I, X). Important for our analysis is the fact that Deception J is again the lone outlier among the positive deceptions. However, since almost all the deceivers achieved the goal for which they deceived in both evaluative categories, no strong relationship appears to exist between achievement of goals and evaluation.

Negative Consequences and Evaluation

The last relationship to consider is that between deceivers' experiencing negative consequences and narrative evaluation.

Table 8. Negative Consequences and Evaluation

Ref	Deceiver-Receiver	Negative consequences?	Evaluation
B	Samuel-Bethlehemites	No	Positive evaluation
C	Michal-Messengers	No	Positive evaluation
D	Michal-Saul	No	Positive evaluation
Q	Nathan-David	No	Positive evaluation
S	Hushai-Absalom 1	No	Positive evaluation
T	Hushai-Absalom 2	No	Positive evaluation
E	Jonathan-Saul	No	Positive characterization
F	David-Achish 1	No	Positive characterization
G	David-Achish 2	No	Positive characterization
H	Bahurim-Servants	No	Positive characterization
J	David-Achish 3	No	Positive characterization
R	Joab/Tekoite-David	No	Positive characterization
K	Joab-Abner	Yes	Negative evaluation
L	Recab/Baanah-Palace	Yes	Negative evaluation
M	David-Uriah	Yes	Negative evaluation
P	Joab-Amasa	Yes	Negative evaluation
U	Saul-Uncle	No	Negative evaluation

Ref	Deceiver-Receiver	Negative consequences?	Evaluation
V	David-Ahimelech	No (but the people of Nob did)	Negative evaluation
W	Saul-Necromancer	No (but Samuel reiterated judgment)	Negative evaluation
Y	Absalom-Men of Israel	No (but revolt ended in death)	Negative evaluation
Z	Absalom-David	No (but revolt ended in death)	Negative evaluation
α	Ziba-David	No (but David changed his decision)	Negative evaluation
A	Jabeshites-Nahash	No	Negative characterization
I	Saul-David	No	Negative characterization
N	Amnon-David/Tamar	Yes	Negative characterization
O	Absalom-David/Amnon	Yes	Negative characterization
X	Amalekite-David	Yes	Negative characterization
β	Ahimaaz-David	No	Unclear

As this table shows, in none of the positive deceptions did the deceiver experience any negative consequences. However, in almost half of the negative deceptions, the deceiver experienced negative consequences (K, L, M, N, O, P, X). Furthermore, in five other negative episodes, although the deceivers did not experience any negative consequences immediately related to their deception, their deception resulted in either a negative situation for them (W, Y, Z), a negative situation for someone else that the deceiver recognized was wrong (V), or a partial retraction of the deceiver's achieved goal (α). This leaves only three negative deceptions with no negative post-deception circumstances attached (A, I, U).[5] Therefore, generally speaking, it seems that the deceivers' post-deception circumstances may reflect the author's evaluation of their deception. Along these lines, Moshe Garsiel writes,

> In the world of the Bible, an essential thematic connection exists between a person's actions and his recompense. This basic biblical principle leads the reader to examine the characters' deeds—comparing or contrasting—in relation to what happens to them later on.[6]

According to this principle, the positive and negative post-deception circumstances reinforce the corresponding narrative evaluations. However, the variegated nature of the negative post-deception circumstances, ranging from the immediate execution of the deceiver (L, X) to only a partial retraction of a deceiver's undeserved reward (α), and the fact that three negative deceptions reflect no negative consequences or circumstances, show that this principle is not applied rigidly. Nevertheless, that none of the positive deceivers experienced any negative consequences, while the majority of negative deceptions resulted in some form of negative circumstance, coheres with the theory that the deceiver's motive is determinative for evaluation.

Now that we have suggested that the author depicted these deceptions based on the deceivers' motives, we need to determine what distinguishes the motives in the positive deceptions from those in the negative ones, while also accounting for the anomalous episodes J and A. To do this we will turn for insight to the ethics of deception found in the explicit statements studied in chapter 2 and analyze the element of justice in these deception accounts.

Justice and Deception Evaluation

In chapter 2, I concluded that the OT never categorically prohibits deception, but only deception that brings unjust harm or disadvantage to another person. This theology of deception explains the depictions of deception in the books of Samuel. If a person's motive for deceiving was just, the author depicted the deception positively; if a person's motive was unjust, the author depicted it negatively. In this section we will look at both the positive and negative deceptions to see how this ethic of deception explains the data.

---

5. However, it is possible that Deception A should not be understood negatively; see discussion below.

6. Garsiel, *First Book of Samuel*, 21.

Positive Deceptions

With the exception of Deception J, which I will discuss below, every positive deception in Samuel was committed either to prevent death or harm or to benefit someone else. In none of these cases was the deceiver attempting to bring unjust harm or disadvantage to another person. Samuel deceived to protect himself from being unjustly harmed by Saul (B). Michal deceived to protect David (C) and herself (D) from being unjustly harmed by Saul. Jonathan deceived to confirm Saul's unjust intentions to harm David (E). David deceived to protect himself from the Philistines as he fled from Saul's unjust pursuit (F, G). The woman of Bahurim deceived to protect David's men from Absalom's spies during a revolt that was unjust given David's anointed status (H). Nathan deceived by his parable to make David realize the unjust harm he had brought against Uriah and Bathsheba (Q). The Tekoite deceived so David would restore Absalom from exile (R). Hushai's two deceptions were to subvert Absalom's unjust revolt (S, T). None of these deceptions violate the OT's proscriptions of deception and therefore the author's positive depiction of them is consistent with this biblical ethic.

As noted above, among the positive deceptions, Deception J has the anomalous motive of causing death or harm. However, considering the OT's explicit proscriptions of deception, we should ask if the death or harm intended by this deception would be considered unjust from the author's perspective. If the author considered it just, this deception would fall properly into place with the other positive deceptions. In this episode David deceived Achish of Gath into believing falsely that he would join him in battle against Israel, when in reality David planned to turn and fight against him and the Philistines (1 Sam 28:1–2; 29:1–11). When we look at prior Israelite military engagement with the Philistines in 1 Samuel, it is clear that the author had no scruples against Israelites fighting and killing Philistines. Two episodes especially support this. First, in 1 Samuel 7, the Philistines engaged Israel in battle after the latter gathered to repent and confess at Mizpah. In response to this Philistine threat, Samuel sacrificed a burnt offering and cried out to YHWH, and "while Samuel was sacrificing the offering and the Philistines approached to fight against Israel, YHWH thundered with a great sound against the Philistines that day so they were confused and struck down before Israel" (v. 10). This divine intervention resulted in the Israelites pursuing the Philistines and striking them down (v. 11), and the narrator summarizes this event as YHWH's hand being against the Philistines (v. 13). Second, in 1 Samuel 14, Jonathan prepared his armor-bearer for their attack on a Philistine outpost near Gibeah by saying, "Perhaps YHWH will act for us" (v. 6). After perceiving a sign that "YHWH had given them into the hands of Israel" (v. 12), Jonathan and his armor-bearer fought and killed twenty Philistines (vv. 13-14). The narrator then notes that a "trembling" (חרדה) came upon the entire Philistine army, "and it was a trembling of God" (ותהי לחרדת אלהים, v. 15). Although this latter phrase could be understood as a superlative ("a very great panic" [NRSV]), most agree that YHWH caused this trembling, whether implicitly or explicitly.[7] This trembling resulted in the Philistines experiencing "exceedingly great confusion, each man's sword against his neighbor" (v. 20). That this was a divinely inspired trembling is demonstrated by the narrator's conclusion in v. 23: "So YHWH saved Israel on that day." In both of these narratives, the author depicts YHWH as supporting Israelite military engagement against the Philistines, and even fighting for them, both defensively (1 Samuel 7) and offensively (1 Samuel 14). This indicates that the author of Samuel viewed Israelite battles against the Philistines as justified, and therefore David's motive in Deception J of killing the Philistines in battle would not have been considered unjust. Thus Deception J does not violate the OT's theology of deception and is rightly categorized as a positive deception.

Negative Deceptions

Inversely, when we consider the negative deceptions in Samuel, in many cases the deceivers clearly intended to bring unjust harm or disadvantage to another person (I, K, L, M, N, O, P, Y, Z, α). In other cases it seems the deceivers were acting more from selfish motives than malicious intent (U, V, W, X). However, even in these latter episodes, some element of injustice was involved in the deceptions. Saul deceived his uncle concerning what Samuel said, thereby not rightly representing the prophetic word (U). David deceived Ahimelech concerning his business in Nob, thereby endangering the priest's life, as David later confessed (V). Saul deceived the necromancer concerning his identity, thereby leading her to break both civil and divine law (W). The Amalekite deceived David concerning his role in Saul's death in an attempt to receive a reward for services not rendered (X). Although in these cases bringing unjust harm or disadvantage to another person was not the deceiver's primary intention, each of these deceptions unjustly disadvantaged another person in some way.[8] Therefore the negative deceptions

---

7. See, e.g., Gordon, *I & II Samuel*, 107; Youngblood, "1, 2 Samuel," 662; Alter, *David Story*, 78; Tsumura, *First Book of Samuel*, 363.

8. In the case of the Amalekite it may be better to say that he intended to advantage himself unjustly. However, had he succeeded in getting the reward he wanted, he would have unjustly disadvantaged David, since the latter would have rewarded a

in the books of Samuel are also consistent with the theology of deception derived from the explicit statements.

The only negative episode that is questionable in this respect is Deception A, the Jabeshites' deceptions of Nahash. Since Nahash and the Ammonites were oppressing Jabesh, it seems that the Israelite attack on Ammon was justified. Supporting this is the fact that Nahash stated that his intention in gouging out the right eye of all the Jabeshites was to "bring disgrace upon all Israel" (ושמתיה חרפה על־כל־ישראל, 1 Sam 11:2). The only other place in the OT where "disgrace upon Israel" is mentioned is David's objection to Goliath's taunts: "What will be done for the man who strikes down this Philistine and removes this *disgrace from Israel* (חרפה מעל ישראל)?" (1 Sam 17:26a). David followed this with a rhetorical question: "Who is this uncircumcised Philistine that *disgraces* (חרף, Piel) *the armies of the living God?*" (v. 26b). In this context, bringing "disgrace upon Israel" also involved "disgracing the armies of the living God" and thus was an affront not only against the people but against YHWH. This reflects the widespread ancient belief that battles between nations were also battles between the nations' deities.[9] This is demonstrated later in David's climactic speech as he faced Goliath. There he said that by killing Goliath and removing the disgrace from Israel, "the whole world will know that there is a God in Israel" (v. 46, NIV). Thus for Nahash to seek to "bring disgrace upon all Israel" meant that he was simultaneously seeking to bring disgrace upon YHWH, and therefore the Israelite attack against the Ammonites was justified. For this reason, the Jabeshite deception that facilitated this attack did not bring unjust harm or disadvantage to another person and thus fits the criteria for positive deception, even if the Jabeshites were characterized negatively because of their offer of vassalage to Nahash.[10] The fact that the author depicts every other deception intended to prevent death or harm positively reinforces this conclusion.

---

person under false pretenses.

9. For further discussion see Long, "1 and 2 Samuel," 291, 295.

10. This possibility of a discrepancy between deceiver characterization and deception evaluation obtains in every other episode in which we are relying on characterization as the primary evaluative means (E, F, G, H, I, J, N, O, R, X). However, in all but one of these other episodes (I), the post-deception circumstances support the deceiver characterization. That is, no positively characterized deceiver experienced any negative consequences (E, F, G, H, J, R), while three of the other four negatively characterized deceivers experienced negative consequences (N, O, X). This agreement between the deceivers' recompense after their deception and their characterization increases confidence that the deception evaluations match the characterizations in these cases.

Summary

This study concludes that the narrative depictions of deception in the books of Samuel are consistent with the theology of deception derived from the explicit statements of the OT. This theology condemns deception only when it brings unjust harm or disadvantage to another person. On this reading, the unclear evaluation of Ahimaaz's deception (β) would most likely be negative, since his motive was to receive a reward while disadvantaging David by claiming ignorance concerning the status of Absalom.

Comparison with Prior Views of Deception

In the introduction we surveyed several views concerning the propriety of lying and deception in general, in the OT, and in the books of Samuel. In light of the preceding analysis, we are now in a position to enter this discussion and offer some conclusions. First, this study argues against the position that it is never right to lie. As we have seen, the OT never proscribes lying or deception outright, and, conversely, the majority of positive deceptions in the books of Samuel used lies as a tactic.[11] As we concluded above, it is not the tactic but the *motive* of the deceiver that both undergirds the OT's explicit proscriptions and directs how the author of Samuel depicts acts of deception. Aquinas's threefold scheme for lies (mischievous, jocose, and officious) and Luther's ethical evaluations (mischievous neither should nor may be told, jocose may be told, and officious should be told) seem to be appropriate outworkings of this theology of deception.

Second, as we saw in the introduction, several have argued that deception in the OT is appropriate as a means for the weak to use against the strong. Prouser suggests such deception "allows an underdog to accomplish a positive

---

11. Grudem objects that many of these passages "simply *report that someone lied* ... without indicating God's approval of the lie (these passages include Michal's lie to protect David in 1 Samuel 19:14, and her lie to protect herself in verse 17; David's counsel to Jonathan to lie in 1 Samuel 20:6; and a woman's lie to protect David's messengers in 2 Samuel 17:20)" ("Why It is Never Right to Lie," 795, emphasis his). However, as we have seen, a poetics of biblical narrative provides indicators for the reader to evaluate characters' actions in relation to the *author's* perspective (see, e.g., Sternberg, *Poetics of Biblical Narrative*, 155. Note that Sternberg refers to the "narrator" here, though he does not distinguish the narrator from the author [ibid., 75]). This approach presupposes that the author has a perspective (i.e., he is not "simply reporting" what happened in a detached fashion), and that he may convey this perspective through a variety of means, only one of which is explicit divine approval within the narrative. More often, authors evaluate narrative action through subtler, depictive means.

goal he or she would not have been able to achieve by direct means."[12] At first glance this thesis seems to hold in the books of Samuel. In none of the positive deceptions was the deceiver more powerful than the receiver. However, in several negative deceptions the deceivers acted from weaker (L, X, α) or relatively equal (K, P) social positions with respect to the receiver, so social standing itself does not seem to determine evaluation. Additionally, as Marcus and Frontain note, it is generally true that "young David" successfully deceived (F, G, J, V), but that after the Bathsheba affair (M) he became the receiver of deception (N, O, Q, R, X, Z, α, β). However, this observation does not explain the various *depictions* of deception. Deception V is negative, as are many of the post-Bathsheba deceptions against David (N, O, X, Z, α), all of which should be positive if David's changing social position determined the author's evaluation.[13] Rather than the social relationship between deceiver and receiver, the determinative factor seems to be the "positive goal" of the deceiver mentioned in Prouser's statement above, which she leaves unelaborated, but which I suggest is best perceived as a *just* goal.

Third, Prouser argues that "those who lie in negative circumstances are unsuccessful,"[14] and from this principle concludes that God's supposed failure to deceive Ahab in 1 Kings 22 indicates that the author is condemning God's actions as a misuse of power.[15] However, the present study has examined fifteen successful[16] deceptions that were depicted negatively, six of which used lies (A, I, V, X, Y, α). This shows that Prouser's claim cannot be sustained in the books of Samuel. Moreover, in all but two of these negative deceptions (I, X), the deceivers successfully achieved the goals for which they deceived, which further contradicts the conclusion that those who lie or deceive in negative circumstances are unsuccessful.

Fourth, David Marcus has suggested that a trend of "measure for measure" is evident in the deceptions involving David, whereby a deceiver often became a receiver of deception.[17] However, only eleven of the twenty-eight episodes examined in this study could even potentially support this view (F, G, I, J, M, N, O, U, V, Y, Z), since in the majority of cases the deceivers never

12. Prouser, "Phenomenology of the Lie," 181.

13. Williams has shown how this thesis is not sustainable for deception in Genesis either, as Joseph twice deceived his brothers from a position of great power and authority in Egypt (Gen 42:7–28; 44:1–34), yet is evaluated positively (*Deception in Genesis*, 51–52).

14. Prouser, "Phenomenology of the Lie," 181.

15. Ibid., 198.

16. Based on the definition provided in chapter 1, deception is a perlocutionary act and therefore successful by its very existence.

17. Marcus, "David the Deceiver," 165.

reappear in the narrative as receivers. Even if one were to concede that the four deceivers[18] who later became receivers were deceived *because of their previous deception(s)* ("retributive deception" as Marcus calls it[19]), which is not self-evident, the preponderance of data would still not support Marcus's contention that Uriah should be viewed as deceptive in 2 Samuel 11 based on this alleged trend.[20] Although in certain circumstances a measure-for-measure principle is possible, it is not prevalent enough in the books of Samuel to assume its validity and base interpretive conclusions on it.

Lastly, we considered the work of Michael Williams, with whose conclusions the present study most closely aligns. As noted in the introduction, Williams argues that in Genesis, "deception is justified when it is used by one previously wronged against the one who has done the wrong in order to restore *shalom*."[21] He does not see these criteria operating outside of Genesis, but suggests that positive deception in the rest of the OT is that which "benefits a third (Israelite) party by removing a threat to that party's physical or spiritual well-being" or "directly safeguards the physical well-being of the Israelite perpetrator(s)."[22] Concerning this latter statement, it is difficult to see how Nathan's deception of David (Deception Q) fits these criteria. Nathan deceived not to remove a threat to himself or someone else but to *promote justice* after David's unjust act. However, rather than strictly disagreeing with Williams's conclusions, the thesis of the present study accounts for them. Williams finds three episodes in Genesis in which deception is positively evaluated: (1) Tamar's deception of Judah, when she disguised herself as a prostitute (Gen 38:1–26), (2) Joseph's deception of his brothers in Egypt, when he pretended not to recognize them and accused them of being spies (Gen 42:7–28), and (3) Joseph's deception of his brothers on their second trip to Egypt, when he planted a divining cup in Benjamin's sack and used it as falsely incriminating evidence (Gen 44:1–34).[23] Williams correctly observes that in each case the deceiver was previously wronged by the receiver(s) and deceived to restore their former situation without harming the receiver(s). However, while this observation is correct, its narrowness leads Williams to posit multiple standards for evaluating deception in the OT.

---

18. Only Saul (I, U), David (F, G, J, M, V), Amnon (N), and Absalom (O, Y, Z) reappear as receivers, and only after these episodes mentioned here.

19. Marcus, "David the Deceiver," 165.

20. Ibid., 165–67.

21 Williams, *Deception in Genesis*, 55.

22. Ibid., 74.

23. Ibid., 53–54.

However, the principal finding of this study, that deception is only prohibited and depicted negatively when it brings unjust harm or disadvantage to another person, accounts for these positive deceptions in Genesis. As Williams rightly acknowledges, Tamar deceived Judah "to continue the line of her dead husband, which had been prevented by her husband's family" (see Gen 38:14; cf. vv. 8–9).[24] Such a motive was just, as Judah's later evaluation of her actions attested: "She is more *righteous* (צדקה) than I" (v. 26, NIV). Similarly, in Joseph's two deceptions, Williams notes that his motive was "to accomplish family reunification by testing for the prerequisite change of heart on the part of the brothers."[25] While it is true that Joseph's brothers had previously wronged him, and that his deception gave him insight toward restoring the situation, it is also true that his deception did not bring unjust harm or disadvantage to his brothers. Rather, like Jonathan's deception of Saul in 1 Samuel 20 (Deception E), Joseph's motive was to determine whether or not unjust inclinations remained in the receivers. Viewed within this rubric, rather than being evaluated according to unique ethical criteria, these positive deceptions in Genesis comport with the broader theology of deception that is present in the explicit statements of the OT and evident in the narrative depictions in the books of Samuel.

Comparison with Deception Elsewhere in the Bible

Since a biblical-theological approach seeks "to survey and synthesize the results of both OT and NT studies,"[26] it is necessary briefly to explore the remaining biblical passages that discuss deceptive activity and see if the foregoing conclusion adequately accounts for this phenomenon across the canon. The question we are asking in this section is this: "Does the thesis that deception is only prohibited when it brings unjust harm or disadvantage to another person explain the various depictions and descriptions of deception in these other texts?" Since relevant passages are numerous, limitations of space preclude detailed exploration of each case. Therefore I will restrict my comments to a broad survey of the data. To do this, I will first

---

24. Ibid., 26.

25. Ibid., 28. At the beginning of the fraternal conflict, Judah had suggested that the brothers sell Joseph, Jacob's favorite and only son by Rachel, into slavery (37:26–27). Here at the end of the fraternal conflict, Judah pled for Joseph to enslave him instead of Benjamin (Gen 44:18–34), Jacob's new favorite and "only" son by Rachel (42:38). Immediately after Judah's speech, Joseph revealed his identity to his brothers (45:1), which shows that he was convinced by Judah's offer that the brothers had changed their hearts. See the helpful discussion in Sternberg, *Poetics of Biblical Narrative*, 302–3.

26. Scobie, *Ways of Our God*, 77.

CONCLUSION 195

examine *deception elsewhere in OT narrative*, followed by *deception in NT narrative*, and finally *deception in the explicit statements of the NT*.

Deception Elsewhere in Old Testament Narrative

In this section we will look at narrative accounts of deception outside of Samuel and Genesis, since we have already dealt with deception in those books. First, we will survey accounts in which deception did not bring unjust harm or disadvantage to another person, and then we will explore accounts in which deception either did or was intended to do so.

Deception That Did Not Cause Unjust Harm or Disadvantage

In Exodus 1, the midwives deceived Pharaoh to cover up their disobedience to his death sentence against the Hebrew boys (v. 19), an action the narrator seemingly affirms by commenting, "So God was good to the midwives" (v. 20), and, "He gave them families" (v. 21). In Exod 3:18, YHWH instructed Moses to ask Pharaoh for a "three-day journey" into the desert. This seems to have been deceptive, since YHWH had just told Moses that he was concerned about Israel's unjust suffering[27] at the hands of the Egyptians and was going to bring them out of Egypt and into Canaan (vv. 7-10).[28] Rahab deceived her king concerning the Hebrew spies' whereabouts (Josh 2:4-6), was rewarded by being spared in the destruction of Jericho (6:17, 25), and is praised in the NT for her faithfulness (Heb 11:31; Jas 2:25). At the battle of Ai, Joshua sent a contingent of men behind the city while the rest of the army retreated deceptively, causing the men of Ai to believe falsely that they were fleeing (Josh 8:6) and thus to pursue them away from the city (vv. 15-17). At YHWH's command, Joshua held out his javelin to coordinate the ambush on the unguarded city, resulting in its destruction (vv. 18-19). The Gibeonites deceived the Israelites into believing falsely that they had traveled from a great distance, when they were actually Israel's neighbors (Josh 9:3-15). The Gibeonites did this because they had heard (and

---

27. In Exod 3:7 YHWH saw Israel's "affliction" (עֲנִי), and in 3:9 he saw "the *oppression* (לַחַץ) with which Egypt was *oppressing* (לֹחֲצִים) them." In Deut 26:6-8 Moses clearly evaluates this Egyptian treatment as evil: "But the Egyptians *did evil* (רעע) to us and *afflicted* (ענה) us, putting upon us hard labor. Then we cried out to YHWH, the God of our fathers, and YHWH heard our voice and saw our *affliction* (עֲנִי), toil, and *oppression* (לַחַץ)."

28. So also Prouser, "Phenomenology of the Lie," 169-70; Esau, "Divine Deception in the Exodus Event?" 8; Nicholas, *Trickster Revisited*, 68.

evidently believed) that YHWH had given Israel the land and thus feared for their lives (v. 24).

Ehud deceived Eglon in order to kill him (Judg 3:16-23), but did so to deliver Israel from Moabite subjugation, for which YHWH had raised him up (vv. 14-15). Jael deceived Sisera into believing falsely that she would hide and protect him, but she killed him when he fell asleep (Judg 4:17-22), an act for which she is praised in the subsequent chapter (5:24-27). Samson deceived Delilah three times concerning the secret of his great strength (Judg 16:6-15). Solomon deceived two prostitutes, each claiming to be the mother of a particular baby, into believing falsely that the child would be cut in half. When the baby's true mother gave up her claim so the child would live, Solomon decreed that the baby be given to her (1 Kgs 3:16-28). In 1 Kings 22, as judgment for the unjust death of Naboth (v. 38; cf. 1 Kgs 21:19), YHWH put a "deceiving spirit" (רוח שקר) in the mouths of Ahab's prophets to entice him to go up to his death at Ramoth Gilead (vv. 19-23).[29] At Elisha's request, YHWH blinded the Aramean army, whom Elisha then deceived into following him into the city of Samaria (2 Kgs 6:18-20). However, rather than killing them, Elisha instructed that they be fed and returned to Aram, after which the Aramean raids against Israel ceased (vv. 21-23). Jehu "acted deceptively to destroy the servants of Baal" (2 Kgs 10:19), after which YHWH told him, "You have done well in doing what is right in my eyes" (הטיבת לעשות הישר בעיני, v. 30). Lastly, Esther concealed her Jewish identity and deceived Haman into believing falsely that she was honoring him by inviting him to her banquet (Esth 5:8-12). However, rather than honoring Haman, she used the banquet to solicit the king's help in protecting the Jews from Haman's unjust plans, resulting in his death (7:1-10).

None of these deceptions brought unjust harm or disadvantage to another person. They were committed either in response to a current or impending threat (Exod 1:17; 3:7-8, 16-18; Josh 9:3-15;[30] Judg 3:15;

---

29. Significantly, although the LXX usually translates שקר with the ἀδικ* word-group (see chapter 2, n. 117), connoting injustice, here both occurrences of רוח שקר are rendered with πνεῦμα ψευδές (1 Kgs 22:22-23).

30. Although the Israelite conquest is depicted as YHWH's just judgment on the Canaanites (Gen 15:16; Josh 1:1-9), the sparing of Rahab shows that this judgment was rightly withheld from those who submitted to Israel's God and thus would not be a religious snare (see Deut 7:16). In Joshua 9, the Gibeonites' stated reason for deceiving was their belief that YHWH would give over the whole land to Israel (v. 24), which clearly resembles Rahab's earlier confession of faith (2:9-11) and thus similarly characterizes them positively (so also Creach, *Joshua*, 83-84). Furthermore, later narratives never depict the Gibeonites as a snare to Israel, and Neh 3:7 and 7:25 even suggest that over time they were fully assimilated (see Howard, *Joshua*, 230). For these reasons, it seems that their deception did not unjustly disadvantage Israel.

Judg 4:17–22; 16:5; 2 Kgs 6:18–23; Esth 7:3–4) or to assist in just judgment at YHWH's command (Josh 2:1–21 [cf. Gen 15:16; Josh 1:1–3]; 8:1; 1 Kgs 22:19–23), with his wisdom (1 Kgs 3:28), or with his approval (2 Kgs 10:30). Furthermore, in almost every case we may view the deception as positively depicted, either because YHWH commanded it (Exod 3:18; 1 Kgs 22:22), YHWH participated in it (Josh 8:18–19), YHWH approved of the deceivers' actions (Exod 1:20–21; 2 Kgs 10:30), Scripture elsewhere affirms the deceiver's actions (Joshua 2; cf. Heb 11:31; Jas 2:25), the narrator refers to the deceiver's actions as "doing justice" (לעשות משפט, 1 Kgs 3:28), the deceivers are characterized positively (Josh 9:3, 24),[31] or the deceivers experienced positive post-deception circumstances (Josh 9:23;[32] Judg 3:30; 4:23–24; 2 Kgs 6:23; Esth 9:1). The case of Samson is less clear, since he is characterized negatively as an unfaithful Nazirite and lover of Philistine women.[33] Nevertheless, it is significant that Samson's circumstances became increasingly negative after he told Delilah the truth (Judg 16:17), since at that point "YHWH left him" (v. 20).

Deception That Caused Unjust Harm or Disadvantage

As Williams points out, Pharaoh repeatedly deceived Moses by saying he would release the Israelites from slavery, but then not doing so (Exod 8:4–11

---

31. After summarizing the coalition of western kings that came to make war against Israel, the narrator introduces the Gibeonites with a disjunctive clause, contrasting this people with these antagonistic kings: "*But the Gibeonites* (וישבי גבעון) heard what Joshua had done to Jericho and Ai . . ." (v. 3). However, the strongest evidence for a positive characterization is the Gibeonites' stated reason for deceiving (Josh 9:24), noted above in n. 30.

32. In this verse, Joshua cursed the Gibeonites and sentenced them to serve as "woodcutters and water carriers (וחטבי עצים ושאבי־מים) in the house of my God." Although Williams sees this as an "unfavorable end" and thus concludes that this deception was negatively evaluated (*Deception in Genesis*, 60), this result was certainly better for the Gibeonites than the annihilation they would have faced otherwise. Moreover, the language used to describe the Gibeonites' service here alludes to Deut 29:10 [11], which describes the sojourner who joined Israel in entering the covenant with YHWH as "the cutter of your wood and carrier of your water" (מחטב עציך עד שאב מימיך). In addition, similar to the other part of Josh 9:23, the psalmist declared that he would "rather be a doorkeeper *in the house of my God* than dwell in the tents of the wicked" (Ps 84:11 [10], NIV). All this indicates that the Gibeonites' post-deception circumstances should not be viewed negatively. For further discussion, see Gordon, "Gibeonite Ruse and Israelite Curse," 83; Creach, *Joshua*, 86; Howard, *Joshua*, 230.

33. See the discussion of von Rad, *Old Testament Theology*, 1:333–34.

[8-15], 21-28 [25-32]; 9:27-35; 10:16-20).[34] Samson's wife deceived him to help the Philistines cheat in answering his riddle correctly (Judg 14:15-19), and Delilah deceived him into revealing the true source of his strength so the Philistines could tie him up and oppress him (Judg 16:4-5). In 1 Kings 13, an old prophet from Bethel deceived a man of God, claiming to have received an oracle that the latter could consume bread and water (v. 18). As a result, the man of God ate and drank contrary to God's command, which led to his death (vv. 23-24). Ahab and Jezebel deceptively acquired Naboth's vineyard by using false witnesses to execute a "judicial murder" (1 Kgs 21:1-16), a crime for which both would experience a shameful death (vv. 19, 23). Gehazi deceived Naaman into giving him money and clothing, claiming that Elisha had requested them (2 Kgs 5:20-24). When Gehazi returned, he lied to Elisha, who knew what Gehazi had done, and as punishment Gehazi became leprous (vv. 25-27). In 2 Chr 35:22, Josiah "disguised himself" (התחפש) to enter battle against Pharaoh Neco, but the narrator immediately says, "He did not listen to the words of Neco from the mouth of God." Despite his disguise, archers shot Josiah, resulting in his death (vv. 23-24).

Each of these deceptions involved or resulted in some sort of injustice, whether unjust harm (Exod 8:28 [32];[35] Judg 16:21;[36] 1 Kgs 21:10-14), disadvantage (2 Kgs 5:23), misrepresentation of YHWH's word (1 Kgs 13:18), or rebellion against YHWH's word (2 Chr 35:22). Moreover, in each episode we may view the deception as negatively depicted, since negative post-deception circumstances followed either for the deceiver (Exod 11:1-16; Judg 15:6; 16:26-30; 1 Kgs 22:38; 2 Kgs 5:27; 9:35-37; 2 Chr 35:23-24) or someone else (1 Kgs 13:23-25).[37]

Deception in New Testament Narrative

In this section we will survey depictions of deception in NT narrative. Here we will not study passages in which a character teaches about or comments

---

34. Williams, *Deception in Genesis*, 60.

35. Concerning the injustice of Pharaoh's oppression of Israel, see n. 27 above.

36. In this case the deception also resulted in false worship, as the Philistines attributed their victory over Samson to Dagan (Judg 16:23-24).

37. Although many believe that Nathan and Bathsheba deceived David into naming Solomon king in 1 Kgs 1:1-35 (e.g., Gunn, "David and the Gift of the Kingdom," 31; Hagan, "Deception as Motif," 302; Marcus, "David the Deceiver," 166; Frontain, "The Trickster Tricked," 188; Prouser, "Phenomenology of the Lie," 105-8; McKenzie, *King David*, 178; Halpern, *David's Secret Demons*, 396-97; Van Seters, *Biblical Saga*, 333), elsewhere I have argued at length against the presence of deception here (see Newkirk, "Reconsidering the Role of Deception," 703-13).

on deception, but only those texts in which a deception actually occurs in the narrative. I will include teaching and comments about deception in NT narrative in the final section with the other explicit statements of the NT. As in the previous section, first we will look at deception that did not cause unjust harm or disadvantage, followed by deception that did so.

Deception That Did Not Cause Unjust Harm or Disadvantage

In all three Synoptic Gospels, Jesus alluded to Isa 6:9-10 when giving his reason for speaking in parables (Matt 13:13-15; Mark 4:11-12; Luke 8:10). In Matthew's account, Jesus did not indicate a causal connection between his parables and the people's lack of understanding, but in both Mark and Luke he stated that the purpose of his parables was to create false understanding:

> And he said to them, "To you has been given the secret of the kingdom of God, but for those outside, everything comes in parables; *in order that* (ἵνα) 'they may indeed look, but not perceive, and may indeed listen, but not understand; *so that* (μήποτε) they may not turn again and be forgiven'" (Mark 4:11-12, NRSV; cf. Luke 8:10).

Although scholars debate how the ἵνα functions here, in conjunction with μήποτε it most naturally indicates the purpose for which Jesus spoke in parables.[38] Since Jesus' parables engendered false understanding "for those outside," it follows that his use of parables was deceptive. After his resurrection, while walking with two disciples on the road to Emmaus, Jesus deceived them by pretending not to know what had happened recently in Jerusalem (Luke 24:17-19a). When they neared their destination, Jesus deceived them again: "As they approached the village to which they were going, Jesus *acted as if he were going farther* (προσεποιήσατο πορρώτερον πορεύεσθαι)" (v. 28, NIV). This prompted the disciples to invite him to stay with them, during which time his identity was revealed (vv. 29-31).

None of these deceptions brought unjust harm or disadvantage to another person. The deceptive function of the parables facilitated God's just judgment on unbelievers, and Jesus' deceptions in Luke 24 add dramatic suspense to the post-resurrection narrative. Since Jesus committed each deception, the authorial evaluation of each is positive.

---

38. Osborne, *Hermeneutical Spiral*, 238; France, *Mark*, 199; Stein, *Mark*, 209-11.

Deception That Caused Unjust Harm or Disadvantage

The first two Gospels record how the Jewish leaders plotted "to arrest Jesus *by stealth* (δόλῳ) and kill him" (Matt 26:4; Mark 14:1, NRSV), and how they gathered false witnesses who testified against him (Matt 26:59-62; Mark 14:56-59). Similarly, Stephen was convicted on the basis of false testimony (Acts 6:13). In both of these situations, the victims were unjustly killed and the deceivers are obviously depicted negatively.[39]

Deception in the Explicit Statements of the New Testament

In this section I will summarize the explicit statements concerning deceptive activity in the NT. Jesus affirmed the abiding applicability of the ninth command (Matt 19:18; Mark 10:19; Luke 18:20). Elsewhere the NT associates deception with persecution (Matt 5:11; 2 Tim 3:12-13) and various other actions that involve unjust wrong to others, such as murder, adultery, theft, greed, sexual immorality, malice, slander, and violence.[40] Paul denounced Elymas the sorcerer as "full of all deceit and every wrongdoing, a son of the devil, *an enemy of all justice/righteousness*" (ἐχθρὲ πάσης δικαιοσύνης, Acts 13:10), and condemned those who divided the Roman church by their deception (Rom 16:17-18). James associates lying with harboring "bitter envy and selfish ambition" (Jas 3:14, NRSV), and John connects it to "walking in the darkness," "not *doing* what is true" (οὐ ποιοῦμεν τὴν ἀλήθειαν, 1 John 1:6), and denying that Jesus is the Messiah (1 John 2:21-22; 2 John 7). The NT speaks negatively about false worship (Rom 1:25, 27; Rev 13:14), false apostles (2 Cor 11:13-15; Rev 2:2), false brothers (2 Cor 11:26; Gal 2:4), false prophets,[41] false messiahs,[42] and false teachers/teaching,[43] the lat-

---

39. The story of Ananias and Sapphira (Acts 5:1-11) does not depict a deception, since Peter did not believe their lie. Nevertheless, since their motive for lying was to keep part of the proceeds from the sale of their property while appearing to give the whole sum to the community, had they deceived they would have unjustly advantaged themselves in the eyes of others. Peter locates their sin in the fact that they "lied to the Holy Spirit" (ψεύσασθαί σε τὸ πνεῦμα τὸ ἅγιον, v. 3; cf. v. 4). The apostolic rebuke of their actions and their swift negative consequences reflect the author's negative evaluation.

40. Matt 15:19; Mark 7:20-23; Rom 1:29-31; 3:13-17; Titus 1:12-13; 3:1-3; 1 Pet 2:1; 3:10-12; 2 Pet 2:13; Rev 18:23-24.

41. Matt 7:15; 24:11; Luke 6:26; Acts 13:6; 1 John 4:1; Rev 16:13; 19:20; 20:10.

42. Matt 24:4-5, 24; Mark 13:5-6, 22; Luke 21:8.

43. 2 Cor 11:3-4; Eph 4:14-15; 1 Tim 4:1-2; 6:20; Titus 1:10-11; 2 Pet 2:1; 1 John 2:26; 4:6; Rev 2:20.

ter concerning which the Epistles warn readers not to be deceived.[44] In his letters Paul repeatedly states that he is not lying[45] or using deception to minister the gospel (2 Cor 4:2; 1 Thess 2:3), and through sarcasm denies that his collection efforts among the Corinthians were deceptive (2 Cor 12:16).

Two NT passages seem to proscribe lying categorically. Ephesians 4:25 says, "Therefore, *putting off falsehood* (ἀποθέμενοι τὸ ψεῦδος), let each speak truthfully with his neighbor," and Col 3:9 says, "*Do not lie to one another* (μὴ ψεύδεσθε εἰς ἀλλήλους), having taken off the old self with its practices." The first passage alludes to Zech 8:16, which says, "Let each of you speak truthfully with his neighbor; *render true and sound judgment* (אמת ומשפט שלום שפטו) in your gates." This reveals a judicial context for the OT command, which coheres with both epistolary contexts, since each suggests that the falsehood in view is that which brings unjust harm or disadvantage to others. In both texts, Paul grounds his command to refrain from false speech in the fact that believers have put off "the old self" (Eph 4:22; Col 3:9b), which in both cases he associates with "anger" (ὀργή), "rage" (θυμός), "evil" (κακία), and "blasphemy" (βλασφημία, Eph 4:31; Col 3:8)—all actions that wrong others. This suggests that Paul's prohibitions of lying in both passages similarly pertain to actions that wrong others. His later command to the Ephesians agrees with this: "Let no evil talk come out of your mouths, but only what is useful for building up, as there is need, so that your words may give grace to those who hear" (4:29, NRSV).

Jesus connected falsehood especially with the devil, referring to him as "the father of lies" (John 8:44, NIV). However, in this verse, Jesus closely associated this falsehood with *murder*:

> You belong to your father, the devil, and you want to carry out your father's desire. He was a *murderer* from the beginning, not holding to the truth, for there is no truth in him. When he lies, he speaks his native language, for he is a liar and the father of lies (NIV).

Syntactically, the devil's "not holding to the truth" is closely connected to his identity as a "murderer" (ἐκεῖνος ἀνθρωποκτόνος ἦν ἀπ' ἀρχῆς καὶ ἐν τῇ ἀληθείᾳ οὐκ ἔστηκεν). As D. A. Carson observes, this description of the devil as a murderer and liar "from the beginning" probably refers to his deception in the Garden of Eden that led to humanity's death (cf. Gen

---

44. 1 Cor 6:9–10; 15:33; Gal 6:7; Eph 5:6; Col 2:4, 8; 2 Thess 2:3; Jas 1:15–17; 1 John 3:7.

45. Rom 9:1; 2 Cor 11:31; Gal 1:20; 1 Tim 2:7.

2:17; 3:1–6).⁴⁶ Therefore, the context of truth and falsehood here pertains particularly to the devil's harmful actions against humanity, which is reinforced by the references in Revelation to the devil as "*that ancient serpent . . . who deceives the whole world*" (Rev 12:9; cf. 20:3, 8, 10). Elsewhere in Revelation, Jesus encourages the Philadelphian church that "those of the synagogue of Satan, who say they are Jews, though they are not, but are *liars*," will bow down before them (3:9). The context suggests that these "liars" had been persecuting the Philadelphian believers, who had not denied Jesus' name (v. 8) and had kept his command for patient endurance (v. 10).⁴⁷ Also associating deception with Satan, Paul writes:

> The coming of the lawless one will be according to the work of Satan with all kinds of false power, signs, and wonders, *and with every unjust deception* (καὶ ἐν πάσῃ ἀπάτῃ ἀδικίας) for those who are perishing. They perish because they refused to love the truth and so be saved (2 Thess 2:9–10).

Paul goes on to say that, in response to this, God engages in deception:

> For this reason, God sends them a *powerful deception so that they will believe the lie* (ἐνέργειαν πλάνης εἰς τὸ πιστεῦσαι αὐτοὺς τῷ ψεύδει), in order that all will be judged who have not believed the truth but have taken pleasure in *injustice/unrighteousness* (ἀδικία, vv. 11–12).

This passage makes it clear that Paul connects Satan's work with "unjust deception" (ἀπάτῃ ἀδικίας), but that God deceives justly in order to judge the unjust.⁴⁸

This text helps clarify two other NT passages that seem to say that God would never engage in any kind of falsehood. The first is Heb 6:17–18:

> In the same way, when God desired to show even more clearly to the heirs of the promise the unchangeable character of his purpose, he guaranteed it by an oath, so that through *two unchangeable things, in which it is impossible that God would prove false* (δύο πραγμάτων ἀμεταθέτων, ἐν οἷς ἀδύνατον ψεύσασθαι [τὸν] θεόν), we who have taken refuge might be strongly encouraged to seize the hope set before us (NRSV).

Contextually, that which God cannot lie about (or as the NRSV renders it, "prove false") is the antecedent of the plural relative pronoun in the

---

46. Carson, *John*, 353.
47. So also Beale, *Revelation*, 285–87; Osborne, *Revelation*, 189–92.
48. For further discussion, see Chisholm, "Does God Deceive?" 11–28.

preceding prepositional phrase (ἐν οἷς), which is the "two unchangeable things," i.e., his promise and oath. Interpreting ἐν with a "reference/respect" function,[49] this results in the translation, "two unchangeable things, *with respect to which* it is impossible for God to prove false." Understood thus, these verses do not teach that every kind of falsehood is a metaphysical impossibility for God.[50] Rather, when God promises and swears that he will act—as he did for Abraham (cf. vv. 13-15)—it is impossible that he will prove false concerning his word.[51]

The second passage that appears to imply that God could never lie is Titus 1:2. Here Paul refers to "the hope of eternal life, which *the 'unfalse' God* (ὁ ἀψευδὴς θεός) promised before the ages." In this verse the grammar does not indicate that God's lack of falsity has any exceptions. However, as was the case in Heb 6:18, the context suggests that the falsity in view here pertains to the impossibility of God proving false with respect to his promises. Whereas v. 2 says that God promised eternal life before the ages, in v. 3 Paul continues, "and in his appointed time he made his word known by the preaching entrusted to me according to the authority of God our Savior." Here Paul is saying that God has not proven false concerning his promise of eternal life, which is demonstrated by the apostolic gospel. Therefore, although this text allows for the interpretation that God is categorically "unfalse," it does not require it, and the context suggests that God's fidelity to his promises is primarily in view. Supporting this is the observation that by referring to God as ἀψευδής, Paul may have been critiquing the Cretan religion. According to Philip H. Towner, the Cretans claimed that Zeus's tomb was on their island, but the poet Callimachus had said it was "unfalse" (ἀψευδής) to say that the tomb in Crete was empty (i.e., the Cretans were lying).[52] Paul later quotes a Cretan poet who said that "Cretans are always liars" (Κρῆτες ἀεὶ ψεῦσται, v. 12), which reinforces this theme in the text and raises the probability that Paul's use of the *hapax legomenon* ἀψευδής may have alluded to Callimachus's critique. If this were the case, the fact that the poet in v. 12 described Cretan liars as "vicious brutes" (κακὰ θηρία, NRSV) may provide helpful background for understanding the significance of Paul's description of God as "unfalse."

49. Wallace, *Greek Grammar Beyond the Basics*, 372. Paul Ellingworth argues that this verse implies the complete impossibility of God lying, though he admits that the grammar of the prepositional phrase is weak in supporting this (*Hebrews*, 343).

50. *Contra* Spicq, *L'Épitre Aux Hébreux*, 162.

51. See Chisholm ("Does God 'Change His Mind'?" 389-96) for similar argumentation concerning Num 23:19 and 1 Sam 15:29, both of which initially seem to reject categorically the idea that God would lie or change his mind.

52. Towner, *Timothy and Titus*, 671.

The remaining references to deceptive activity in the NT are all nondescript. In describing Christ's suffering, Peter alludes to the Isaianic servant who had no deceit in his mouth (1 Pet 2:22).[53] The book of Revelation says that the 144,000 had "no lie" in their mouths (14:5), that liars will not be permitted in the New Jerusalem (21:27; 22:15), but instead will be cast into the lake of burning sulfur, along with "murderers," "the sexually immoral," and "idolaters" (21:8). Therefore, as was the case in the OT, the explicit statements of the NT only condemn deception in the context of the unjust harm or disadvantage that it brings to other people.

Summary

As this survey shows, none of the remaining narratives of the OT or the narratives of the NT depicts deception in such a way that contradicts the thesis of this study. Rather, these narratives comport well by portraying just deceptions positively and unjust deceptions negatively. Similarly, like the explicit statements of the OT, the explicit statements of the NT never categorically condemn deception. Rather, they describe deception approvingly if committed for just purposes (e.g., 2 Thess 2:11–12), but condemn it when it results in injustice. Although not all of these passages clearly demonstrate that justice is the criterion by which deception is evaluated, applying this rubric to them adequately accounts for their varied perspectives. However, since this section has only been a brief survey, a fuller exploration of all these relevant texts is needed either to confirm this thesis more confidently or to qualify it.

Concluding Remarks

In this study I have argued that the author of the books of Samuel evaluated acts of deception based on whether or not the deceivers had just motives. If a deception was for just purposes, the author depicted it positively; if a deception was for unjust purposes, the author depicted it negatively. This criterion of justice also explains the depictions of deception in Genesis, removing the need to posit unique evaluative criteria for that book. Moreover, a survey of deception in the rest of the Bible indicates that this thesis seems to apply across the Christian canon. On a theological level, this suggests that, despite popular Christian assumption, not all lying and deception is wrong. Rather, a biblically based ethic of deception should fundamentally

---

53. Although, cf. Isa 53:9, which parallels "deceit" (מרמה) with "violence" (חמס).

be concerned with the motive for which it is committed. This means that in certain situations, Christians can and should be *just deceivers*. Although this study concludes that a biblical evaluation of deception depends upon the situation in which it is committed, such a view should not be confused with "situation ethics." According to Joseph Fletcher,

> The situationist enters into every decision-making situation fully armed with the ethical maxims of his community and its heritage, and he treats them with respect as illuminators of his problems. Just the same he is prepared in any situation to compromise them or set them aside *in the situation* if love seems better served by doing so.[54]

In contrast to this, the author of Samuel's depictions of deception are consistent with the theology of deception found in the explicit statements of the OT, and thus he was not compromising or setting aside the "ethical maxims of his community" by depicting certain deceptions positively. Similarly, a Christian who deceives for just purposes is not setting aside the ethical maxims of his or her community. Rather, the ethical maxims of the Bible require one to determine whether or not deception is warranted in any given situation based on whether it serves just or unjust ends.

---

54. Fletcher, *Situation Ethics*, 26 (emphasis his).

Bibliography

Ackerman, J. S. "Knowing Good and Evil: A Literary Analysis of the Court History in 2 Samuel 9-20 and 1 Kings 1-2." *JBL* 109 (1990) 41-60.
Ackroyd, Peter R. *The First Book of Samuel*. CBC. Cambridge: Cambridge University Press, 1971.
———. *The Second Book of Samuel*. CBC. Cambridge: Cambridge University Press, 1977.
———. "The Succession Narrative (So-Called)." *Int* 35 (1981) 383-96.
———. "The Verb Love: *'āhēb* in the David-Jonathan Narratives: A Footnote." *VT* 25 (1975) 213-14.
Adler, Jonathan. "Lying, Deceiving, or Falsely Implicating." *JPhil* 94 (1997) 435-52.
Allbee, Richard A. "Asymmetrical Continuity of Love and Law between the Old and New Testaments: Explicating the Implicit Side of a Hermeneutical Bridge, Leviticus 19.11-18." *JSOT* 31 (2006) 147-66.
Alonso-Schökel, Luis. "David y la mujer de Tecua: 2 Sm 14 como modelo hermenéutico." *Bib* 57 (1976) 192-205.
Alter, Robert. *The Art of Biblical Narrative*. Rev. ed. New York: Basic, 2011.
———. *The David Story*. New York: Norton, 1999.
Althann, Robert. "An Unrecognized Repetition at 2 Samuel 15,8." *JSem* 9 (1997) 179-84.
———. "The Meaning of ארבעים שנה in 2 Samuel 15:7." *Bib* 73 (1992) 248-52.
Altpeter, Gerda. "2 Sam 12,1-15a: eine strukturalistische Analyse." *TZ* 38 (1982) 46-52.
Amit, Yairah. *Reading Biblical Narratives: Literary Criticism and the Hebrew Bible*. Translated by Yael Lotan. Minneapolis: Fortress, 2001.
Anderson, A. A. *2 Samuel*. WBC 11. Dallas: Word, 1989.
Anderson, John E. *Jacob and the Divine Trickster: A Theology of Deception and YHWH's Fidelity to the Ancestral Promise in the Jacob Cycle*. Siphrut 5. Winona Lake, IN: Eisenbrauns, 2011.
———. "Jacob, Laban, and a Divine Trickster? The Covenantal Framework of God's Deception in the Theology of the Jacob Cycle." *PRSt* 36 (2009) 3-23.
Anderson, William H. U. "David as a Biblical 'Good-Fella' and 'The Godfather.'" *SJOT* 18 (2004) 60-76.
Andersson, Greger. *Untamable Texts: Literary Studies and Narrative Theory in the Books of Samuel*. LHBOTS 514. London: T. & T. Clark, 2009.
Andrew, Maurice E. "Falsehood and Truth: An Amplified Sermon on Exodus 20:16." *Int* 17 (1963) 425-38.
Angert-Quilter, Theresa, and Lynne Wall. "The 'Spirit Wife' at Endor." *JSOT* 92 (2001) 55-72.

Ap-Thomas, D. R. "Saul's Uncle." *VT* 11 (1961) 241–45.
Aquinas, Thomas. "Of Lying." In *Summa Theologica, Vol. 12*, 85–98. London: Burns, Oates, and Washbourne, 1922.
Arnold, Bill T. *1 & 2 Samuel*. NIVAC. Grand Rapids: Zondervan, 2003.
———. "Necromancy and Cleromancy in 1 and 2 Samuel." *CBQ* 66 (2004) 199–213.
———. "The Amalekite's Report of Saul's Death: Political Intrigue or Incompatible Sources?" *JETS* 32 (1988) 289–98.
Auerbach, Elias. "Das Zehngebot—Allgemeine Gesetzes-Form in Der Bibel." *VT* 16 (1966) 255–76.
Augustine. "Against Lying." In *The Fathers of the Church: A New Translation*, edited by Roy J. Deferrari, translated by Mary Sarah Muldowney, 125–78. Vol. 16. New York: Fathers of the Church, 1952.
———. "Lying." In *The Fathers of the Church: A New Translation*, edited by Roy J. Deferrari, translated by Mary Sarah Muldowney, 53–110. Vol. 16. New York: Fathers of the Church, 1952.
Auld, A. Graeme. *I & II Kings*. The Daily Study Bible Series. Philadelphia: Westminster, 1986.
———. *I & II Samuel*. OTL. Louisville: Westminster John Knox, 2011.
Austin, J. L. *How to Do Things with Words*. Oxford: Oxford University Press, 1965.
Bach, Alice. *Women, Seduction, and Betrayal in Biblical Narrative*. Cambridge: Cambridge University Press, 1997.
Baer, D. A., and R. P. Gordon. "חסד." In *NIDOTTE* 2:211–18.
Bailey, Randall C. *David in Love and War: The Pursuit of Power in 2 Samuel 10–12*. JSOTSup 75. Sheffield, UK: JSOT, 1990.
Baker, David L. *Tight Fists or Open Hands? Wealth and Poverty in Old Testament Law*. Grand Rapids: Eerdmans, 2009.
Baker, David W. "רעע." In *NIDOTTE* 3:1154–58.
Baldick, C. *The Concise Dictionary of Literary Terms*. Oxford: Oxford University Press, 1990.
Baldwin, Joyce G. *1 & 2 Samuel: An Introduction and Commentary*. TOTC. Downers Grove, IL: IVP, 1988.
Ball, E. "The Co-Regency of David and Solomon." *VT* 27 (1977) 268–79.
Bar-Efrat, Shimon. "The Death of King Saul: Suicide or Murder? Diachronic and Synchronic Interpretations of ISam 31—IISam 1." In *David und Saul im Widerstreit: Diachronie und Synchronie im Wettstreit: Beiträge zur Auslegung des ersten Samuelbuches*, edited by Walter Dietrich, 272–79. OBO 206. Göttingen: Vandenhoeck & Ruprecht, 2004.
———. *Das Erste Buch Samuel: Ein narratologisch-philologischer Kommentar*. Translated by Johannes Klein. BWANT 176. Stuttgart: Kohlhammer, 2007.
———. *Narrative Art in the Bible*. London: T. & T. Clark, 1989.
———. "Some Observations on the Analysis of Structure in Biblical Narrative." *VT* 30 (1980) 154–73.
———. *Das Zweite Buch Samuel: Ein narratologisch-philologischer Kommentar*. Translated by Johannes Klein. BWANT 181. Stuttgart: Kohlhammer, 2009.
Barclay, William. *The Ten Commandments*. Louisville: Westminster John Knox, 1998.
Barr, James. *The Concept of Biblical Theology: An Old Testament Perspective*. London: SCM, 1999.

Bauck, Peter. "1 Samuel 19: David and the *Teraphim*: יהוה עם דוד and the Emplotted Narrative." *SJOT* 22 (2008) 212–36.
Bellefontaine, Elizabeth. "Customary Law and Chieftainship: Judicial Aspects of 2 Samuel 14:4–21." *JSOT* 8 (1987) 47–72.
Bentham, Jeremy. *An Introduction to the Principles of Morals and Legislation*. Oxford: Clarendon, 1823.
Bergen, Robert D. *1, 2 Samuel*. NAC 7. Nashville: Broadman & Holman, 1996.
Berlin, Adele. "Characterization in Biblical Narrative: David's Wives." *JSOT* 23 (1982) 69–85.
———. *Poetics and Interpretation of Biblical Narrative*. BLS 9. Sheffield, UK: Almond, 1983.
Bettenzoli, Giuseppe. "Samuel und das Problem des Königtums: die Tradition von Gilgal." *BZ* ns 30 (1986) 222–36.
Beuken, W. A. M. "1 Samuel 28: The Prophet as 'Hammer of Witches.'" *JSOT* 6 (1978) 3–17.
Birch, Bruce C. "The Choosing of Saul at Mizpah." *CBQ* 37 (1975) 447–57.
———. "The Development of the Tradition on the Anointing of Saul in I Sam 9:1—10:16." *JBL* (1971) 55–68.
———. "The First and Second Books of Samuel." In *The New Interpreter's Bible*, Vol. 2. Nashville: Abingdon, 1998.
———. *The Rise of the Israelite Monarchy: The Growth and Development of 1 Samuel 7–15*. SBLDS 27. Missoula, MT: Scholars, 1976.
Bledstein, Adrien J. "Was *Habbiryā* a Healing Ritual Performed by a Woman in King David's House?" *BR* 37 (1992) 15–31.
Blenkinsopp, Joseph. "Saul and the Mistress of the Spirits (1 Samuel 28.3–25)." In *Sense and Sensitivity: Essays on Reading the Bible in Memory of Robert Carroll*, edited by Alastair G. Hunter and Philip R. Davies, 49–61. JSOTSup 348. Sheffield, UK: Sheffield Academic Press, 2002.
Blocher, Henri. "The Biblical Concept of Truth." *Themelios* 6 (1969) 47–61.
Block, Daniel I. *Deuteronomy*. NIVAC. Grand Rapids: Zondervan, 2012.
———. "Empowered by the Spirit of God: The Holy Spirit in the Historiographic Writings of the Old Testament." *SBJT* 1 (1997) 42–61.
———. *Judges, Ruth*. NAC 6. Nashville: Broadman & Holman, 1999.
———. "Reading the Decalogue Right to Left: The Ten Principles of Covenant Relationship in the Hebrew Bible." In *How I Love Your Torah, O Lord! Studies in the Book of Deuteronomy*, 21–60. Eugene, OR: Cascade, 2011.
———. "What Has Delphi to do with Samaria? Ambiguity and Delusion in Israelite Prophecy." In *Writing and Ancient Near Eastern Society: Papers in Honour of Alan R. Millard*, edited by Piotr Bienkowski et al., 189–216. London: T. & T. Clark, 2005.
Bock, Darrell L. *Luke, Volume 1: 1:1—9:50*. BECNT. Grand Rapids: Baker, 1994.
———. *Luke, Volume 2: 9:51—24:53*. BECNT. Grand Rapids: Baker, 1996.
Bodner, Keith. *1 Samuel: A Narrative Commentary*. HBM 19. Sheffield, UK: Sheffield Phoenix, 2009.
———. "Crime Scene Investigation: A Text Critical Mystery and the Strange Death of Ishbosheth." *JHebS* 7 (2007) 2–18.
———. *David Observed: A King in the Eyes of His Court*. HBM 5. Sheffield, UK: Sheffield Phoenix, 2008.
———. "Layers of Ambiguity in 2 Samuel 11:1." *ETL* 80 (2004) 102–11.

———. "Nathan: Prophet, Politician and Novelist?" *JSOT* 95 (2001) 43–54.

———. *National Insecurity: A Primer on the First Book of Samuel*. Toronto: Clements, 2003.

———. *Power Play: A Primer on the Second Book of Samuel*. Toronto: Clements, 2004.

Booth, Wayne C. *The Rhetoric of Fiction*. 2nd ed. Chicago: University of Chicago, 1983.

Bovati, Pietro. *Re-Establishing Justice: Legal Terms, Concepts and Procedures in the Hebrew Bible*. Translated by Michael J. Smith. JSOTSup 105. Sheffield, UK: JSOT, 1994.

Bowen, Nancy. "The Role of Yhwh as Deceiver in True and False Prophecy." Ph.D. diss., Princeton Theological Seminary, 1994.

Bowman, Richard G. "The Fortune of King David/The Fate of Queen Michal: A Literary Critical Analysis of 2 Samuel 1–8." In *Telling Queen Michal's Story*, edited by David J. A. Clines and Tamar C. Eskenazi, 97–120. JSOTSup 119. Sheffield, UK: Sheffield Academic Press, 1991.

Bright, John. *Jeremiah*. AB 21. Garden City: Doubleday, 1965.

Brown, F., S. R. Driver, and C. A. Briggs. *A Hebrew and English Lexicon of the Old Testament*. Oxford, 1907.

Brown, Robert M. "The Nathan Syndrome: Stories with a Moral Intention." *RelLit* 16 (1984) 49–59.

Brueggemann, Walter. *David and His Theologian: Literary, Social, and Theological Investigations of the Early Monarchy*. Edited by K. C. Hanson. Eugene, OR: Cascade, 2011.

———. *David's Truth in Israel's Imagination and Memory*. 2nd ed. Minneapolis: Fortress, 2002.

———. *1 & 2 Kings*. SHBC. Macon, GA: Smyth & Helwys, 2000.

———. *First and Second Samuel*. IBC. Louisville: John Knox, 1990.

———. "Narrative Coherence and Theological Intentionality in 1 Samuel 18." *CBQ* 55 (1993) 225–44.

———. "Narrative Intentionality in 1 Samuel 29." *JSOT* 43 (1989) 21–35.

———. "Truth-Telling as Subversive Obedience." In *The Ten Commandments: The Reciprocity of Faithfulness*, edited by William P. Brown, 291–300. Louisville: Westminster John Knox, 2004.

Budde, D. Karl. *Die Bücher Samuel*. Tübingen and Leipzig: Mohr (Siebeck), 1902.

Callaham, Scott N. *Modality and the Biblical Hebrew Infinitive Absolute*. AKM 71. Stuttgart: Harrassowitz, 2010.

Calvin, John. *Institutes of the Christian Religion*. Translated by Henry Beveridge. Grand Rapids: Eerdmans, 2001.

Camp, Claudia V. "The Wise Women of 2 Samuel: A Role Model for Women in Early Israel?" *CBQ* 43 (1981) 14–29.

Campbell, Antony F. *1 Samuel*. FOTL 7. Grand Rapids: Eerdmans, 2003.

———. "The Reported Story: Midway Between Oral Performance and Literary Art." *Semeia* 46 (1989) 77–85.

———. *2 Samuel*. FOTL 8. Grand Rapids: Eerdmans, 2005.

———. "The Storyteller's Role: Reported Story and Biblical Text." *CBQ* 64 (2002) 427–41.

Campbell, Antony F., and Mark A. O'Brien. *Unfolding the Deuteronomistic History: Origins, Upgrades, and Present Text*. Minneapolis: Augsburg, 2000.

Caquot, André, and Philippe de Robert. *Les Livres de Samuel*. CAT VI. Genève: Labor et Fides, 1994.
Carmichael, Calum M. "David at the Nob Sanctuary." In *For and Against David: Story and History in the Books of Samuel*, edited by A. Graeme Auld and Erik Eynikel, 201–12. BETL 232. Leuven: Peeters, 2010.
———. "Laws of Leviticus 19." *HTR* 87 (1994) 239–56.
Carpenter, Eugene and Michael A. Grisanti. "אוֶן." In *NIDOTTE* 1:309–15.
———. "שׁקר." In *NIDOTTE* 4:247–49.
Carson, D. A. *The Gospel according to John*. PNTC. Grand Rapids: Eerdmans, 1991.
Carson, Thomas L. *Lying and Deception: Theory and Practice*. New York: Oxford University Press, 2010.
———. "Lying, Deception, and Related Concepts." In *The Philosophy of Deception*, edited by Clancy Martin, 153–87. New York: Oxford University Press, 2009.
Cartledge, Tony W. *1 & 2 Samuel*. SHBC. Macon, GA: Smyth & Helwys, 2001.
Cassuto, Umberto. *A Commentary on the Book of Exodus*. Translated by Israel Abrahams. Jerusalem: Magnes, 1967.
Cathcart, Kevin J. "The Trees, the Beasts and the Birds: Fables, Parables and Allegories in the Old Testament." In *Wisdom in Ancient Israel: Essays in Honour of J. A. Emerton*, edited by John Day et al., 212–21. Cambridge: Cambridge University Press, 1995.
Childs, Brevard S. *The Book of Exodus: A Critical, Theological Commentary*. OTL. Philadelphia: Westminster, 1974.
Chisholm Jr., Robert B. "Does God 'Change His Mind?'" *BSac* 152 (1995) 387–99.
———. "Does God Deceive?" *BSac* 155 (1998) 11–28.
———. "Ehud: Assessing an Assassin." *BSac* 168 (2011) 274–82.
———. "שׁנה." In *NIDOTTE* 4:190–91.
Chisholm, Roderick M., and Thomas D. Feehan. "The Intent to Deceive." *JPhil* 74 (1977) 143–59.
Christensen, Duane L. *Deuteronomy 1:1—21:9*. WBC 6A. Nashville: Thomas Nelson, 2001.
———. *Deuteronomy 21:10—34:12*. WBC 6B. Nashville: Thomas Nelson, 2002.
Clifford, Richard J. *Proverbs: A Commentary*. OTL. Louisville: Westminster John Knox, 1999.
Clines, David J. A. "Michal Observed: An Introduction." In *Telling Queen Michal's Story*, edited by David J. A. Clines and Tamar C. Eskenazi, 24–63. JSOTSup 119. Sheffield, UK: Sheffield Academic, 1991.
Coats, George W. "Parable, Fable, and Anecdote: Storytelling in the Succession Narrative." *Int* 35 (1981) 368–82.
———. "2 Samuel 12:1–7a." *Int* 40 (1986) 170–74.
Cogan, Mordechai. *1 Kings: A New Translation with Introduction and Commentary*. AB 10. New York: Doubleday, 2000.
Coggins, Richard J. "On Kings and Disguises." *JSOT* 50 (1991) 55–62.
Cole, Alan. *Exodus*. TOTC. London: IVP, 1973.
Conrad, Joachim. "Davids Königtum als Paradoxie: Versuch zu 1 Sam 21,2–10." In *Gott und Mensch im Dialog. Festschrift für Otto Kaiser zum 80. Geburtstag*, edited by Markus Witte, 413–23. BZAW 345/1–2. Berlin: de Gruyter, 2005.
———. "Der Gegenstand und die Intention der Geschichte von der Thronfolge Davids." *TLZ* 108 (1983) 161–76.

Conroy, Charles. *Absalom Absalom! Narrative and Language in 2 Sam 13-20*. AnBib 81. Rome: Biblical Institute, 1978.

———. *1-2 Samuel, 1-2 Kings*. OTM 6. Wilmington, DE: Glazier, 1983.

Coxon, Peter W. "A Note on 'Bathsheba' in 2 Samuel 12:1-16." *Bib* 62 (1981) 247-50.

Craig, Kenneth M. "Rhetorical Aspects of Questions Answered with Silence in 1 Samuel 14:37 and 28:6." *CBQ* 56 (1994) 221-39.

Craigie, Peter C. *The Book of Deuteronomy*. NICOT. Grand Rapids: Eerdmans, 1976.

Craigie, Peter C., et al. *Jeremiah 1-25*. WBC 26. Dallas: Word, 1991.

Craven, T. "Women Who Lied for the Faith." In *Justice and the Holy: Essays in Honor of Walter Harrelson*, edited by D. A. Knight and P. A. Paris, 35-49. Atlanta: Scholars, 1989.

Creach, Jerome F. D. *Joshua*. IBC. Louisville: John Knox, 2003.

Cribb, Bryan Howard. *Speaking on the Brink of Sheol: Form and Message of Old Testament Death Stories*. Gorgias Dissertations 43. Piscataway, NJ: Gorgias, 2009.

Crüsemann, Frank. "Zwei alttestamentliche Witze: 1 Sam 21:11-15 und 2 Sam 6:16, 20-23 als Beispiele einer biblischen Gattung." *ZAW* 92 (1980) 215-27.

Cryer, Frederick. "David's Rise to Power and the Death of Abner: An Analysis of 1 Samuel 26:14-16 and Its Redaction-Critical Implications." *VT* 35 (1985) 385-94.

Culley, Robert C. "Themes and Variations in Three Groups of OT Narratives." *Semeia* 3 (1975) 3-13.

Currid, John D. *A Study Commentary on Exodus: Volume 2: Exodus 19-40*. Auburn, MA: Evangelical, 2001.

Daube, David. "Absalom and the Ideal King." *VT* 48 (1998) 315-25.

———. "Nathan's Parable." *NovT* 24 (1982) 275-88.

Deboys, David G. "1 Samuel 29:6." *VT* 39 (1989) 214-19.

Delekat, Lienhard. "Tendenz und Theologie der David-Salomo-Erzählung." In *Das ferne und nahe Wort: Festschrift für Leonhard Rost zum 70. Geburtstag*, edited by F. Maass, 26-36. BZAW 105. Berlin: Töpelman, 1967.

DeVries, Simon J. *1 Kings*. WBC 12. Waco, TX: Word, 1985.

Dhorme, Le P. Paul. *Les Livres de Samuel*. Paris: Gabalda, 1910.

Driver, S. R. *A Critical and Exegetical Commentary on Deuteronomy*. 3rd ed. ICC. Edinburgh: T. & T. Clark, 1996.

———. *Notes on the Hebrew Text of the Books of Samuel*. Oxford: Clarendon, 1890.

Durham, John I. *Exodus*. WBC 3. Waco, TX: Word, 1987.

Edelman, Diana Vikander. *King Saul in the Historiography of Judah*. JSOTSup 121. Sheffield, UK: JSOT, 1991.

———. "Saul's Rescue of Jabesh-Gilead (I Sam 11 1-11): Sorting Story from History." *ZAW* 96 (1984) 195-209.

Ellingworth, Paul. *The Epistle to the Hebrews: A Commentary on the Greek Text*. NIGNT. Grand Rapids: Eerdmans, 1993.

Engar, Ann W. "Old Testament Women as Tricksters." In *Mappings of the Biblical Terrain: The Bible as Text*, edited by Vincent L. Tollers and John Maier, 143-57. Lewisburg, PA: Bucknell University Press, 1990.

Enns, Peter. *Exodus*. NIVAC. Grand Rapids: Zondervan, 2000.

Esau, Ken. "Divine Deception in the Exodus Event?" *Direction* 34 (2006) 4-17.

Eschelbach, Michael A. *Has Joab Foiled David? A Literary Study of the Importance of Joab's Character in Relation to David*. StBL 76. New York: Lang, 2005.

Esler, Philip F. *Sex, Wives, and Warriors: Reading Biblical Narrative with its Ancient Audience*. Eugene, OR: Cascade, 2011.
Eslinger, Lyle M. *Kingship of God in Crisis: A Close Reading of 1 Samuel 1–12*. BLS 10. Sheffield, UK: Almond, 1985.
———. "Viewpoints and Point of View in 1 Samuel 8–12." *JSOT* 26 (1983) 61–76.
Evans, Mary J. *1 and 2 Samuel*. NIBC. Peabody, MA: Hendrickson, 2000.
Exum, J. Cheryl. *Fragmented Women: Feminist (Sub)versions of Biblical Narratives*. Valley Forge, PA: Trinity, 1993.
Eynikel, Erik. "The Parable of Nathan (II Sam 12,1–4) and the Theory of Semiosis." In *Rethinking the Foundations: Historiography in the Ancient World and in the Bible: Essays in Honour of John Van Seters* (in collaboration with Hans Heinrich Schmid), edited by Steven L. McKenzie and Thomas Römer, 71–90. BZAW 294. Berlin: de Gruyter, 2000.
Fallis, Don. "What is Lying?" *JPhil* 106 (2009) 29–56.
Farmer, Kathleen Anne. "The Trickster Genre in the Old Testament." Ph.D. diss., Southern Methodist University, 1978.
Firth, David G. *1 & 2 Samuel*. AOTC 8. Nottingham, UK: Apollos, 2009.
———. "David and Uriah (with an Occasional Appearance by Uriah's Wife) Reading and Re-Reading 2 Samuel 11." *OTE* 21 (2008) 310–28.
———. "Testimonies True (?) and False (?) in 1 Samuel 21–22." *SABJT* 15 (2006) 20–27.
Fischer, Alexander. "David und Batseba: ein literarkritischer und motivgeschichtlicher Beitrag zu 2 Sam 11." *ZAW* 101 (1989) 50–59.
Fischer, David Hackett. *Historians' Fallacies: Toward a Logic of Historical Thought*. New York: Harper & Row, 1970.
Fletcher, Joseph. *Situation Ethics: The New Morality*. Philadelphia: Westminster, 1966.
Fokkelman, Jan P. *Narrative Art and Poetry in the Books of Samuel: A Full Interpretation Based on Stylistic and Structural Analysis, Vol. 1: King David (II Sam. 9–20 & 1 Kings 1–2)*. SSN 20. Assen: Van Gorcum, 1981.
———. *Narrative Art and Poetry in the Books of Samuel: A Full Interpretation Based on Stylistic and Structural Analysis, Vol. II: The Crossing Fates (I Sam. 13–31 & II Sam. 1)*. SSN 23. Assen: Van Gorcum, 1986.
———. *Narrative Art and Poetry in the Books of Samuel: A Full Interpretation Based on Stylistic and Structural Analysis, Vol. III: Throne and City (II Sam. 2–8 & 21–24)*. SSN 27. Assen: Van Gorcum, 1990.
———. *Narrative Art and Poetry in the Books of Samuel: A Full Interpretation Based on Stylistic and Structural Analysis, Vol. IV: Vow and Desire (I Sam. 1–12)*. SSN 31. Assen: Van Gorcum, 1993.
———. *Reading Biblical Narrative: An Introductory Guide*. Leiderdorp: Deo, 1999.
———. "Saul and David: Crossed Fates." *BRev* 5 (1989) 20–32.
Fox, Michael V. *Proverbs 10–31*. AB 18B. New Haven: Yale University Press, 2009.
Frame, John M. *The Doctrine of the Christian Life*. Phillipsburg, NJ: P. & R., 2008.
France, R. T. *The Gospel of Mark: A Commentary on the Greek Text*. NIGTC. Grand Rapids: Eerdmans, 2002.
Fretheim, Terence E. *Exodus*. IBC. Louisville: John Knox, 1991.
———. *First and Second Kings*. WBC. Louisville: Westminster John Knox, 1999.
Freund, Richard A. "Lying and Deception in the Biblical and Post-Biblical Judaic Tradition." *SJOT* 1 (1991) 45–61.

Frontain, Raymond-Jean. "The Trickster Tricked: Strategies of Deception and Survival in the David Narrative." In *Mappings of the Biblical Terrain: The Bible as Text*, edited by Vincent L. Tollers and John Maier, 170–89. Lewisburg, PA: Bucknell University Press, 1990.

Fuchs, Esther. "'For I Have the Way of Women': Deception, Gender, and Ideology in Biblical Narrative." *Semeia* 42 (1988) 68–83.

———. "Who is Hiding the Truth? Deceptive Women and Biblical Androcentrism." In *Feminist Perspectives on Biblical Scholarship*, edited by A. Yarbro Collins, 137–44. Chico: Scholars, 1985.

Galil, Gershon. "The Jerahmeelites and the Negeb of Judah." *JANES* 28 (2001) 33–42.

Garsiel, Moshe. *The First Book of Samuel: A Literary Study of Comparative Structures, Analogies and Parallels*. Jerusalem: Revivim, 1983.

———. "Puns Upon Names as a Literary Device in 1 Kings 1–2." *Bib* 72 (1991) 378–86.

———. "A Review of Recent Interpretations of the Story of David and Bathsheba." *Immanuel* 2 (1973) 18–20.

———. "The Story of David and Bathsheba: A Different Approach." *CBQ* 55 (1993) 244–62.

Gass, Erasmus. "Achisch von Gat als politische Witzfigur." *TQ* 189 (2009) 210–42.

Gerstenberger, Erhard S. *Leviticus: A Commentary*. Translated by Douglas W. Stott. OTL. Louisville: Westminster John Knox, 1996.

Gispen, Willem Hendrik. *Exodus*. Translated by Ed van der Maas. BSC. Grand Rapids: Zondervan, 1982.

Glueck, Nelson. *Hesed in the Bible*. Translated by Alfred Gottschalk. Cincinnati: Hebrew Union College, 1967.

Goldberg, Michael L. "The Story of the Moral: Gifts or Bribes in Deuteronomy?" *Int* 38 (1984) 15–25.

Goldingay, John. *Men Behaving Badly*. Carlisle, UK: Paternoster, 2000.

———. *Old Testament Theology: Israel's Faith*. Downers Grove, IL: IVP, 2006.

———. *Old Testament Theology: Israel's Gospel*. Downers Grove, IL: IVP, 2003.

Good, Edwin M. "Deception and Women: A Response." *Semeia* 42 (1988) 117–32.

Gordon, Robert P. "Covenant and Apology in 2 Samuel 3." In *Hebrew Bible and Ancient Versions: Selected Essays of Robert P. Gordon*, 38–46. Farnham, UK: Ashgate, 2006.

———. *I & II Samuel: A Commentary*. LBI. Exeter, UK: Paternoster, 1986.

———. "Gibeonite Ruse and Israelite Curse in Joshua 9." In *Hebrew Bible and Ancient Versions: Selected Essays of Robert P. Gordon*, 80–100. Farnham, UK: Ashgate, 2006.

———. "In Search of David: The David Tradition in Recent Study." In *Faith, Tradition, and History: Old Testament Historiography in its Near Eastern Context*, edited by A. R. Millard et al., 285–98. Winona Lake, IN: Eisenbrauns, 1994.

———. "Simplicity of the Highest Cunning: Narrative Art in the Old Testament." In *Hebrew Bible and Ancient Versions: Selected Essays of Robert P. Gordon*, 22–32. Farnham, UK: Ashgate, 2006.

Grassi, Joseph A. "Five Loaves of the High Priest." *NovT* 7 (1964) 119–22.

Gray, John. *I & II Kings: A Commentary*. OTL. Philadelphia: Westminster, 1963.

Gray, Mark. "Amnon: A Chip off the Old Block? Rhetorical Strategy in 2 Samuel 13:7–15: The Rape of Tamar and the Humiliation of the Poor." *JSOT* 77 (1998) 39–54.

Green, Barbara. "The Engaging Nuances of Genre: Reading Saul and Michal Afresh." In *Relating to the Text: Interdisciplinary and Form-Critical Insights on the Bible*, edited

by Timothy J. Sandoval and Carleen Mandolfo, 141–59. JSOTSup 384. London: T. & T. Clark, 2003.
———. *How Are the Mighty Fallen? A Dialogical Study of King Saul in 1 Samuel.* JSOTSup 365. Sheffield, UK: Sheffield Academic Press, 2003.
Greenberg, Moshe. *Ezekiel 1–20.* AB 22. Garden City, NY: Doubleday, 1983.
Gressmann, Hugo. "The Oldest History Writing in Israel." In *Narrative and Novella in Samuel: Studies by Hugo Gressmann and Other Scholars, 1906–1923,* edited by David M. Gunn, translated by David E. Orton, 9–58. JSOTSup 116. Sheffield, UK: Sheffield Academic Press, 1991.
Grønbæk, Jakob H. *Die Geschichte vom Aufstieg Davids (1. Sam. 15–2. Sam 5) Tradition und Komposition.* Copenhagen: Prostant Apud Munksgaard, 1971.
Gros Louis, Kenneth R. R. "The Difficulty of Ruling Well: King David of Israel." *Semeia* 8 (1977) 15–33.
Grudem, Wayne. "Why It is Never Right to Lie: An Example of John Frame's Influence on My Approach to Ethics." In *Speaking the Truth in Love: The Theology of John M. Frame,* edited by John J. Hughes, 778–801. Phillipsburg, NJ: P. & R., 2009.
Gunn, David M. "David and the Gift of the Kingdom." *Semeia* 3 (1975) 14–45.
———. *The Fate of King Saul: An Interpretation of a Biblical Story.* JSOTSup 14. Sheffield, UK: JSOT, 1980.
———. "From Jerusalem to the Jordan and Back: Symmetry in 2 Samuel 15–20." *VT* 30 (1980) 109–13.
———. *The Story of King David: Genre and Interpretation.* JSOTSup 6. Sheffield, UK: JSOT, 1978.
———. "Traditional Composition in the 'Succession Narrative.'" *VT* 26 (1976) 214–29.
Haelewyck, Jean-Claude. "La Mort d'Abner: 2 Sam 3,1–39." *RB* 102 (1995) 161–92.
———. "L'assassinat d'Ishbaal (2 Samuel IV 1–12)." *VT* 47 (1997) 145–53.
Hagan, Harry. "Deception as Motif and Theme in 2 Sm 9–20; 1 Kgs 1–2." *Bib* 60 (1979) 301–26.
Halbe, Jörn. "Gemeinschaft, die Welt unterbricht: Grundfragen und -inhalte deuteronomischer Theologie und Uberlieferungsbildung im Lichte der Ursprungsbedingungen alttestamentlichen Rechts." In *Das Deuteronomium: Entstehung, Gestalt und Botschaft,* edited by Norbert Lohfink, 55–75. Louvain: Peeters, 1985.
Halpern, Baruch. *David's Secret Demons: Messiah, Murderer, Traitor, King.* Grand Rapids: Eerdmans, 2001.
Hammond, Gerald. "Michal, Tamar, Abigail and What Bathsheba Said: Notes toward a Really Inclusive Translation of the Bible." In *Women in the Biblical Tradition,* edited by George J. Brooke, 53–70. Lewiston, NY: Mellen, 1992.
Hansen, Tracy. "My Name is Tamar." *Theology* 95 (1992) 370–76.
Harris, Gregory H. "Does God Deceive? The 'Deluding Influence' of Second Thessalonians 2:11." *MSJ* 16 (2005) 73–93.
Harrison, R. K. *Introduction to the Old Testament.* Grand Rapids: Eerdmans, 1969.
———. *Leviticus: An Introduction and Commentary.* TOTC. Leicester, UK: IVP, 1980.
Hartley, John E. *Leviticus.* WBC 4. Dallas: Word, 1992.
Haupt, Paul. "Deal Gently with the Young Man." *JBL* 45 (1926) 357.
Hertzberg, Hans Wilhelm. *I & II Samuel.* Translated by J. S. Bowden. OTL. Philadelphia: Westminster, 1964.

Hill, Andrew E. "A Jonadab Connection in the Absalom Conspiracy." *JETS* 30 (1987) 387–90.
Hoffner Jr., Harry A. "The Linguistic Origins of Teraphim." *BSac* 124 (1967) 230–38.
———. "Second Millennium Antecedents to the Hebrew 'ōḇ." *JBL* 86 (1967) 385–401.
Hoftijzer, Jacob. "David and the Tekoite Woman." *VT* 20 (1970) 419–44.
Holladay, William L. *Jeremiah I: A Commentary on the Book of the Prophet Jeremiah Chapters 1–25*. Hermeneia. Philadelphia: Fortress, 1986.
Holloway, Steven W. "Distaff, Crutch or Chain Gang: The Curse of the House of Joab in 2 Samuel 3:29." *VT* 37 (1987) 370–75.
Holmstedt, Robert D. "The Relative Clause in Biblical Hebrew: A Linguistic Analysis." Ph.D. diss., University of Wisconsin-Madison, 2002.
Howard Jr., David M. *Joshua*. NAC 5. Nashville: Broadman & Holman, 1998.
Hubbard, David A. *Proverbs*. The Communicator's Commentary. Dallas: Word, 1989.
Humphreys, W. Lee. "The Tragedy of King Saul: A Study of the Structure of 1 Samuel 9–31." *JSOT* 6 (1978) 18–27.
Hütter, Reinhard. "The Tongue—Fallen and Restored: Some Reflections on the Three Voices of the Eighth Commandment." In *I Am the Lord Your God: Christian Reflections on the Ten Commandments*, edited by Carl E. Braaten and Christopher R. Seitz, 189–205. Grand Rapids: Eerdmans, 2005.
Hyman, Ronald T. "Power of Persuasion: Judah, Abigail, and Hushai." *JBQ* 23 (1995) 9–16.
Irwin, W. A. "Truth in Ancient Israel." *JR* 9 (1929) 357–88.
Janzen, David. "The Condemnation of David's 'Taking' in 2 Samuel 12:1–14." *JBL* 131 (2012) 209–20.
Jenni, Ernst, and Claus Westermann. *Theological Lexicon of the Old Testament*. Translated by Mark E. Biddle. 3 vols. Peabody, MA: Hendrickson, 1997.
Jensen, Hans J. L. "Desire, Rivalry and Collective Violence in the Succession Narrative." *JSOT* 55 (1992) 39–59.
Jenson, Philip P. "חמש." In *NIDOTTE* 2:190–91.
Jobling, David. *1 Samuel: Studies in Hebrew Narrative & Poetry*. Berit Olam. Collegeville, MN: Liturgical, 1998.
———. "David and the Philistines: With Methodological Reflections." In *David und Saul im Widerstreit: Diachronie und Synchronie im Wettstreit*, edited by W. Dietrich, 74–85. OBO 206. Göttingen: Vandenhoeck & Ruprecht, 2004.
Jones, Gwilym H. *The Nathan Narratives*. JSOTSup 80. Sheffield, UK: JSOT, 1990.
Jonker, Louis C. *Exclusivity and Variety: Perspectives on Multidimensional Exegesis*. CBET 19. Kampen: Kok Pharos, 1996.
Josephus. Translated by H. St. J. Thackeray et al. 10 vols. LCL. Cambridge: Harvard University Press, 1926–65.
Kaiser Jr., Walter C. *Toward Old Testament Ethics*. Grand Rapids: Zondervan, 1983.
Kant, Immanuel. *The Metaphysics of Morals*. Translated and edited by Mary Gregor. Cambridge: Cambridge University Press, 1996.
Keefe, Alice A. "Rapes of Women/Wars of Men." *Semeia* 61 (1993) 79–97.
Kidner, Derek. *The Proverbs: An Introduction and Commentary*. TOTC. London: IVP, 1964.
King, Philip J., and Lawrence E. Stager. *Life in Biblical Israel*. LAI. Louisville: Westminster John Knox, 2001.

Kiuchi, Nobuyoshi. *The Purification Offering in the Priestly Literature: Its Meaning and Function*. JSOTSup 56. Sheffield, UK: Sheffield Academic, 1987.
Klein, Johannes. "Davids Flucht zu den Philistern (1 Sam xxi 11ff; xxvii–xxix)." *VT* 55 (2005) 176–84.
Klein, Lillian R. "Michal, the Barren Wife." In *Samuel and Kings: A Feminist Companion to the Bible*, edited by Athalya Brenner, 37–46. Sheffield, UK: Sheffield Academic, 2000.
Klein, Ralph W. *1 Samuel*. WBC 10. Waco, TX: Word, 1983.
Klopfenstein, Martin A. *Die Lüge nach dem Alten Testament: Ihr Begriff, ihre Bedeutung und ihre Beurteilung*. Zürich: Gotthelf, 1964.
———. "שקר." In *TLOT* 3:1399–1405.
Knierim, R. "און." In *TLOT* 1:60–62.
———. "עול." In *TLOT* 2:849–51.
Koehler, Ludwig. *Old Testament Theology*. London: Lutterworth, 1957.
Labuschagne, C. J. "Teraphim: A New Proposal for its Etymology." *VT* 16 (1966) 115–17.
Langlamet, François. "1 Samuel 13–2 Samuel 1? Fokkelman et le prêtre de Nob." *RB* 99 (1992) 631–75.
Lasine, Stuart. "Judicial Narratives and the Ethics of Reading: The Reader as Judge of the Dispute between Mephibosheth and Ziba." *HS* 30 (1989) 49–69.
———. "Melodrama as Parable: The Story of the Poor Man's Ewe-Lamb and the Unmasking of David's Topsy-Turvy Emotions." *HAR* 8 (1984) 101–24.
Lategan, Bernard C. "Reference: Reception, Redescription, and Reality." In *Text and Reality: Aspects of Reference in Biblical Texts*, edited by Bernard C. Lategan and Willem S. Vorster, 67–93. Philadelphia: Fortress, 1985.
Lawton, Robert B. "1 Samuel 18: David, Merob, and Michal." *CBQ* 51 (1989) 423–25.
———. "Saul, Jonathan, and the 'Son of Jesse.'" *JSOT* 58 (1993) 35–46.
Layton, Scott C. "A Chain Gang in 2 Samuel 3:29?" *VT* 39 (1989) 81–86.
Lehmann, Paul L. *The Decalogue and a Human Future: The Meaning of the Commandments for Making and Keeping Human Life Human*. Grand Rapids: Eerdmans, 1995.
Leithart, Peter J. *A Son to Me: An Exposition of 1 & 2 Samuel*. Moscow, ID: Canon, 2003.
Leonard, Jeanne Marie. "La Femme de Teqoa et le fils de David: Etude de 2 Samuel 14/1–20." *CV* 23 (1980) 135–48.
Lescow, Theodore. "Die Komposition der Tamar-Erzählung II Sam 13,1–22." *ZAW* 114 (2002) 110–11.
Levine, Baruch A. *Leviticus*. JPS Torah Commentary. Philadelphia: Jewish Publication Society, 1989.
Lewis, T. J. "Teraphim." In *DDD*, 844–50.
Long, V. Philips. *The Art of Biblical History*. FCI 5. Grand Rapids: Zondervan, 1994.
———. "1 and 2 Samuel." In *Zondervan Illustrated Bible Backgrounds Commentary*, edited by John H. Walton, 266–491. Vol. 2. Grand Rapids: Zondervan, 2009.
———. *The Reign and Rejection of King Saul: A Case for Literary and Theological Coherence*. SBLDS 118. Atlanta: Scholars, 1987.
Longman III, Tremper. *Proverbs*. BCOTWP. Grand Rapids: Baker Academic, 2006.
Lust, Johann. "On Wizards and Prophets." In *Studies on Prophecy: A Collection of Twelve Papers*, 133–42. VTSup 26. Leiden: Brill, 1974.

Lyke, Larry L. *King David with the Wise Woman of Tekoa: The Resonance of Tradition in Parabolic Narrative*. JSOTSup 255. Sheffield, UK: Sheffield Academic, 1997.

Mabee, C. "David's Judicial Exoneration." *ZAW* 92 (1980) 89–107.

———. "Judicial Instrumentality in the Ahimelech Story." In *Early Jewish and Christian Exegesis*, edited by Craig A. Evans and William F. Stinespring, 17–32. Atlanta: Scholars, 1987.

Magonet, Jonathan. "The Structure and Meaning of Leviticus 19." *HAR* 7 (1983) 151–67.

Mahon, James Edwin. "A Definition of Deceiving." *IJAP* 21 (2007) 181–94.

———. "The Truth About Kant on Lies." In *The Philosophy of Deception*, edited by Clancy Martin, 201–24. New York: Oxford University Press, 2009.

———. "Two Definitions of Lying." *IJAP* 22 (2008) 211–30.

Marcus, David. "David the Deceiver and David the Dupe." *Prooftexts* 6 (1986) 163–71.

Marshall, I. Howard. *The Gospel of Luke: A Commentary on the Greek Text*. NIGTC. Exeter, UK: Paternoster, 1978.

Mastéy, Emmanuel. "A Linguistic Inquiry Solves an Ancient Crime: Re-examination of 2 Samuel 4:6." *VT* 61 (2011) 82–103.

Matthews, Victor H., and Don C. Benjamin. *Social World of Ancient Israel, 1250–587 BCE*. Peabody, MA: Hendrickson, 1993.

Matthews, Victor H. "Female Voices: Upholding the Honor of the Household." *BTB* 24 (1994) 8–15.

Matties, Gordon H. "Reading Rahab's Story: Beyond the Moral of the Story (Joshua 2)." *Direction* 24 (1995) 57–70.

Mauchline, John. *1 and 2 Samuel*. NCB. London: Oliphants, 1971.

Mayes, A. D. H. *Deuteronomy*. NCB. Grand Rapids: Eerdmans, 1979.

McCarter Jr., P. Kyle. *I Samuel: A New Translation with Introduction, Notes and Commentary*. AB 8. Garden City, NY: Doubleday, 1980.

———. *II Samuel: A New Translation with Introduction, Notes and Commentary*. AB 9. Garden City, NY: Doubleday, 1984.

———. "The Apology of David." *JBL* 99 (1980) 489–504.

———. "'Plots, True or False': The Succession Narrative as Court Apologetic." *Int* 35 (1981) 355–67.

McConville, J. Gordon. *Deuteronomy*. AOTC 5. Leicester, UK: Apollos, 2002.

McEvenue, Sean E. "The Basis of Empire: A Study of the Succession Narrative." *ExAud* 2 (1986) 34–45.

McKay, J. W. "Exodus XXIII 1–3, 6–8: A Decalogue for the Administration of Justice in the City Gate." *VT* 21 (1971) 311–25.

McKenzie, Steven L. *King David: A Biography*. New York: Oxford University Press, 2000.

Meibauer, Jörg, "Lying and Falsely Implicating." In *Cultures of Lying: Theories and Practice of Lying in Society, Literature, and Film*, edited by Jochen Mecke, 79–114. Berlin: Galda & Wilch, 2007.

Merrill, Eugene H. *Deuteronomy*. NAC 4. Nashville: Broadman & Holman, 1994.

Mettinger, Tryggve N. D. *King and Messiah: The Civil and Sacral Legitimation of Israelite Kings*. ConBOT 8. Lund: Gleerup, 1976.

Milgrom, Jacob. *Cult and Conscience: The Asham and the Priestly Doctrine of Repentance*. SJLA 18. Leiden: Brill, 1976.

———. *Leviticus: A Book of Ritual and Ethics*. Minneapolis: Fortress, 2004.

———. *Leviticus 1–16*. AB 3. New York: Doubleday, 1991.
———. *Leviticus 17–22*. AB 3A. New York: Doubleday, 2000.
Mill, John Stuart. *Utilitarianism*. Edited by Oskar Piest. New York: Liberal Arts, 1957.
Miller, J. Maxwell. "Geba/Gibeah of Benjamin." *VT* 25 (1975) 145–66.
———. "Saul's Rise to Power: Some Observations concerning 1 Samuel 9:1—10:16; 10:26—11:15 and 13:2—14:46." *CBQ* 36 (1974) 157–74.
Miller, Patrick D. *Deuteronomy*. IBC. Louisville: John Knox, 1990.
———. *The Ten Commandments*. Interpretation. Louisville: Westminster John Knox, 2009.
Miscall, Peter D. *1 Samuel: A Literary Reading*. Bloomington, IN: Indiana University Press, 1986.
———. "Literary Unity in Old Testament Narrative." *Semeia* 15 (1979) 27–44.
———. *The Workings of Old Testament Narrative*. Philadelphia: Fortress, 1983.
Moberly, R. W. L. "אמן." In *NIDOTTE* 1:427–33.
Mommer, I. "David und Merab—eine historische oder eine literarische Beziehung?" In *David und Saul im Widerstreit: Diachronie und Synchronie im Wettstreit*, edited by W. Dietrich, 196–204. OBO 206. Göttingen: Vandenhoeck & Ruprecht, 2004.
Moore, Michael S. "Bathsheba's Silence (1 Kings 1:11–31)." In *Inspired Speech: Prophecy in the Ancient Near East. Essays in Honour of Herbert B. Huffmon*, edited by John Kaltner and Louis Stulman, 336–46. JSOTSup 378. London: T. & T. Clark, 2004.
Moran, William L. "The Ancient Near Eastern Background of the Love of God in Deuteronomy." *CBQ* 25 (1963) 77–87.
Morgenstern, Julian. "The Book of the Covenant." *HUCA* 33 (1962) 59–105.
Murray, John. *Principles of Conduct: Aspects of Biblical Ethics*. Grand Rapids: Eerdmans, 1991.
Na'aman, Nadav. "The Pre-Deuteronomistic Story of King Saul and Its Historical Significance." *CBQ* 54 (1992) 638–58.
Neiderhiser, Edward A. "2 Samuel 20:8–10: A Note for a Commentary." *JETS* 24 (1981) 209–10.
Nelson, Richard D. *Deuteronomy: A Commentary*. OTL. Louisville: Westminster John Knox, 2002.
———. *First and Second Kings*. IBC. Louisville: John Knox, 1987.
Newkirk, Matthew. "Reconsidering the Role of Deception in Solomon's Ascent to the Throne." *JETS* 57 (2014) 703–13.
Nicholas, Dean Andrew. *The Trickster Revisited: Deception as a Motif in the Pentateuch*. StBL 117. New York: Lang, 2009.
Nicholson, Sarah. *Three Faces of Saul: An Intertextual Approach to Biblical Tragedy*. JSOTSup 339. Sheffield, UK. Sheffield Academic Press, 2002.
Nicol, George G. "The Alleged Rape of Bathsheba: Some Observations on Ambiguity in Biblical Narrative." *JSOT* 73 (1997) 43–54.
———. "David, Abigail, and Bathsheba, Nabal and Uriah: Transformations within a Triangle." *SJOT* 12 (1998) 130–45.
———. "The Wisdom of Joab and the Wise Woman of Tekoa." *ST* 36 (1982) 97–104.
Niditch, Susan. *Underdogs and Tricksters: A Prelude to Biblical Folklore*. San Francisco: Harper & Row, 1987.
Nihan, Christophe L. "1 Samuel 28 and the Condemnation of Necromancy in Persian Yehud." In *Magic in the Biblical World: From the Rod of Aaron to the Ring of Solomon*, edited by Todd Klutz, 23–54. JSNTSup 245. London: T. & T. Clark, 2003.

Noll, K. L. *The Faces of David*. JSOTSup 242. Sheffield, UK: Sheffield Academic, 1997.
Noth, Martin. *Exodus*. Translated by J. S. Bowden. OTL. Philadelphia: Westminster, 1962.
———. *Leviticus: A Commentary*. Translated by J. E. Anderson. OTL. Philadelphia: Westminster, 1965.
Osborne, Grant R. *The Hermeneutical Spiral: A Comprehensive Introduction to Biblical Interpretation*. Downers Grove, IL: IVP, 1991.
Park, Song-Mi Suzie. "The Frustration of Wisdom: Wisdom, Counsel, and Divine Will in 2 Samuel 17:1–23." *JBL* (2009) 453–67.
Parsons, Michael. "Bathsheba: Readings Then and Now." *SABJT* 15 (2006) 43–47.
———. "Luther and Calvin on Rape: Is the Crime Lost in the Agenda?" *EvQ* 74 (2002) 123–42.
Patrick, Dale. *Old Testament Law*. Atlanta: John Knox, 1985.
Patterson, Richard D. "The Old Testament Use of an Archetype: The Trickster." *JETS* 42 (1999) 385–94.
Payne, David F. *Deuteronomy*. Philadelphia: Westminster, 1985.
———. *I & II Samuel*. Philadelphia: Westminster, 1982.
Perdue, Leo G. "'Is There Anyone Left of the House of Saul ...?' Ambiguity and the Characterization of David in the Succession Narrative." *JSOT* 30 (1984) 67–84.
Petersen, David L. "Portraits of David: Canonical and Otherwise." *Int* 40 (1986) 130–42.
Phillips, Anthony. *Ancient Israel's Criminal Law: A New Approach to the Decalogue*. New York: Schocken, 1970.
———. "Another Look at Adultery." *JSOT* 20 (1981) 3–25.
———. "Interpretation of 2 Samuel 12:5–6." *VT* 16 (1966) 242–44.
———. "The Undetectable Offender and the Priestly Legislators." *JTS* 36 (1985) 146–50.
Pigott, Susan M. "Wives, Witches, and Wise Women: Prophetic Heralds of Kingship in 1 and 2 Samuel." *RevExp* 99 (2002) 145–74.
Plass, Ewald M., ed. *What Luther Says: An Anthology*. 3 vols. Saint Louis, MO: Concordia, 1959.
Polzin, Robert. *David and the Deuteronomist: A Literary Study of the Deuteronomic History*. Bloomington, IN: Indiana University Press, 1993.
———. *Samuel and the Deuteronomist: A Literary Study of the Deuteronomic History*. San Francisco: Harper & Row, 1989.
Porter, J. R. *Leviticus*. CBC. Cambridge: Cambridge University Press, 1976.
Pressler, Carolyn. *The View of Women Found in the Deuteronomic Family Laws*. BZAW 216. Berlin: de Gruyter, 1993.
Pritchard, James B., ed. *Ancient Near Eastern Texts Relating to the Old Testament*. 3rd. ed. Princeton: Princeton University Press, 1969.
Propp, William H. *Exodus 19–40*. AB 2A. New York: Doubleday, 2006.
———. "Kinship in 2 Samuel 13." *CBQ* 55 (1993) 39–53.
Prouser, Ora Horn. "The Phenomenology of the Lie in Biblical Narrative." Ph.D. diss., The Jewish Theological Seminary of America, 1991.
———. "Suited to the Throne: The Symbolic Use of Clothing in the David and Saul Narratives." *JSOT* 71 (1996) 27–37.
———. "The Truth About Women and Lying." *JSOT* 61 (1994) 15–28.
Provan, Iain W. *1 and 2 Kings*. NIBC. Peabody, MA: Hendrickson, 1995.

Provan, Iain W., V. Philips Long, and Tremper Longman III. *A Biblical History of Israel.* Louisville: Westminster John Knox, 2003.
Pyper, Hugh S. *David as Reader: 2 Samuel 12:1-15 and the Poetics of Fatherhood.* BIS 23. Leiden: Brill, 1996.
———. "The Enticement to Re-Read: Repetition as Parody in 2 Samuel." *BibInt* 1 (1993) 153–66.
Ramsdell, Edward Thomas. "The Old Testament Understanding of Truth." *JR* 31 (1951) 264–73.
Reinhartz, Adele. "Anonymity and Character in the Books of Samuel." *Semeia* 63 (1993) 117–41.
Reis, Pamela Tamarkin. "Collusion at Nob: A New Reading of 1 Samuel 21–22." *JSOT* 61 (1994) 59–73.
———. "Cupidity and Stupidity: Woman's Agency and the 'Rape' of Tamar." *JANES* 25 (1997) 43–60.
———. "Eating the Blood: Saul and the Witch of Endor." *JSOT* 73 (1997) 3–23.
———. "Killing the Messenger: David's Policy or Politics?" *JSOT* 31 (2006) 167–91.
Rendsburg, Gary A. "Hebrew Philological notes (II)." *HS* 42 (2001) 187–95.
Ridderbos, J. *Deuteronomy.* Translated by Ed van der Maas. BSC. Grand Rapids: Zondervan, 1984.
Ridout, George. "The Rape of Tamar." In *Rhetorical Criticism, Essays in Honor of James Muilenburg*, edited by Jared J. Jackson and Martin Kessler, 75–84. Pittsburgh: Pickwick, 1974.
Rinquist, Linzay. "Necromancing Samuel: Saul Asks Witch Which? A Narrative Perspective of 1 Samuel 28." *SABJT* 15 (2006) 37–42.
Roberts, J. J. M. "Does God Lie? Divine Deceit as a Theological Problem in Israelite Prophetic Literature." In *Congress Volume*, edited by J. A. Emerton, 211–20. VTSup 40. Leiden: Brill, 1988.
Robinson, Gnana. *Let Us Be Like the Nations: A Commentary on the Books of 1 and 2 Samuel.* ITC. Grand Rapids: Eerdmans, 1993.
Rofé, Alexander. "The Tenth Commandment in the Light of Four Deuteronomic Laws." In *Ten Commandments in History and Tradition*, edited by Ben-Zion Segal and Gershon Levi, 45–65. Jerusalem: Magnes, 1990.
Rooker, Mark F. *Leviticus.* NAC 3A. Nashville: Broadman & Holman, 2000.
Rosenberg, Joel. "The Institutional Matrix of Treachery in 2 Samuel 11." *Semeia* 6 (1989) 103–16.
Rost, Leonhard. *The Succession to the Throne of David.* Translated by Michael D. Rutter and David M. Gunn. Sheffield, UK: Almond, 1982.
Roth, Martha T. *Law Collections from Mesopotamia and Asia Minor.* 2nd ed. Edited by Piotr Michalowski. SBLWAW 6. Atlanta: Scholars, 1997.
Roth, Wolfgang. "You Are the Man: Structural Interaction in 2 Samuel 10–12." *Semeia* 8 (1977) 1–13.
Rouillard, Hedwige, and J. Tropper. "*Trpym*, rituals de guérison et culte des ancêtres d'après 1 Samuel 19:11–17 et les texts parallèles d'Assur et de Nuzi." *VT* 37 (1987) 340–61.
Routledge, Robin. "*Hesed* as Obligation: A Re-Examination." *TynBul* 46 (1995) 179–96.
Rowe, Jonathan. *Michal's Moral Dilemma: A Literary, Anthropological and Ethical Interpretation.* LHBOTS 533. London: T. & T. Clark, 2011.

Rudman, Dominic. "The Commissioning Stories of Saul and David as Theological Allegory." *VT* 50 (2000) 519–30.

———. "Reliving the Rape of Tamar: Absalom's Revenge in 2 Samuel 13." *OTE* 11 (1998) 326–39.

Sarna, Nahum M. *Exploring Exodus: The Heritage of Biblical Israel*. New York: Schoken, 1987.

Schäfer-Lichtenberger, Christa. "Michal—eine literarische Figur mit Vergangenheit: In Memoriam Hans Joachim Stoebe (1909–2002)." *WD* 27 (2003) 87–105.

Schipper, Jeremy. "Did David Overinterpret Nathan's Parable in 2 Samuel 12:1–6?" *JBL* 126 (2007) 383–91.

———. *Parables and Conflict in the Hebrew Bible*. New York: Cambridge University Press, 2009.

———. "'Why Do You Still Speak of Your Affairs?': Polyphony in Mephibosheth's Exchanges with David in 2 Samuel." *VT* 54 (2004) 344–51.

Schunk, K.-D. "Das 9. Und 10. Gebot—Jüngstes Glied des Dekalogs?" *ZAW* 96 (1984) 104–9.

Scobie, Charles H. H. *The Ways of Our God: An Approach to Biblical Theology*. Grand Rapids: Eerdmans, 2003.

Seebass, Horst. "Nathan und David in II Sam 12." *ZAW* 86 (1974) 203–11.

Seibert, Eric A. *Subversive Scribes and the Solomonic Narrative: A Rereading of 1 Kings 1–11*. LHBOTS 436. London: T. & T. Clark, 2006.

Seiler, Stefan. *Die Geschichte von der Thronfolge Davids (2 Sam 9–20; 1 Kön 1–2)*. BZAW 267. Berlin: de Gruyter, 1998.

Sheldon, Rose Mary. "Spy Tales." *BRev* 19 (2003) 12–19, 41–42.

Shemesh, Yael. "David in the Service of King Achish of Gath: Renegade to His People or a Fifth Column in the Philistine Army?" *VT* 57 (2007) 73–90.

———. "Lies By Prophets and Other Lies in the Hebrew Bible." *JANES* 29 (2002) 81–95.

———. "Measure for Measure in the David Stories." *SJOT* 17 (2003) 89–109.

Sherwood, Aaron. "A Leader's Misleading and a Prostitute's Profession: A Re-examination of Joshua 2." *JSOT* 31 (2006) 43–61.

Simon, Uriel. "Poor Man's Ewe-Lamb: An Example of a Juridical Parable." *Bib* 48 (1967) 207–42.

Smith, Henry Preserved. *A Critical and Exegetical Commentary on the Books of Samuel*. ICC. Edinburgh: T. & T. Clark, 1898.

Smith, Jenny. "The Discourse Structure of the Rape of Tamar (2 Samuel 13:1–22)." *VE* 20 (1990) 21–42.

Smith, Richard G. *The Fate of Justice and Righteousness During David's Reign: Rereading the Court History and Its Ethics according to 2 Samuel 8:15b—20:26*. LHBOTS 508. London: T. & T. Clark, 2010.

Spicq, Ceslas. *L'Épitre Aux Hébreux: II - Commentaire*. Paris: Gabalda, 1953.

Sprinkle, Joe M. *'The Book of the Covenant': A Literary Approach*. JSOTSup 174. Sheffield, UK: JSOT, 1994.

Stamm, J. J., and M. E. Andrew. *The Ten Commandments in Recent Research*. Naperville, IL: Allenson, 1967.

Stein, Robert H. *Luke*. NAC 24. Nashville: Broadman & Holman, 1992.

———. *Mark*. BECNT. Grand Rapids: Baker Academic, 2008.

Stek, John H. "Rahab of Canaan and Israel: The Meaning of Joshua 2." *CTJ* 37 (2002) 28–48.
Sternberg, Meir. *The Poetics of Biblical Narrative: Ideological Literature and the Drama of Reading*. Bloomington, IN: Indiana University Press, 1985.
Stoebe, Hans Joachim. "David und Uria: Überlegungen zur Überlieferung von 2 Sam 11." *Bib* 67 (1986) 388–96.
———. *Das Erste Buch Samuelis*. KAT 8.1. Gütersloh: Gütersloher, 1973.
———. *Das Zweite Buch Samuelis*. KAT 8.2. Gütersloh: Gütersloher, 1994.
———. "חסד." In *TLOT* 2:449–64.
———. "רעע." In *TLOT* 3:1249–54.
Stone, Ken. *Sex, Honor, and Power in the Deuteronomistic History*. JSOTSup 234. Sheffield, UK: Sheffield Academic, 1996.
Sturdy, John. "The Original Meaning of 'Is Saul Also Among the Prophets?' [1 Samuel x 11, 12; xix 24]." *VT* 20 (1970) 206–13.
Taggar-Cohen, Ada. "Political Loyalty in the Biblical Account of 1 Samuel XX–XXII in Light of Hittite Texts." *VT* 55 (2005) 251–68.
Thompson, J. A. *Deuteronomy: An Introduction and Commentary*. TOTC. London: IVP, 1974.
———. "The Significance of the Verb *Love* in the David-Jonathan Narratives in 1 Samuel." *VT* 24 (1974) 334–38.
Tigay, Jeffrey H. *Deuteronomy*. JPS Torah Commentary. Philadelphia: Jewish Publication Society, 1996.
Towner, Philip H. *The Letters to Timothy and Titus*. NICNT. Grand Rapids: Eerdmans, 2006.
Trebolle-Barrera, Julio C. "Espías contra consejeros en la revuelta de Absalón." *RB* 86 (1979) 524–43.
Trible, Phyllis. *Texts of Terror: Literary-Feminist Readings of Biblical Narratives*. OBT 13. Philadelphia: Fortress, 1984.
Tsumura, David Toshio. *The First Book of Samuel*. NICOT. Grand Rapids: Eerdmans, 2007.
Turner, David L. *Matthew*. BECNT. Grand Rapids: Baker Academic, 2008.
Van der Bergh, Ronald H. "A Narratological Analysis of Time in 2 Samuel 11:2–27a." *OTE* 21 (2008) 498–512.
Van der Merwe, Christo H. J., et al. *A Biblical Hebrew Reference Grammar*. Biblical Languages: Hebrew 3. Sheffield, UK: Sheffield Academic Press, 1999.
Van der Toorn, Karel. "The Nature of the Biblical Teraphim in the Light of Cuneiform Evidence." *CBQ* 52 (1990) 203–22.
———. "Saul and the Rise of Israelite State Religion." *VT* 43 (1993) 519–42.
Van Dijk-Hemmes, Fokkelien. "Tamar and the Limits of Patriarchy: Between Rape and Seduction: On 2 Samuel 13 and Genesis 38." In *The Double Voice of Her Desire*, edited by J. Bekkenkamp and F. Dröes, translated by D. E. Orton, 68–88. Tools for Biblical Study 6. Leiden: Deo, 2004.
Van Pelt, Miles V., and Walter C. Kaiser, Jr. "אוב." In *NIDOTTE* 1:303–4.
Van Seters, John. *The Biblical Saga of King David*. Winona Lake, IN: Eisenbrauns, 2009.
———. *A Law Book for the Diaspora: Revision in the Study of the Covenant Code*. New York: Oxford University Press, 2003.
Van Staalduine-Sulman, Eveline. *The Targum of Samuel*. SAIS 1. Leiden: Brill, 2002.

VanderKam, James C. "Davidic Complicity in the Deaths of Abner and Eshbaal: A Historical and Redactional Study." *JBL* 99 (1980) 521-39.
VanGemeren, Willem A., ed. *New International Dictionary of Old Testament Theology and Exegesis*. 5 vols. Grand Rapids: Zondervan, 1997.
Vanhoozer, Kevin J. "Ezekiel 14: 'I, the Lord, Have Deceived That Prophet': Divine Deception, Inception, and Communicative Action." In *Theological Commentary: Evangelical Perspectives*, edited by R. Michael Allen, 73-98. London: T. & T. Clark, 2011.
Vârtejanu-Joubert, Madalina. "Les 'anciens du peuple' et Saül: temps, espace et rite de passage dan Nombres xi et 1 Samuel x." *VT* 55 (2005) 542-63.
Veijola, Timo. "David und Meribaal." *RB* 85 (1978) 338-61.
Vette, Joachim. "Der letzte Richter? Methodische Überlegungen zur Charaktergestaltung in 1 Sam 11." *CV* 51 (2009) 184-97.
Vogt, Peter T. *Deuteronomic Theology and the Significance of Torah: A Reappraisal*. Winona Lake, IN: Eisenbrauns, 2006.
Von Rad, Gerhard. *Deuteronomy: A Commentary*. Translated by Dorothea Barton. OTL. Philadelphia: Westminster, 1966.
———. *Old Testament Theology Volume I: The Theology of Israel's Historical Traditions*. Translated by D. M. G. Stalker. New York: Harper & Row, 1962.
Vorster, Willem S. "Reader-Response, Redescription, and Reference: 'You Are the Man' (2 Sam 12:7)." In *Text and Reality: Aspects of Reference in Biblical Texts*, edited by Bernard C. Lategan and Willem S. Vorster, 95-112. Philadelphia: Fortress, 1985.
Wadsworth, Tom. "Is There a Hebrew Word for Virgin? *Bethulah* in the Old Testament." *ResQ* 23 (1980) 161-71.
Wallace, Daniel B. *Greek Grammar Beyond the Basics: An Exegetical Syntax of the New Testament*. Grand Rapids: Zondervan, 1996.
Waltke, Bruce K. *The Book of Proverbs: Chapters 1-15*. NICOT. Grand Rapids: Eerdmans, 2004.
———. *The Book of Proverbs: Chapters 15-31*. NICOT. Grand Rapids: Eerdmans, 2005.
———. *Genesis: A Commentary*. Grand Rapids: Zondervan, 2001.
———. *An Old Testament Theology: An Exegetical, Canonical, and Thematic Approach*. Grand Rapids: Zondervan, 2007.
———. "Righteousness in Proverbs." *WTJ* 70 (2008) 225-37.
Waltke, Bruce K. and M. O'Connor. *An Introduction to Biblical Hebrew Syntax*. Winona Lake, IN: Eisenbrauns, 1990.
Walton, John H. "בתולה." In *NIDOTTE* 1:781-84.
Weinfeld, Moshe. *Deuteronomy 1-11: A New Translation with Introduction and Commentary*. AB 5. New York: Doubleday, 1991.
Weingreen, Jacob. "Rebellion of Absalom." *VT* 19 (1969) 263-66.
Weiser, Artur. "Die Legitimation des Königs David: zur Eigenart und Entstehung der sogen. Geschichte von Davids Aufstieg." *VT* 16 (1966) 325-54.
Wellhausen, Julius. *Prolegomena to the History of Israel*. Translated by J. Sutherland Black and Allan Menzies. Edinburgh: Black, 1885.
Wells, Bruce. *The Law of Testimony in the Pentateuchal Codes*. BZABR 4. Harassowitz: Wiesbaden, 2004.
———. "Sex, Lies, and Virginal Rape: The Slandered Bride and False Accusation in Deuteronomy." *JBL* 124 (2005) 41-72.
Wenham, Gordon J. "$B^{E}T\hat{U}L\bar{A}H$ 'A Girl of Marriageable Age.'" *VT* 22 (1972) 326-48.

―――. *The Book of Leviticus*. NICOT. Grand Rapids: Eerdmans, 1979.
Wénin, André. "Marques linguistiques du point de vue dans le récit biblique: l'example du marriage de David (1 S 18,17–29)." *ETL* 83 (2007) 319–37.
―――. *Samuel et l'instauration de la monarchie (1 S 1–12) Une recherché littéraire sur le personage*. Frankfurt: Lang, 1988.
Westbrook, Raymond. "Prohibition on Restoration of Marriage in Deut 24:1–4." In *Studies in Bible 1986*, edited by Sara Japhet, 387–405. Jerusalem: Magnes, 1986.
Wharton, James A. "A Plausible Tale: Story and Theology in 2 Samuel 9–20, 1 Kings 1–2." *Int* 35 (1981) 341–54.
White, Ellen. "Michal the Misinterpreted." *JSOT* 31 (2007) 451–64.
Whitelam, Keith W. *The Just King: Monarchical Judicial Authority in Ancient Israel*. JSOTSup 12. Sheffield, UK: JSOT, 1979.
Whybray, R. N. *The Succession Narrative: A Study of II Samuel 9–20; I Kings 1 and 2*. SBT 9. London: SCM, 1968.
Willey, Patricia K. "The Importunate Woman of Tekoa and How She Got Her Way." In *Reading between Texts: Intertextuality and the Hebrew Bible*, edited by Danna Nolan Fewell, 115–31. LCBI. Louisville: Westminster John Knox, 1992.
Willi-Plein, I. "1 Sam 18–19 und die Davidshausgeschichte." In *David und Saul im Widerstreit: Diachronie und Synchronie im Wettstreit*, edited by W. Dietrich, 138–77. OBO 206. Göttingen: Vandenhoeck & Ruprecht, 2004.
―――. "Anmerkungen zur Frage der Herkunft des Terafim." *ZAH* 15.16 (2002/2003) 172–75.
―――. "Michal und die Anfänge des Königtums in Israel." In *Congress Volume Cambridge 1995*, edited by J. A. Emerton, 401–19. VTSup 66. Leiden: Brill, 1997.
Williams, Michael James. *Deception in Genesis: An Investigation into the Morality of a Unique Biblical Phenomenon*. StBL 32. New York: Lang, 2001.
―――. "Lies, Lies, I Tell You! The Deceptions of Genesis." *CTJ* 43 (2008) 9–20.
Willis, Timothy M. *The Elders of the City: A Study of the Elders-Laws in Deuteronomy*. SBLMS. Atlanta: Society of Biblical Literature, 2001.
Wong, Gregory T. K. "Ehud and Joab: Separated at Birth?" *VT* 56 (2006) 399–411.
Woudstra, M. H. *The Book of Joshua*. NICOT. Grand Rapids: Eerdmans, 1981.
Wozniak, Jerzy. "Drei verschiedene literarische Beschreibungen des Bundes zwischen Jonathan und David." *BZ* 27 (1983) 213–18.
Wright, Christopher J. H. *Old Testament Ethics for the People of God*. Downers Grove, IL: IVP, 2004.
Yadin, Yigael. "Some Aspects of the Strategy of Ahab and David." *Bib* 36 (1955) 332–51.
Yamada, Frank M. *Configurations of Rape in the Hebrew Bible: A Literary Analysis of Three Rape Narratives*. StBL 109. Frankfurt: Lang, 2008.
Yee, Gale A. "Fraught with Background: Literary Ambiguity in 2 Samuel 11." *Int* 42 (1988) 240–53.
Yoder, Christine Roy. "On the Threshold of Kingship: A Study of Agur (Proverbs 30)." *Int* 63 (2009) 254–63.
Youngblood, Ronald F. "1, 2 Samuel." In *The Expositor's Bible Commentary*, edited by F. E. Gaebelein. Vol. 3. Grand Rapids: Zondervan, 1992.
Zimmerli, Walther. *Ezekiel 1: A Commentary on the Book of the Prophet Ezekiel Chapters 1–24*. Hermeneia. Philadelphia: Fortress, 1969.

Scripture Index

Old Testament/Hebrew Bible

Genesis

2:17	201–2	44:1–34	192n13, 193
3:1–6	202	44:18–34	194n25
11:6	27n47	45:1	194n25
15:16	196n30, 197	45:8	102
18:15	17	49:17	161n76
20:12	111	50:11	79n92
21:23	15, 52n116		
24:2–4	143n8		
24:15	143n8		

Exodus

27:35	19, 157n65	1:15–21	ix
29:25	18, 65n48	1:17	196
30:33	22n26	1:19	1, 195
31	161	1:20–21	197
31:19	62	1:20	2, 195
31:20	161	1:21	2, 195
31:26–27	161	3:7–10	195
31:26	162	3:7–8	196
31:34–35	62	3:7	195n27
31:34	62	3:9	195n27
34:13	19n20	3:16–18	196
34:30	79n92	3:18	195, 197
35:18	156n63	7:22	87n4
36:20	79n92	8:3 [7]	87n4
37:26–27	194n25	8:4–11 [8–15]	197–98
38:1–26	193	8:14 [18]	87n4
38:8–9	194	8:21–28 [25–32]	198
38:13–18	1	8:28 [32]	198
38:14	194	9:27–35	198
38:26	1, 194	10:16–20	198
41:1	162n78	11:1–16	198
42:7–28	192n13, 193	12:41	162n78
42:38	194n25	14:9—15:21	161n76
		20:7	22n28

Exodus (continued)

20:16	ix, 1, 1n1, 1n3, 16n3, 21, 22n26
22:10–11	40
22:15–16	112
23:1–9	23
23:1–8	1
23:1–3	23, 33n64
23:1–2	23
23:1	1n3, 22n28, 24, 27, 35
23:2	24, 24n35, 25
23:3	23, 24n35, 32–33, 33n64
23:4–5	23, 33n64
23:6–9	23, 33n64
23:6	1n3, 23, 23n31, 24n35, 32–33, 33n64, 36
23:7	24n35, 34–35, 45n91, 52n116
23:8–9	24n35
23:8	35, 36
23:31	79n92
34:12	79n92
34:15	79n92
26:30	38n71

Leviticus

5:1	31, 32
5:20–26 [6:1–7]	39–42, 49
5:21–22 [6:2–3]	17, 41
5:21 [6:2]	41–42
5:22 [6:3]	16n4, 41, 52n116
5:23–24 [6:4–5]	41
5:24 [6:5]	16n4, 41, 52n116
5:25–26 [6:6–7]	41
15:16	106
15:18	106
18:9	111
18:11	111
19:1–2	34
19:11–12	41–42, 49
19:11	16–17, 41, 83
19:12	16n4, 41, 52n116
19:13	42
19:14	42n80
19:15	33, 33n64, 34, 34n65, 38
19:16	25–26
19:31	154
19:35–36	37
19:35	38
19:36	38
20	115
20:2	115n112
20:4–5	115
20:6	154
20:9	115n112
20:10	115n112
20:11	115n112
20:12	115n112
20:13	115n112
20:15	115n112
20:16	115n112
20:17	111, 115
20:27	115n112, 154
24:8–9	147
26:8	150n42

Numbers

14:14	79n92
15:30–31	41n77
16:48–50	138n64
21:21–24	79n92
23:19	18, 203n51
25:8–9	138n64
25:18–19	138n64
31:7–8	79n92
31:16	138n64
32:17	79n92
33:52	79n92
33:55	79n92
35:26–27	97
35:30	21, 24

Deuteronomy

1:16	34n65

1:17	34n66	29:10 [11]	197n32
2:22	79n92	30:12	46n93
2:34–35	78–79	34:10	46n93
3:6–7	79n91		
4:2	46n93		
5:11	22n28	**Joshua**	
5:20	ix, 1n1, 16, 21, 22n26, 22n28		
		1:1–9	196n30
7:16	196n30	1:1–3	197
10:17	36	2	82, 197
11:4	161n76	2:1–21	197
16:18	34n65, 36, 36n69	2:1–7	ix
16:19	35–36, 36n69	2:2	82
16:20	52	2:3	82
17:6	20, 24	2:4–6	2, 195
18:10	155	2:4–5	82
18:15	46n93	2:4	82
19:1–10	97	2:5	82
19:11–13	97	2:7	82
19:14	38	2:9–11	84, 196n30
19:15–21	ix	2:9	79n92, 84
19:15	24	2:24	79n92
19:16–21	26, 30	6:17	82, 195
19:16–19	22, 24	6:25	2, 82, 195
19:16	16, 21	7:9	79n92
19:18	16, 16n3, 21, 21n23, 27, 35n68, 52n116	7:11	17
		7:14–26	146
19:19	27	8:1	197
20:1	161n76	8:6	195
20:4	161n76	8:15–17	195
21:2	35n67	8:18–19	195, 197
22:13–21	27, 35n67	8:26	79
22:13–19	29–30, 30n55, 31	8:27	79
22:13	30	8:33	35n67
22:14	29–31	9	166
22:20–21	30–31	9:3–15	195–96
22:20	30, 35	9:3	197, 197n31
22:28–29	112	9:5	19n17
23:11	106	9:16	166
23:21	163n80	9:17–18	101
25:13–16	37–38	9:22	18, 65n48
25:15	38	9:23	197, 197n32
25:16	38	9:24	79n92, 196, 196n30, 197, 197n31
26:6–8	195n27		
27:17	39	11:4–9	161n76
27:18	42, 42n80	13:1–2	79
27:22	111	13:2	76
27:25	36		

Joshua (continued)

13:21	79n92
15:31	80
19:5	80
20:4	97
20:7	97
23:2	35n67
24:1	35n67
24:6	161n76
24:18	79n92
24:27	17n14

Judges

1:32	79n92
1:33	79n92
2:2	79n92
2:13	133n46
3:10	57n13
3:14–15	196
3:15	196
3:16–23	196
3:30	197
4:11	150n45, 151n45
4:15	161n76
4:17–22	196, 197
4:21	87
4:23–24	197
5:19–22	161n76
5:24–27	196
6:34	57n13
7:16–20	57n13
9:43	57n13
11:21	79n92
11:29	57n13
14:6	57n13
14:15–19	198
14:19	57n13
15:6	198
15:14	57n13
16:4–5	198
16:5	197
16:6–15	196
16:10	18
16:13	18
16:17	197
16:20	197
16:21	198
16:23–24	198n36
16:26–30	198
19–21	57n13, 58
19:29	57n13
20–21	57

Ruth

3:7	87
3:8	87n5

1 Samuel

2:10	144n11
2:12–17	154
2:13	80n95
2:18	154
2:19	154
2:28	159n70
4:9	133n46
4:17	138n64, 173n112
4:20	156n63
6:2	155
7	188–89
7:3	133n45
7:4	133n45
7:10	188
7:11	188
7:13	188
8:3	23n31
8:5	141
8:7	141
8:8	133n45
8:9	80n95
8:11	80n95
8:20	56
8:22	141
9–15	58
9:1—10:16	144n10
9	141
9:3	144
9:5	144

9:6	144	13:13	71
9:7	144	14	188–89
9:8	144	14:6	188
9:17	141	14:12	189
9:21	127n23	14:13–14	189
9:27	142	14:15	189
10	145	14:20	189
10:1	141, 144, 144n11	14:23	189
10:2–6	144	14:38–44	146
10:4–6	141	14:50–51	141n1
10:5	144–45	14:50	141n1
10:7–8	144–45	15	60, 67, 77
10:7	141, 144, 144n13	15:3	78–79
10:8	144n13	15:7–8	158
10:9	141, 144	15:7	78
10:10–13	141	15:10–35	149n41
10:13–16	145	15:15	60
10:13	145n16	15:21	60
10:14–16	140–41	15:23	67, 154
10:14	141	15:27–28	154
10:15	141	15:28	67
10:16	141–43, 143n8, 144, 177	15:29	16, 203n51
		16	71, 148–49
10:17–25	145	16:1–5	53, 58, 83, 83n103, 157n65
10:18	145		
10:19	145	16:1	58–59, 144n11
10:20–24	145, 146n21	16:2	58–60
10:20	55, 159n70	16:3	71n63
10:24	55	16:5	59n24, 71n63
11	53, 57n13, 58, 193	16:6–10	71
11:1–11	53, 55, 157n65	16:8–13	132n42
11:1	57, 57n11, 133n45	16:10	71
11:2	53, 190	16:11	71
11:3	54–57	16:12	71
11:4	56	16:13	144n11
11:6	57n13	16:22	86n1
11:7	57n13	17	150
11:9–10	54	17:9	133n45
11:10	54–55, 57	17:21	79n92
11:11	57, 57n13	17:26	190
12:3	21n26	17:27	127n23
12:10	133n45	17:30	127n23
12:14	133n45	17:34–37	138
12:20	133n45	17:46	190
12:24	133n45	17:54	91
13:3	145	17:57	91
13:4	145	18	85
13:10–14	149n41	18:1	164n86

1 Samuel (continued)

18:3–5	93
18:3–4	75
18:4	154
18:5	75, 89, 177
18:6–7	72, 74–75, 93
18:7	86n1
18:8	86n1, 127n23
18:9	86n1
18:10	89
18:11	86n1
18:12	86n1, 89
18:14–15	89
18:14	89
18:15	86n1, 89
18:16	89, 177
18:17–23	10n48
18:17–19	85
18:17	86, 86n1
18:20–27	85
18:20	64, 85, 88
18:21	85–86, 88
18:22	86–88, 177
18:23	87–88
18:25	87–88
18:26	88
18:28–29	89
18:28	64, 89
18:29	89
19	60, 62, 72, 148
19:1	149, 149n41
19:10	74n75
19:11–17	53, 60, 67, 74n75
19:11–12	60, 65
19:11	60, 64–67, 74n75, 149, 149n41
19:12–17	10n48
19:12	65, 68, 74n75
19:13–16	61, 64, 67
19:13–14	65
19:13	19n17, 62, 154
19:14	61–64, 191n11
19:15	63
19:16	62–63
19:17	18, 53, 60n27, 61, 64–66, 69, 69n60, 74n75, 191n11
19:18	68, 74n75, 149
19:19–20	149, 149n41
19:24	154
20	68, 71, 146, 148, 194
20:1–7	71
20:1	149
20:2	127n23
20:3	70
20:4	72
20:6	69, 71n63, 191n11
20:7	68
20:9	71
20:13	71, 152
20:14–17	167
20:24	68
20:27–34	53, 68, 157n65
20:27	68, 72
20:28–29	66, 68–69
20:28	72
20:29	70–71, 71n63, 74n75
20:30–33	149, 149n41
20:30–31	68
20:30	70–72
20:31	70–72
20:32–33	68
20:32	72
20:33	64, 72
20:34	70, 72
20:35–42	70, 72
20:42	147
21:2–10 [1–9]	140, 146, 151, 157n65
21:2 [1]	148
21:3 [2]	146–47
21:4 [3]	148
21:5 [4]	146–47
21:6 [5]	106
21:7 [6]	106n72, 148
21:8 [7]	146, 148, 150, 151n45
21:10 [9]	72
21:11–16 [10–15]	53, 72, 74, 76, 147, 151
21:11 [10]	72, 74, 152
21:12 [11]	75, 91–93
21:13 [12]	72, 74
21:14 [13]	73
21:15–16 [14–15]	75, 91
21:15 [14]	74
21:16 [15]	73

SCRIPTURE INDEX 233

22:1	74	28:4–5	152
22:8	164	28:8	19n17, 153–54
22:9–10	152	28:9	153
22:10	151	28:10	127n23, 155
22:13	164	28:11–12	153
22:14	151	28:12	18, 65n48, 67, 153
22:15	151	28:17–19	153–54
22:17–20	152	28:17	67
22:20	74n75	28:18	127n23
22:22	152	29–30	89n10
23:1–5	151n50	29	90
23:6–14	151n50	29:1–11	85, 89, 188
23:13	74n75	29:1	89n10
24	77	29:3–4	90
24:5 [4]	87	29:3	91–92
24:7 [6]	127n23	29:4	90–91
24:9 [8]	92	29:5	91–93
25	129	29:8	90, 92–93
25:3	130n35	29:9	90, 168–69
25:23	129	29:11	93
25:24	66, 129	30:1–2	159
25:25	126n18, 129	30:17	74n75
25:35	130	30:24	127n23
26	77	31	89n10, 155–57
26:15	92	31:4	156
26:16	127n23	31:5	156, 157n65
26:17	92	31:6	156
26:19	92, 133n45	31:7–10	156
27:1	74n75, 75		
27:2–4	76		
27:3	77	## 2 Samuel	
27:5	77		
27:6	80	1	103n57, 172, 174
27:7–12	53, 75, 157n65	1:1–16	140, 155
27:8–12	91	1:1	159
27:8–11	92	1:2	158
27:8	76, 78–79	1:3	74n75
27:9	77–78	1:5	157
27:10–12	91	1:6	157–58
27:10	76, 90	1:8	158–59
27:11	78, 80, 91, 92n18	1:13	157, 159
27:12	76–77, 80, 89	1:16	21n26, 158
28	89n10, 152, 154	2–3	99
28:1–2	85, 89, 188	2	97, 97n30, 118n119
28:1	77, 89n10, 90	2:6	127n23
28:2	90–91, 93	2:12	117
28:3–25	89n10, 90, 140, 152	2:19	95
28:3	89n10, 153		

2 Samuel (continued)

2:21	95	10:1–8			9n44
2:23	95	10:18			161n76
3–4	100	10:19			133n45
3:1	97n30	11–14			127, 127n23
3:2–5	120n1	11–12			104
3:3	113	11		104, 107n78, 121–22
3:7	93	11:4			121n3, 123
3:10	94	11:6–13			107n78
3:17–19	94	11:7		85, 104–5, 107n78
3:17–18	96n29	11:8–13			104
3:17	96n29	11:8			105
3:20–25	96n29	11:9			105
3:21	94, 96, 96n29, 118	11:10			106
3:22–26	94	11:11		105–6, 107n76, 125, 127, 127n23
3:22	96, 96n29, 97n30, 99, 118	11:13			105
3:23	96, 96n29, 97n30, 118	11:14–17			123
3:24	96n29	11:14–15			85, 104
3:26	96	11:14		105, 107, 121n3
3:27	85, 93–94, 94n22, 95, 100, 103, 118n119	11:24			108
		11:25		108, 127, 127n23
3:36–37	96n29	11:27—12:1			121–22
3:37	96	11:27			108, 121n3
3:30	94n22, 100	12		104, 109n82, 126
4	172	12:1–7			120–21
4:1–2	101, 103	12:1			121, 124–25
4:2	99, 101, 103	12:3			125
4:3	101	12:4			123
4:4	98, 99n38	12:5			121, 124
4:5	101, 103	12:6		121, 127, 127n23
4:6	74n75, 85, 97–98, 99n38, 100, 102–3	12:7–12			124n12
		12:7–8			124n12
4:7	100, 102	12:7			121, 124–25
4:8	101	12:9–10			124n12
4:9–11	103n57	12:9			108, 123, 127
4:10	101, 158, 173–74	12:11–12			124n12
4:11	98, 104	12:12			127n23
4:12	104	12:13			121
5:1	159n70	12:14		108, 127, 127n23
5:6	79n92	12:21			127n23
6:16	64n44	13:1–22			85, 109
6:21	132n42	13:1			109, 111
8:4	161n76	13:2			109
9:1	167	13:5			109, 111
9:7	165	13:6–7			10n48
9:10	133n45	13:6			110–12
		13:7			110–11
		13:8			110–11

13:10	111	14:19	126, 127n24
13:11	111, 114	14:20	126n19, 127n23, 127n24, 129, 168–69
13:13	111		
13:14–15	112	14:21	10n49, 127n23, 129
13:14	112	14:22	128
13:15	115n110	14:23	128
13:17	112, 115	14:24	10n49, 126n18, 128
13:18	112	14:33	128
13:19	115n110	15:1–6	140, 159, 162–63
13:20	109, 127n23	15:1	160
13:22	113	15:2	159, 159n70, 160
13:23–39	85, 113, 163	15:3–4	160
13:23–29	112	15:3	159–61
13:23–24	164	15:4	159, 161
13:23	113, 164	15:5	159
13:24	113	15:6	127n23, 159, 159n70, 160–62
13:25	114		
13:26–28	10n48	15:7–12	140, 162
13:26	114	15:7–9	10n48
13:27	114	15:7–8	162–64
13:28	113–15, 164	15:7	162n78, 164, 164n83
13:29	115n110	15:8	133n45, 162–63
13:31	115n110	15:9	162, 164
13:34	115n110	15:10	159n70, 162–64
13:36	115n110	15:11	159n70, 162–63, 163n81, 164, 164n85
13:37–38	113		
13:38	125	15:12	162, 164–65
13:39—14:1	125n18	15:13–14	164
14	159, 168	15:13	159n70, 161
14:1–21	120, 125	15:19–22	169–70
14:1	126, 126n19, 129	15:24–37	170n102
14:2–21	10n49, 157n65	15:24–29	170
14:2	128	15:30–37	170
14:3	126, 127n23	15:30	135
14:4	129	15:31	10n48, 164
14:5–7	126, 128	15:32–37	131
14:7	126	15:32	137
14:8	126–28, 130, 160	15:34	121n2, 130–31, 134, 137
14:9	129		
14:10	126–28, 160	15:35–36	130
14:11	126–28, 160	15:37	131
14:12	127n24, 129	16:1–4	140, 165, 169
14:13	120n1, 126, 127n23, 127n24	16:2	135
		16:3	169
14:15	127n23, 127n24	16:4	169
14:17	127n24, 168–69	16:5–14	169
14:18–21	126	16:11–12	170
14:19–21	126	16:14	135, 137

2 Samuel (continued)

16:16–19	120, 130
16:16	130
16:17	130–31, 133
16:18–19	130–31
16:18	132–33
16:19	132–33
16:20	134
16:21–22	134
17:1–3	134, 138n66
17:1–2	135n53
17:5–14	120, 134, 157n65
17:5	136
17:6	127n23, 136
17:7–16	131
17:7–14	10n48, 81
17:7	134, 137
17:8–9	137
17:8	137–38
17:10	138
17:11–13	134
17:11	138
17:12–14	82
17:12	138
17:13	138
17:14	121n2, 134–35, 137, 139
17:15–21	53, 81, 157n65
17:15–17	81
17:15	136
17:16	135–36
17:17	81
17:18–20	136
17:18	82, 136
17:19	82
17:20	81–82, 191n11
17:21	81–82, 135–37
17:22	136, 139
17:23	135
17:24	135–36
17:27–29	139
17:28–29	139n69
18:5	128, 173n110
18:7	138n64
18:12	128, 173n110
18:14–15	161, 164
18:19—19:8	174
18:19–30	x, 140, 171
18:19	171
18:20	171–73
18:22	172–74
18:23	171–73
18:25	173
18:27	173–74
18:28	171
18:29	171–72
18:30	172
19:6 [5]	74n75
19:10 [9]	74n75
19:14 [13]	10n49, 101, 116
19:17–24 [16–23]	169
19:17–19 [16–18]	170
19:25–31 [24–30]	140, 165, 169
19:25 [24]	157n65, 165–66, 167n94, 168, 170
19:27 [26]	19, 168
19:28 [27]	19, 165, 168–69
19:30 [29]	170
19:31 [30]	165, 167, 167n94, 168n94, 170
19:32–40 [31–39]	169–70
19:41–44 [40–43]	116
19:43 [42]	127n23
20	118n119
20:1–2	116
20:8–10	85, 116
20:8	118, 118n120
20:9	117–18
20:10	100, 117
20:14–22	9n44
21:1–2	101
21:5–6	101
22:44	133n45
24:2	159n70
24:3	127n23
24:16	168n99
24:21	138n64
24:25	138n64

1 Kings

1:1–35	198n37
1:42	174

2:5–6	95, 115, 118
2:5	118, 118n120
2:28–34	95
2:39	162n78
3:16–28	196
3:28	197
4:5	131n36
8:16	132n42
11:34	132n42
13:18	17, 157n65, 198
13:23–25	198
13:23–24	198
21:1–16	198
21:10–14	198
21:19	196, 198
21:23	198
22	8, 192, 196
22:19–23	196–97
22:22–23	16, 196n29
22:22	197
22:38	196, 198

2 Kings

4:16	18
5:20–24	198
5:23	198
5:25–27	198
5:27	198
6:18–23	197
6:18–20	196
6:21–23	196
6:23	197
7:9	173n112
9:12	16, 52n116
9:35–37	198
10:19	196
10:30	196–97

1 Chronicles

8:33	141n1
9:39	141n1
10:13–14	155
12:18 [17]	19

18:21–22	16
21:17	138n64
21:22	138n64
27:33	131n36
28:4	132n42

2 Chronicles

6:5–6	132n42
8:1	162n78
19:6	36
19:7	36
35:22	198
35:23–24	198

Nehemiah

3:7	196n30
7:25	196n30

Esther

5:8–12	196
7:1–10	196
7:3–4	197
9:1	197

Job

7:3	17n13
8:18	17
11:11	17, 45
13:7	19
15:6	21n26
15:34	44
15:35	19, 45
24:2	44
27:4	19, 45
31:5–6	46
31:28	17n14
34:5–6	44
34:6	18
35:13	17n13

Psalms

Reference	Page
5:7 [6]	18, 19n20, 47n98
5:10 [9]	47n98
7:5 [4]	49n108
7:15 [14]	16, 47n101
9:10 [9]	44
10:7-8	47n98
10:7	19
10:18	44
12:2-6 [1-5]	47n97
15:3	47n99
15:5	47
24:4	48
25:3	49
26:4-5	47n100
26:10	47
27:12	16, 16n3, 21n23, 47
28:3	47n99, 48
31:7 [6]	17
31:14 [13]	27
31:18-19 [17-18]	47n97
32:2	47n101
34:14 [13]	19, 47n99
35:11-12	24
35:11	47
35:19-20	47n97
35:19	52n116
35:20	19
36:4-5 [3-4]	47n101
36:4 [3]	19
36:6 [5]	45n87
37:12	27
38:13 [12]	19n20, 47n97
38:20-21 [19-20]	47n97
38:20 [19]	52n116
41:6-7 [5-6]	47n97
43:1	19, 47n97
44:18 [17]	16
49:6 [5]	47n101
50:19	19, 47n99
52:3-6 [1-4]	47n98
52:4 [2]	19
52:5 [3]	16
52:6 [4]	19n20
55:12 [11]	19n20, 47n98
55:21-24 [20-23]	47n98
55:24 [23]	19n20
58:2-4 [1-3]	47
58:4 [3]	18
59:13 [12]	17, 47n97
60:13 [11]	17n13
62:5 [4]	47n97
63:11-12 [10-11]	47n97
69:5 [4]	47n97
74:21	44
78:34-37	18
78:36	48
78:37	48n106
78:56-57	48n106
78:57	48
78:70	132n42
84:11 [10]	197n32
88:12 [11]	45n87
89:2-3 [1-2]	45n87
89:23 [22]	47n97
89:25 [24]	45n87
89:34-35 [33-34]	15
89:34 [33]	45n87
89:36 [35]	18
89:50 [49]	45n87
92:3 [2]	45n87
96:13	45n88
98:3	45n87
100:5	45n87
101:7-8	47n101
101:8	48n102
106:29-30	138n64
108:13 [12]	17n13
109:1-5	47n97
109:2	16, 19
116:8	48
116:10	48
116:11	48
119:29-30	48
119:67-71	48
119:75	45n88
119:104	48
119:115-18	47n100
119:128	48
119:138	45n88
119:161-63	48
120:1-7	47n97
120:2-3	19
127:1-2	17n13
144:7-8	47n97

144:8	16
144:11	16, 47n97

Proverbs

6:17–19	46
6:17	45–46, 52n116
6:19	16n3, 18, 21n23, 44n84, 47, 52n116
10:18	16, 44
11:1	19, 44
11:13	44
11:18	16, 44, 52n116
12:5–6	44
12:5	19, 45n90
12:6	45n90
12:17	16n3, 21n23, 44n84, 45n88, 52n116
12:18	45n90
12:19	52n116
12:20	19, 45, 45n90
12:22	45, 83
13:5	45, 45n91, 52n116
14:5	16n3, 18, 21n23, 44n84
14:8	46
14:25	18, 19n20, 44n84
16:11	44
17:4	44
17:7	45
17:23	44
19:5	16n3, 18, 21n23, 44n84, 47
19:9	16n3, 18, 21n23, 44n84, 47
19:22	47
19:28	44n84
20:10	44
20:17	44
20:19	44
20:23	19, 44
21:6	44
21:28	18, 44n84
22:28	44
23:10	44
24:23–25	44
24:28	44n84
25:18	21n23, 22n26, 44n84
26:18–19	19, 44
26:24–28	44
26:24	19n20, 44
26:26	44
26:28	16, 44
29:12	16, 45, 45n91
30:4	46n93
30:5–8	46
30:6	46n93
30:8	46
30:9	17n14
30:32	27n47

Ecclesiastes

7:7	44

Song of Songs

4:9	110

Isaiah

1:23	50
3:9	21n26
5:18	17, 50
5:23	50
6:9–10	199
9:14 [15]	16n6, 50n113
11:5	45n88
23:17	162n78
28:15–17	50
28:15	18
29:21	49
30:9	17
30:17	150n42
32:1	45
32:7	50, 52n116
33:15	50
41:27	173n112
52:7	173n112

Isaiah (continued)

53:9	50n112, 204n53
57:4	16
57:11	18
59:3	16, 50n112
59:4	17, 22n30, 45n88, 50
59:12–15	50
59:12	21n26
59:13	17n14, 52n116
60:6	173n112
61:1	173n112
63:7–8	15

Jeremiah

2:30	17n13
4:30	17n13
5:1	50n111
5:2	16n4, 49n110, 49n111
5:12	17, 50n113
5:26	50
5:27	50
5:31	16n6, 50n113, 52n116
6:13	50
6:28	25, 50
6:29	17n13
7:4–10	51
7:4	16n6
7:8	16n6
7:9	16n4, 49n110, 51, 52n116
8:10	50
9:3–8 [4–9]	50
9:7 [8]	19n20
10:14	16n7
12:6	49n108
13:25	16n7
14:7	21n26
14:14	16n6, 50n113
16:19	16n7
18:15	17
20:6	16n6, 50n113
20:7–10	3n11
23:14	16n6, 50n113
23:25–26	50n113
23:25	16n6
23:26	16n6
23:32	16n6, 50n113
27:10	16n6, 50n113
27:14–16	16n6, 50n113
27:15–16	52n116
28:15	16n6, 50n113, 52n116
29:8–9	50n113
29:9	16n6, 52n116
29:21	16n6, 50n113
29:23	16n6, 50n113
29:31	16n6, 50n113
37:14	16
40:16	16
43:2	16n6
44:3	133n46
46:11	17n13
51:17	16n7

Lamentations

1:19	19
2:14	17n12, 50n113

Ezekiel

12:24	17n12
13:6–9	17n12, 18, 46, 50n113
13:6	50
13:8	50
13:10	46
13:19–23	50n113
13:19	18
13:22	16n6, 52n116
13:23	17n12
21:34 [29]	17n12, 18, 46, 50n113
22:9	25, 50
22:12	50
22:28	17n12, 18, 46, 50n113
45:9–10	50

Daniel

8:24–25	19n20

Hosea

4:1–2	51, 51n115
4:2	17
5:5	21n26
5:10	50
7:3	17, 50
7:10	21n26
10:4	49n110
10:13	17, 50
11:12	17
12:2 [1]	18, 50n112
12:8 [7]	19, 50
12:12 [11]	17

Amos

8:5	19, 50

Jonah

2:9 [8]	17

Micah

2:11	16n6, 18, 50n113
3:11	50
6:3	21n26
6:11	19, 50
6:12	16, 19, 50n112
7:3	50

Nahum

3:1	17, 50n112

Habakkuk

2:3	18
2:18	16n7

Zephaniah

1:9	19n20, 50n112
3:13	50

Zechariah

5:3–4	49n110, 49n111
5:4	16n4
8:16	50, 201
8:17	16, 50
10:2	16, 16n6, 22n28, 50n113
13:3–4	50n113
13:3	16n6
13:4	50
14:12	138n64
14:15	138n64
14:18	138n64

Malachi

3:5	49n110, 49n111
3:14	17n13

New Testament

Matthew

1:5	2
5:11	200
7:15	200n41
12:1–8	147n26
13:13–15	199
15:19	200n40
19:18	200
24:4–5	200n42
24:11	200n41
24:24	200n42
26:4	200
26:59–62	200

Mark

2:23–28	147n26
4:11–12	199
7:20–23	200n40
10:19	200
13:5–6	200n42
13:22	200n42
14:1	200
14:56–59	200

Luke

6:1–5	147n26
6:26	200n41
8:10	199
18:20	200
21:8	200n42
24	199
24:17–19	199
24:28	199
24:29–31	199

John

8:44	201

Acts

5:1–11	ix, 200n39
5:3	200n39
5:4	200n39
6:13	200
13:6	200n41
13:10	200

Romans

1:25	200
1:27	200
1:29–31	200n40
3:7–8	83
3:13–17	200n40
9:1	201n45
16:17–18	200

1 Corinthians

6:9–10	201n44
10:13	83
15:33	201n44

2 Corinthians

4:2	201
11:3–4	200n43
11:13–15	200
11:26	200
11:31	201n45
12:16	201

Galatians

1:20	201n45
2:4	200
6:7	201n44

Ephesians

4:14–15	200n43
4:22	201
4:25	83, 201
4:29	201
4:31	201
5:6	201n44

Colossians

2:4	201n44
2:8	201n44
3:8	201
3:9	201

1 Thessalonians

2:3	201

2 Thessalonians

2:3	201n44
2:9–10	202
2:11–12	202, 204

1 Timothy

2:7	201n45
4:1–2	200n43
6:20	200n43

2 Timothy

3:12–13	200

Titus

1:2	203
1:3	203
1:10–11	200n43
1:12–13	200n40
1:12	203
3:1–3	200n40

Hebrews

6:13–15	203
6:17–18	202
6:18	203
11:31	2, 83, 195, 197

James

1:15–17	201n44
2:25	83, 195, 197
3:14	200

1 Peter

2:1	200n40
2:22	204
3:10–12	200n40

2 Peter

2:1	200n43
2:13	200n40

1 John

1:6	200
2:21–22	200
2:26	200n43
3:7	201n44
4:1	200n41
4:6	200n43

2 John

7	200

Revelation

2:2	200	16:13	200n41
2:20	200n43	18:23–24	200n40
3:8	202	19:20	200n41
3:9	202	20:3	202
3:10	202	20:8	202
12:9	202	20:10	200n41, 202
13:14	200	21:8	204
14:5	204	21:27	204
		22:15	204

www.ingramcontent.com/pod-product-compliance
Lightning Source LLC
Chambersburg PA
CBHW050438240426
43661CB00055B/2424